"Woodcock's thoughtful appraisals, careful research, and graceful writing skillfully demonstrate the importance of anarchism as a historical movement. At the same time, his compassion and generosity of spirit make plain the relevance of anarchism to our own age of capital, empire, and the surveillance state. His book remains the essential introduction to the classical anarchist thinkers."

Mark Leier, Director, Centre for Labour Studies,
Simon Fraser University

To what degree can anarchism be an effective organized movement? Is it realistic to think of anarchist ideas ever forming the basis for social life itself? These questions are widely being asked again today in response to the forces of economic globalization. The framework for such discussions was given perhaps its most memorable shape, however, in George Woodcock's classic study of anarchism—now widely recognized as the most significant twentieth-century overview of the subject.

Woodcock surveys all of the major figures that shaped anarchist thought, from Godwin and Proudhon to Bakunin, Goldman, and Kropotkin, and looks as well at the long-term prospects for anarchism and anarchist thought. In Woodcock's view "pure" anarchism—characterized by "the loose and flexible affinity group which needs no formal organization"—was incompatible with mass movements that require stable organizations, that are forced to make compromises in the face of changing circumstances, and that need to maintain the allegiance of a wide range of supporters. Yet Woodcock continued to cherish anarchist ideals; as he said in a 1990 interview, "I think anarchism and its teachings of decentralization, of the coordination of rural and industrial societies, and of mutual aid as the foundation of any viable society, have lessons that in the present are especially applicable to industrial societies."

This classic work of intellectual history and political theory (first published in the 1960s, revised in 1986) is now available exclusively from Broadview Press.

George Woodcock (1912-1995), internationally acclaimed intellectual historian and man of letters, was the author of dozens of books, including the classic biography *Gabriel Dumont: The Métis Chief and His Lost World* (also available from Broadview) and the Governor-General's Award-winning *George Orwell: The Crystal Spirit*.

Anarchism

A History of Libertarian Ideas and Movements

George Woodcock

University of Toronto Press

Previously published by Broadview Press © 2004 George Woodcock with permission from the Writers' Trust of Canada c/o The Woodcock estate

LIBRARY AND ARCHIVES CANADA CATALOGUING IN PUBLICATION

Woodcock, George, 1912-1995
Anarchism : a history of libertarian ideas and movements / George Woodcock.

(Broadview encore editions)
Includes index.

ISBN 978-1-55111-629-7

    1. Anarchism — History I. Title II. Series

HX828.W6 204   335'83   C204-905498-8

We welcome comments and suggestions regarding any aspect of our publications—please feel free to contact us at news@utphighereducation.com or visit our Internet site at www.utphighereducation.com.

The University of Toronto Press acknowledges the financial support for its publishing activities of the Government of Canada through the Book Publishing Industry Development Program (BPIDP).

North America
5201 Dufferin Street
North York, Ontario, Canada, M3H 5T8

2250 Military Road
Tonawanda, New York, USA, 14150

ORDERS PHONE: 1-800-565-9523
ORDERS FAX: 1-800-221-9985
ORDERS E-MAIL: utpbooks@utpress.utoronto.ca

UK, Ireland, and continental Europe
NBN International
Estover Road, Plymouth, PL6 7PY, UK
TEL: 44 (0) 1752 202301
FAX ORDER LINE: 44 (0) 1752 202333
enquiries@nbninternational.com

Inteior design by George Kirkpatrick
Cover design by Lisa Brawn

Contents

Preface to the 1986 Edition

A SERIES of events, of which the book itself was part, have made necessary this new and considerably revised edition of *Anarchism*. I wrote the original version during 1960 and 1961; it was published in the United States in 1962 and in the first British Penguin edition in 1963; subsequently it was translated into many languages, including Italian, Swedish, Japanese, Spanish and Portuguese.

When I wrote *Anarchism*, the most striking recent event in the history of the tradition I discussed had been the Spanish Civil War, in which for the last time anarchism had inspired a genuine mass following. The destruction of the Spanish Republic in 1939, and the virtually unopposed entry of Franco's troops into the traditional anarchist stronghold of Barcelona, seemed to mark the end of the movement that Bakunin had founded during the internal struggles of the International in the 1860s; everywhere but in Spain it had, for various reasons, become moribund. 1939 seemed to me the year that marked the death of classic anarchism, and I chose it as the end point of my narrative.

But even as I did so I made the distinction between a movement and an idea; I pointed out that over the two centuries before Bakunin organized his first conspiratorial cells in post-Risorgimento Italy very similar ideas to his had been formulated, by the Differs in the English and the Enragés in the French Revolutions, by Godwin and Proudhon, and that there was no reason to assume that this perennially renewable anarchist *idea* would not re-emerge once again in a new and different form even after the *movement*, as the world up to 1939 knew it, had faded into history.

But since in 1960-61 the few small groups that represented the vestigial tradition hardly represented a renaissance of the idea, *Anarchism* concentrated on the historic movement, and took on a somewhat elegiac tone, so that one reviewer at the time described it rather felicitously as a threnody. It was indeed, as I then conceived it, a kind of Periclean oration, an expansion into a whole commemorative volume of the old Italian anarchist lament, 'Flowers for the rebels who failed ...' I ended in a peroration that would be inappropriate as a termination to the book as it now appears in revision but which is too just a tribute to the great anarchists to be abandoned. When I voiced it I took for granted that the movement which ended in Barcelona in 1939 must be treated as a piece of past history, and I remarked that the thought of re-creating obsolete forms of organization or imitating insurrectional methods that had failed in the past would in the future be less important than the impact of the more general and enduring lessons of anarchism on receptive minds. And then I voiced the tribute that I still sustain and would not like to omit entirely from the book it once brought to a close:

> The heritage that anarchism has left to the modern world is to be found in a few inspiring lives of self-sacrifice and devotion like those of Melatesta and Louise Michel, but most of all in the incitement to return to a moral and natural view of society which we find in the writings of Godwin and Tolstoy, of Proudhon and Kropotkin, and in the stimulation such writers give to that very taste for free choice and free judgement which modern society has so insidiously induced the majority of men to barter for material goods and the illusion of security. The great anarchists call on us to stand on our own moral feet like a generation of princes, to become aware of justice as an inner fire, and to learn that the still, small voices of our own hearts speak more truly than the choruses of propaganda that daily assault our outer ears. 'Look into the depths of your own being,' said Peter Arshinov, the friend of Makhno. 'Seek out the truth and realize it yourselves. You will find it nowhere else.' In this insistence that freedom and moral self-realization are interdependent, and one cannot live without the other, lies the ultimate lesson of true anarchism.

Those words are still true, but this book is no longer a threnody. Since it was written, anarchism has re-emerged in new forms, adapted to a changing world. Few readers will not have seen, appended to some wall graffito that challenges our complacency as well as that of our society, the symbol of the circled A. it is a sign the classic anarchists did not even know. It was first used in 1964 by a small French group, Jeunesse Libertaire, taken up in 1966 by another youth group, the Circolo Sacco e Vanzetti in Milan, and then in 1968 it suddenly became popular in Italy, whence it spread rapidly around the world, so that nowadays one is as likely to see it in some small town of the Australian outback or the Canadian prairie as in the capitals of Europe.

The spread of the circled A, and of the libertarian fraternity it represents, is merely one manifestation of the resurgence of anarchist ideas that has made it necessary to revise this book, since one can no longer validly argue that anarchism in any final sense came to an end in 1939, though the old traditional anarchism did. The idea has revived astonishingly, assuming new manifestations over the past two decades. The earliest clear signs began to emerge in the very year the first edition of *Anarchism* was published in Britain. The small nucleus that had attracted some of the British literati during World War II and had continued tenuously ever since suddenly began to proliferate under the stimulus of the Campaign for Nuclear Disarmament, and I remember in 1963 reading with astonishment a report from London of a contingent five hundred strong marching twenty abreast behind the black banner of the London anarchists in one of the street demonstrations of that year. 'The London anarchists came ringleted and bearded and pre-Raphaelite,' enthused one reporter. 'It was a frieze of non-conformists enviable in their youth and gaiety and personal freedom.' There had not even been fifty active anarchists in London when I had been involved in editing *Freedom* twenty years before.

As the decade went on the evidence of new upsurges of anarchism increased, not only in Britain but also in the United States, where anarchist ideas played an important role in the counter-culture of the 1960s, in France, where the black flag was prominent in the great revolt of May 1968, and in Holland, where the Provos gave a new twist to the old idea of propaganda by deed through deliberately goading governments into showing their most brutal faces. The weak provoke; the strong unwillingly expend themselves.

> Through provocation [said one Provo manifesto] we force authority to tear off its mask. Uniforms, boots, helmets, sabres, truncheons, fire hoses, police dogs, tear gas and all the other means of suppression they have lined up for us must be produced. The authorities must be forced to rage, threatening us right and left, commanding, forbidding, condemning, convicting. They will become more and more unpopular and the popular spirit will ripen for revolution. A revolutionary feeling will once again be in the air: crisis.
>
> A crisis of provoked authority.
>
> Such is the gigantic provocation we call for from the International Provotariat.

At first, when such reports reached me from all over the Western world, I began to think I had been rash in so officiously burying the historic anarchist movement. But in fact what was happening in the 1960s was not a knock in the coffin of the past. The anarchists of the 1960s were not the historic anarchist movement resurrected; they were something quite different—a series of new manifestations of the idea. Anarchism spread into classes and regions that had never welcomed it before. It seized on the new issues of the times. It produced a whole fresh literature of its own, with writers like Paul Goodman and Colin Ward and Murray Bookchin adding new insights to the old anarchist arguments. And it became for the first time a matter of interest to political scientists and historians; books on its personalities and its old and new manifestations proliferated. Even when it was not welcome, anarchism was at last taken seriously as a political alternative.

In what happened *Anarchism* itself played a role as the first comprehensive history of libertarian ideas and movements; it is still the fullest. It has continued to be read over the two decades since it first appeared and has been in print throughout that period; this will be the eighth printing in Britain alone. In 1973 I decided that something must be done to recognize what had taken place in anarchist terms since 1939, and I wrote a postscript that in a rather general way outlined recent developments; it appeared in the 1975 edition. Now it seems to me that more extensive changes are needed, and I have accordingly carried out a general revision and updating of the book. This has made little difference to the first eight chapters, dealing with the general idea of anarchism and the particular contributions of the classic anarchist thinkers. But it has involved considerable revision and additions to the next six chapters, which deal with anarchism as a changing and developing movement, both internationally and in various specific countries. Finally, the original epilogue and much of the more general material in the 1975 postscript have been combined in a new epilogue with fresh material to offer a more adequate comparison between what one might call old and new anarchism.

The extension of the scope of anarchism beyond 1939 has led to a change in my relation to the book. I am no longer the sympathetic though objective observer looking from the present into a past in which I had no part. I did play a role in the anarchist movement during the 1940s, which means that in the book as revised I appear as an actor, if only a minor one, and that at times an element of subjectivity enters in, since I am looking at events in which I was involved and to which I reacted personally. In dealing with myself as a figure in the book, I have followed the practice of talking of 'George Woodcock' whenever it is merely a question of recording what I did and of talking of 'I' when I am expressing a personal view of a situation in which I was involved.

2 September (Labor Day) 1985

1. Prologue

'WHOEVER denies authority and fights against it is an anarchist,' said Sébastien Faure. The definition is tempting in its simplicity, but simplicity is the first thing to guard against in writing a history of anarchism. Few doctrines or movements have been so confusedly understood in the public mind, and few have presented in their own variety of approach and action so much excuse for confusion. That is why, before beginning to trace the actual historical course of anarchism, as a theory and a movement, I start with a chapter of definition. What is anarchism? And what is it not? These are the questions we must first consider.

Faure's statement at least marks out the area in which anarchism exists. All anarchists deny authority; many of them fight against it. But by no means all who deny authority and fight against it can reasonably be called anarchists. Historically, anarchism is a doctrine which poses a criticism of existing society; a view of a desirable future society; and a means of passing from one to the other. Mere unthinking revolt does not make an anarchist, nor does a philosophical or religious rejection of earthly power. Mystics and stoics seek not anarchy, but another kingdom. Anarchism, historically speaking, is concerned mainly with man in his relation to society. Its ultimate aim is always social change, its present attitude is always one of social condemnation, even though it may proceed from an individualist view of man's nature; its method is always that of social rebellion, violent or otherwise.

But even among those who recognize anarchism as a social-political doctrine, confusion still exists. Anarchism, nihilism, and terrorism are often mistakenly equated, and in most dictionaries will be found at least two definitions of the anarchist. One presents him as a man who believes that government must die before freedom can live. The other dismisses him as a mere promoter of disorder who offers nothing in place of the order he destroys. In popular thought the latter conception is far more widely spread. The stereotype of the anarchist is that of the cold-blooded assassin who attacks with dagger or bomb the symbolic pillars of established society. Anarchy, in popular parlance, is malign chaos.

Yet malign chaos is clearly very far from the intent of men like Tolstoy and Godwin, Thoreau and Kropotkin, whose social theories have all been described as anarchist. There is an obvious discrepancy between the stereotype anarchist and the anarchist as we most often see him in reality; that division is due partly to semantic confusions and partly to historical misunderstandings.

In the derivation of the words 'anarchy', 'anarchism', and 'anarchist', as well as in the history of their use, we find justifications for both the conflicting sets of meanings given to them. *Anarchos*, the original Greek word, means merely 'without a ruler', and thus anarchy itself can clearly be used in a general context to mean either the negative condition of unruliness or the positive condition of being unruled because rule is unnecessary for the preservation of order.

It is when we come to the use of the three words in a social-political context that we encounter important shifts of meaning. 'Anarchy' and 'anarchist' were first used freely in the political sense during the French Revolution. Then they were terms of negative criticism, and sometimes of abuse, employed by various parties to damn their opponents, and usually those to the Left. The Girondin Brissot, for example, demanding the suppression of the Enragés, whom he called anarchists, declared in 1793, 'it is necessary to define this anarchy'. He went on to do so:

Laws that are not carried into effect, authorities without force and despised, crime unpunished, property attacked, the safety of the individual violated, the morality of the people corrupted, no constitution, no government, no justice, these are the features of anarchy.

Brissot at least attempted a definition. A few years later, turning upon the Jacobins it had destroyed, the Directory descended to partisan abuse, declaring:

By 'anarchists' the Directory means these men covered with crimes, stained with blood, and fattened by rapine, enemies of laws they do not make and of all governments in which they do not govern, who preach liberty and practise despotism, speak of fraternity and slaughter their brothers ...; tyrants, slaves, servile adulators of the clever dominator who can subjugate them, capable in a word of all excesses, all basenesses, and all crimes.

Used moderately by Brissot or violently by the Directory, 'anarchism' was clearly a word of condemnation both during and after the French

Revolution; at best it described those whose politics one considered destructive and disastrous, at worst it was a term to be used indiscriminately for the smearing of one's rivals. And so the Enragés, who distrusted excessive power, and Robespierre, who loved it, were tarred by the same invidious brush.

But, like such titles as Christian and Quaker, 'anarchist' was in the end proudly adopted by one of those against whom it had been used in condemnation. In 1840, Pierre-Joseph Proudhon, that stormy, argumentative individualist who prided himself on being a man of paradox and a provoker of contradiction, published the work that established him as a pioneer libertarian thinker. It was *What Is Property?*, in which he gave his own question the celebrated answer: 'Property is theft.' In the same book he became the first man willingly to claim the title of anarchist.

Undoubtedly Proudhon did this partly in defiance, and partly in order to exploit the word's paradoxical qualities. He had recognized the ambiguity of the Greek *anarchos*, and had gone back to it for that very reason—to emphasize that the criticism of authority on which he was about to embark need not necessarily imply an advocacy of disorder. The passages in which he introduces 'anarchist' and 'anarchy' are historically important enough to merit quotation, since they not merely show these words being used for the first time in a socially positive sense, but also contain in germ the justification by natural law which anarchists have in general applied to their arguments for a non-authoritarian society.

> What is to be the form of government in the future? [he asks]. I hear some of my readers reply: 'Why, how can you ask such a question? You are a republican.' A republican! Yes, but that word specifies nothing. *Res publica*; that is, the public thing. Now, whoever is interested in public affairs—no matter under what form of government, may call himself a republican. Even kings are republicans. 'Well, you are a democrat.' No ... 'Then what are you?' I am an anarchist!

Proudhon goes on to suggest that the real laws by which society functions have nothing to do with authority; they are not imposed from above, but stem from the nature of society itself. He sees the free emergence of such laws as the goal of social endeavour.

> Just as the right of force and the right of artifice retreat before the steady advance of justice, and must finally be extinguished in equality, so the sovereignty of the will yields to the sovereignty of reason and must at last be lost in scientific socialism ... As man seeks justice

in equality, so society seeks order in anarchy. Anarchy—the absence
of a master, of a sovereign—such is the form of government to which
we are every day approximating.

The seeming paradox of order in anarchy—here indeed we have the
key to the change in connotation of this whole group of words. Proudhon,
conceiving a natural law of balance operating within society, rejects
authority as an enemy and not a friend of order, and so throws back at the
authoritarians the accusations levelled at the anarchists; in the process he
adopts the title he hopes to have cleared of obloquy.

As we shall later see, Proudhon was a voluntary hermit in the political
world of the nineteenth century. He sought no followers, indignantly
rebuffed the suggestion that he had created a system of any kind, and
almost certainly rejoiced in the fact that for most of his life he accepted
the title of anarchist in virtual isolation. Even his immediate followers
preferred to call themselves mutualists, and it was not until the later 1870s,
after the split in the First International between the followers of Marx and
those of Bakunin, that the latter—who were also the indirect followers of
Proudhon—began, at first rather hesitantly, to call themselves anarchists.

It is the general idea put forward by Proudhon in 1840 that unites him
with the later anarchists, with Bakunin and Kropotkin, and also with certain earlier and later thinkers, such as Godwin, Stirner, and Tolstoy, who
evolved anti-governmental systems without accepting the name of anarchy; and it is in this sense that I shall treat anarchism, despite its many
variations: as a system of social thought, aiming at fundamental changes in
the structure of society and particularly—for this is the common element
uniting all its forms—at the replacement of the authoritarian state by
some form of non-governmental cooperation between free individuals.

But even when one has established the view of anarchism as a definite
current of social philosophy, crystallizing at certain times into action,
there remain misunderstandings which arise from historical rather than
semantic confusion. First, there is the tendency to identify anarchism with
nihilism, and to regard it as a negative philosophy, a philosophy of
destruction simply. The anarchists themselves are partly responsible for
the misunderstanding, since many of them have tended to stress the
destructive aspects of their doctrine. The very idea of abolishing authority
implies a clean sweep of most of the prominent institutions of a typical
modern society, and the strong point in anarchist writings has always been
their incisive criticism of such institutions; in comparison their plans of
reconstruction have been oversimplified and unconvincing.

Yet in the mind of no anarchist thinker has the idea of destruction ever stood alone. Proudhon used the phrase *Destruam et Aedificabo* as the motto for the attack on industrial Caesarism embodied in his *Economic Contradictions* (1846): 'I destroy and I build up.' And Michael Bakunin ended his essay on *Reaction in Germany* with a celebrated invocation: 'Let us put our trust in the eternal spirit which destroys and annihilates only because it is the unsearchable and eternally creative source of all life. The passion for destruction is also a creative passion!'

The tradition has continued into our own generation. In 1936, almost a hundred years after Bakunin published *Reaction in Germany*, the Spanish anarchist leader Buenaventura Durutti, standing among the destruction caused by the Civil War, boasted to Pierre van Paassen:

> We are not in the least afraid of ruins. We are going to inherit the earth. There is not the slightest doubt about that. The bourgeoisie may blast and ruin its own world before it leaves the stage of history. We carry a new world, here in our hearts. That world is growing this minute.

The anarchist, then, may accept destruction, but only as part of the same eternal process that brings death and renewed life to the world of nature, and only because he has faith in the power of free men to build again and build better in the rubble of the destroyed past. It was Shelley, the greatest disciple of Godwin, who gave eloquent expression to this recurrent anarchist dream of renewal:

> The earth's great age begins anew,
>   The golden years return,
> The earth doth like a snake renew
>   Her winter weeds outworn;
> Heaven smiles, and faiths and empires gleam
> Like wrecks in a dissolving dream.

It is through the wrecks of empires and faiths that the anarchists have always seen the glittering towers of their free world arising. That vision may be naïve—we have not yet come to the point of judging it in such terms—but it is clearly not a vision of destruction unmitigated.

Certainly no man capable of such a vision can be dismissed as a nihilist. The nihilist, using the term in a general sense, believes in no moral principle and no natural law; the anarchist believes in a moral urge powerful

enough to survive the destruction of authority and still to hold society
together in the free and natural bonds of fraternity. Nor is the anarchist a
nihilist in the narrow historical sense, since the particular group somewhat
inaccurately called nihilists in Russian history were terrorists who
belonged to the People's Will, an organized conspiratorial movement
which sought during the later nineteenth century to achieve constitutional
government—an unanarchistic aim—by a programme of organized assassination directed against the autocratic rulers of Tsarist Russia.

This last statement begs a familiar question. If anarchists are not
nihilists, are they not terrorists in any case? The association of anarchism
with political terrorism is still well established in the popular mind, but it
is not a necessary association, nor can it be historically justified except in a
limited degree. Anarchists may be substantially agreed on their ultimate
general aims; on the tactics needed to reach that aim they have shown singular disagreement, and this is particularly the case with regard to violence. The Tolstoyans admitted violence under no circumstances; Godwin
sought to bring change through discussion and Proudhon and his followers through the peaceful proliferation of cooperative organizations;
Kropotkin accepted violence, but only reluctantly and because he felt it
occurred inevitably during revolutions and that revolutions were unavoidable stages in human progress; even Bakunin, though he fought on many
barricades and extolled the bloodthirstiness of peasant risings, had also
times of doubt, when he would remark, in the tones of saddened idealism:

> Bloody revolutions are often necessary, thanks to human stupidity;
> yet they are always an evil, a monstrous evil and a great disaster, not
> only with regard to the victims, but also for the sake of purity and
> the perfection of the purpose in whose name they take place.

In fact, where anarchists did accept violence it was largely because of
their adherence to traditions that stem from the French, American, and
ultimately the English Revolutions—traditions of violent popular action
in the name of liberty which they shared with other movements of their
time such as the Jacobins, the Marxists, the Blanquists, and the followers of
Mazzini and Garibaldi. With time—and particularly as the memory of
the Commune of 1871 began to fade—the tradition acquired a romantic
aura; it became part of a revolutionary myth and in many countries had
little relation to actual practice. There were, indeed, special situations,
particularly in Spain, Italy, and Russia, where violence had long been
endemic in political life, and here the anarchists, like other parties,

accepted insurrectionism almost as a routine; but among the celebrities of anarchist history the heroes of violent action have been far outnumbered by the paladins of the word.

Nevertheless, through the shadowy confusion of attitudes regarding violence and non-violence there move unmistakably those dark angels of anarchism, the terrorist assassins. Outside the special conditions of Spain and Russia, they were few in number and they operated mostly during the 1890s. The distinction of their victims—for several royal personages as well as Presidents of France and the United States were among those executed by these self-appointed judges of the crimes of authority—gave their acts a notoriety out of all proportion to their numbers. But at no time was a policy of terrorism adopted by anarchists in general. The terrorists, as we shall see, were mostly lonely men driven by a curious blend of austere idealism and apocalyptic passion, the black aspect of the same passion that turned other anarchists, like Peter Kropotkin and Louise Michel, into secular saints.

Yet there is no doubt that the assassinations carried out by men like Ravachol and Émile Henry and Leon Czolgosz, to name only three of the most notorious, did enormous harm to the anarchist cause by implanting in the popular mind an identification which lingers long after its justification has vanished. What seems curious is that other assassinations of the same period should have been so much more easily forgotten than those of the anarchists. The name of the Russian Social Revolutionaries, whose victims were far more numerous, arouses no reminiscent shudder, and few people who associate anarchists with daggers and infernal machines pause to remember that only one of the four assassins of American presidents claimed to be an anarchist; of the others one was a Confederate, the second a disappointed Republican, and the third was a former communist.

The lingering prejudice can possibly be explained by the disturbance that is created in the minds of the insecure by any doctrine of logical extremity. The anarchists attack the principle of authority which is central to contemporary social forms, and in doing so they arouse a guilty kind of repugnance in ordinary people; they are rather like Ivan Karamazov crying out in the court-room, 'Who does not desire his father's death?' The very ambivalence of the average man's attitude to authority makes him distrust those who speak openly the resentments he feels in secret, and thus it is in the psychological condition which Erich Fromm has named 'fear of freedom' that we may find the reason why—against the evidence of history—so many people still identify anarchism with unmitigated

destruction and nihilism and political terror. What anarchism really is we
shall now begin to consider.

To describe the essential theory of anarchism is rather like trying to
grapple with Proteus, for the very nature of the libertarian attitude—its
rejection of dogma, its deliberate avoidance of rigidly systematic theory,
and, above all, its stress on extreme freedom of choice and on the primary
of the individual judgement—creates immediately the possibility of a
variety of viewpoints inconceivable in a closely dogmatic system.
Anarchism, indeed, is both various and mutable, and in the historical perspective it presents the appearance, not of a swelling stream flowing on to
its sea of destiny (an image that might well be appropriate to Marxism),
but rather of water percolating through porous ground—here forming for
a time a strong underground current, there gathering into a swirling pool,
trickling through crevices, disappearing from sight, and then re-emerging
where the cracks in the social structure may offer it a course to run. As a
doctrine it changes constantly; as a movement it grows and disintegrates,
in constant fluctuation, but it never vanishes. It has existed continuously in
Europe since the 1840s, and its very protean quality has allowed it to survive where many more powerful but less adaptable movements of the
intervening century have disappeared completely.

The peculiar fluidity of anarchism is reflected in its attitude toward
organization. By no means all anarchists reject organization, but none
seeks to give it an artificial continuity; the fluid survival of the libertarian
attitude itself is what is important. In fact, the basic ideas of anarchism,
with their stress on freedom and spontaneity, preclude the possibility of
rigid organization, and particularly of anything in the nature of a party
constructed for the purpose of seizing and holding power. 'All parties
without exception, in so far as they seek for power, are varieties of abso-
lutism,' said Proudhon, and none of his descendants has thought otherwise. For the idea of partisan organization the anarchists substitute their
mystique of individual and popular impulse, which in practice has found
its expression in a succession of loose and impermanent groups and confederations of propagandists who see their duty not to lead the people so
much as to enlighten and give example to them. Even the anarchist insurrectionaries in Italy and Spain carried out their small uprisings not
because they thought revolutions under their control would ensue, but
because they considered such acts to be 'propaganda by deed', aimed at
showing the people a course of action that might lead to their liberation.
In practice, of course, anarchist militants have often come dangerously
near to the authoritarian stance of the revolutionary leader, but their basic

theory has always rejected any such position, and has sought to eliminate its necessity by posing the idea of the spontaneous origin of revolutions.

> Revolutions [said Bakunin] are not made, either by individuals or by secret societies. They come automatically, in a measure; the power of things, the current of events and facts, produces them. They are long preparing in the depth of the obscure consciousness of the masses— then they break out suddenly, not seldom on apparently slight occasion.

Kropotkin gave the same thought a scientific twist in accordance with the mode of the later nineteenth century:

> Evolution never advances so slowly and evenly as has been asserted. Evolution and revolution alternate, and the revolutions—that is, the times of accelerated evolution—belong to the unity of nature as much as do the times when evolution takes place more slowly.

Both Bakunin's mystical faith in unreasoning mass impulse and Kropotkin's adapted social Darwinism imply that rigid organization and rigid theoretical systems are drags on progress—whether revolutionary or evolutionary; at the same time they encourage the flexibility of approach that makes men sensitive to currents of discontent and aspiration.

Hence freedom of interpretation and variety of approach are elements one would naturally expect to find in the world of the anarchist. The congealing elements of dogmatism and orthodoxy have not been absent even in that world—for these are matters of personality as much as of theory— but in the relatively short run they have always dissolved in the renewed urge toward change, an urge unhindered by the power of personal leaders or sacred texts. Respected as individuals like Kropotkin and Malatesta and Louise Michel may have been in their time, none of them wielded or attempted to wield the same hypnotic influence over a whole movement as either Blanqui or Marx; and, though anarchism has produced its quota of notable books—Godwin's *Political Justice*, Kropotkin's *Mutual Aid*, Proudhon's *General Idea of the Revolution*—none of these has been accorded or has seemed to demand a niche in the tabernacle such as the faithful keep for the canonical texts of Marxism.

Yet, despite the recurrent impulse toward individualism of approach and interpretation, common circumstances and personal affinities have induced even among anarchists a modified tendency to group thinking,

s possible to identify a number of fairly well-defined 'schools' of
thought.

ne end of the series—Left or Right according to one's predilec-
tio. —stands individualist anarchism. Max Stirner, preaching insurgent
self-assertion and foreseeing a Union of Egoists drawn together by respect
for each other's ruthlessness, carries this trend as far as logical fanaticism
will go; William Godwin, in his vision of a Thebaid of free men sharing
their means according to the dictates of abstract justice, offers a rather
coldly benevolent variation of the same vision.

The next point along the spectrum of anarchist attitudes is Proudhon's
mutualism. Proudhon differs from the true individualist anarchists
because he sees history in social form and, despite his fierce defence of
individual freedom, thinks in terms of association. 'That I may remain
free, that I may be subject to no law but my own, and that I may govern
myself,' he says, 'the edifice of society must be rebuilt on the idea of
Contract.' He seeks to *rebuild* society, not to abolish it, and he envisages the
world of the future as a great federation of communes and workers' cooperatives, based economically on a pattern of individuals and small groups
possessing (not owning) their means of production, and bound by contracts of exchange and mutual credit which will assure to each individual
the produce of his own labour.

Beyond mutualism we reach the three more familiar varieties of
anarchist thought—collectivism, anarchist communism, and anarcho-
syndicalism. These all retain some of the elements of Proudhon's
theory—particularly his federation and the emphasis on workers' associations which led his mutualist followers to establish the first French sections of the International in 1865. But Bakunin and the collectivists of the
later 1860s, seeking to adapt anarchist attitudes to a society of growing
industry, replaced Proudhon's insistence on individual possession by the
idea of possession by voluntary institutions, with the right to the enjoyment of his individual product or its equivalent still assured to the individual worker. During the later 1870s, Kropotkin and his fellow anarchist
communists took the development a logical stage further. They not only
envisaged the local commune and similar associations as the proper
guardians of the means of production; they also attacked the wage system
in all its forms, and revived the idea—already put forward by Sir Thomas
More—of a literal communism that would allow everyone to take, according to his wishes, from the common store-houses, on the basis of the slogan: 'From each according to his means, to each according to his needs.'
The main difference between the anarchist communists and the anarcho-
syndicalists, who appeared a decade later in the French trade unions, was

that the latter emphasized the revolutionary trade union both as an organ of struggle (the general strike its most potent tactic) and also as a foundation on which the future free society might be constructed.

Finally, somewhat aside from the curve that runs from anarchist individualism to anarcho-syndicalism, we come to Tolstoyanism and to the pacifist anarchism that appeared, mostly in Holland, Britain, and the United States, before and during the Second World War and which has continued since then in the deep anarchist involvement in protests against nuclear armament. Tolstoy, who associated anarchism with violence, rejected the name, but his complete opposition to the state and other authoritarian forms brings his ideas clearly within the orbit of anarchistic thought. His followers and the modern pacifist anarchists, who accept the label he rejected, have tended to concentrate their attention largely on the creation of libertarian communities—particularly farming communities—within present society, as a kind of peaceful version of the propaganda by deed. They divide, however, over the question of action. Tolstoy preached non-resistance and his greatest disciple, Gandhi, who sometimes called himself an anarchist, attempted to give practical expression to this doctrine. The pacifist anarchists have accepted the principle of resistance and even revolutionary action, provided it does not incur violence, which they see as a form of power and therefore non-anarchist in nature. This change in attitude has led the pacifist anarchists to veer toward the anarcho-syndicalists, since the latter's concept of the general strike as the great revolutionary weapon made an appeal to those pacifists who accepted the need for fundamental social change but did not wish to compromise their ideal by the use of negative (i.e. violent) means.

The differences between the various anarchist schools, though at first sight they appear considerable, actually lie in two fairly limited regions; revolutionary methods (especially the use of violence) and economic organization. All recognize that if anarchist hopes are fulfilled and political domination is brought to an end, economic relations will become the main field in which organization is necessary; the differences we have encountered between the various schools of thought reflect differing views of how far cooperative 'administration of things' (to use a Saint-Simonian phrase which anarchist writers have borrowed extensively) can then be applied without danger to individual independence. At one extreme, the individualists distrust all cooperation beyond the barest minimum for an ascetic life; at the other, the anarchist communists envisage an extensive network of interconnecting mutual-aid institutions as a necessary safeguard for individual interests.

Despite these differences, the various anarchist schools are united by a group of common assumptions which form the kernel of their philosophy. These begin with a naturalistic view of society.

All anarchists, I think, would accept the proposition that man naturally contains within him all the attributes which make him capable of living in freedom and social concord. They may not believe that man is naturally good, but they believe very fervently that man is naturally social. His sociality is expressed, according to Proudhon, in an immanent sense of justice, which is wholly human and natural to him:

> An integral part of a collective existence, man feels his dignity at the same time in himself and in others, and thus carries in his heart the principle of a morality superior to himself. This principle does not come to him from outside; it is secreted within him, it is immanent. It constitutes his essence, the essence of society itself. It is the true form of the human spirit, a form which takes shape and grows toward perfection only by the relationship that every day gives birth to social life. Justice, in other words, exists in us like love, like notions of beauty, of utility, of truth, like all our powers and faculties.

Not merely is man naturally social, the anarchists contend, but the tendency to live in society emerged with him as he evolved out of the animal world. Society existed before man, and a society living and growing freely would in fact be a natural society, as Kropotkin emphasizes in *Modern Science and Anarchism*:

> The anarchists conceive a society in which all the mutual relations of its members are regulated, not by laws, not by authorities, whether self-imposed or elected, but by mutual agreements between the members of that society, and by a sum of social customs and habits— not petrified by law, routine, or superstition, but continually developing and continually readjusted, in accordance with the ever-growing requirements of a free life, stimulated by the progress of science, invention, and the steady growth of higher ideals. No ruling authorities, then. No government of man by man; no crystallization and immobility, but a continual evolution—such as we see in Nature.

If man is naturally capable of living in such a free society, if society is in fact a natural growth, then clearly those who attempt to impose man-made laws, or to create what Godwin called 'positive institutions', are the real enemies of society, and the anarchist who rebels against them, even to the extent of violence and destruction, is not antisocial after all; according to anarchist reasoning he is the regenerator, a responsible individual striving to adjust the social balance in its natural direction.

The emphasis on the natural and prehuman origin of societies has made almost every anarchist theoretician, from Godwin to the present, reject Rousseau's idea of a Social Contract. It also makes them reject not merely the authoritarian communism of Marx, with its emphasis on a dictatorship of the proletariat to impose equality by external force, but also the various pre-Marxist Utopian socialisms. In fact the very idea of Utopia repels most anarchists, because it is a rigid mental construction which, successfully imposed, would prove as stultifying as any existing state to the free development of those subjected to it. Moreover, Utopia is conceived as a perfect society, and anything perfect has automatically ceased growing; even Godwin qualified his rash claims for the perfectibility of man by protesting that he did not mean men could be made perfect, but that they were capable of indefinite improvement, an idea which, he remarked, 'not only does not imply the capacity for being brought to perfection, but stands in express opposition to it'.

The general distaste for the rigidity of Utopian thinking has not prevented the anarchists from adopting some ideas contained within Utopias. We have already seen that the anarchist communists echoed the suggestions on communistic distribution put forward by More in the original *Utopia*, while certain of Fourier's ideas on how to induce men to work for passion rather than profit have entered deeply into anarchist discussions on such questions as 'What to do with the lazy man?' and 'Who will do the dirty work?' But the only complete Utopian vision that has ever appealed generally to anarchists is *News From Nowhere*, in which William Morris, who came remarkably near to Kropotkin in his ideas, presented a vision—charmingly devoid of any suspicion of compulsion—of the kind of world that might appear if all the anarchist dreams of building harmony on the ruins of authority had the chance to come true.

One of the most interesting features of Morris's vision in *News From Nowhere* is the curious feeling it induces in the reader of having passed into a continuum where ordinary time relationships have ceased; the Middle Ages are in fact more real to the inhabitants of Nowhere than the chronologically much nearer nineteenth century. The idea of progress as a necessary good has vanished, and all happens, not in the harsh white light of perfection, which Morris denies, but in the mellow stillness of a long summer afternoon which ends only for the unfortunate visitor to the future who has to return to Victorian life and London and the acrimonious debates that were wrecking the Socialist League.

The golden sunlight of that long summer afternoon when time paused on the edge of eternity haunted the anarchists too. Admittedly, like most nineteenth-century men of the Left, they talked often of Progress. Godwin dreamed of men improving indefinitely, Kropotkin sedulously linked anarchism with evolution, and Proudhon actually wrote a *Philosophie du progrès*. Yet it is only with qualifications that anarchism can be regarded either as progressive in the ordinary Victorian sense, or as evolutionary in the commonly understood sense of desiring development toward more complex forms—in this case social forms.

The Marxists, indeed, have always denied the existence of a progressive element in anarchism, and have even accused anarchists of reactionary tendencies. From their own standpoint they are not entirely wrong, for in its attitude toward social development anarchism often seems to float like Mohammed's coffin, suspended between the lodestones of an idealized future and an idealized past. The past the anarchist sees may not be the golden age of Hesiod and Plato, but it resembles that antique vision; it is a kind of amalgam of all those societies which have lived—or are supposed to have lived—by cooperation rather than by organized government. Its components come from all the world and from all history. The peasant communism of the Russian *mir*, the village organization of the Kabyles in the Atlas Mountains, the free cities of the European Middle Ages, the communities of the Essenes and the early Christians and the Doukhobors, the sharing of goods implied in the customs of certain primitive tribes: all these attract the anarchist theoretician as examples of what can be done without the apparatus of the state, and they draw him nostalgically to a contemplation of man as he may have been in these fragments of a libertarian past. The accuracy of the interpretations which Kropotkin in particular made of these early societies may well be questioned on the grounds that insufficient account was taken of the extent to which a tyranny of custom becomes a substitute for overt authority. But here we are less concerned with the flaws in this view of the past than with the attitude it represents, an attitude which not only seeks to establish a continuity—almost a tradition—uniting all non-authoritarian societies, but also regards simplicity of life and nearness to nature as positive virtues.

Here we reach another important difference between anarchists and Marxists. The Marxist rejects the primitive as representing a stage in social evolution already past; for him, tribesmen, peasants, small craftsmen, all belong with the bourgeoisie and the aristocracy on the scrap heap of history. Communist *realpolitik* may at times demand a *rapprochement* with the peasants, as now in the Far East, but the end of such a policy is always to turn the peasants into proletarians of the land. The anarchists, on the other hand, have placed great hopes in the peasant. He is near to the earth, near to nature, and therefore more 'anarchic' in his reactions; Bakunin regarded the Jacqueries as rough models for the spontaneous popular uprising which was his ideal for the revolution. The peasant, moreover, is the heir to a long tradition of cooperation forced upon him by historical circumstances; in approving this tendency in peasant societies the anarchist theoreticians tend to forget that, as they become more prosperous, peasant societies being to show—like any other developing society so far known in history—differences in wealth and status that end in the establishment of a class hierarchy of rich peasants, poor peasants, and labourers. It is significant that anarchism became a powerful mass movement among the poor peasants of Andalusia and the Ukraine, but failed to gain any appreciable success among more prosperous peasants; it was only fear of Durutti and his militia columns that forced the vine-growers of Aragón to adopt the collectivist organization favoured by the Spanish anarchists in the early years of the Civil War.

The anarchist's cult of the natural, the spontaneous, the individual, sets him against the whole highly organized structure of modern industrial and statist society, which the Marxist sees as the prelude to his own Utopia. Even efforts to encompass the industrial world by such doctrines as anarcho-syndicalism have been mingled with a revulsion against that world, leading to a mystic vision of the workers as moral regenerators; even the syndicalists could not foresee with equanimity the perpetuation of anything resembling industrial society as it exists at present.

Indeed, except for pockets of industrial workers in Paris, the Lyons region, Marseilles, Barcelona, and Milan, the appeal of anarchism has always been strongest among the very classes that remain outside the general trend toward mechanism and conformity in the industrial world. A high proportion of celebrated anarchists came from the aristocracy or the country gentry; Bakunin, Kropotkin, Cherkesov, and Tolstoy in Russia, Malatesta and Cafiero in Italy, are typical examples. Others, like Godwin, Domela Nieuwenhuis, and Sébastien Faure, were former clergymen or seminarists. Among the rest, members of the artisan class—the traditional handcraftsmen—have been perhaps the most important; anarchist militants include an astonishing proportion of shoemakers and printers. At certain times—the 1890s in France, the 1940s in Britain and the United States, and the 1960s widely in the Western countries—intellectuals and artists in rebellion against mass values have been attracted in considerable numbers. Finally, anarchists have tended to welcome as natural rebels the *déclassé* elements whom Marx despised most of all because they fitted

nowhere into his neat pattern of social stratification; as a result the anarchist movement has always had its links with that shadowy world where
rebellion merges into criminality, the world of Balzac's Vautrin and his
originals in real life.

These elements unite mainly in their opposition to the modern state
and the modern capitalist or communist economy. They represent a rebellion, not necessarily in favour of the past, but certainly in favour of an
ideal of individual freedom which belongs outside the present in which
they find themselves. This fact alone should make us look cautiously at
anarchist progressivism. What it implies is certainly not progress in terms
of society as it now exists. On the contrary, the anarchist contemplates
what in some ways is a retreat—a retreat along the lines of simplification.

This appears, of course, in his proposals for social reconstruction. He
seeks to break down, to get back to the roots, and to base any organization
that may be necessary on—to use a favourite anarchist phrase—'the point
of production'. This dissolution of authority and government, the decentralization of responsibility, the replacement of states and similar monolithic organizations by a federalism which will allow sovereignty to return
to the intimate primal units of society—this is what in their various ways
the anarchists have all desired, and such a desire necessarily implies a policy of simplification. But we should miss the essence of the anarchist attitude if we ignored the fact that the urge toward social simplification arises
not from any desire for the more efficient working of society, nor even
entirely from a wish to eliminate the organs of authority that destroy individual freedom, but largely from a moral conviction of the virtues of a
simpler life.

The deeply moralistic element in anarchism, which makes it much
more than a mere political doctrine, has never been explored adequately,
and this is due partly to the reluctance of the anarchists themselves, who
have rejected conventional moralities, to stress this aspect of their own
philosophy. Nevertheless, the urge to simplicity is part of an ascetic attitude which permeates anarchist thought. The anarchist does not merely
feel anger against the wealthy; he feels anger against wealth itself, and in
his eyes the rich man is as much a victim of his luxury as the poor man of
his destitution. To enable all men to live in luxury, that vision which
bedevils North American democracy, has never appealed to the anarchists.
Their attitude was expressed by Proudhon when, in *La Guerre et la paix*, he
pointed out the distinction between pauperism and poverty. Pauperism is
destitution; poverty is the state in which a man gains by his work enough
for his needs, and this condition Proudhon praises in lyrical terms as the

ideal human state, in which we are most free, in which, being masters of our senses and our appetites, we are best able to spiritualize our lives.

The sufficiency that will allow men to be free—that is the limit of the anarchist demand on the material world. That it has not been a merely theoretical limit is emphasized by the extraordinary accounts Franz Borkenau has given of those Andalusian villages which, having chased out authority in the early days of the Spanish Civil War, set out to create the anarchist Eden. Quite deliberately, they aimed at the simplification even of the poor life that had been theirs in the unregenerate past, closing the *cantinas*, and, in their plans for exchange with neighbouring communes, deciding that they had no further need even for such innocent luxuries as coffee. These men were not all fanatical apostles of anarchism; most of them were ordinary villagers inspired at a historic moment by the moral dimensions of a faith that had long given them hope.

Proudhon and the village ascetics of Andalusia have not been isolated in the movement to which they both belong. Throughout anarchist literature one finds echoes of their conception of a society where, once simple needs have been satisfied, men will have the leisure to cultivate their minds and their sensibilities. Kropotkin includes in *The Conquest of Bread* a chapter on 'The Need for Luxury' which might seem to negate this contention, but when we examine it we find that he sees luxury, not as material enjoyment, but as 'the higher delights, the highest within man's reach, of science, and especially of scientific discovery; of art, and especially of artistic creation'. By simplifying existence so that toil is reduced, the anarchist believes that man can turn his attention to such noble activities and achieve the philosophic equilibrium in which death will cease to have terror. Again, it is Proudhon who presents the vision most concisely when, in *De la justice*, he remarks that human life enters its fullness when it contains love, work, and 'social communion or Justice'. 'If these conditions are fulfilled,' he declares, 'existence is full; it is a feast, a song of love, a perpetual enthusiasm, an endless hymn to happiness. At whatever hour the signal may be given, man is ready; for he is always in death, which means that he is in life and in love.'

This digression into the vision of the simplified life will have made it evident that the anarchist sees progress not in terms of a steady increase in material wealth and complexity of living, but rather in terms of the moralizing of society by the abolition of authority, inequality, and economic exploitation. Once this has been achieved, we may return to a condition in which natural processes resume their influence over the lives of societies and individuals, and then man can develop inwardly in accordance with the spirit that raises him above the beasts. And thus we see Proudhon, in the *Philosophie du progrès*, insisting that the presence of equilibrium is the inevitable complement to the unending movement in the universe. Progress is indefinite, but it has no end, nor, in the ordinary sense, does it appear to have a goal; it is 'an incessant metamorphosis', a negation of the Absolute, 'the affirmation of universal movement and in consequence the negation of immutable forms and formulae, of all doctrines of eternity, permanence, or impeccability, of all permanent order, not excepting that of the universe, and of every subject or object, spiritual or transcendental, that does not change'. The formula is almost Heraclitean; it suggests the flux of never-ending change rather than the dialectical forward movement of the Hegelians and the Marxists; it suggests a world in which history loses all its rigidity in the interflow of balancing forces; it suggests contradiction as a positive and productive element, and equilibrium as a dynamic condition in a world that changes constantly and never reaches the stillness of perfection because imperfection is a cause and a consequence of its everlasting movement.

But I would misrepresent anarchism as it has appeared in history if I ended this introductory chapter by leaving the impression that there is anything in the theory which suggests a passive acceptance of inevitable process. To the anarchist, despite the scientific determination that at times has inconsistently found its way into his teachings, no specific event is inevitable, and certainly no specific event in human society. For him history does not move, as it does for the Marxist, along the steel lines of dialectical necessity. It emerges out of struggle, and human struggle is a product of the exercise of man's will, based on the spark of free consciousness within him, responding to whatever impulse—in reason or in nature—provokes the perennial urge to freedom.

It is the consciousness of the need for struggle, of the need to take practical steps to achieve the liberation of society, that takes anarchism into the world of politics. Here I raise a controversial question, since, although anarchists differ in their ideas of the tactics to be used in achieving social change, they are united in regarding themselves as apolitical or even antipolitical. The bitterest battles between anarchists and Marxists were fought over the question of whether an egalitarian society could be created by workers' political parties aiming at seizure of the state machine. The anarchists have all denied political action, and have declared that the state must not be taken over, but abolished; that the social revolution must lead, not to the dictatorship of any class, even the proletariat, but to the abolition of all classes.

Such an attitude can indeed be described as anti-political, but, just as anti-Utopias like *Brave New World* and *Nineteen Eight-Four* are part of Utopian literature, so the antipolitics of the anarchist is part of political history, conditioned by the very governmental institutions against which it fights. The development of anarchism ran parallel to the development of the centralized state and for a century or more in varying degrees anarchism was an integral part of the political pattern of Europe and the Americas.

The sharp difference between the anarchist conception of strategy in a politically dominated world and that of the movements with which it has competed arises partly from libertarian individualism and partly from the conviction we have already observed, that, in the larger sense at least, means profoundly affect ends. Sharing metaphorically Christ's contention that one cannot cast out devils by Beelzebub, the anarchists regard all institutions and parties based on the idea of regulating social change by governmental action and man-made laws as counter-revolutionary. In proof of this argument, they point to the fact that all revolutions carried out by political means have ended in dictatorships; the resort to coercion has transformed them and betrayed the revolutionary ideal. It is for this reason that the anarchists not only reject political action as such, but also attack reformism—the idea that society can be changed by piecemeal measures—and deny the theory of a transitional period between the capitalist state and the anarchic society. It may indeed be impossible for society to move in one step to complete freedom, but the anarchist believes that he should accept no less as his aim, and should continue to struggle and use every weakness of the unfree society to reach his ultimate goal.

The anarchists therefore base their tactics on the theory of 'direct action', and claim that their means are essentially social and economic. Such means embrace a whole varied range of tactics—from the general strike and resistance to military service to the formation of cooperative communities and credit unions—which aim to dissolve the existing order and either prepare for the social revolution or make sure that once it has begun it may not proceed in an authoritarian course. But the distinction between social-economic and political means is in fact less clearly defined than the anarchists usually maintain, since a general strike aimed at a change in the political structure of society—or a dissolution of that structure—is really, as Clausewitz said of war, politics carried on by other means, and the same applies to the insurrectionism advocated at various periods by the violent anarchists and the assassinations practised by the terrorist minority of the 1880s and the 1890s.

But this question of definition should not be allowed to obscure the fact that a real difference does exist between anarchist direct-actionism and the methods of other left-wing movements. For what unites and characterizes all the various tactics advocated by the anarchists, however they may differ on points of violence and non-violence, mass action and individual action, is the fact that they are based on direct individual decisions. The individual takes part voluntarily in a general strike; of his own free will he becomes a member of a community, or refuses military service, or takes part in an insurrection. No coercion or delegation of responsibility occurs; the individual comes or goes, acts or declines to act, as he sees fit. It is true that the anarchist image of the revolution does indeed take most frequently the form of a spontaneous rising of the people; but the people are not seen as a mass in the Marxist sense—they are seen as a collection of sovereign individuals, each of whom must make his own decision to act.

The means of revolutionary action, based on the spontaneous will of the individual, is of course paralleled by the end of the free society, in which the administration of social and economic affairs will be carried out by small local and functional groups demanding of the individual the minimum sacrifice of sovereignty necessary for a life that has been decentralized, debureaucratized, and highly simplified. Individuals, in fact, will federate themselves into communes and working associations, just as these will be federated into regional units, and overriding authorities will be replaced by coordinating secretariats. In this organic network of balancing interests, based on the natural urge of mutual aid, the artificial patterns of coercion will become unnecessary.

The extreme concern for the sovereignty of individual choice not only dominates anarchist ideas of revolutionary tactics and of the future structure of society; it also explains the anarchist rejection of democracy as well as autocracy. No conception of anarchism is farther from the truth than that which regards it as an extreme form of democracy. Democracy advocates the sovereignty of the people. Anarchism advocates the sovereignty of the person. This means that automatically the anarchists deny many of the forms and viewpoints of democracy. Parliamentary institutions are rejected because they mean that the individual abdicates his sovereignty by handing it over to a representative; once he has done this, decisions may be reached in his name over which he has no longer any control. This why anarchists regard voting as an act that betrays freedom, both symbolically and actually. 'Universal Suffrage is the Counter-Revolution,' cried Proudhon, and none of his successors has contradicted him.

But the anarchist opposition to democracy goes deeper than a dispute over forms. It involves a rejection of the idea of the people as an entity distinct from the individuals who compose it; it also involves a denial of popular government. On this point Wilde spoke for the anarchists when he said: 'There is no necessity to separate the monarchy from the mob; all authority is equally bad.' Particularly, the anarchist rejects the right of the majority to inflict its will on the minority. Right lies not in numbers, but in reason; justice is found not in the counting of heads but in the freedom of men's hearts. 'There is but one power,' said Godwin, 'to which I can yield a heart-felt obedience, the decision of my own understanding, the dictate of my own conscience.' And Proudhon was thinking of democracies as well as of the Emperor Napoleon III when he proudly declared: 'Whoever puts his hand on me to govern me is a usurper and a tyrant; I declare him my enemy!'

In reality the ideal of anarchism, far from being democracy carried to its logical end, is much nearer to aristocracy universalized and purified. The spiral of history here has turned full circle, and where aristocracy—at its highest point in the Rabelaisian vision of the Abbey of Thelème—called for the freedom of noble men, anarchism has always declared the nobility of free men. In the ultimate vision of anarchy these free men stand godlike and kingly, a generation of princes, as Shelley has described them:

> The loathsome mask has fallen, the man remains
> Sceptreless, free, uncircumscribed, but man
> Equal, unclassed, tribeless, and nationless
> Exempt from awe, worship, degree, the king
> Over himself; just, gentle, wise, but man
> Passionless?—no, yet free from guilt or pain,
> Which were, for his will made or suffered them,
> Nor yet exempt, though ruling them like slaves,
> From chance, and death, and mutability.
> The clogs of that which else might oversoar
> The loftiest star of unascended heaven
> Pinnacled deep in the intense inane.

But that is the anarchist vision of man in a world which still lies outside history and outside time. Now we will turn to the somewhat different picture of anarchism as history so far contains it.

PART ONE: THE IDEA

2. The Family Tree

ANARCHISM is a creed inspired and ridden by paradox, and thus, while its advocates theoretically reject tradition, they are nevertheless very much concerned with the ancestry of their doctrine. This concern springs from the belief that anarchism is a manifestation of natural human urges, and that it is the tendency to create authoritarian institutions which is the transient aberration. If one accepts this view, then anarchism cannot merely be a phenomenon of the present; the aspect of it we perceive in history is merely one metamorphosis of an element constant in society. It is to tracing this constant but elusive element that anarchist historians, such as Peter Kropotkin, Max Nettlau, and Rudolf Rocker, have largely devoted themselves.

The family tree which these writers have cultivated so carefully is indeed a magnificent growth, and in the shade of its branches one encounters some astonishing forefathers. Kropotkin was perhaps the most extreme of all the anarchist genealogists, for he sought the real origin of his creed not among individual thinkers, but among the anonymous mass of the folk. 'Anarchism,' he declared, 'originated among the people, and it will preserve its vitality and creative force so long only as it remains a movement of the people.'

In *Modern Science and Anarchism* this belief is elaborated in historical terms. 'From all times,' Kropotkin claims in this book, 'two currents of thought and action have been in conflict in the midst of human societies.' These are, on the one hand, the 'mutual aid' tendency, exemplified in tribal custom, village communities, medieval guilds, and, in the fact, all institutions 'developed and worked out, not by legislation, but by the creative spirit of the masses', and, on the other hand, the authoritarian current, beginning with the 'magi, shamans, wizards, rain-makers, oracles, and priests' and continuing to include the recorders of laws and the 'chiefs of military bands'. 'It is evident,' Kropotkin concluded dogmatically, 'that anarchy represents the first of these two currents ... We can therefore say that from all times there have been anarchists and statists.' Elsewhere Kropotkin conjectures that the roots of anarchism must be found in 'the remotest stone-age antiquity', and from this highly personal view of pre-history he goes on through all the gamut of rebellious movements to the early English trade unions, reaching the eventual conclusion that 'these are the main popular anarchist currents which we know of in history'.

Parallel with Kropotkin's search for an unnamed and inarticulate anar-chism of the people runs the search of other historians of the movement for anarchist elements in the thoughts of philosophers and writers in the past. Lao-Tsu, Aristippus and Zeno, Étienne de la Boëtie, Fénelon and Diderot are recruited in this way and the delightful chivalric Utopia of the Abbey of Thelème admits Rabelais on the strength of its libertarian motto, 'Do what you will!' Religious movements like the Anabaptists, the Hussites, the Doukhobors, and the Essenes are claimed *en masse*, and the French Tolstoyan Lechartier has by no means been alone in declaring that 'the true founder of anarchy was Jesus Christ and ... the first anarchist society was that of the apostles'. Two recent historians of anarchism, Alain Sergent and Claude Harmel, have discovered the first anarchist in Jean Meslier, the eighteenth-century curé of Étrepigny, whose resentment against the ecclesiastical and civil authorities of his time festered into a great Testament which he left to his rural parishioners (it was intercepted after his death by the Church authorities and never reached the farmers for whom it was meant) and in which he denounced authority of every kind and advocated a bucolic society based on friendship among peasant communities. And the American professor James A. Preu recently proved to his own satisfaction that the gist of Godwin's *Political Justice*—and by implication of all anarchist thought—is to be found in Book IV of *Gulliver's Travels*; he is not the first writer to have recognized in the Tory Dean an anarchist forefather in disguise.

But the roots of this spreading genealogical tree are far too weak for the crown of branches they are expected to bear. Even a cursory study of the writers claimed shows that what has so often been represented as the pre-history of anarchism is rather a mythology created to give authority to a movement and its theories in much the same way as a primitive clan or tribe creates its totemic myths to give authority to tradition or taboo. It is supported by the failure to realize that, though rebellion and the desire for freedom are both ancient elements in human society, they change their forms in accordance with changing historical situations. If, for example, we consider such great typical rebels of classical antiquity as Brutus and Spartacus, we realize that each of these men strove sincerely for his own idea of liberty, yet neither Brutus, fighting for the interests of a patrician oligarchy against the threat of dictatorship, nor Spartacus, seeking to liberate the slaves so that they could take up again their broken lives in their own countries, would have shared or understood the particular conceptions of economic equality and classless liberty which the nineteenth-century anarchists developed in reaction against an increasingly centralized and mechanized capitalist state.

In general, the anarchist historians have confused certain attitudes which lie at the core of anarchism—faith in the essential decency of man, a desire for individual freedom, an intolerance of domination—with anarchism as a movement and a creed appearing at a certain time in history and having specific theories, aims, and methods. The core attitudes can certainly be found echoing back through history at least to the ancient Greeks. But anarchism as a developed, articulate, and clearly identifiable trend appears only in the modern era of conscious social and political revolutions.

Its peculiar combination of moral visions with a radical criticism of society only begins to emerge in a perceptible form after the collapse of the medieval order. This collapse was to lead on one side to the rise of nationalism and of the modern centralized state, but on the other to the emergence of a revolutionary trend which early began to develop the authoritarian and libertarian currents that matured during the nineteenth century in the conflict between Marxism and anarchism.

Just as the great dissolution of medieval society took on ecclesiastical, social, and political forms, which are very difficult to disentangle, so the movements of revolt retained until the end of the seventeenth century a similar triple aspect. The extreme criticisms of society during this period were voiced not by humanists, but by fundamentalist religious dissenters, who attacked both the Church and the current systems of authority and property-owning on the basis of a literal interpretation of the Bible. Implied in their demands was the longing for a return to the natural justice of the Garden of Eden. Whether or not the hedge priest John Ball actually recited it, the famous couplet—

> When Adam delved and Eve span,
> Who was then the gentleman?

—is symptomatic of an urge toward a lost simplicity that still, almost three hundred years later, echoed in the pamphlets of the Commonwealth period.

The demands of the peasants who revolted in England in the fourteenth century and in Germany during the early sixteenth century were not in themselves revolutionary. The malcontents wished for an end to impositions by the clergy and the lords; they wished most of all for the final destruction of the moribund institutions of serfdom. But few of them went beyond such simple reformist demands, and a naïve faith in certain aspects of feudalism was shown by the trust the English peasants placed in the promises of King Richard II even after the slaying of their leader Wat Tyler. One can compare their attitude with that of the illiterate Russians who marched behind Father Gapon to the Winter Palace in 1905, in the tragically foolish hope that they would encounter, not the bullets that were actually awaiting them, but the understanding compassion of the Tsar, that symbolic Father in their still semi-feudal world.

Yet among the leaders of the English and the German peasants there did appear the first signs of the kind of social criticism that was to end in anarchism. The fragment of John Ball's speech which Froissart has preserved—almost all we know of the opinions of that tempestuous man whose presence only half emerges from the medieval shadows—attacks both property and authority and implies a link between them that anticipates the arguments developed by the nineteenth-century anarchists.

> Things cannot go well in England, nor ever will, until all goods are held in common, and until there will be neither serfs nor gentlemen, and we shall be equal. For what reason have they, whom we call lords, got the best of us? How did they deserve it? Why do they keep us in bondage? If we all descended from one father and one mother, Adam and Eve, how can they assert or prove that they are more masters than ourselves? Except perhaps that they make us work and produce for them to spend!

The tone of this speech seems authentic, even if the chronicler sharpened the details; it has that peculiar mixture of religious exaltation and social denunciation with which we become familiar as the Reformation develops into its more radical forms. But, though Ball denounces private property and demands equality, he does not appear to make a specific rejection of government as such. And for a long time we see demands for egalitarian communism emerging within what remains an authoritarian framework. The first literary presentation of an ideal egalitarian society, Sir Thomas More's *Utopia* (1516), is governed by a complicatedly elected authority and imposes extraordinarily stringent rules on individual behaviour. And, though efforts have been made to discover anarchistic elements in the German peasant revolt, led by Thomas Münzer, and in the

Anabaptist commune of Münster, the practice of these movements seems in each case to negate the anti-authoritarian attitudes suggested in the statements of some of their leaders. Münzer, for instance, denounced authority, but made no concrete suggestions for a form of society that might do without it, and when he attempted to set up his ideal commonwealth at Mülhausen, nothing resembling an anarchistic society in fact emerged. Engels has summed up the situation very clearly in *The Peasant War in Germany*.

> Communism of all possessions, universal and equal labour duty, and the abolition of all authority were proclaimed. In reality Mülhausen remained a republican imperial city with a somewhat democratic constitution, with a senate elected by universal suffrage and under the control of a forum, and with the hastily improvised feeding of the poor. The social change, which so horrified the Protestant middle-class contemporaries, in reality never went beyond a feeble and unconscious attempt prematurely to establish the bourgeois society of a later period.

As for the Anabaptists, their denunciations of earthly authority were negated by their theocratic inclinations, and there was little evidence of a genuine libertarian trend in the attempt to impose communism forcibly in Münster, or in the expulsion from the city of those who refused to become Anabaptists, or in the puritanical iconoclasm which led to the destruction of manuscripts and musical instruments. A small group of Anabaptist saints appears to have exercised a rather ruthless authority during most of the stormy history of the Münster commune, and in the end Jan of Leyden became not only the spiritual leader but also the temporal ruler of the city, claiming to be King of the Earth, destined to usher in the Fifth Monarchy which would prepare the Second Coming of Christ.

What seems to have been lacking in these movements, from an anarchist point of view, was the element of individualism that would have balanced their egalitarianism. The shaking free from the medieval tendency to see man as a member of a community ordained by God was a slow process, and perhaps slowest of all among the landworker and artisan classes—used to a communitarian pattern of guild and village life—on whom the peasant revolts and the Anabaptist movement were mostly based. Here the anarchist historiographers fall into the error of assuming that the primitive or medieval folk community, based on mutual aid and roughly egalitarian by nature, is also individualistic; most frequently, of course, it is the reverse, inclined toward a traditional pattern in which conformity is expected and the exceptional resented.

The individualist trend in post-medieval Europe emerges first among the cultured classes of the Italian cities during the Quattrocento; it appears as a cult of personality which has nothing to do with ideas of social reform, and it leads as often to the pride of the despot as to the desire for many-sided fulfilment of the humanist scholar. But it creates a new interest in man as an individual rather than as a mere member of the social order; from the time of Dante it permeates the literature of southern Europe, and from Chaucer that of England, until it leads to such individualist literary forms as the Elizabethan drama, the biography and autobiography, and, eventually, the novel, all based on a steadily deepening interest in the emotional and psychological nature of man defined against, rather than in, his social background.

Parallel to this secular exaltation of the individual, the later stages of the Reformation culminate in a religious radicalism which goes beyond such chiliastic sects as the Anabaptist and which, particularly among the Quakers, develops a personalistic view of religion, rejecting organized forms, and basing itself on the idea of the 'inner light', or, as George Fox called it, 'that of God in every man', an idea resembling Tolstoy's and not very far from some anarchist conceptions of immanent justice.

These secular and religious tendencies all helped to propel the seventeenth century toward a deepening consciousness of the value of individual liberty. And it was during the English Civil War that this trend produced the earliest recognizably anarchistic movement.

The men who fought the Civil War were—on both sides—more thoroughly the heirs of Renaissance individualism than is commonly recognized; there is perhaps no more magnificent example of the Baroque cult of personality than Milton's Satan. In another direction the rise of the Independents in opposition to the Calvinists shows the increasing swing toward an emphasis on the personal conscience as director of religious and moral choice, and here again, in *Areopagitica*, Milton drew a conclusion that is more libertarian than liberal. Economic and social changes, the rise of early capitalism and the consolidation of the squirearchy, all pointed in the same direction, and combined to produce the state of extreme political tension that led through rebellion to the first modern revolutionary dictatorship—Cromwell's prototype of the totalitarian state—but also to its contradiction.

For the very individualism that plunged the middle classes into a political and military struggle for the creation of a class oligarchy veiled by democratic pronouncements resulted among the lower classes in the emergence of two radical movements. The larger was that of the Levellers, ancestors of the Chartists and advocates of universal suffrage. Though some of them, like Walwyn, suggested community of property, their general demand was for political rather than economic equality, and for a democratic constitution that would do away with the privileges arrogated to themselves by the higher officers of the New Model Army. In curious anticipation of French Revolutionary invective, one Cromwellian pamphleteer stigmatized the Levellers as 'Switzerizing anarchists'. But it was not the Levellers who represented the really anarchistic wing of the English revolutionary movement in the seventeenth century. Rather, it was the ephemeral group whose peculiar form of social protest earned them the name of Diggers.

The Levellers were drawn mainly from the lower ranks of the New Model Army, who wanted their share in governing the country they had fought to liberate from the rule of Divine Right Kings. The Diggers, on the other hand, were mostly poor men, victims of the economic recession that followed the Civil War, and their demands were principally social and economic. They considered they had been robbed by those who remained rich, not only of political rights, but even of the elementary right to the means of survival. Their protest was a cry of hunger, and their leaders, Gerrard Winstanley and William Everard, had both suffered from the troubles of the time. Winstanley was a former Lancashire mercer who had come to London, set himself up in the cloth trade, and been ruined by the recession. 'I was beaten out both of estate and trade, and forced to accept the goodwill of friends crediting to me, to lead a country life.' Everard was an old soldier of the Civil War who had been cashiered for spreading Leveller propaganda.

The Diggers began with theory in 1648, and proceeded to action in 1649. Winstanley's early pamphlet, *Truth Lifting Up Its Head Above Scandals*, established the philosophic basis of the movement as a rationalistic one. God, in Winstanley's view, was none other than 'the incomprehensible spirit, Reason'. 'Where does that Reason dwell?' he asks. 'He dwells in every creature, according to the nature and being of the creature, but supremely in man. Therefore man is called a rational creature ... This,' he continues in an interesting anticipation of Tolstoy, 'is the Kingdom of God within man.'

From this almost pantheistic conception of God as immanent Reason there arises a theory of conduct which suggests that if man acts in accordance with his own rational nature he will fulfil his duty as a social being.

Let reason rule the man and he dares not trespass against his fellow creatures, but will do as he would be done unto. For Reason tells him is thy neighbour hungry and naked today, do thou feed him and clothe him, it may be thy case tomorrow and then he will be ready to help thee.

This is near to literal Christianity, but it is just as near to Kropotkin's view of the motivation of mutual aid, and in his most radical pamphlet, *The New Law of Righteousness*, Winstanley emerges with a series of propositions which reinforce the anarchistic elements in his thought.

Equating Christ with 'the universal liberty', he begins with a statement on the corrupting nature of authority, and here he criticizes not only political power, but also the economic power of the master over his servant and the familial power of the father over the child and the husband over the wife.

Everyone that gets an authority into his hands tyrannizes over others; as many husbands, parents, masters, magistrates, that live after the flesh do carry themselves like oppressing lords over such as are under them, not knowing that their wives, children, servants, subjects are their fellow creatures, and hath an equal privilege to share them in the blessing of liberty.

But the 'equal privilege to share in the blessing of liberty' is not an abstract privilege. Its conquest is linked with the attack on property rights, and here Winstanley is emphatic in his insistence on the intimate link between economic and political power.

And let all men say what they will, so long as such are rulers as call the land theirs, upholding this particular property of mine and thine, the common people shall never have their liberty, nor the land be freed from troubles, oppressions and complainings; by reason thereof the Creator of all things is continually provoked.

If Winstanley's criticism of society as he sees it at this crucial point in his career ends in a libertarian rejection of both authority and property, his vision of the kind of egalitarian society he would like to create embodies many features of the ideal society envisaged by the anarchists two centuries later.

When this universal law of equity rises up in every man and woman, then none shall lay claim to any creature and say, This is mine, and that is yours. This is my work, that is yours. But everyone shall put to their hands to till the earth and bring up cattle, and the blessing of the earth shall be common to all; when a man hath need of any corn or cattle, take from the next store-house he meets with. There shall be no buying and selling, no fairs or markets, but the whole earth shall be a common treasury for every man, for the earth is the Lord's … When a man hath eat, and drink, and clothes, he hath enough. And all shall cheerfully put to their hands to make these things that are needful, one helping another. There shall be none lords over others, but everyone shall be a lord of himself, subject to the law of righteousness, reason and equity, which shall dwell and rule in him, which is the Lord.

Work done in common and its products shared equally; no rulers, and men living peacefully with each other according to the promptings of their own consciences; commerce abolished and in its place a system of open store-houses; it all reads like a primitive sketch of Kropotkin's anarchist-communist society, and the sketch is given the last touch that turns it into a recognizable likeness when we find Winstanley anticipating the whole line of libertarian thinkers by condemning punishment and contending that crime arises from economic inequality.

For surely this particular property of mine and thine hath brought in all misery upon people. For first, it hath occasioned people to steal one from another. Secondly, it hath made laws to hang those that did steal. It tempts people to do an evil action and then kills them for doing of it. Let all judge if this not be a great devil.

Winstanley insists that the only way to end social injustice is for the people themselves to act, and he talks with apocalyptic fervour of the role of the poor in regenerating the world. 'The Father is now raising up a people to himself out of the dust that is out of the lowest and most despised sort of people … In these and from these shall the Law of Righteousness break forth first.' The people should act, Winstanley contends, by seizing and working the land, which represents the principal source of wealth. He does not think it necessary to seize forcibly the estates of rich men. The poor can settle the commons and the waste lands (which he estimates occupy two-thirds of the country) and work them together. From their example men can learn the virtues of communal life, and the earth become a 'common treasury' providing plenty in freedom for all. The best pages of *The New Law of Righteousness* rise to a level of prophetic fervour.

> And when the Lord doth shew unto me the place and manner, how He will have us that are called common people to manure and work upon the common lands, I will then go forth and declare it in my action, to eat my bread with the sweat of my brows, without either giving or taking hire, looking upon the land as freely mine as another's.

The Lord did not delay. *The New Law of Righteousness* appeared in January 1649, and early in April Winstanley and his associates initiated their campaign of direct action by proceeding to St George's Hill, near Walton-on-Thames, where they began to dig the waste land and sow it with wheat, parsnips, carrots, and beans. They numbered in all between thirty and forty people, and Winstanley invited the local landworkers to join them, prophesying that very shortly their numbers would increase to five thousand. But the Diggers seem to have aroused little sympathy even among their poor neighbours, and a great deal of hostility among the local clergy and landowners. They were beaten by paid hooligans and fined by magistrates; their cattle were driven away, their seedlings torn up, and their flimsy huts burned down; they were called before General Fairfax, who failed to intimidate them, and troops of soldiers were sent to investigate them, but were withdrawn when a number of them showed evident interest in the Digger doctrine. Through all these difficult months Winstanley and his followers refused to be provoked into the violence which they abhorred. Their pamphlets appeared one after the other during 1649, full of righteous complaint against a world that refused to acknowledge them; they even sent out apostles into the country, who instigated occupations of waste lands at several places in the Home Counties and even as far afield as Gloucestershire.

But even Digger endurance was not proof against unrelenting persecution. In March 1650 the settlers left St George's Hill, and abandoned their attempt to win England to agrarian communism by the power of example. The other colonies were then shorter-lived, and as a movement the Diggers had disappeared by the end of 1650.

For a little while Winstanley continued to spread his ideas, now entirely by literary means, and in 1652 he aimed at the most unlikely convert of all by addressing to Cromwell his last and longest work—*The Law of Freedom in a Platform, or True Magistracy Restored*. The relative moderation of this pamphlet suggests that Winstanley's enthusiasm and his extremity of views had both been sapped by the experience of St George's Hill. For, though he continues to advocate almost complete communism, he puts forward a political plan little different from that of the extreme Levellers, calling for annual Parliaments, and providing for various kinds of officers and overseers, introducing compulsion to work and even admitting the death penalty for certain offences against the community. *The Law of Freedom* aroused little attention, and after publishing it Winstanley retreated into an obscurity so dense that even the place and date of his death are unknown.

The Digger movement left no heritage to later social and political movements, though it may have influenced the Quakers, toward whom some of its supporters were drawn. So completely was it forgotten, indeed, that even William Godwin, writing his *History of the Commonwealth*, does not appear to have realized how similar the Digger doctrine was to that which he himself developed in *Political Justice*. Only at the end of the nineteenth century was Winstanley's importance as a precursor of modern social ideologies recognized, and then, on the strength of his communistic ideas, some of the Marxists tried to claim him as their ancestor. But there is nothing Marxian about the peasant paradise that Winstanley envisions in *The New Law of Righteousness*. Its communism is entirely libertarian, and the effort of Winstanley and his friends to follow out its principles on St George's Hill stands at the beginning of the anarchist tradition of direct action.

No incident or movement in either the American or the French Revolution presented so prophetic a miniature of the anarchist future as the Diggers created in 1648 and 1649. During the nineteenth century both the United States and France were to be rich in varieties of anarchist thought and deed, but the manifestations of this tendency in the great eighteenth-century revolutions were impulsive and incomplete.

Some writers have seen an anarchistic element in the democracy of Thomas Jefferson, but, while he and many of his followers, notably Joel Barlow, admired Godwin's *Political Justice*, there is little evidence in his writings that he accepted Godwin's views in their extremity, or that he was ever much more than an opponent of excessive government. When he made his famous statement—'That government is best which governs least'—he did not reject authority. On the contrary, he thought it might be made harmless if the people participated thoroughly in its operation.

The influence over government must be shared among the people. If
every individual which composes their mass participates in the ultimate authority, the government will be safe; because the corrupting
of the whole mass will exceed any private resources of wealth.

Such passages make it clear that Jefferson looked to a system of universal suffrage in which the people would as far as possible be the rulers—a
condition as opposed to anarchist ideas as any other type of authority.
And, while he also spoke of 'a little rebellion, now and then' as 'a good
thing and as necessary in the political world as storms in the physical', he
evidently saw this as a corrective rather than a revolutionary force. 'It pre-
vents the degeneracy of government and nourishes a general attention to
the public affairs.'

Indeed, all of Jefferson's career, as an expansionist president, as a slave-
owning Virginian gentleman, as a political leader adept at compromise,
reinforces the authoritarian undertone of his writing, and tells strongly
against his claim to a place in the pantheon of anarchist ancestors.

A more genuine claim can be put for Thomas Paine, whose life made
him a personification of the common ideas that linked the British,
American, and French revolutionary movements of the later eighteenth
century. Paine's extreme distrust of government undoubtedly influenced
Godwin, who associated with him during the crucial years from 1789 to
1792, and his discussions of its demerits actually became, by quotation, part
of the fabric of *Political Justice*. Paine was one of those who thought that
government was indeed a necessity, but a most unpleasant one, brought
upon us by the corruption of man's original innocence. At the very beginning of the American War of Independence, in the historic pamphlet
entitled *Common Sense*, he made a distinction between society and government that brought him close to the viewpoint later established by Godwin.

Some writers have so confounded society with government as to
leave little or no distinction between them; whereas they are not
only different, but have different origins. Society is produced by our
wants, and government by our wickedness; the former promotes our
happiness *positively* by uniting our affections, the latter *negatively* by
restraining our vices. The one encourages intercourse, the other creates distinctions. The first is a patron, the last is a punisher.

Society in every state is a blessing, but government even in its best
state is but a necessary evil; in its worst state an intolerable one; for
when we suffer, or are exposed to the same miseries by a *government*

which we might expect in a country without government our calamity is heightened by reflecting that we furnish the means by which we suffer. Government, like dress, is the badge of lost innocence; the palaces of kings are built on the ruins of the bowers of paradise.

Paine's distrust of government was persistent; indeed, it was probably increased by the difficulties into which his honesty led him even with revolutionary governments. Sixteen years later, in *The Rights of Man*, he set in opposition to the claims of government the beneficial influence of those natural social urges which Kropotkin later made the subject of *Mutual Aid*.

Great part of that order which reigns among mankind is not the effect of government. It has its origin in the principles of society and the natural constitution of men. It existed prior to government and would exist if the formality of government was abolished. The mutual dependence and reciprocal interest which man has upon man, and all the parts of civilized community upon each other, create that great chain of connexion which holds it together. The landholder, the farmer, the manufacturer, the merchant, the tradesman, and every occupation, prospers by the aid which each receives from the other, and from the whole. Common interest regulates their concerns and forms their law; and the laws which common usage ordains, have a greater influence than the laws of government.

In the same work Paine speaks, like Godwin, of government as a hindrance to 'the natural propensity of society', and asserts that 'the most perfect civilization is, the less occasion has it for government, because the more does it regulate its own affairs and govern itself'. Here we have the point of view that we have already seen characterizing the typical anarchist; he stands in an evil, government-dominated present, looking back to a lost paradise of primitive innocence and forward to a future whose civilized simplicity will rebuild the golden age of liberty. In temperament and ideals Paine came very near to the anarchists; only his lack of optimism in the immediately foreseeable future prevented him from becoming one of them.

The American Revolution's lack of native expressions of anarchism is perhaps due to the masking of the kind of deep social divisions which parted the Diggers from the Grandees in the English Revolution by a common urge toward freedom from foreign oppression; these divisions only became really evident during the nineteenth century.

In the French Revolution, on the other hand, the clash between libertarian and authoritarian trends was evident and at times assumed violent
form. Kropotkin devoted one of his most scholarly books, *The Great French
Revolution*, to an interpretation of popular movements during the stormy
years from 1789 to the end of the Jacobin rule in 1793. His anarchistic bias
led him to overemphasize the libertarian elements, but it also enabled him
to see the events of the Revolution stereoscopically, thrown into relief by
social and economic causes, rather than as a mere struggle between political parties and personalities.

Certainly we can follow Kropotkin in seeing the emergence during this
period of some of the ideas that were eventually to crystallize into nineteenth-century anarchism. Condorcet, one of the great seminal minds of
the age, who believed in the indefinite progress of man toward a classless
liberty, already put forward while he was hiding from the Jacobins the idea
of *mutualité*, which was to be one of the twin pillars of Proudhon's anarchism; he conceived the plan of a great mutual-aid association among all
the workers that would save them from the perils of those economic crises
during which they were normally forced to sell their labour at starvation
prices.

The other Proudhonian pillar, federalism, was the subject of much discussion and even experiment during the Revolution. The Girondins
conceived it as a political expedient. While the Paris Commune in 1871 was
to see in a federal republic the means of saving Paris from a reactionary
France, the Girondins imagined that it might save France from a Jacobin
Paris. A more genuinely social federalism emerged among the various
semi-spontaneous revolutionary institutions of the time, first in the 'districts' or 'sections' into which the capital had been divided for electoral
purposes and out of which the Commune of Paris arose, and later in the
network of 'Popular Societies and Fraternal Societies, as well as
Revolutionary Committees', which tended to take the place of the sections
as the latter became subordinate political organs, dominated by the
Jacobins. In this connection Kropotkin quotes an interesting passage from
Sigismond Lacroix's *Actes de la commune*:

The state of mind of the districts ... displays itself both by a very
strong sentiment of communal unity and by a no less strong tendency toward self-government. Paris did not want to be a federation of
sixty republics cut off haphazard each in its territory; the Commune
is a unity composed of its united districts ... But side by side with
this undisputed principle, another principle is disclosed ... which is,

that the Commune must legislate and administer for itself, directly, as much as possible. Government by representation must be reduced to a minimum; everything that the Commune can do directly must be done by it, without any intermediary, without any delegation, or else it may be done by delegates reduced to the role of special commissioners, acting under the uninterrupted control of those who have commissioned them ... The final right of legislating and administering for the Commune belongs to the districts—to the citizens who come together in the general assemblies of the districts.

In such an organization Kropotkin sees an early expression of 'the principles of anarchism', and concludes that these principles 'had their origin, not in theoretic speculations, but in the *deeds* of the Great French Revolution'. But here again he allows his anxiety to prove the folk origins of anarchism to lead him into exaggeration. What he misses is the fact that the 'right of legislating', even if it is brought down to the level of general assemblies, still exists; the people *rule*. And so we must regard the revolutionary years as an attempt at direct democracy rather than at anarchy. Yet, even if it was not anarchist in any true sense, the Commune was—like its successor in 1871—federalist, and here it anticipated Proudhon by developing sketchily the kind of practical framework in which he thought an anarchist society might develop.

But we have to look beyond Condorcet's mutualism and the federalism of the Commune to find the real proto-anarchists of the French Revolution. Kropotkin was so concerned with tracing popular manifestations that he neglected unduly the individuals who came nearest to expressing an anarchistic attitude toward the events of their times. He paid only scant attention to Jacques Roux, Jean Varlet, and the Enragés who gathered round them; yet if there are any anarchist ancestors in the French Revolution, it is among these courageous intransigents, unsuccessful and historically obscure as they were, that we must find them.

The movement of the Enragés appeared during 1793, and ran like a sullen ground bass through the year of the Terror. Like the Digger movement during the English Civil War, it emerged at a time of economic recession; to a great extent it was a response to the economic distress of the poor people of Paris and Lyons, but it was also a reaction against the social distinctions which marked the hardening power of the ascendant middle class.

The Enragés were not a party in the modern sense. They had no organization, no agreed common policy. They were a loose group of like-minded revolutionaries who cooperated in the most rudimentary manner, yet who were united in rejection of the Jacobin conception of state author- ity, who advocated that the people act directly, and who saw in communis- tic economic measures rather than in political action a way to end the sufferings of the poor. The accusation brought against Roux by the Jacobins, that he told the people that 'every kind of government must be proscribed', is in effect true of them all.

Jacques Roux, the most celebrated of the Enragés, was one of the priests of the Revolution, a country clergyman who, even before he reached Paris in 1790, had been accused of inciting the peasants of his district to burn and pillage the châteaux of landowners who attempted to enforce their rights to seigneurial dues. 'The land belongs to all equally,' he is said to have told his parishioners. He remained a priest after the Revolution, in which he appears to have seen a reflection of the pure spirit of Christianity; he once defined its task as 'making men equal between each other as they are to all eternity before God'. But it is difficult to believe that a man of Roux's temperament and attitude remained an orthodox Roman Catholic; his idea of God was probably not far from Gerrard Winstanley's.

Roux's sincerity made him as poor as the strictest of Christian ascetics, and his compassion for the workers of the Gravilliers quarter in which he lived seems to have been one of the causes for the extremity of his radical- ism, yet there was a hard fanatical edge to his character which led him into the one action that odiously mars his memory. While Thomas Paine pleaded for the life of Louis XVI, Roux was among those who were charged with witnessing the King's execution. Before leaving the prison, Louis asked if he could confide his will to him as a priest. Roux replied coldly: 'I am here only to lead you to the scaffold.' Yet the man who gloat- ed on the destruction of the King as the living manifestation of authority later protested from his own prison cell against the brutalities which the Terror was inflicting on men and women whose only crime was the rank into which they were born by chance.

From the beginning Roux was active in the revolutionary life of Paris. He frequented the Club of the Cordeliers, and in March 1792 hid Marat in his own house, an act which did not save him later from the attacks of the self-styled 'friend of the people'. He ran unsuccessfully as a candidate for the Convention, and eventually became a member of the General Council of the Commune.

It was not until the end of 1792 that Roux began to show the extremity of views he had evolved while working among the shoemakers and carpenters of Gravilliers, who were his closest associates. The failure of the Revolution to fulfil the demands he had made on it during its first year was weighing on his mind, and he delivered a speech at this time in which he gave a first hint of anarchistic tendencies by declaring that 'senatorial despotism is as terrible as the sceptre of kings because it chains the people without their knowing it and brutalizes and subjugates them by laws they themselves are supposed to have made'. During the unruly weeks that followed, when petitioners appeared at the bar of the Convention with demands for the control of prices, and the poor people of Gravilliers rioted against profiteering shopkeepers, Roux defended them, and may even have played some part in inciting them.

During March 1793 Roux was joined by the young revolutionary orator Jean Varlet. Like Roux, Varlet was an educated man. He came of good family, had studied at the Collège d'Harcourt, and at the time of the Revolution had a modest private income as well as a post in the Civil Service. The Revolution filled him with the kind of enthusiasm that can turn to bitterness when it is frustrated. He became a popular orator, and then, in March 1793, emerged as a leader of the earliest attacks on the Girondins. But, just as behind Roux's agitation over prices lay the idea of common ownership, so behind Varlet's attack on the most conservative group in the Convention lay a general condemnation of the idea of government by representation.

Though there is no evidence that Varlet and Roux had collaborated beforehand—and even some evidence of mutual jealousy between these two popular agitators—by June 1793 they were together in a new agitation over the cost of living, and Jacques Roux made a series of speeches in which he not only denounced the class structure which the Revolution had allowed to survive—'What is liberty, when one class of men starve another?'—but also suggested that the law protects exploitation, which prospers 'in its shadow'. Because he did not trust legislators, he demanded that the condemnation of profiteering be written into the constitution in such a way as to be safe from meddling governments.

Through 1793 the agitation of the Enragés continued. They were joined by Théophile Leclerc from Lyons and by the beautiful and talented actress Claire Lacombe with her organization of women, La Société des Républicaines Révolutionaires. At the same time, the hostility of the Jacobins narrowed around them, particularly when their voices were raised against the state-operated Terror. To Robespierre the anti-government implications of the Enragés' speeches and of their ephemeral journals (Roux's *Le Publiciste* and Leclerc's *L'Ami du peuple*) were as evident as they seem to us today; he had no intention of tolerating their agitation indefinitely. Roux and Varlet were arrested. Claire Lacombe's society was suppressed, despite a protest demonstration of six thousand angry women. Roux, called before the Revolutionary Tribunal and realizing that his death was inevitable, cheated the guillotine by painfully committing suicide. 'I do not complain of the tribunal,' he said before he died. 'It has acted according to the law. But I have acted according to my liberty.' To die placing liberty above law is the death of an anarchist.

Yet it was reserved for Varlet, who survived the Terror, to state explicitly the anarchistic conclusions that are to be drawn from the movement of the Enragés. After Robespierre had fallen and the surviving Enragés had rejoiced over his passing, Varlet witnessed the subsequent tyranny of the Directory, and in anger he published what we must regard as the earliest anarchist manifesto in continental Europe. Appropriately, it was entitled *Explosion*; the title-page bore an engraving showing clouds of smoke and flame billowing around a burning classical structure, and above the engraving an epigraph: 'Let revolutionary government perish, rather than a principle.'

Surveying the years of the Revolution, Varlet declares:

Despotism has passed from the palace of kings to the circle of a committee. It is neither the royal robes, nor the sceptre, nor the crown that makes kings hated, but ambition and tyranny. In my country there has only been a change in dress.

Why, he goes on to ask, should a revolutionary government have in this way become as much a tyranny as the rule of a king? Partly, he suggests, because the intoxication of power makes men wish to see it remain for ever in their own hands. But there is more to the matter than the mere weakness of men; here is a contradiction within the very institution of government.

What a social monstrosity, what a masterpiece of Machiavellianism, this revolutionary government is in fact. For any reasoning being, Government and Revolution are incompatible, at least unless the people wishes to constitute the organs of power in permanent insurrection against themselves, which is too absurd to believe.

Here, at the very end of their movement, the last of the Enragés makes clear its implications. It is interesting to observe how tardily these early

French libertarians brought themselves to the open rejection of government. Even in comparison with Winstanley, their lack of a developed programme or philosophy is remarkable. But their time was short—a few packed months of action—and they worked too near the centre of the revolution they had helped to make for their ideas to crystallize sharply in such a period. Winstanley had been able to stand on the edge of events and to formulate his theories as far as his knowledge would allow, and then to proceed to action with a philosophy to inspire him in his deeds.

Yet the French Revolution was not so unproductive in anarchist thought as this account may have made it appear. In the same year as Jean Varlet published his *Explosion*, William Godwin in England published the first great treatise on the evils of government, *Political Justice*. And it is doubtful indeed if *Political Justice* would even have been conceived if the French Revolution had not happened when it did.

3. The Man of Reason

Like Tolstoy and Stirner, William Godwin is one of the great libertarian thinkers who stand outside the historical anarchist movement of the nineteenth century, yet, by their very isolation from it, demonstrate the extent to which it sprang from the spirit of the age. He had little direct influence on that movement, and many of its leaders, whose theories so closely resembled his own, were unaware of the extent to which he had anticipated them. Proudhon knew Godwin by name, but his single reference to him in *Economic Contradictions* (1846), in which he dismissed him as a 'communist' of the same school as Robert Owen, suggests that he was not familiar with his work. There is no evidence that Bakunin knew even as much about him as Proudhon, while it was not until comparatively late in Kropotkin's life, after his own theories were fully formed, that the latter encountered *Political Justice* and realized the deep affinity between his own thought and Godwin's. After Kropotkin, Godwin became recognized by the more intellectual anarchists as one of their predecessors, but his influence, which was potent, has lain mostly elsewhere.

Godwin never called himself an anarchist; for him 'anarchy' retained the negative meaning given to it by the polemicists of the French Revolutionary period. It meant, whenever he referred to it, the disorder that results from the breakdown of government without the general acceptance of a 'consistent and digested view of political justice'. Like subsequent libertarian thinkers, Godwin saw society as a naturally developing phenomenon which can operate in complete freedom from government, but he did not share the faith of his successors in the spontaneous instincts of the untutored people. In this sense he remained a man of the Enlightenment; education was his real key to liberation, and he feared that without it man's 'ungoverned passions will often not stop at equality but incite them to grasp at power'.

Yet so rooted was his conviction of the life-destroying propensities of authority, that he would not wholly condemn even an anarchy conceived in negative terms. Extreme disorder, for this believer in an ordered life under the aegis of impartial reason, was infinitely more to be desired than extreme subordination.

Anarchy is transitory, but despotism tends towards permanence. Anarchy awakens mind, diffuses energy and enterprise through the community, though it does not effect this in the best manner ... But in despotism mind is trampled into an equality of the most odious sort. Everything that promises greatness is destined to fall under the exterminating hand of suspicion and envy.

In the positive sense in which anarchism is now understood, Godwin stands at the head of the tradition, for the arguments he put forward in 1793 with the publication of his *Enquiry Concerning Political Justice* embraced all the essential features of an anarchistic doctrine. He rejected any social system dependent on government. He put forward his own conception of a simplified and decentralized society with a dwindling minimum of authority, based on a voluntary sharing of material goods. And he suggested his own means of proceeding towards it by means of a propaganda divorced from any kind of political party or political aim. Essentially, this doctrine, which thrilled the Romantic poets from Coleridge to Shelley, and for a brief period during the 1790s became a kind of secular gospel for English radicals, was the same as that which Proudhon proclaimed during the revolutionary 1840s. Godwin anticipated the whole of nineteenth-century anarchism when he summarized in his resounding Latinized language the hope that lay at the core of his doctrine:

With what delight must every well-informed friend of mankind look forward to the dissolution of political government, of that brute engine which has been the only perennial cause of the vices of mankind, and which has mischiefs of various sorts incorporated with its substance, and no otherwise to be removed than by its utter annihilation!

In Godwin one can see, more clearly than in later libertarian writers, the various currents that came together to produce the anarchist point of view. The French Revolution certainly gave Godwin the immediate impulse to write *Political Justice*, and provided the audience ready to receive it with an enthusiasm which still astonishes us when we look back on those years in which, as Hazlitt said in an oft-quoted passage of recollection, William Godwin 'blazed in the firmament of reputation'. But the ideas put forward in *Political Justice* had been established in Godwin's mind long before the French Revolution.

As early as 1783, when his passion for education ran on more conventional lines, he planned to set up a private school, and published a curious little prospectus entitled *An Account of the Seminary That Will Be Opened on Monday the Fourth Day of August at Epsom in Surrey.* For reasons which are evident when one reads it, this school prospectus did not attract a single pupil, but it has its place among the more curious early examples of anarchist literature. Godwin devoted very little space to the kind of practical details parents expect to find, and was much more concerned with putting forward his theories on the nature of society and the general function of education. As a result, *An Account of the Seminary* reads in places like a preliminary exercise in the arguments regarding government which Godwin was to extend in *Political Justice* and in the proposals on free education that he was to elaborate in *The Enquirer* (1797). The following paragraph clearly reveals the direction which his thought had taken five years before the outbreak of the French Revolution:

> The state of society is incontestably artificial; the power of one man over another must be always derived from convention or from conquest; by nature we are equal. The necessary consequence is, that government must always depend upon the opinion of the governed. Let the most oppressed people under heaven once change their mode of thinking, and they are free ... Government is very limited in its power of making men either virtuous or happy; it is only in the infancy of society that it can do any thing considerable; in its maturity it can only direct a few of our outward actions. But our moral dispositions and character depend very much, perhaps entirely, upon education.

Here the key ideas of *Political Justice* already exist in embryo. A natural, egalitarian society is opposed to an artificial, governmental society. The power of thought is stressed. Education is given a peculiar importance because of Godwin's idea that human character is determined by environment rather than heredity, and that human faults are imparted by bad training. (Elsewhere in the same prospectus he remarks: 'The vices of the young spring not from nature, who is equally the kind and blameless mother of all her children; they derive from the defects of education.') And, while Godwin had not yet reached the logical destination of deciding that government is positively evil, he is already prepared to argue that it contains little that is positively good.

The language and even the framing of ideas in *An Account of the Seminary* have a French ring, reminiscent of the writers—Helvétius, d'Holbach, and Rousseau—whom Godwin had been reading since 1781. But it would be wrong to assume that Godwin was ever a mere disciple of the French social philosophers of the eighteenth century; to the utilitarianism of Helvétius and d'Holbach (and of Bentham as well, for that matter), he opposed the view of man as part of a system of universal moral order and maintained that immutable truths must be the criteria of our actions; to the social contract of Rousseau he opposed the idea of a society living according to moral law, and to Rousseau's idea of education as a process of imposing a certain cast upon the pupil's mind he opposed an interplay between master and student which would encourage the mind of the child to develop according to its natural bent. 'The gentle yoke of the preceptor should be confounded as much as possible with the eternal laws of nature and necessity.'

In fact, Godwin shows, perhaps more than any other writer of his time, the modification of French eighteenth-century liberal thought by the radical elements in English dissent. He belonged to a family of dissenting ministers. His grandfather and one of his uncles had been famous preachers; his father was the uneloquent but strict pastor of a series of rural Independent congregations. Godwin himself showed early a tendency to follow the family profession. His favourite childhood game was the preaching of heartrending sermons by which he hoped to convert his schoolfellows. Later, like Hazlitt, he attended Hoxton Academy, the best of those excellent colleges which the Dissenters founded during the eighteenth century when their beliefs still debarred them from the universities. He emerged with his intention of following the ministry unchanged, and from 1778 to 1783 he presided, with a growing conviction of unsuitability, over a succession of small nonconformist chapels in East Anglia and the Home Counties. At Beaconsfield he finally decided that he had lost whatever vocation he might have had in the beginning, and set off to London to live as a writer. To the end of his life he continued to dress and to look like a nonconformist minister.

Godwin's abandonment of the ministry was preceded by his conversion—through the arguments of Joseph Priestley—from his original Calvinism to the doctrines of Socinius, who denied the divinity of Christ and held that the soul of man was born pure—a belief that accorded with Godwin's later idea of the infant as a kind of *tabula rasa* on which experience writes its story. But it was not until 1790, the very year before the beginning of *Political Justice*, that he finally abandoned any kind of Christian belief and, under the influence of his close friend Thomas Holcroft, became an avowed atheist, a position which he only modified so far as to retreat into a vague pantheism that dominated his later life.

But, though the 1780s show Godwin progressively shedding the actual dogmas of his youthful religion, we should not assume that he shed also the intellectual influence of the dissenting tradition. His individualism, his distrust of the state, his stress on sincerity as a rule for the conduct of human relations, were all acquired in his youth among the Independents and were eventually to become the most prominent pillars of the anarchistic vision he constructed in *Political Justice*. But there is one particular influence to which students of Godwin have in the past paid too little heed.

When he was eleven, Godwin's parents withdrew him from the last of a succession of rural schools and sent him to Norwich to become the sole pupil of Samuel Newton, pastor of the Independent congregation. Newton was one of those men, curiously combining political radicalism and religious bigotry, whose presence has been one of the distinctive features of English left-wing movements since the Civil War. He was a supporter of John Wilkes; he was also a disciple of Robert Sandeman, the linen-draper apostle of a small fundamentalist sect which had been expelled by the Presbyterians for opposition to any form of Church government and had eventually become attached to the Independents. The Sandemanians remained Calvinists at heart; their conception of election was so rigorous, Godwin claimed, that 'after Calvin had damned ninety-nine in a hundred of mankind', Sandeman had 'contrived a scheme for damning ninety-nine in a hundred of the followers of Calvin'.

To this creed Godwin was early converted, and he remained faithful to it from his early teens until his middle twenties, for he tells us that he came out of Hoxton at the age of twenty-three with his Sandemanian beliefs unchanged and only began to abandon them some time afterwards. In fact, he never wholly shed the influence of this radical sect, and a glance at some of their basic beliefs and practices suggests that many aspects of *Political Justice* were little more than Sandemanianism secularized.

Sandeman held that the Bible contained all that was necessary for salvation; here, of course, Godwin parted from him, but he agreed with many of the conclusions drawn from this belief. The Sandemanians denied the validity of Church government; Godwin denied the validity of all government. They maintained that the religious man had no business with the state; Godwin maintained the same for the moral man. They established an organization of independent congregations, with no ordained ministers; Godwin envisaged a network of independent parishes, without rulers, as the ideal basic structure for a libertarian society. Finally, the Sandemanians believed in community of property as a desirable ideal and taught that it was sinful to save money, since a surplus should be distributed to those who needed it; it appears to have been a practice in Sandemanian congregations for poor members to be supported by their relatively better-off co-religionists. Once again there is a close parallel with the Godwinian system, which envisages a community of goods to be shared according to need, which lays specific stress on the moral evils of 'accumulated property', and which maintains, not so much that a poor man has a right to be supported by those more fortunate, but rather that the latter have a positive duty to support him.

Sandeman's doctrine was only one among the many influences that contributed to the eventual form of *Political Justice*. Yet it clearly contains the first sources of some of the most important elements in Godwin's system; it also demonstrates that Godwin was familiar since boyhood with one form or another of the anti-authoritarian and communistic ideas he later developed. He became an anarchistic thinker by no sudden conversion, but by a gradual process of drawing the logical conclusions from concepts with which his receptive mind had long been familiar. In this sense the French social philosophers, and even such English writers as John Locke and Thomas Paine, were not so much giving him new ideas as providing the rational arguments and the logical framework in which he could develop the individualism that reached him by way of the dissenting tradition. Of dissent in its radical form he retains almost all but the religious element—the sense that all we do is a preparation for a Heavenly Kingdom.

Political Justice is in fact linked with religion only in terms of its discarded origins. In itself it presents a characteristically anarchistic combination of the political and the moral, criticizing forms of governmental organization but also achieving a solution based on the changing of personal opinion and the reformation of personal conduct. And thus Godwin appears as the earliest important social writer to pose consciously within his own work the extreme implications of that post-Reformation world in which, as F.W. Maitland said, 'for the first time the Absolute State faced the Absolute Individual'.

Thus, springing from the stem of English dissent, nurtured by two decades of assiduous reading in the Greek classics and in English and French literature from the late seventeenth century onward, *Political Justice* finally bore fruit in the energizing sunlight with which the French Revolution first rose upon the Western world.

In the early phase of the Revolution, when bloodshed was slight and the factional struggle had not yet culminated in the Terror, Godwin's enthusiasm was almost unalloyed.

My heart beat high with great swelling sentiments of Liberty, [he
later recollected, in words reminiscent of Wordsworth's confession].
I had read with great satisfaction the writings of Rousseau, Helvétius
and others, the most popular authors of France. I observed in them a
system more general and simply philosophical than in the majority
of English writers on political subjects, and I could not refrain from
conceiving sanguine hopes of a revolution of which such writings
had been the precursors.

Yet he continued, as he remarked, to disapprove of 'mob government
and violence,' and to desire 'such political changes only as should flow
purely from the clear light of the understanding and the erect and generous feelings of the heart'.

But, as we have seen, it was not the French Revolution itself that made
Godwin a libertarian; he merely saw it as an event by which his already
developing ideas might be realized; and this fact largely explains the
steadfastness with which, in the days after 1797 when political reaction
reigned in England and most of the former friends of the revolution
became its enemies, he maintained his radical beliefs. His ideas had been
conceived independently of events in France, and when the revolution
declined into violence and dictatorship, this did not force him to abandon
any of his basic beliefs; on the contrary, it offered a support to his original
contention that political changes are fruitless unless they emerge from
changes in moral attitudes.

While the French Revolution produced an appropriate climate, there is
some doubt as to the precise impulse which started Godwin on the writing
of *Political Justice*. He himself claimed that the original conception 'proceeded on a feeling of the imperfections and errors of Montesquieu, and a
desire of supplying a less faulty work' than the French writer's *L'Esprit des
lois*. On the other hand, it has generally been thought, without any actual
confirmation in Godwin's own words, that *Political Justice* was meant as a
comprehensive answer to Burke's *Reflections on the French Revolution*. Godwin
was certainly conscious of the need for Burke to be answered, since he
served on a small committee which arranged for the publication of Paine's
Rights of Man, an avowed reply to the *Reflections*. But this tells us nothing
about his own intentions in writing *Political Justice*, and the most we can
fairly assume is that a desire to refute Burke may have been one among a
number of motives that set Godwin to work.

Once begun, the whole conception of *Political Justice* developed in the
process of writing, and, like most of the great seminal works in the world's

literature, it took on a life of its own which carried it far beyond Godwin's original intent. Indeed, the logically developed structure of anarchist thought that now seems to distinguish the book only appeared as the theme was gradually worked out in the process of writing. Godwin was conscious of this, particularly since the chapters of *Political Justice* were printed as soon as they were written, a process which did not allow him to eliminate the inevitable contradictions that appeared as his opinions matured.

> The ideas of the author became more perspicacious and digested as his inquiries advanced [he explained in an apologetic preface]. He did not enter upon the work without being aware that government by its very nature counteracts the improvement of individual mind; but he understood the full meaning of this proposition more completely as he proceeded, and saw more distinctly into the nature of the remedy.

Political Justice appeared in February 1793. Already the political reaction had begun, and the government was persecuting radicals who had sympathized with the French Revolution. Barely two months before, Paine had been sentenced to death for publishing *The Rights of Man*; he had already crossed to France, thanks to William Blake's timely warning that the officers of the crown were searching for him. Godwin had to expect that he too might suffer for a book as direct as *Political Justice*, but moral cowardice was not one of his faults, and his preface embodies a calm challenge to the enemies of literary freedom.

> It is to be tried, whether a project is formed for suppressing the activity of mind and putting an end to the disquisitions of science. Respecting the event in a personal view the author has formed his resolution. Whatever conduct his countrymen may pursue, they will not be able to shake his tranquillity. The duty he is most bound to discharge is the assisting the progress of truth; and if he suffer in any respect for such a proceeding, there is certainly no vicissitude that can befall him that can ever bring along with it a more satisfactory consolation.

Such philosophy in the face of possible persecution was perhaps another gift of his dissenting heritage; some at least among Godwin's ancestors must have faced similar moments of risk for the sake of their nonconformity. In the event, *Political Justice* went unprosecuted. A famous tale runs that when the possibility of proceeding against it was discussed in the Cabinet, Pitt brushed it aside with the remark that a book that sold at three guineas would have little influence. How far Pitt was wrong we shall see later.

In the account of *Political Justice* that follows I shall concentrate as far as possible on the aspects that establish Godwin at the beginning of the anarchist intellectual tradition. The astonishing completeness with which the book anticipates the various facets of the libertarian point of view—so that it still remains one of the most thorough expositions of anarchistic beliefs—will explain the space I devote at this point to a single memorable treatise.

It is impossible to begin a satisfactory discussion of Godwinian anarchism without considering the idea of Necessity which pervades his masterpiece. Necessity, as Godwin saw it, was really the immutable and impersonal moving force of the universe which expresses itself through natural laws and determines the actions of human beings. Necessitarian beliefs of various kinds have not been uncommon among anarchists, for many of Godwin's successors accepted the scientific determinism of the nineteenth-century evolutionists. Indeed, the general anarchist tendency to rely on natural law and to imagine a return to an existence based on its dictates leads by a paradoxical logic toward determinist conclusions which, of course, clash in a very obvious way with the belief in the freedom of individual action.

It is clear from *Political Justice* that Godwin's own idea of Necessity was by no means uncomplicated by such contradictions. A Necessitarian viewpoint came easily to a former Calvinist, and was also comforting for a man who longed for philosophic detachment, who preferred to pity people as victims of circumstance rather than as wilful transgressors. But, while his intellectual heritage and his own nature impelled Godwin toward Necessitarianism, he was quite evidently aware of the difficulties that assail any attempt to wed anarchism and determinism. If Necessity exists, and is the law of nature, how are we to explain that the human situation went so far astray that artificial systems of authority have replaced natural social organizations? How, on the other hand, if government is inevitable—as all things that exist must be to a complete Necessitarian— can we condemn it realistically? Finally, how can personal freedom and responsible choice, for which all the anarchists, Godwin included, have struggled, have any meaning in a Necessitarian world? Can one in fact be a political libertarian and a philosophic Necessitarian at the same time?

Anarchists have tried to solve this problem in a variety of ways. Few have taken what one might have thought the logical step of accepting the absurdist or existentialist view of an undetermined world where natural law does not exist. Most of them seem to have elected for an attitude which relegates determination to certain limited aspects of life. Natural determination cannot be avoided. We grow old and die; we must recognize our physical and perhaps even our moral weaknesses. Once we voluntarily accept such limitations we are free within them, and then it is only the avoidable that can enslave us. The greatest kingdom of the avoidable and the artificial is human society, and this precisely is the realm where freedom is possible, since it is the realm where will can operate effectively. Men, in other words, cannot deny their physical or even their psychological determination, just as they cannot deny natural disasters; on the other hand, they can deny slavery to human institutions and to other human beings.

In practice Godwin, like these later anarchists, presented a compromise between determination and freedom which is not always evident when one listens to his invocations of Necessity as if it were some blind, mechanical, and all-ruling goddess. No one has better explained this aspect of Godwin's thought than Dr F.E.L. Priestley in his introduction to the 1946 facsimile edition of *Political Justice*. Priestley suggests that Godwin places so much emphasis on Necessity because, following Hume, Hartley, and d'Holbach, he conceives of free will as meaning 'complete irresponsibility of behaviour, the ability "to will or choose without motive, or to be able to prevent motives from acting upon the will"'. To such a conception, Dr Priestley opposes, as more truly representing the idea of liberty, Locke's definition of freedom 'as determination by the "last result of our own minds" ... with its logical difficulty of a free but determined will'. What Godwin is anxious to avoid, he suggests, is making 'the will independent of the idea of understanding', and there is nothing in his application of the idea of Necessity that would contradict a limited but genuine freedom of the will as defined by Locke.

Of the two sorts of determination, that in which the mind is determined by past experience, and that in which it is determined by a judgement of the future [Dr Priestley continues], the latter is the greater fundamental importance to Godwin's scheme. At the same time, his eagerness to construct an exact science of morality, based on predictability of behaviour, discovery of general principles, and control of process, leads him towards the more empirical form. The distinction he draws between voluntary and involuntary actions suggests that involuntary behaviour exhibits one sort of necessity, that dictated by past experience, while voluntary actions are always determined by a judgement, and proceed 'upon the apprehended truth of some proposition'. This second type of determinism, rational and teleological, is hard to distinguish from what is usually considered free will. In fact, Godwin's whole doctrine is essentially the same as the Thomist doctrine of free will as outlined by Professor Taylor; we are usually biased in our choice of actions by the factors upon which the various sciences lay stress, but we can on occasion eliminate this bias and impartially weigh the merits of alternatives. In making the estimate of their various merits, the will is determined solely by the superior goodness of the alternative chosen. This ability to be determined solely by the good is all that the advocate of free will can fairly claim. Upon this view, Godwin must be classed with the upholders of free will.

Dr Priestley's view is confirmed by Godwin's later writings, particularly *Thoughts on Man* (1831), the last volume of essays published during his life. Man's actions, he contends there, are indeed involved in a necessary chain of cause and effect, but the human will is emergent from this process and in turn takes its place in the series of causes; man's actions become voluntary—and by implication free—in so far as he can alter the direction of the chain, even if he can never break it asunder.

> Will, and a confidence in its efficiency, 'travel through, nor quit us till we die'. It is this which inspires us with invincible perseverance and heroic energies, while without it we should be the most inert and soulless of blocks, the shadows of what history records and poetry immortalizes, and not men.
>
> Free will is an integral part of the science of man and may be said to constitute its most important chapter ... But, though the doctrine of the necessity of human actions can never form the rule of our intercourse with others, it will still have its use. It will moderate our excesses, and point out to us that middle path of judgement which the soundest philosophy inculcates ... We shall view with pity, even with sympathy, the men whose frailties we behold, or by whom crimes are perpetrated, satisfied that they are parts of one great machine, and, like ourselves, are driven forward by impulses over which they have no real control.

Godwin, in other words, accepts in his old age the essential division in the Necessitarian attitude—that, though philosophically one may see no alternative to determination, in practice one acts as if men were free. He admits that 'we can never divest ourselves of the delusive sense of liberty of human actions', and that 'it is not desirable that we should do so'. In other words, he grants the contradiction between a universe dominated by immutable law and man's sense of his own freedom, and he pragmatically welcomes the contradiction, thus creating one of those states of equilibrium between opposing conditions or ideas that delighted many of his libertarian successors, particularly, of course, Proudhon.

It is within this chosen region of suspense between the necessary and the voluntary that Godwin builds the structure of *Political Justice*. He begins with the assumption that 'the happiness of human species is the most desirable object for human science to pursue', and of all forms of happiness he gives pride of place to the 'intellectual and moral'. The most potent enemy of such happiness he detects in 'erroneous and corrupt government', and so his book has really a double purpose; it is an inquiry into the political functioning of society, but it will also be, Godwin hopes, 'an advantageous vehicle of moral improvement ... from the perusal of which no man should rise without being strengthened in habits of sincerity, fortitude, and justice.' From a melancholy consideration of the historical record of governments, of their endless wars abroad, of the endemic poverty and periodical repression they produce at home, Godwin concludes that, while the evils of political life may possibly never be ended, the faintest hope of replacing that 'history of crimes' by a society of 'true freedom and perfect equity' is worth following. But the confidence with which he proceeds suggests that Godwin, at least in this noontide of his career, was far from believing himself the spokesman of a forlorn hope.

He begins with four basic propositions. First, he claims that 'the moral characters of men are the result of their perceptions', and that neither good nor bad is born into us. If this is the case, the elimination of harmful external factors can also eliminate criminal tendencies from the characters of human beings. But it is not merely a question of acting upon people by changing their environments. We have to awaken their minds as well, for voluntary actions originate in judgements of goodness or desirability, and are therefore acts of reason. As such, they can be changed by rational persuasion, and even the power of environment can often be countered by the proper influencing of opinion.

This brings Godwin to his second basic proposition. Of all the means of 'operating upon mind', the most potent is government. Here is a significant shift from *An Account of the Seminary*, in which he had given education the advantage. He now explains that 'political institution is peculiarly strong in that very point in which the efficacy of education was deficient, the extent of its operation'. It is only this power of 'positive institutions', Godwin claims, that keeps error so long alive in the world, for, like all anarchists, he believes that, left to itself, the human mind will naturally tend to detect error and to approach steadily nearer to truth.

> Injustice therefore by its very nature is little fitted for a durable existence. But government 'lays its hand upon the spring that is in society and puts a stop to its motion'. It gives substance and permanence to our errors. It reverses the genuine propensities of mind, and instead of suffering us to look forward, teaches us to look backward for perfection. It prompts us to seek the public welfare, not in innovation and improvement, but in a timid reverence for the decisions of our ancestors, as if it were the nature of mind always to degenerate and never to advance.

Godwin's third proposition is really a corollary of the second; government is as bad in practice as it is in principle. In demonstrating this, he concentrates mostly on the vast economic differences between the classes of his own eighteenth-century world. Both legislation and the operation of laws work in favour of the rich, and, indeed, it is in the nature of political institutions, by giving power and privilege to individuals, 'greatly to enhance the imagined excellence of wealth'. Godwin was one of the first to describe clearly the intimate link between property and power which has made the anarchists enemies of capitalism as well as of the state.

The fourth basic proposition is the celebrated statement on the perfectibility of man. 'Perfectibility is one of the most unequivocal characteristics of the human species, so that the political as well as the intellectual state of man may be presumed to be in a course of progressive improvement.' Godwin reinforces this bold statement by a comparison between the primitive and the civilized states of man, and maintains, with a naïvety worthy of the early Ruskin, that even in the arts a constant improvement has been evident. Subsequently, as we have seen in an earlier chapter, he was to deny any such Utopian intent and to maintain that he meant merely that man was capable of indefinite improvement. And even here his progressivism differs from the customary Victorian type in that it is primarily moral, and envisages as its principal goal an inner change in the individual that will take him to the condition of natural justice from which his subjection to political institutions had diverted him.

It is on Justice that Godwin lays the stress as he begins to develop from his four basic statements a discussion of the principles of society. Society, he maintains, originated in men's consciousness of the need for mutual assistance, and its moving principle—a moral principle—is Justice, which Godwin defines as 'a rule of conduct originating in the connexion of one percipient being with another.' Justice demands that we do everything in our power to assist other individuals according to their need and worth; it sees our persons and our property as things we hold in trust for mankind. 'I am bound,' Godwin declares, 'to employ my talents, my understanding, my strength, and my time for the production of the greatest quantity of general good.' Yet we should beware of setting up the general good, or society itself, as something above or outside individuals. It is always what is good and just between individuals that is good and just for society. For 'society is nothing more than an aggregation of individuals. Its claims and duties must be the aggregate of their claims and duties, the one no more precarious and arbitrary than the other.' The purpose of society is to do for its members 'everything that can contribute to their welfare. But the nature of their welfare is defined by the nature of mind. That will most contribute to it which enlarges the understanding, supplies incitements to virtue, fills us with a generous conscience of our independence and carefully removes whatever can impede our exertions.'

Society, in other words, is best employed when it assists man to be a moral being. But here we come to another direction of relationship. If man's links with society are a kind of horizontal pattern of magnified connections between individuals, his relationship to morality is a vertical one. For, Godwin insists,

> Morality is, if anything can be, fixed and immutable; and there must surely be some strange deception that should induce us to give an action eternally and unchangeably wrong the epithets of rectitude, duty and virtue.

The difficulty arises when we come to consider how man, bounded by the limits of his perception, is to establish the vertical relationship with those absolute truths that constitute ideal morality. Clearly, duty can only demand that we serve the general good according to the full extent of our capacities. On the other hand, neither incapacity nor ignorance can give the quality of justice to an unjust act. And so, while men cannot expect to be absolutely virtuous, they should endeavour to form 'virtuous dispositions.' But a virtuous disposition cannot be imposed; it can only be cultivated by each man within himself. It 'is principally generated by the uncontrolled exercise of private judgement and the rigid conformity of every man to the dictates of his conscience'.

If we insist on this autonomy of the individual judgement, then we follow the path of the radical Dissenters to a declaration of the moral equality of men. Physically and mentally men may be unequal, though Godwin believes that such differences are exaggerated, but morally all men are equal because of their essential independence. Justice must be applied to them in equal measure, and opportunities and encouragement should be given without discrimination.

Man has duties to truth and to morality, which is an aspect of truth. But has he rights? No man, Godwin, answers, has the right 'to act anything but virtue and to utter anything but truth'. What he does have, strictly speaking, are not rights, but claims on the assistance of his fellows under reciprocal justice. Many things commonly regarded as rights, such as freedom of conscience or speech, should be sought not because men have a right to them but because they are essential for the attainment of moral truth.

Society and government have neither claims nor rights. They exist only for the convenience of individuals. And here Godwin comes to the perennial confusion between justice and human law. The first, he argues, is based on immutable moral truths, the second on the fallible decisions of political institutions. Man must recognize what is right by his own understanding, and here it is evidence, not authority, that should move him. It follows from this reasoning that governments have no right to our obedience. Reason, exercised independently in the discovery of justice, is the only true role of conduct. If every man listened to its voice, there would be a society of unconstrained concord.

But it may be granted that in the present imperfect state of human judgement these principles cannot always be applied. Crime occurs, and, though punishment is in its nature unjust, restraint may be unavoidable. Yet men are what they are, Godwin insists, because of the environment that has shaped them, and we must therefore abolish the social causes that make restraint necessary. 'He that would reconcile a perfect freedom in this respect with the interest of the whole, ought to propose at the same time the means of extirpating selfishness and vice.'

In considering the question of necessary restraint, Godwin asks in what manner the supercession of private judgement for the sake of public good may, where necessary, be carried out. And this in turn leads him 'to ascertain the foundation of political government'. He begins with three hypotheses commonly advanced. The first two—that government originates in the right of might and that it originates in divine right—he dismisses as alien to the concept of an immutable justice. The third hypothesis is that of the social contract, deriving from Locke and Rousseau and commonly held by radicals in the eighteenth century. Godwin departs emphatically from the men of his age on this point, and anticipates the anarchists of the nineteenth century by dismissing the social contract also as a basis for political justice. It seeks to bind one generation by the promises of another. It negates the obligation of each individual to exercise his private judgement on what is right. It is based on the fallacious idea that we must fulfil our promises, whereas we should make no promises at all, but perform acts only because they are just.

Godwin hastens to add that an emphasis on the duty of private judgement does not preclude common action. Indeed, when measures have to be adopted for the general good, they must be deliberated in common, and there is a close resemblance between the exercise of private judgement and common deliberations properly carried out. Both are 'means of discovering right and wrong, and of comparing particular propositions with the standards of eternal truth'. But they are no more than this, and neither an individual nor a deliberative body has the authority to make laws. The only just law is the law of Reason: 'Her decrees are irrevocable and uniform. The functions of society extend, not to the making, but to the interpreting of law; it cannot decree, it can only declare that which the nature of things has already decreed ...' Thus the authority of the community is strictly executive, and is confined to 'the public support of justice'. Where it assures this, every reasonable man must cooperate; where it does not, every reasonable man must resist its decisions.

With the idea of resistance we come to the beginning of the long anarchist controversy on ends and means. Godwin stands with Tolstoy, and to an extent with Proudhon, among those who place moral persuasion and passive resistance above violent and active resistance. He does not actually deny active resistance. But he counsels extreme caution in its use. Force is no substitute for reason, and its use by people who seek to establish justice does not make it any better. It should never be used without the prospect of success, and even then only 'where time can by no means be gained, and the consequences instantly to ensue are unquestionably fatal'. Violence, then, is the last, desperate resort of just men.

The appropriate form of resistance, which should be attempted in every instance, is the spreading of truth, the 'censuring in the most explicit manner every proceeding that I perceive to be adverse to the true interests of mankind'. The revolutions we should desire are those which proceed by changing human opinions and dispositions; used with sincerity and persistence, reason will accomplish all that violence can only attempt with the most dubious chance of success.

But persuasion must as far as possible be direct and individual. Godwin distrusts political associations, which seek to persuade by the weight of numbers rather than by propagating the truth. The only associations he admits are those created in an emergency to resist encroachments on freedom, but these should be dispersed as soon as the need for them has ended, lest they ossify into institutions. The method Godwin suggests is the formation of loose discussion-groups of people awakened to the pursuit of truth; these might eventually form a universal movement, acting potently for the improvement of individuals and 'the amelioration of political institutions'. But any attempt to create a uniformity of thought in such groups should be avoided. 'Human beings should meet together not to enforce but to inquire. Truth disclaims the alliance of marshalled numbers.' By such means social change may be gradual and tranquil. But this does not mean necessarily that 'the revolution is at an immeasurable distance'. 'The kingdom of truth comes not with ostentation,' and its growth may produce great results when these are least expected.

Such extreme faith in the power of unaided reason is almost peculiar to Godwin's century. We find few even among anarchists in the nineteenth century maintaining it quite so trustfully. But in his opposition to highly organized political parties and his insistence on small, loosely formed groups, coalescing naturally into a wider movement, Godwin was sketching out the first plan of all later forms of anarchist organization.

Having laid the moral foundations of his argument, Godwin proceeds to discuss what he calls 'the practical details of political institution', and here he deals in turn with four aspects of political life: general administration, or government; education; crime and law; and the regulation of property. His discussion of government begins with an uncompromising statement of clear opposition:

> Above all, we should not forget that government is an evil, an usurpation upon the private judgement and individual conscience of mankind; and that, however we may be obliged to admit it as a necessary evil for the present, it behoves us, as the friends of reason and the human species, to admit as little of it as possible, and carefully to observe whether, in consequence of the gradual illumination of the human mind, that little may not hereafter be diminished.

Thus, in his examination of the various forms of government which he distinguishes—monarchy, aristocracy, and democracy—Godwin is seeking not the greatest good but the least evil. His objections to monarchy and aristocracy do not depart materially from criticisms of these forms of government voiced by other eighteenth-century thinkers. It is in discussing democracy that he is original and characteristically anarchistic.

Democracy clearly is the form of government under which we have the best prospect of advancing to something better, and, as Godwin presents it in his ideal definition, it has already within it the seeds of a better society. It is 'a system of government according to which every member of society is considered as a man and nothing else. So far as positive regulation is concerned, if indeed that can with any propriety be termed regulation which is the mere recognition of the simplest of all principles, every man is regarded as equal.' In history there have been at best only approximations to this ideal, yet even imperfect and turbulent democracies have been infinitely superior in their achievements to monarchies and aristocracies.

> Democracy restores to man a consciousness of his value, teaches him by the removal of authority and oppression to listen only to the dictates of reason, gives him confidence to treat other men as his fellow beings, and induces him to regard them no longer as enemies against whom to be upon his guard, but as brethren whom it becomes him to assist.

Yet so far democracy has never produced a condition of true social justice. This failure, Godwin suggests, stems partly from the lack of a due sense of the power of truth and the value of sincerity; it is this which makes democracies cling to the support of institutional forms, which makes them loath to accept with Godwinian confidence the proposition that 'the contest between truth and falsehood is of itself too unequal for the former to stand in need of support from any political ally'. For this reason we have the lingering not only of religious fictions, but also of political myths, with all this implies in the division of men between an enlightened élite and an ignorant subject caste. Here Godwin stands far apart from Plato, with his theory of the 'noble falsehood'.

> Why divide men into two classes [he asks], one of which is to think and reason for the whole, and the other to take the conclusions of their superiors on trust? This distinction is not founded in the nature of things; there is no such inherent difference between man and man as it thinks proper to suppose. The reasons that should convince us that virtue is better than vice are neither complicated nor abstruse;

and the less they be tampered with by the injudicious interference of political institutions, the more they will come home to the understanding and approve themselves to the judgement of every man.

Turning to the actual functioning of democratic government, Godwin advocates the simplification and decentralization of all forms of administration. Great, complex, centralized states are harmful and unnecessary for the good of mankind. As they dissolve, localized forms of administration should take their place, in which the disadvantages of government may immediately be mitigated by a diminished scope for ambition. 'Sobriety and equity are the obvious characteristics of a limited circle.' An enlightened localism of this kind, Godwin thinks, would not lead to a narrow parochialism; on the contrary, it would turn the world into a single great republic in which men could move and discuss freely without the impediment of national barriers.

In the local units of society—the 'parishes' as Godwin calls these ancestors of the 'communes' of later anarchists—legislation would rarely be needed; the whole community would participate as far as possible in administration, and officials—where they existed—would be concerned with providing information and attending to concerns of practical detail. The only form of parish organization really necessary would be some kind of jury to deal with offences against justice and to arbitrate in controversies.

In exceptional emergencies it might indeed be necessary to be beyond the parishes and to call a general assembly. But Godwin sees great dangers in such bodies, and in his warnings anticipates the anti-parliamentary tone characteristic of the anarchist tradition. Under the best circumstances assemblies present grave disadvantages. Their actions are based on the fictitious unanimity of majority decisions. Even more sinister is the real unanimity which arises when delegates form themselves into parties and accept the shackling of individual thought. As for the practice of voting, Godwin declares with great moral indignation that 'the deciding upon truth by the casting up of numbers' is an 'intolerable insult upon all reason and justice'. For these various reasons, national assemblies, even while they are still necessary, should be used 'as sparingly as the case will admit'.

At first, in the extreme democracy which Godwin envisages, both assemblies and juries may have to issue commands. But the need for force arises not 'out of man's nature, but out of the institutions by which he has already been corrupted'. When these institutions are reduced to a dwindling remnant, men will progress to the condition in which it will be necessary merely to invite them to refrain from acting prejudicially to their fellows. And in the end we shall reach a society where wisdom can be transmitted without the intervention of any institution, the society of moral men living in just relations—or, as we may say in modern phraseology, the society of pure anarchy.

All this depends on our attitude to education, and it is to this aspect of political life that Godwin now proceeds. He begins with a discussion of how the vital process of forming just opinions may be carried out. Society is unqualified by its very nature for this function, for its acts are conditioned by the men who compose it, the vicious as well as the virtuous, the just as well as the unjust, and it has therefore no claim to moral superiority. Society's only advantage lies in its authority. But we do not make a man virtuous by command, and in using force we do positive harm by inhibiting sincere human intercourse and limiting freedom.

Godwin contends that in all these respects the small social group has the advantage over the extensive political institution. But the way he talks of the operations of such groups arouses one's deepest misgivings. In circles of this kind, he says, 'opinion would be all sufficient; the inspection of every man over the conduct of his neighbours, when unstained by caprice, would constitute a censorship of the most irresistible nature. But the force of this censorship would depend upon its freedom, not following the positive dictates of law, but the spontaneous decisions of the understanding.' Even Godwin's assurance that such a process would be free and spontaneous does not entirely erase the distasteful picture of a future where mutual inspection and censorship will be the order of the day and public opinion will reign triumphant. Perhaps this passage reflects the influence on Godwin's mind of a Puritan childhood, during which his own actions were so far censored—without any corporal punishment—that he was rebuked by his father for caressing the cat on a Sunday. But the image he creates recurs with disquieting frequency as we pass on through anarchist history.

In this connection, George Orwell once wrote an essay on Swift (a writer, incidentally, much admired by Godwin), in which he pointed out that in the anarchistic society of the Houyhnhnms in *Gulliver's Travels*, 'exhortation' was as powerful as compulsion in any other society. Orwell continued:

This illustrates very well the totalitarian tendency which is implicit in the anarchist or pacifist vision of Society. In a Society where there is no law, and in theory no compulsion, the only arbiter of behaviour is public opinion. But public opinion, because of the tremendous urge to conformity in gregarious animals, is less tolerant than any system of law. When human beings are governed by 'thou shalt not', the individual can practise a certain amount of eccentricity; when they are supposedly governed by 'love' and 'reason', he is under continuous pressure to make him behave and think in exactly the same way as everyone does.

There is a good deal of truth in what Orwell says, even if his way of saying it is characteristically dogmatic. The anarchists accept much too uncritically the idea of an active public opinion as an easy way out of the problem dealing with anti-social tendencies. Few of them have given sufficient thought to the danger of a moral tyranny replacing a physical one, and the frown of the man next door becoming as much a thing to fear as the sentence of the judge. And some of them have undoubtedly been positively attracted by the idea of radiating moral authority; anarchism has had its Pharisees like every other movement for human regeneration.

However, while Godwin places an unwise stress on the virtues of mutual censorship, his criticism of state interference in the cultivation of opinion is acute enough, and when he comes to discuss the application of such interference by the foundation of state educational systems, he points to dangers which have only become more obvious during a century of experience. Here a long quotation seems justified, since in developing a point of view held fairly consistently by his dissenting forebears, Godwin at the same time sketches out an attitude that recurs among his successors, most of whom have taken the problems of education just as seriously. He comes to the care of the problem when he indicates the dangerous uses to which governments may put education once its control falls into their hands.

The project of a national education ought uniformly to be discouraged on account of its obvious alliance with national government. This is an alliance of a more formidable nature than the old and much contested alliance of Church and state. Before we put so powerful a machine under the direction of so ambiguous an agent, it behoves us to consider well what it is that we do. Government will not fail to employ it to strengthen its hands and perpetrate its institutions. If we could even suppose the agents of government not to propose to themselves an object which will be apt to appear in their eyes not merely innocent but meritorious, the evil would not the less happen. Their views as institutors of a system of education will not fail to be analogous to their views in their political capacity; the data on which their conduct as statesmen is vindicated will be the data upon which their instructions are founded. It is not true that our youth ought to be instructed to venerate the commonwealth, however excellent; they should be instructed to venerate truth, and the constitution only so far as it corresponded with their independent deductions of truth. Had the scheme of a national education been adopted when despotism was most triumphant, it is not to be believed that it could have for ever stifled the voice of truth. But it would have been the most formidable and profound contrivance for that purpose that imagination can suggest. Still, in the countries where liberty chiefly prevails, it is reasonably to be assumed that there are important errors, and a national education has the most direct tendency to perpetrate those errors and to form all minds upon one model.

The practice of totalitarian states in our own time leaves no reason to suggest that Godwin in any way exaggerated the perils of education falling into the hands of political leaders. For him the small, independent school, like the small discussion group, remained the desirable unit, and individual instruction was the best of all.

The last book of *Political Justice*, in which Godwin examines the institution of property, is the most celebrated section of his masterpiece, because of its supposed anticipations of socialist economics. But only in his exposure of the effects of private property and in his insistence on the close relationship between property and systems of government does Godwin really anticipate socialism, if we use that word in its present connotation of state ownership. His positive suggestions about changes in the property system are uniformly anarchistic.

Godwin begins by remarking that the abolition of 'the system of coercion and punishment is intimately connected with the circumstance of property's being placed on an equitable basis'. Hence every man is 'entitled, so far as the general stock will suffice, not only to the means of being, but of well-being'. But this claim to an equitable share of the common property presupposes a duty to assume a full share of the common tasks.

Justice directs that each man, unless perhaps he be employed more beneficially to the public, should contribute to the cultivation of the common harvest, of which each man consumes a share. This reciprocity ... is of the very essence of justice.

In Godwin's roughly sketched picture of the functioning of a propertyless society one sees the same agrarian vision as runs through More, Winstanley, Morris, and Kropotkin—the vision of men working together in the fields and then taking, according to their own estimates of their just needs, from the common barns and store-houses, without any mechanism of currency or exchange, for exchange is 'of all practices the most perni-cious'. Like later anarchist writers, Godwin envisages a drastic simplification of life, for luxury is a corrupting condition—we must pity the rich as much as the poor—and work is necessary for human happiness. The ideal situation is that in which a man has 'independence of mind, which makes us feel that our satisfactions are not at the mercy either of men or of fortune, and activity of mind, the cheerfulness that arises from industry properly employed about objects of which our judgement acknowledges the intrinsic value'.

'Accumulated property'—Godwin's pre-Marxist phrase for what we call capitalism—is hostile to the qualitative enrichment of life. By its per-petuation of economic inequality it 'treads the powers of thought in the dust, extinguishes the sparks of genius, and reduces the great mass of mankind to be immersed in sordid cares'. Against its baleful reign Godwin paints the idyllic picture of his own Utopia. With luxury brought to an end,

> the necessity for the greater part of the manual industry of mankind would be superseded; and the rest, being amicably shared among all the active and vigorous members of the community, would be bur-thensome to none. Every man would have a frugal yet wholesome diet: every man would go forth to that moderate exercise of his cor-poral functions that would give hilarity to the spirits; none would be made torpid with fatigue, but all would have leisure to cultivate the kindly and philanthropical affections of the soul and to let loose his faculties in the search of intellectual improvement ... Genius ... would be freed from those apprehensions that perpetually recall us to the thought of personal emolument, and of consequence would expatiate freely among sentiments of generosity and public good.

Such a system, Godwin contends, would also remove the principal causes of crime, which arises mainly from 'one man's possessing in abun-dance that of which another man is destitute'. Envy and selfishness would vanish along with anxiety and insecurity; corruption would disappear, and the principal incentive to war would be removed. 'Each man would be united to his neighbour in love and mutual kindness a thousand times more than now; but each man would think and judge for himself.'

As Godwin continues, he fills out the details of his egalitarian Arcadia. He anticipates Veblen by remarking that property is usually desired, not for its own sake, but for the distinction it confers; in an egalitarian society, however, men will seek distinction in the service of the public good. He also goes into a long disquisition on the length of the desirable working day, and presents the rather surprising estimate that, in a life without luxury, it may well be reduced to half an hour!

In reaching his conclusions he is assisted by a prophetic glance at the industrial developments of the future, which also prompts him to suggest a way in which excessive cooperation may be avoided. For, like Proudhon and Stirner, and unlike Bakunin and Kropotkin, Godwin was led by his individualism to a profound distrust of any kind of collaboration that might harden into institutional form. In this connection he indulges in some delightful absurdities, doubting whether a man of independent judgement can play in an orchestra or act in a play, but he does make a valid point that a free man should not be tied more than he can help to the convenience of others. And he sees in technological progress a possible means of providing the individual with greater independence.

At present, to pull down a tree, to cut a canal, to navigate a vessel requires the labour of many. Will it always require the labour of many? When we look at the complicated machines of human contrivance, various sorts of mills, of weaving engines, of steam engines, are we not astonished at the compendium of labour they produce? Who shall say where this species of improvement must stop? ... The conclusion of the progress which has here been sketched is something like a final close to the necessity of human labour.

Standing at the beginning of the Industrial Revolution, Godwin has the same kind of wondering vision as H.G. Wells at the beginning of the Technological Revolution.* Science, he even ventures to suggest, may yet discover the secret of immortality!

---

*Up to now history has not entirely followed Godwin's vision. The effect of industrial development has been in the main to tighten the net of cooperation by increasing the division of labour. Moreover, Godwin's view ignores the fact that complex machinery, even if it can be operated by one man, must be made by many men. However, it is worth remarking that some of the more imaginative modern writers on social and economic relations, such as Lewis Mumford, have suggested that the eventual result of technological progress may well be a breakup of the monolithic structures of contemporary industry, accompanied by geographical decentralization, a dissolution of the metropolis, and a return to an organic social order in which the individual will develop more freely than in the recent past. If this happens, Godwin may well be vindicated in his long view of the machine as a liberator.

In spite of his distrust of cooperation, Godwin is far from seeing liberated humanity living in mutual isolation and suspicion. On the contrary,
he envisages the possibility of specialization in the various crafts, which
would lead to a man's following the task for which he had the greatest
aptitude, and distributing his surplus products to whomever might need
them, receiving what he himself needs of other things from the surplus
produced by his neighbours, but always on the basis of free distribution,
not of exchange. It is evident that, despite his speculations on the future of
machinery, Godwin's ideal society is based on the economics of handcrafts
and cultivation.

But above all, intercourse between men remains necessary for the
maturing of thought and building of character by means of frank conversation and the exchange of ideas. Such intercourse, of course, precludes
possessive personal relationships, and it is for this reason that Godwin
makes his celebrated condemnation of marriage, which endeavours to give
permanence to a past choice and which is, moreover, 'the worst of proper-
ties'. Men and women will live as equals in friendship, and the propagation
of the species 'will be regulated by the dictates of reason and duty'. As for
children, they too must be liberated from the domination of parents and
teachers. 'No creature in human form will be expected to learn anything
but because he desires it and has some conception of its utility and value.'

This is Godwin's sketch of the world of universal benevolence, toward
which justice marches, and which it behoves every man of wisdom to
advance by his teaching. In a tone of majestic rhetoric and in a mood of
calm confidence in the powers of reason, *Political Justice* draws to its end.
In it, as Sir Alexander Gray has said, 'Godwin sums up, as no one else
does, the sum and substance of anarchism, and thus embodies a whole tradition.' More astonishingly, he embodies it prophetically. *Political Justice*
was to remain for a half century an isolated work. Godwin himself wrote
nothing else like it, though his first novel, *Caleb Williams*, a pursuit story of
almost Kafkaesque power, in which an innocent man is hunted by all the
hostile forces of society, has a claim to be considered an anarchist parable.
But after *Caleb Williams* had appeared in 1794 its author began to recede
into the shadows of Grub Street, and his later novels, his painstaking
biographies, and his bad plays (which he perversely considered the best of
all his works) belong to the history of minor English literature.

Nor did he leave any movement of social protest behind him to link in
recognizable form with that which grew up in the 1860s from the seed of
Proudhon's thought. *Political Justice* was immensely popular for a few years
after its publication, until the political sky became clouded over by war

between Britain and revolutionary France. The year when Godwin's brief and idyllic marriage with Mary Wollstonecraft came to a tragic end, 1797, marked the turning-point. The popular vogue of *Political Justice* ended abruptly. Coleridge and Wordsworth and Southey, fair-weather Godwinians all, recanted quickly, and their fleeting adherence to the principles of *Political Justice* merits no more than a mention in a history of anarchism. The circles of working men, who clubbed their threepences to buy copies of *Political Justice* for reading and discussion, disappeared with the rest of the radical movement in the dark days at the end of the century. Godwin himself, clouded in calumny, reduced to lifelong indebtedness, and writing mostly for the means of sustenance, maintained his views with exemplary fortitude, supported by the regard of men like Hazlitt and Lamb and Coleridge, who departed as a disciple and returned as a friend. Though Godwin twice revised *Political Justice* for new editions, he never, despite the sensational accusations of writers like De Quincey, withdrew or mitigated the anarchistic conclusions he had drawn in the first edition.

It was, in fact, not in the years of what Hazlitt aptly called 'a sultry and unwholesome popularity' that Godwin wielded his most important influence, but in the period when his public reputation had sunk to its lowest ebb. In 1811 it was with astonishment that Shelley found the author of *Political Justice* to be still alive. There followed a relationship scarred by the sensational facts of Shelley's elopement with Godwin's daughter, and Godwin's endless borrowing from Shelley, but also marked by the consolidation of a Godwinian strain in Shelley's verse which even the Platonism of the poet's final phase never completely displaced. On one level at least, *Queen Mab*, *The Revolt of Islam*, and *Prometheus Unbound* are all transmutations into verse of the creed of *Political Justice*, and even *Hellas* could not have been what it is without the Godwinian influence. Other writers— H.N. Brailsford and Frank Lea in particular—have traced the poet's intellectual debt to the philosopher, which more than cancels out the philosopher's financial debt to the poet. Here it is enough to say that, through Shelley's Godwinism, anarchism first appears as a theme of world literature. And, though Shelley must perhaps cede to Tolstoy the honour of being the greatest of anarchist writers, he remains the greatest of anarchist poets.

A less obvious influence leads from Godwin to the English labour movement. It is likely that many of the working men who had read *Political Justice* in the 1790s remained Godwinians at heart, while at least three influential socialists came under Godwin's sway in his later years. One was Robert Owen, who knew him personally. Owen was no anarchist, but he

absorbed Godwin's distrust of political movements, and through him a libertarian element was transmitted to the early trade unions and particularly to the Grand National Consolidated. Francis Place, another devoted
fighter for the right of workers to combine, was also a disciple of Godwin
and at one time undertook the thankless task of trying to disentangle his
financial affairs. William Thompson, the early socialist economist, developed his ideas on property largely from Book VIII of *Political Justice*, and it
may have been through Thompson, who certainly influenced the economic theories of Karl Marx, that the frail anarchistic phantom known as 'the
withering away of the state' came to haunt the imagination of that most
authoritarian of socialists.

When English socialism revived during the 1880s, it took on a peculiarly
libertarian tone, and echoes of Godwin appear in the works of many of its
leading exponents. Morris's *News from Nowhere* reads like a medievalized
adaptation of the Godwinian Utopia, and, as Dr F.E.L. Priestley has pointed out, Oscar Wilde's *The Soul of Man Under Socialism* is 'a thorough
rehearsal of Godwin's whole system'. Bernard Shaw picked a Godwinian
theme for development in *Back to Methuselah*, and H.G. Wells, in *Men Like
Gods*, brought the ideal Godwinian society into line with the speculations
of Edwardian scientists.

After the Second World War, English writers returned to Godwin with
greatly renewed interest. John Middleton Murry, Herbert Read, and
Charles Morgan have all pointed out how timely his criticism of 'positive
institutions' appears in a state-ridden world, and critics like Angus Wilson,
Walter Allen, and Roy Fuller have recognized in his pioneer novel of
crime and pursuit, *Caleb Williams*, a remarkable anticipation of the anxi-
eties that haunt a great deal of contemporary fiction. A century and a half
after his death in 1836, Godwin is more securely established than at any
time since 1797 as a landmark not merely in the development of political
thought, but also in the history of English literature.

Yet the irony remains that the influence of *Political Justice*, the most
complete early exposition of anarchist ideas, should have been diffused in
English literature and in the English socialist movement, but should have
been absent from the anarchist movement itself until very late in its history. For Stirner and Proudhon do not take up where Godwin left off; each
of them begins anew on his own road to freedom.

4. The Egoist

THE pervasiveness of anarchistic ways of thinking in the age that followed the French Revolution, and which established both the capitalist system of production and the modern centralized state, is shown strikingly in the variety of points from which writers in many countries started independently on their journeys to similar libertarian destinations. Godwin, as we have seen, came to the rejection of government by way of the English Dissenting tradition, modified by the French Enlightenment. Josiah Warren in the United States and Pierre-Joseph Proudhon in France independently reached anarchism during the 1840s largely by criticizing Utopian socialist doctrines, particularly those of Charles Fourier and Robert Owen. And during the same decade in Germany Max Stirner, in his single important work, *The Ego and His Own*, proceeded from Hegelianism to its almost complete inversion in a doctrine that denied all absolutes and all institutions, and based itself solely on the 'ownness' of the human individual. It is true that Stirner had studied Proudhon's earlier works but—like Proudhon himself in dismissing Godwin—he failed to see the similarity between his own conclusions and those implied in the writings of the French anarchist. His arguments, and the extreme individualism to which they led him, can therefore reasonably be regarded as the independent outgrowth of a general tendency of the age.

At first sight Stirner's doctrine seems strikingly different from that of other anarchist thinkers. These tend, like Godwin, to conceive some absolute moral criterion to which man must subordinate his desires in the name of justice and reason, or, like Kropotkin, to pose some innate urge which, once authority is brought to an end, will induce men to cooperate naturally in a society governed by invisible laws of mutual aid. Stirner, on the other hand, draws near to nihilism and existentialism in his denial of all natural laws and of a common humanity; he sets forth as his ideal the egoist, the man who realizes himself in conflict with the collectivity and with other individuals, who does not shrink from the use of any means in 'the war of each against all', who judges everything ruthlessly from the viewpoint of his own well-being, and who, having proclaimed his 'ownness', may then enter with like-minded individuals into a 'union of egoists', without rules or regulations, for the arrangement of matters of common convenience.

There is no need to point out the resemblance between Stirner's egoist and the superman of Nietzsche; Nietzsche himself regarded Stirner as one of the unrecognized seminal minds of the nineteenth century. Yet there are elements in Stirner's thought that bring him clearly into the anarchist tradition and which have given him a considerable influence in libertarian circles during the present century. As much as any of the more typical anarchist thinkers, he criticizes existing society for its authoritarian and anti-individual character; he poses a desirable condition that can come about only with the overthrow of governmental institutions; he calls for equality between egoists even if he sees it in terms of the tension created by a balance of might; and he suggests—however vaguely—insurrectionary means by which the change in society can be brought about. At the same time, there have been few anarchists so extreme as Stirner in their worship of force, or so joyful in their view of life as a perpetual and amoral conflict of wills.

Yet a curious insight into the character of theoretical extremists is presented when we come to observe this fanatic of individualism, who alarmed even some of the anarchists, such as Kropotkin, by the ferocity of his teachings. For the great egoist, the poet of everlasting conflict, who praised crime and exalted murder, was in real life, when he published *The Ego and His Own* in 1845, a mild-mannered and long-suffering teacher in Madame Gropius's Berlin academy for young ladies. He was called Johann Caspar Schmidt. The *nom de plume* which he substituted for such a commonplace name was derived from the extraordinary development of his forehead; *Stirne* is the German word for brow, and Max Stirner might reasonably be translated as Max the Highbrow.

Just as Schmidt assumed a new name to publish his book, so he appeared to create a new personality to write it, or at least to call up some violent, unfamiliar self that was submerged in his daily existence. For in the unhappy, luckless, and ill-ordered career of the timid Schmidt there was nothing at all of the free-standing egoist of Max Stirner's passionate dream; the contrast between the man and his work seems to provide us with a classic example of the power of literature as a compensatory daydream.

The known facts of Schmidt's life, pieced together with difficulty by the individualist poet John Henry Mackay in the 1890s, are scanty and pathetic. He was a Bavarian, born in 1806 in Bayreuth, then an obscure town untouched by the fame that Wagner and Richter were later to bring it. His parents were poor, his father died when he was young, and his mother's second marriage led to a period of wandering in northern Germany, broken by intermittent sickness. Later, when the family returned to Bayreuth, Johann Caspar followed his studies at the local gymnasium, and then he embarked on a long, interrupted, and undistinguished university career.

From 1826 to 1828 he studied philosophy at the University of Berlin, where he attended the lectures of Hegel, the first intellectual hero against whom he was later to react decisively. There followed a single semester at Erlangen, and a registration at Königsberg, where he did not attend a single lecture, being called to Kulm to look after his mother, who was now sinking into insanity. Only three years afterward, in 1832, could he return to the University of Berlin, where eventually he passed narrowly the examination for a certificate to teach in Prussian gymnasia.

For a year and a half Schmidt worked as an unpaid training teacher at the Berlin Königsberg Realschule, at the end of which time the Prussian government refused to appoint him to a salaried post. He did not protest; indeed, this period of his life was characterized by a resigned apathy that seemed to prevent any serious effort to overcome his misfortunes. And the misfortunes continued. Despite his lack of employment, Schmidt married his landlady's daughter in 1837; she died a few months later in childbirth. Then he resumed the task of caring for his mad mother, and waited almost two years before he was finally taken on as a teacher in Madame Gropius's school, where he remained, and taught well, for five years.

These were the least unlucky years of Stirner's life, the years during which he associated with some of the most vital intelligences of Germany, and, under their stimulation, emerged from the stagnation of his life to write *The Ego and His Own*, a book which, whatever its faults, can never be accused of lacking force and fire.

The environment that summoned these unexpected qualities from the hitherto unproductive mind of Johann Caspar Schmidt was Hippel's Weinstube on Friedrichstrasse where, during the early 1840s, the Young Hegelians of Berlin would gather to discuss and amend and eventually refute the teachings of the Master. They called themselves Die Freien— the Free Ones—and formed a kind of irregular debating society under the leadership of the brothers Bruno and Edgar Bauer. Marx and Engels, and the poets Herwegh and Hoffman von Fallersleben, were occasional visitors. The debates were brilliant, extravagant, and noisy. Visiting dignitaries were treated with disrespect, and one evening Arnold Ruge, who had set himself up as a kind of high priest among the Left Hegelians, became involved in a bitter dispute with the Berlin group, which Engels celebrated in a pencil sketch. The sketch has survived. Ruge, portly and pompous, is shouting angrily at the Berliners among a welter of overturned chairs and trampled papers, while outside the fray a lonely figure, highbrowed, bespectacled, negligently smoking a cigarette, looks on ironically. It is Stirner, caught in the silent, detached role he played in the company of the Free Ones, the role of the critical, smiling listener, on good terms with all and the friend of none.

Only in one way did the armour of detachment break apart, and that was after the arrival from Mecklenburg of a pretty, brilliant, and superficially emancipated young woman named Marie Dahnhardt, who frequented Hippel's Weinstube and was accepted by the Free Ones as a good comrade who could drain her stein and smoke her cigar with the best of them. Stirner saw in Marie a hope of the happiness he had so far missed in life, and in 1843 they were married; the ceremony, which took place in Stirner's apartment, was bohemianly chaotic, for the pastor arrived to find the bridegroom and witnesses playing cards in their shirtsleeves, the bride came late, in her everyday clothes, and, since no one had remembered to buy wedding rings, the ceremony was completed with the copper rings from Bruno Bauer's purse. It was two years after the marriage that *The Ego and His Own* appeared.

This was not Stirner's first published work; Karl Marx had already printed in the *Rheinische Zeitung* an essay on educational methods. But it was the book that brought Stirner fame, brief and scandalous. In its pages he not merely advocated an egoism and an amorality repugnant to most nineteenth-century minds; he also attacked the whole spectrum of con-temporary thought. Not only Hegel, but also Feuerbach, Marx, and Proudhon—already an avowed anarchist—were rejected. The habitués of Hippel's Weinstube—and especially Bruno Bauer—were condemned with the rest. Stirner set out to demolish not merely all religious beliefs, but also every political or social or philosophical doctrine that seemed to him, by posing anything outside the individual, whether an absolute prin-ciple, or a party, or even a collective abstraction like Man, to start the reli-gious process all over again. By their very extremity his arguments pro-voked such celebrities as Feuerbach and Moses Hess to reply in print.

But Stirner's success was as insubstantial as most of those that proceed from notoriety. His book faded quickly from the public attention, and it was only fifty years later, after the vogue for Nietzsche had prepared the readers for the cult of unlimited self-will, that a popular revival of *The Ego and His Own* took place. During the 1890s and the Edwardian era it was read widely, both within and outside anarchist circles; there was something in the book's undisciplined vigour that appealed particularly to the rebellious auto-didacts of that time, the stalwarts of the Mechanics' Institutes. As late as the 1940s I encountered a group of anarchist working men in Glasgow for whom it was still a belated gospel.

This vogue, however, took place long after Stirner's death, and for him ephemeral success was followed by renewed misfortune. He left Madame Gropius's school; though the cause of his departure is not known, it was very probably due to the discovery that the mild Herr Schmidt had for *alter ego* the terrible Herr Stirner who recommended rebellion and gloried in violence. To earn a living, he began a series of translations of French and English economists, and actually published several volumes of J.-B. Say and Adam Smith; it was an unremuneratively arduous task and, in a desperate attempt to make some easy money, he invested what was left of his wife's dowry in a dairy, which in its turn failed from his lack of business experience. By 1847 Marie Dahnhardt had endured enough of Stirner's ineffectual dealings with life, and she departed, first to England and later to Australia. Long afterward, in London during the 1890s, John Henry Mackay visited her and found that the memory of those days half a century ago still rankled; she would not talk of Stirner except to say that he was 'very sly' and impossibly egotistical.

Left alone, Stirner sank gradually into poverty and obscurity, living in a series of poor lodgings, earning some kind of miserable living by arranging deals between small businessmen, and publishing a *History of Reaction* whose pedestrian dullness bears the mark of Johann Caspar Schmidt rather than that of Max Stirner. Twice he was imprisoned for debt, and the last years of his life, until he died in 1856, were spent mostly in evading his numerous creditors.

It was the career of a man whose proneness to failure clearly sprang from something more personal than mere ill luck, from some flaw of will that gave his one considerable book, seen against the grey background of his life, the aspect of a violent effort to break free from a natural and suffocating apathy. The apathy closed again over Johann Caspar Schmidt the man and finally engulfed him; Max Stirner the writer survived by the sheer desperation which gave his protest its peculiar vigour.

What strikes one at once about *The Ego and His Own* is its passionate anti-intellectualism. In contrast to Godwin's stress on reason, Stirner speaks for the will and the instincts, and he seeks to cut through all the structures of myth and philosophy, all the artificial constructions of human thought, to the elemental self. He denies the reality of such abstract and generalized concepts as Man and Humanity; the human individual is the only thing of which we have certain knowledge, and each individual is unique. It is this uniqueness that every man must cultivate; the ego is the only law, and no obligations exist to any code, creed, or conception outside it. Rights do not exist; there is only the might of the embattled ego. As for such Godwinian concepts as duty and immutable moral laws, Stirner denies them completely. His own needs and desires provide the sole rule of conduct for the self-realized individual.

Even freedom, the great goal of most anarchists, is, in Stirner's view, surpassed by uniqueness or 'ownness'. Freedom he sees as a condition of being *rid* of certain things, but he points out that the very nature of life makes absolute freedom an impossibility.

> One becomes free from much, not everything. Inwardly one may be free in spite of the condition of slavery, although, too, it is again only from some things, not from everything; but from the whip, the domineering temper, etc., of the master one does not as a slave become *free.* 'Freedom lives only in the realm of dreams!' Ownness, on the contrary, is my whole being and existence, it is I myself. I am free from what I am *rid* of, owner of what I have in my *power* or what I *control. My own* I am at all times and under all circumstances, if I know how to possess myself and do not throw myself away on others. To be free is something that I cannot truly *will,* because I cannot make it, cannot create it; I can only wish it and aspire towards it, for it remains an ideal, a spook. The fetters of reality cut the sharpest welts in my flesh every moment. But *my own* I remain.

Yet in his fight for 'ownness' Stirner finds himself faced with the same enemy as the anarchist in his fight for freedom—the state.

> We two, the state and I, are enemies. I, the egoist, have not at heart the welfare of this 'human society'. I sacrifice nothing to it. I only utilize it; but to be able to utilize it completely I must transform it rather into my property and my creature—i.e., I must annihilate it and form in its place the Union of Egoists.

The state, whether despotic or democratic, is the negation of individual will. It is based on the worship of collective man; moreover, its very systems of legislation and law enforcement result in a stabilization, a freezing of action and opinion, which the man who wishes to possess himself in uniqueness cannot tolerate. Therefore the struggle between the egoist and the state is inevitable.

For the state it is indispensable that nobody have an *own will*; if one had, the state would have to exclude, lock up, or banish him; if all had, they would do away with the state. The state is not thinkable without lordship and servitude; for the state must will to be the lord of all that it embraces, and this will is called the 'will of the State' ... The *own will* in me is the state's destroyer; it is therefore branded by the state as 'self-will'. Own will and the state are powers in deadly hostility, between which no 'eternal peace' is possible.

In the vacuum left by the annihilated state arises the world of the egoists, a world Stirner alarmingly characterized by the liberal use of such words as *force* and *power* and *might*, words most anarchists use only in a pejorative sense. These, as I have already remarked, Stirner opposes to *right*.

I do not demand any right; therefore I need not recognize any either. What I can get by force I get by force and what I do not get by force I have no right to, nor do I give myself airs; or consolation, with talk of my imprescriptible right ... Entitled or unentitled—that does not concern me; if I am only powerful, I am empowered of myself, and need no other empowering or entitling.

The accession of each man to his power, which his uniqueness implies, does not however suggest for Stirner a reign of universal rapacity and perpetual slaughter, nor does it mean the wielding of power over others. Each man defends by force his own uniqueness, but having attained the self-realization of true egoism he does not need to be burdened with more possessions than he requires, and he recognizes that to rule over others would destroy his own independence.

He who, to hold his own, must count on the absence of will in others is a thing made by these others, as the master is a thing made by the servant. If submissiveness ceased, it would be all over with lordship.

In Stirner's world there will be neither masters nor servants, but only egoists, and the very fact of the withdrawal of each man into his uniqueness will prevent rather than foster conflict.

As unique you have nothing in common with the other any longer, and therefore nothing divisive or hostile either; you are not seeking to be in the right against him before a *third* party, and are standing with him neither 'on the ground of right' nor on any other common ground. The opposition vanishes in complete severance or single-ness. This might be regarded as the new point in common or a new parity, but here the parity consists precisely in the disparity.

Egoism does not deny union between individuals. Indeed, it may well foster genuine and spontaneous union. For 'the individual is unique, not as a member of a party. He unites freely and separates again'. Stirner, who despises the practical and always prefers aphorism to argument, does not go into very much detail about the form of social organization that the Union of Egoists might produce. Indeed, anything static enough to be defined by a word like 'organization' lies outside the Stirnerite perspec-tive, and he clearly opposes *society*, as well as the state, because he sees it as an institution based on a collective conception of Man, on the subordina-tion of the individual to the whole. To society all he opposes is a union based on the free coming together of egoists who use their 'intercourse' or 'commercium' for their own advantages and abandon it as soon as it ceases to serve them.

> You bring into a union your whole power, your competence, and *make yourself count*, in a society you are *employed*, with your working power; in the former you live egoistically, in the latter humanly, i.e., religiously, as a 'member in the body of the Lord'; to a society you owe what you have, and are in duty bound to it, are possessed by 'social duties'; a union you utilize, and give it up undutifully and unfaithfully when you see no way to use it further. If a society is more than you, then it is more to you than yourself; a union is only your instrument, or the sword with which you sharpen and increase your natural force; the union exists for you and through you, the society conversely lays claim to you for itself and exists even without you; in short, the society is *sacred*, the union your *own*; the society consumes *you, you* consume the union.

If the world of Stirnerite egoists, that free intercourse of unique begins each embattled in his power, could ever be achieved in real life, it might take on a shape rather similar to the underground Utopia which Bulwer Lytton describes in *The Coming Race*, where every individual possesses power in the form of the deadly energy called *vril*. A kind of equilibrium based on mutual respect has been established, and brotherhood paradoxi-cally emerges from the danger of mutual destruction, so that governments have been rendered unnecessary and have withered away in the face of this union of the powerful.

But the world in which the Union of Egoists will reign cannot be won without a struggle. While the state remains, Stirner contends, the egoist must fight against it with all the means in his power, and the idea of this constant struggle carried on outside all conceptions of morality leads him to a rhapsodic glorification of crime.

> In crime the egoist has hitherto asserted himself and mocked at the sacred; the break with the sacred, or rather of the sacred, may become general. A revolution never returns, but a mighty, reckless, shameless, conscienceless, proud *crime*, does it not rumble in distant thunders, and do you not see how the sky grows presciently silent and gloomy?

Stirner may have had no direct influence on the proud and reckless criminals whose presence darkened the anarchist movement in the Latin countries during the 1880s and the 1890s, but he often anticipates them remarkably, as he also anticipates the later anarchist idea of the spontaneous rising of the people as a gathering of rebellious individuals rather than a mass insurrection.

At the same time, Stirner attacks the socialists and the communists for their belief that the property question can be settled amicably. Force will be necessary. Each man, Stirner declares, must have and take what he requires, and this involves 'the war of each against all', for 'the poor become free and proprietors only when they *rise*'. Here Stirner makes a distinction, fundamental to his point of view, between revolution and rebellion. Like Albert Camus in our own generation, he denies revolution and exalts rebellion, and his reasons are linked closely to his conception of individual uniqueness.

> Revolution and rebellion must not be looked upon as synonymous. The former consists in an overturning of conditions, of the established condition or *status*, the state or society, and is accordingly a *political* or *social* act. The latter has indeed for its unavoidable consequence a transformation of circumstances, yet does not start from that but from men's discontent with themselves; it is not an armed rising, but a rising of individuals, a getting up, without regard for the consequences that spring from it. The Revolution aims at new arrangements; rebellion leads us no longer to let ourselves be

arranged, but to arrange ourselves, and sets no glittering hopes on 'institutions'. It is not a fight against the established, since, if it prospers, the established collapses of itself ... Now, as my object is not the overthrow of an established order but my elevation above it, my purpose and deed are not political and social, but egoistic. The revolution commands one to make arrangements; rebellion demands that one *rise or exalt oneself.*

From Godwin, who placed his faith in immutable moral laws, and saw rational discussion as the best means to change the condition of man, to Stirner, who exalted the amoral individual and called for egoistic and self-assertive rebellion, the way may seem long, yet it ends for both in a society of proud individuals, each secure in his integrity and cooperating with other individuals only in so far as it is convenient to him. Working in isolation, and separated from the main historical stream of anarchism, one of them developed the logical and the other the passionate conclusion of anarchistic thought, and it is significant that two such different thinkers should have found their journeys meeting in the same destination.

It is true that *The Ego and His Own* remains a highly personal book, a product of Stirner's discontent, crying extravagantly against everything that in life bore down upon and destroyed his will. Yet when one has taken all this into account and has endured the appalling verbosity with which the substance of a brilliant essay has been inflated into the most tedious of all the libertarian classics, it remains the expression of a point of view that belongs clearly to one end of the varied spectrum of anarchist theory.

Of anarchist theory—but not of the anarchist movement; for, like Godwin, Stirner was not to be discovered by libertarian writers until after anarchism had taken on definite shape as a creed of the times. Even then, his influence affected only a few small marginal groups of individuals. It is as the appropriately lonely rhapsodist of the uniqueness of every human being that Stirner claims his place in the history of anarchism.

5. The Man of Paradox

'My conscience is mine, my justice is mine, and my freedom is a sovereign freedom,' said Pierre-Joseph Proudhon. No individualist—not even Stirner—was more lonely in the extremity of his thought than this self-taught philosopher who became angry at the suggestion that he had constructed any system of ideas, who passionately avoided the encouragement of any party or sect to support his views, and who proudly displayed the fluctuations and contradictions of his thought as evidence of its vitality. 'Such men,' said his friend Alexander Herzen, 'stand much too firmly on their own feet to be dominated by anything or to allow themselves to be caught in any net.'

But Proudhon was a connoisseur of paradox, an *aficionado* of antinomial thinking, and among all the oppositions he delighted to display in his thought none is more striking than that which made this arch-individualist at the same time a mystagogue of the people. Proudhon, of course, has not been the only Frenchman to stand lonely in his pride and to claim nevertheless that he speaks for his people and for history. We have only to consider the statements of De Gaulle in our own generation to recognize a curious affinity between the nationalist General-President and the printer from the Jura who became the first of the anarchists. Where De Gaulle identifies himself with France, Proudhon identifies himself with the Revolution and the People ('a collective ... an infallible and divine being', as he calls it when he is not dismissing it as an ignorant rabble). 'I regard myself,' he declared proudly in 1848, 'as the most complete expression of the Revolution.' And during the same period he confided to the secrecy of his diary: 'The representative of the people—that am I. For I alone am right.'

The double picture of Proudhon that often comes to us from the contradictions within his writings is no misleading clue either to his significance in the history of social and political thought or to the nature of his contribution to that thought. For Proudhon, who valued individual freedom so much that he distrusted the very word 'association', became the direct ancestor of the organized anarchist movement, which gave his

beliefs collective expression and force, and the actual master of some of
the men who created it. From him the French workers who helped to
found the International, and many leaders of the Commune of 1871, and
most of the syndicalist militants of the French trade unions between 1890
and 1910, were all to take the greater part of their ideas; as Élie Halévy
once remarked, he—and not Marx—was 'the real inspirer of French
socialism', or, at least, of French socialism as it existed up to the 1930s. He
was not the only lonely social philosopher to become the forerunner of
mass movements that would rise after his death—Marx, of course, was
another—but he was almost certainly the only avowed individualist to
whom this has happened.

But Proudhon's post-mortem influence sprang in fact from a sociological strain in his thought which distinguished him sharply from Stirner. If
we define Stirner as an egoistic individualist, we must regard Proudhon as
a social individualist. To Stirner the individual is all, and society his
enemy. To Proudhon the individual is both the starting point and the ultimate goal of our endeavours, but society provides the matrix—the serial
order as he would call it—within which each man's personality must find
its function and fulfilment. In one of his earlier works, *De la création de l'ordre dans l'humanité* (1843), he emphasizes that individual men cannot live on
their own, and that there is no such thing in nature as an isolated being.
All things, and all men, exist within appropriate relationships, or serial
groups, and so society, and all its true organs down to the family, is part of
the natural and universal order. The relationship between man and society
is thus a delicate equilibrium, and society must not become a monolithic
totality in which individual differences are melted and merged into uniformity. Yet at the same time it can never be merely a collection of individuals. Out of it emerges a collective force and a collective character
which are distinct from those of its members. This idea of the emergent
collective force or consciousness brings Proudhon into the central stream
of anarchism considered as a doctrine which sees individual freedom rooted deeply in the natural processes out of which society itself evolves.

Proudhon, of course, was more than an anarchist theoretician. His vigorous prose aroused the admiration of Baudelaire and Flaubert, drew
grudging praise from Victor Hugo—who disliked him personally—and
led his most critical biographer, Arthur Desjardins, to admit in the end
that 'this plebeian sculpts his phrases with a profound art, the art of great
classicists. He, no less than Molière, should have belonged to the
Académie Française.' The complexity of Proudhon's personality and outlook tempted the great critic Sainte-Beuve to write his first biography, and
turned the painter Gustave Courbet into his enthusiastic and lifelong

disciple. His provocative discussions of social and philosophical problems projected his influence far beyond the circle of anarchist thought or the boundaries of France; it can be seen in the whole Russian *narodnik* tradition, it inspired the Spanish federalist leader Pi y Margall and the Italian nationalist hero Carlo Pisacane, and it led Tolstoy not merely to borrow the title of his greatest novel from Proudhon's *La Guerre et la paix*, but also to incorporate in *War and Peace* many Proudhonian views on the nature of war and history. The breadth of his thought, the vigour of his writing, and the penetrative influence he wielded out of his solitude combine to make Proudhon one of the great nineteenth-century Europeans, whose importance has rarely been fully appreciated in English-speaking countries. In sheer greatness of texture only Tolstoy among the anarchists exceeds him.

Perhaps the reason for Proudhon's relative neglect in England and North America is the peculiarly Gallic nature of his genius, which makes even his writing difficult to translate in such a way that more than a suggestion of its strength and style are retained. For this convinced internationalist, this hater of states and frontiers, was also a passionate regionalist, a true patriot who loved his land and its traditions and was never happy in exile even among people who, like the Belgians, spoke his own tongue. He could reject the French state, like all other states, as a 'fictitious being, without intelligence, without passion, without morality', but with equal sincerity he could apostrophize France itself in the most lyrical terms:

O my land, my French land, the land of those who sing the eternal revolution! Land of liberty, for despite your bondages, in no place on earth, either in Europe or in America, is the mind, which is the entire man, so free as on your soil! Land that I love with all that accumulated love which a growing son has for his mother ...

Yet he could say also—and here his sincerity is perhaps deepest of all—'if I were forced to choose between the two I should be man enough to sacrifice my country to justice'.

Justice, indeed was Proudhon's ruling passion, the subject of his greatest book, *De la justice dans la révolution et dans l'église*; in that word was expressed and contained all he strove to attain, all he hoped for man and for society.

Justice is the central star which governs society, the pole around which the political world revolves, the principle and regulator of all transactions. Nothing takes place between men save in the name of right, nothing without the invocation of justice.

The idea of an immanent justice is as central to Proudhon's anarchism
as that of an immutable system of reason is to Godwin's. But when we seek
for the sources of this passion which made Proudhon not only a seeker
after justice but also that very different thing, a just man, we have to turn
again to his French origins. For it is as impossible to imagine Proudhon out
of the French revolutionary tradition as it is to think of Godwin detached
from the heritage of English Dissent or Stirner from the atmosphere of
German Romantic philosophy. Again we see how the common preoccupations of the age produced similar results from different beginnings.

By birth Proudhon was a man of the people. His father was a small
craftsman—a cooper and later a most unsuccessful brewer and tavern-
keeper—and his mother was a cook, but both were of Franc-Comtois
peasant stock. Proudhon was able to boast of his 'rustic blood' and in later
years to recollect with idyllic delight the hard times when the family
would go back to the land and he would run as a nine-year-old cowherd
over the limestone crags of the Jura. Forty years afterward, as a man of the
cities, he wrote with moving simplicity on the frugal merits of a peasant
life enjoyed in freedom.

> In my father's house we breakfasted on maize porridge; at midday we
> ate potatoes; in the evening bacon soup, and that every day of the
> week. And despite the economists who praise the English diet, we,
> with that vegetarian feeding, were fat and strong. Do you know why?
> Because we breathed the air of our fields and lived from the produce
> of our own cultivation.

The ideal of the free peasant life was to become a shaping element in
Proudhon's social and political thought. But, though he had the industry
that might have made a good farmer, circumstances prepared a different
destiny for him. He was born in 1809, and in childhood lived through the
distress that afflicted eastern France at the end of the Napoleonic wars.
Later he went on a scholarship to the Collège in Besançon; despite the
humiliation of being a poor boy in sabots among merchants' sons, he
developed a taste for learning, but had to abandon his education uncompleted because his father's passion for litigation had plunged the family
into destitution.

The trade he chose was printing, and so he entered the ranks of those
craftsmen from whom anarchism has traditionally drawn many of its most
dedicated recruits. Among such working men he found a sense of comradeship which he had never encountered in the snobbish atmosphere of

the Collège, and he took a pride in mastering his trade. 'I still remember with delight,' he said long after he had left the printing shop, 'the great day when my composing stick became for me the symbol and instrument of my freedom.'

There were other ways in which the printing shop was a congenial place for a youth with a great capacity for self-education. Besançon was a centre of theology, and as he proof-read the effusive apologetics of the local clergy, Proudhon found himself slowly converted to atheism by the ineptitude of their defence of Christianity. But he also absorbed much genuine religious scholarship, taught himself Hebrew in his spare time, and encountered one of the men who later helped to shape his social theories—the eccentric socialist and fellow Bisontin, Charles Fourier. Proudhon supervised the printing of Fourier's masterpiece, *Le Nouveau Monde industriel et sociétaire*, that extraordinary amalgam of sound social reasoning and fantasy, and, he recollected later, 'for six weeks I was the captive of this bizarre genius'. Finally, Proudhon's apprenticeship came to an end, and, after a period of wandering as a journeyman printer, he was rash enough to set up his own business in Besançon. It declined into slow failure; one of Proudhon's partners committed suicide in desperation, and he was left with a debt which for the remaining three decades of his life he struggled unsuccessfully to repay.

But hard work and poverty were not the whole of Proudhon's existence even at this point. While he struggled with his printing press he wrote his first published work; it was an *Essai de grammaire générale*, a rather naïve philological brochure which gained him some repute along the intellectuals of the Franche-Comté and earned him the Suard pension, awarded every three years by the Besançon Academy to a young scholar of outstanding promise. In his submission to the academicians he made a celebrated dedication, an oath to his fellows in poverty which sounded the note for the rest of his life:

Born and brought up in the working class, still belonging to it, today and forever, by heart, by nature, by habit, and above all by the community of interests and wishes, the greatest joy of the candidate, if he gains your votes, will be to have attracted in his person your just solicitude for that interesting portion of society, to have been judged worthy of being its first representative before you, and to be able to work henceforward without relaxation, through philosophy and science, and with all the energy of his will and the powers of his mind, for the complete liberation of his brothers and companions.

Soon he began to express these sentiments in a more explicit and disturbing manner. His pension took him to Paris, and there, observing the discontent among the Parisian workers and already moving on the edge of socialist and revolutionary groups, he began to formulate the ideas that had already taken shape dimly in his mind. They first appeared in a form as unexpected as Godwin's *An Account of the Seminary*. The Besançon Academy offered a prize for an essay on the Celebration of Sunday. Proudhon competed, but, as Sainte-Beuve justly remarked, what he presented was a thesis in which the subject had become 'hardly more than a pretext for introducing his system of ideas, still obscure and half-concealed'.

In *De la célébration du dimanche* Proudhon does indeed express his approval of the institution of a day of rest, and devotes much of his essay to an idyllic description of the peaceful rural life; it reads like the nostalgic dream of a man who already feels himself an exile from such innocent pleasures. But the real point of his essay appears when he discusses Moses, the institutor of such a beneficial custom, not merely as a religious leader, but also as the father of social reform. He examines the teachings of the patriarch, and by disputing the translation of the Eighth Commandment, which he interprets as meaning, not 'Thou shalt not steal', but 'Thou shalt not lay anything aside for thyself', he mounts a clear attack on the institution of property, and supports it with a categorical assertion that 'equality of condition is ... the aim of society'. Finally, he declares that 'property is the last of the false gods'. He attacks 'cumulative proprietors' and the 'exploiters of the proletariat', and ends on the challenging note of an imaginary dialogue in which the poor cry out in defiance: 'Proprietors, defend yourselves!' Already, Proudhon had evolved the social attitude he would maintain throughout his life, and had laid down in rough outline the main elements of his thought: his egalitarianism, his theory of the evil of accumulated property, his sense of a natural, immanent justice.

If Proudhon used the oblique approach in *De la célébration du dimanche*, he turned to the direct attack two years later in the work that brought him into the harsh and sudden light of notoriety. As the first book of a self-educated man, *What Is Property?* was in every way remarkable, full of fire and paradox, and containing so many original insights, that Karl Marx, afterward Proudhon's bitterest enemy, called it a 'penetrating work' when he discussed it in the *Neue Rheinische Zeitung*, and later, in *The Holy Family*, described it as 'the first decisive, vigorous, and scientific examination' of property.

What Is Property? begins with a paragraph of Proudhonian challenge that has ensnared many an impatient reader into a wrong judgement of the book's intent:

> If I were asked to answer the question: 'What is slavery?' and I should answer in one word, 'Murder!', my meaning would be understood at once. No further argument would be needed to show that the power to take from a man his thought, his will, his personality, is a power of life and death, and that to enslave a man is to kill him. Why, then, to this other question: 'What is property?' may I not likewise answer, 'Theft!'

'Property is Theft!' was to become one of the great political catchwords of the nineteenth century and to hang like a symbolic albatross on the popular image of Proudhon. But Proudhon, as he made clear even in this first work, did not mean literally what he said. His boldness of expression was intended as a form of shocking emphasis, and what he wished to be understood by *property* was, as he later explained, 'the sum of its abuses'. He was denouncing the property of the man who uses it to exploit the labour of others without any effort of his own. For 'possession', the right of a man to effective control over his dwelling and the land and tools he needed to work and live, Proudhon had only approval; in fact, he regarded it as a necessary keystone of liberty, and his main criticism of the communists was that they wished to destroy it.

These aspects of his theory became clearer in later works, but even in *What Is Property?* a distinction between kinds of property is evident. The man who works has an absolute right over what he produces, but not over the means of production. 'The right to products is exclusive—*jus in re*; the right to means is common—*jus ad rem.*' This is so, not merely because raw materials are provided by nature, but also because of the heritage of installations and techniques which is the real source of human wealth and because of the collaboration that makes each man's contribution so much more effective than if he worked in solitude.

> Now this reproductive leaven—this eternal germ of life, this preparation of the land and manufacture of implements for production—constitutes the debt of the capitalist to the producer, which he never pays; and it is this fraudulent denial which causes the poverty of the labourer, the luxury of idleness, and the inequality of conditions. This it is, above all things, which has been fitly named the exploitation of man by man.

Hence, property is incompatible with justice, since in practice it brings about the exclusion of the majority of producers from their equal rights to the fruits of social work.

But if property in the means of production destroys equality, and offends justice, we must consider an alternative, not merely to property itself, but also to the social organization that is based upon it. Will it be communism, Proudhon asked, thinking of the Utopian systems of Cabet, Owen, and similar thinkers? But communism fails to recognize that, though man is a social being and seeks equality, he also loves independence. Property, in fact, springs from man's desire to free himself from slavery of communism, which is the primitive form of association. But property, in its turn, goes to the extreme, and violates equality by the rights of exclusion and increase, and supports the acquisition of power by the privileged minority. In other words, it leads to unjust authority, and this brings us to the question of legitimate authority, if such exists.

Here Proudhon makes his historic proclamation of anarchist faith, which I have already quoted in the opening pages of this book. He goes on to explain it by tracing the genesis of authority in the tendency of social animals and primitive man always to seek a leader. As man develops reasoning powers, he turns them almost immediately upon authority, and so emerge protest, disobedience, and finally rebellion. Rebellion is canalized by the appearance of political science and the realization that the laws by which society functions are not matters for the opinion of rulers, but exist in the nature of things. At this point the idea of anarchy, the government which is no government, appears.

Communism denies independence, property destroys equality, but in 'anarchy' or 'liberty' Proudhon—at this time under the influence of Hegelian ideas imperfectly transmitted through articles in French reviews—finds a synthesis that eliminates the deficiencies of both, leading to a society where equality, justice, independence, and the recognition of individual merits can all flourish in a world of products bound together by a system of free contacts.

By rejecting government and the non-working proprietor, by advocating economic equality and free contractual relationships between independent workers, *What Is Property?* contains the basic elements from which all later libertarian and decentralist doctrines have been built. But it contains them in an undeveloped form. Throughout his book Proudhon seems to discuss property in a society of peasants and small craftsmen, and pays little attention to industries that cannot be carried on by single 'possessors'. He is, in fact, arguing from the world he knew—the city of

Besançon, still untouched by the railways, a place of artisan workshops in a land of mountain farmers. Very soon, when he moved to industrial Lyons after the final collapse of his printing business, Proudhon was to widen considerably his view of nineteenth-century social and economic problems.

Before he left Besançon, where he had returned in 1841 after the expiry of the Suard pension, he wrote two other memoirs on property in reply to critics of the first. These add little to his basic contentions, though a significant new note of militancy appears in the second, entitled *Avertissement aux propriétaires.* In true anarchist manner Proudhon here declares that the workers alone can renovate society.

> Workers, labourers, men of the people, whoever you may be, the initiative of reform is yours. It is you who will accomplish that synthesis of social composition which will be the masterpiece of creation, and you alone can accomplish it ... And you, men of power, angry magistrates, cowardly proprietors, have you at last understood me? ... Do not provoke the outbreaks of our despair, for even if your soldiers and policemen succeed in suppressing us, you will not be able to stand up before our last resource. It is neither regicide, nor assassination, nor poisoning, nor arson, nor refusal to work, nor emigration, nor insurrection, nor suicide; it is something more terrible than all that, and more efficacious, something which is seen but cannot be spoken of.

In a letter to Ackermann, the Alsatian poet, Proudhon confided that what he meant by this final threat was a revival of something like the German Fehmgericht, the secret popular tribunals which dealt summarily with petty tyrants in the Middle Ages. But to his readers the threat remained all the more sensational because of its vagueness. It was sensational enough, indeed, to induce Louis-Philippe's government to take swift action, and Proudhon was indicted for various crimes against public security. He was fortunate; a jury of his fellow townsmen decided that his ideas were very hard for them to follow, and conscientiously refused to convict the writer for a book they did not understand.

In Lyons Proudhon became managing clerk—and apparently a very efficient one—to a water-transport firm run by an old schoolfellow, Antoine Gauthier. His work kept him closely in touch with the commercial life of this growing centre of the French industrial revolution, and he used his spare time to broaden his knowledge of the rebellious tendencies

among the French workers during the years of ferment that preceded the
Revolution of 1848. Lyons was an ideal city for such a study. Throughout
the nineteenth century its factory workers were extremely receptive to
revolutionary doctrines. When Proudhon arrived in 1842 the followers of
Cabet, Fourier, and Saint-Simon were all very active in the city, and a certain romantic colour was given to its radical life by the presence of the
Peruvian feminist-socialist Flora Tristan, who claimed to be descended
from Montezuma and who in fact became the grandmother of the painter
Gauguin. The largest group among the textile workers was the secret society of the mutualists, led by veteran insurrectionaries who had taken part
in the risings of 1831 and 1834. It was with this group that Proudhon established his closest ties; the fact that they consisted entirely of manual workers, with no admixture of middle-class intellectuals, appealed to his own
sense of identification with the poorest class, and he seems to have seen in
their activities a vindication of his idea that out of the people could arise
the movement to reform society. Moreover, the mutualists—whose very
name Proudhon later adopted to describe his own teachings of the reorganization of society by means of free contractual association—appear to
have shared his view of the primacy of economic change, in contradiction
to the Jacobin emphasis on political evolution, which was later adopted by
the authoritarian socialists.

Proudhon's association with the Lyons mutualists was the only occasion
on which he actually became involved in an underground organization.
His letters and diaries suggest that he established close contacts with
workers' groups not only in Lyons but also in 'the neighbouring towns and
villages for fifty miles around', and saw himself as a man of standing
among them and a mediator between the various socialist sects.

At this time a great deal of attention was being given in Lyons to the
idea of a widespread association of workers; Flora Tristan wrote a book on
the subject, and it recurs constantly in Proudhon's journals during the
mid-1840s. These references anticipate in a significant way the attitude of
the French Proudhonian delegates to the First International in the 1860s
and look forward also to the later anarcho-syndicalist view of a social
change achieved through economic or industrial action. 'The social revolution,' he notes, 'is seriously compromised if it comes through a political
revolution.' And he adds that 'the new socialist movement will begin by ...
the war of the workshops'. Unlike Marx, he hopes that this war may be
carried on without violent revolution, 'invading all through the force of
principle'. Like Winstanley and Godwin, he relies on the power of reason
and example, and even envisages the proprietors being dispossessed 'at
their solicitation and without indemnity'. About the actual nature of the

workers' associations, which he also calls 'progressive societies', he is vague, but he appears to see them partly as educational, intended to give the proletariat a true consciousness of the economic realities that underlie the social situation, and partly as functional, actual cells of the new order, organized on a 'collective and limited liability' basis, for the purpose of regulating a mutualist exchange of goods and services, a network that will embrace all the industrial centres. The possibilities of the idea fill him with the kind of irrational optimism that was still possible in the sociological *terra incognita* that nineteenth-century radicals were exploring. With an over-confidence characteristic of the time as well as the man, he estimated those already ripe for association in the Lyons region at a hundred thousand. 'By 1860,' he added, 'the globe will be overrun in every direction by the association.'

But at this period it was not merely in Lyons that Proudhon found stimulating contacts. His work gave him many opportunities to visit Paris, where he made the acquaintance of men who were to play important parts in his own life and also in the future of European socialism and anarchism. The Russians Alexander Herzen and Michael Bakunin became his close friends in 1844, and remained so until the end of his life, both of them falling under the influence of his personality and his ideas. He also encountered, in an ambiance of metaphysical discussion, many of the German Left Hegelians who had exiled themselves to Paris. They included Arnold Ruge and Karl Grün, both of whom helped to introduce his works to German readers, and also Karl Marx. The meeting between Marx and Proudhon was historically important because it showed the first signs of the irreconcilable conflict between authoritarian socialism and anarchism that was to reach its climax twenty-five years later in the heart of the First International.

I have already remarked on Marx's first favourable reaction to Proudhon's work. Their early meetings appear to have consolidated a good impression, largely because Proudhon was the only one among the leading French socialists of the time willing to pay serious attention to Marx and his fellow Left Hegelians. Marx clearly regarded him as a possible convert to his own schemes for an international revolutionary organization, but evidently did not take into account the fact that Proudhon was not in the least interested in an association for political propaganda of the kind planned by the German socialists, but envisaged instead an association for the encouragement of economic action and cooperation.

How far their various aims were discussed in Paris over the winter of 1844-5 is unrecorded. What we do know is that after Marx was expelled from France to Belgium in 1845 he still regarded Proudhon as a possible collaborator, and on 5 May 1846 wrote a letter asking for his cooperation in the establishment of a 'sustained correspondence' among socialists of various countries to discuss matters of common interest:

> In that manner, differences of opinion can be brought to light; one can achieve an exchange of ideas and an impartial criticism. It will be a step forward for the socialist movement in its 'literary' expression, a step toward shaking off the limitations of 'nationality'. And at the moment of action it is certainly of great importance for each of us to be informed on the state of affairs abroad as well as at home.

Proudhon reacted cautiously. He expressed his willingness to participate in the correspondence Marx suggested, but made a series of reservations which already reveal the important differences that were to divide him more and more deeply from authoritarian socialism.

> First, although my ideas in the matter of organization and realization are at this moment more or less settled, at least as regards principles, I believe it is my duty, as it is the duty of all socialists, to maintain for some time yet the critical or dubitive form; in short, I make profession in public of an almost absolute economic anti-dogmatism.
>
> I applaud with all my heart your thought of bringing to light all opinions; let us give the world the example of a learned and far-sighted tolerance, but let us not, because we are at the head of a movement, make ourselves the leaders of a new intolerance, let us not pose as the apostles of a new religion, even if it be the religion of logic, the religion of reason. Let us gather together and encourage all protests, let us brand all exclusiveness, all mysticism; let us never regard a question as exhausted, and when we have used our last argument, let us begin again, if necessary, with eloquence and irony. On that condition, I will gladly enter into your association. Otherwise—no!
>
> I have also some observations to make on this phrase of your letter: *at the moment of action.* Perhaps you retain the opinion that no reform is at present possible without a *coup-de-main*, without what was formerly called a revolution and is really nothing but a shock. That opinion, which I understand, which I excuse and would willingly discuss, having myself shared it for a long time, my most recent studies have made me completely abandon. I believe we have no need of it in order to succeed; and that consequently we should not

put forward *revolutionary action* as a means of social reform, because that pretended means would simply be an appeal to force, to arbitrariness, in brief, a contradiction. I myself put the problem in this way: *to bring about the return to society, by an economic combination, of the wealth which was withdrawn from society by another economic combination.*

With this letter, which clearly opposes the anarchist ideal of economic action to the Marxist emphasis on political action, all direct contact between Marx and Proudhon came to an end. Marx did not reply, and he is said to have been disappointed by Proudhon's attitude. However, it was more than disappointment that he showed in his next public reference to Proudhon, which occurred after the latter published in the autumn of 1846 his *System of Economic Contradictions: or, The Philosophy of Poverty.* Marx chose this occasion for a complete reversal of his past attitude to Proudhon by publishing *The Poverty of Philosophy*; this was a pretended critique of Proudhon's book which degenerated into a tissue of abusive misrepresentations showing a complete failure to understand the originality and plasticity of thought underlying the apparent disorder of Proudhon's arguments. The dialogue between the two authors showed not merely a complete divergence of theoretical outlook, but also—and perhaps this was more important—an irreconcilable opposition of personalities.

In *Economic Contradictions* Proudhon was in fact using what in his letter to Marx he had called 'the critical or debutive form'. It is true that the title-page bore the epigraph *Destraum et Aedificabo*, but Proudhon destroyed to greater effect than he built up, and by the end of the book he more or less admitted that the constructive side of his approach to society would have to be discussed later. He was concerned basically with illuminating the way in which, in society as it exists, all good possibilities turn to evil conclusions.

> The essential contradiction of our ideas, being realized by work and expressed in society with a gigantic power, makes all things happen in the reverse way to that in which they should, and gives society the aspect of a tapestry seen the wrong way round, or a hide turned inside out...the non-producer should obey, and by a bitter irony it is the non-producer who commands. Credit, according to the etymology of its name and its theoretical definition, should be the provider of work; in practice it oppresses and kills it. Property, in the spirit of its finest prerogative, is the making available of the earth, and in the exercise of the same prerogative it becomes the denial of the earth.

In the same way communism, which takes fraternity for its principle, ends by destroying it and establishing monopoly. In fact, unbalanced monopoly is the end which all solutions attempted up to the present have reached. Here one perceives that Proudhon is really seeking a kind of equilibrium in which economic contradictions will not be eliminated—for they cannot be—but brought into a dynamic equation. This dynamic equation he finds in mutualism, a concept that includes such familiar Proudhonian elements as the dissolution of government, the equalization of property, and the freedom of credit.

Proudhon worked much anger out of his system writing *Economic Contradictions*; in particular, he shocked the respectable with an anti-religious declaration as scandalous in its way as 'Property is Theft!' He examined the idea of Providence, and came to the conclusion that, far from the state of the world confirming the existence of a benevolent deity, it leads one irresistibly to the conclusion embodied in the aphorism: 'God is Evil.' Man, Proudhon urges, becomes what he is by opposing himself to all in the universe that is non-human; but this non-human all is—in the view of the theologians at least—governed by God. If God exists, then, he must be in opposition to Man, and since the only good we can know is human good, God must, by Proudhonian logic, be evil.

> I affirm that God, if there is a God, bears no resemblance to the effigies which the philosophers and the priests have made of him; that he neither thinks nor acts according to the law of analysis, foresight and progress, which is the distinctive characteristic of man; that on the contrary, he seems to follow an inverse and retrograde path; that the intelligence, liberty, personality, are constituted otherwise in God than in us; and that this originality of nature...makes of God a being who is essentially anti-civilized, anti-liberal, anti-human.

If this is true, then the conquest of tyranny and poverty and falsehood lies in opposition to God. 'We reach knowledge in spite of him. Every step forward is a victory in which we overcome the Divine.'

Here Proudhon presents as emphatically as any other of the later anarchists a rebellion against the idea of a ruling God which is the unavoidable corollary of the fight against earthly government. However, the rejection of a transcendental deity, and the accompanying anti-clericism, do not preclude an attitude in some ways religious. And Proudhon was never a true atheist. He disliked the atheist's absolute dogmatism as much as that of the priest, and regarded the idea of God—even if it had been created by man himself—as existing and therefore to be opposed. God and Man in fact represented for Proudhon the ultimate contradiction, the Manichean poles of his cosmos in whose struggle lay the secret of social salvation. In his diary in 1846 there appear two significant notes. The first says: 'God and man, neither is more than the other; they are two incomplete realities, which have no fullness of existence.' The second adds: 'God is necessary to reason but rejected by reason.' Proudhon was not a denier of the idea of God; he was its adversary. And here it is worth emphasizing the persistence of the idea of conflict in Proudhon's thoughts; he lived for the struggle more than for the victory, and in this most of the anarchists have resembled him. At most he sees a possible truce between the contradictory forces in the universe and in society; but stress and tension are inevitable and desirable. It would therefore be most unwise in judging a work like *Economic Contradictions* to forget that Proudhon was a deliberately anti-systematic thinker who distrusted static conclusions and final answers. The dynamic society was always his ideal, the society kept in movement by perpetual change and kept alive by perpetual criticism.

A great leap in the process of perpetual change came when the Orléanist monarchy was overthrown in the February Revolution of 1848. By this time Proudhon had left his post in Lyons to follow a free-lance writing career in Paris. His reputation among the radical working men of the capital was already so high that in January 1848 Engels wrote to Marx complaining of the 'Proudhonistery' rampant among the members of the Communist League in Paris, while in the last months of 1847 he was negotiating with a group of sympathizers to take over the direction of a journal that would continue the tradition of the short-lived *Le Peuple*, edited briefly by a journalist name Ribeyrolles who, like Proudhon, had moved on the edge of socialist circles without becoming closely involved in any particular sect.

Proudhon had foreseen the February Revolution; he had also realized that it would be dominated by sentimental liberals and Jacobins with few thoughts for the radical reconstruction of society. During the days of the insurrection he was stimulated by the example of the rebels and took part in the bloodless storming of the Tuileries, helped to build barricades, and composed placards for the revolutionary junta in a commandeered printing shop. But when he returned to his hotel room and began to write down his impressions for the benefit of friends outside the capital, he came to the conclusion that, as he put it, 'they have made a revolution without ideas'. Victory had come from the weakness of the monarchy rather than the strength of the revolution. 'It is necessary to give a direction to the movement and already I see it lost beneath the waves of discussion.'

He set himself to provide the ideas which seemed so lacking, and in doing so he initiated the process by which, over the next two decades, anarchism ceased to be a merely theoretical trend, detached from immediate events, and turned instead toward propaganda and action aiming at social change without a foreseeable future. His activities during the revolutionary year of 1848 and the reactionary year of 1849 were centred mainly on three ventures: the series of periodicals beginning with the first issue of *Le Représentant du peuple* on 7 February 1848; the attempt to create a People's Bank and a system of mutualist exchange; and the sole disillusioning affray which he made into parliamentary activity when a by-election in June 1848 took him into the Constituent Assembly.

'What is the Producer? Nothing ... What should he be? Everything!' It was with this banner heading that *Le Représentant du peuple* started its course as the first regularly published anarchist periodical.* Proudhon maintained and even flaunted his independence of party and clique, and took his stand as an independent critic whose aim was to show the true ends of the revolution and the errors of the revolutionaries. He was supported by a small but devoted group of associates, many of them printing workers like himself, and in this respect *Le Représentant du peuple* set something of a precedent, for the most enduring type of anarchist organization has in fact been the small functional group devoted to a specific task of propaganda, often that of publication.

It was the independence of *Le Représentant du peuple*, reinforced by Proudhon's astringent style, that made his paper an immediate success.

> Of all the newspapers [commented the Comtese d'Agoult in her *History of 1848*], the only one that was produced with a quite extraordinary originality and talent was *Le Représentant du peuple* ... From the depth of his retreat he [Proudhon] agitated public opinion more strongly, more deeply than was done by the men who mingled most with the multitudes ... His unexpected and striking manner of speaking ... excited the curiosity of the public to the highest degree.

One of the constant themes of Proudhon's articles during 1848 was that 'the proletariat must emancipate itself without the help of the government'. He coupled this with a denunciation of the myth of universal suffrage as a panacea for all social ills, and pointed out that political

---

*The first anarchist periodical of any kind may well have been a sheet called *El Provenir*, which Proudhon's Spanish disciple Ramón de la Sagra published briefly in Galicia in 1845.

democracy without economic changes could easily result in retrogression rather than progress. Nowadays, when we have learned a great deal about the mass appeal of right-wing movements of the fascist type, such a contention does not seem extraordinary, but in April 1848, in the high tide of revolutionary optimism, Proudhon was almost alone in anticipating the situation that would follow within a year when democracy would be submerged by the election of Louis-Napoleon as Prince-President by the very means of universal suffrage which the Republic had set up for its own defence.

This insight makes all the more puzzling Proudhon's own willingness to be elected to the Constituent Assembly. He had already put forward his candidature in April and failed to win election by a small margin; in June he was elected by 77,000 votes with the support, among others, of the poet Charles Baudelaire, who then edited a small newspaper called *La Tribune nationale*. It has been suggested that Proudhon's aim in seeking election was the hope that as a legislator he might win some kind of official support for the People's Bank; he had already solicited in vain the help of the socialist minister Louis Blanc. However that may be, his experience was almost immediately disillusioning. He conscientiously carried out his task as a legislator, attending from morning till night at the various committees and bureaux even when the Assembly itself was not in session. But he found that this work had the effect of isolating him from the currents of real life. 'As soon as I set foot in the parliamentary Sinai,' he recollected a year later in *Les Confessions d'un révolutionnaire*, 'I ceased to be in touch with the masses; because I was absorbed by my legislative work, I entirely lost sight of the current of events.' It was soon clear to Proudhon that, with his anarchistic theories, he was completely out of place in the Assembly. Certainly the experience hardened his distrust of political methods, and helped to create the anti-parliamentarianism that marked his last years and was inherited by the anarchist movement in general.

At the same time, it must be said that he did not remain long in the ignorance he lamented, and that his position within the Assembly soon became as much that of angry independence as it was already in the world of journalism. When the barricades were raised by the discontented workers in the latter part of June 1848, Proudhon at first suspected, like his colleagues, the work of Bonapartist agitators wishing to undermine the Republic. But he set out to find the truth for himself, and took advantage of his representative's insignia to visit the areas where the fighting was in progress. The conclusion he reached was that the uprising had been fundamentally socialist in nature, that 'its first and determining cause is the

social question, the social crisis, work, ideas'. He realized that a new element had entered into revolutionary history with this first uprising of the
working class as distinct from the bourgeois revolutionaries, and he
understood now that, in their different ways, he and the men who fought
at the June barricades had gone beyond the mere political revolutionism of
the Jacobins and were seeking solutions to the economic injustices evident
in the society of their time.

Once he realized this, Proudhon did not hesitate to defend the insurrectionaries. As the repression continued, and the firing squads were
replaced by the tribunals with their innumerable sentences of transportation, he felt the need to express his sympathy with the victims; he did so
with characteristic emphasis in *Le Représentant du peuple* of 6 July:

> Four months of unemployment were suddenly converted into a *casus
> belli*, into an insurrection against the government of the Republic;
> there is the whole truth of these funereal days ... The French worker
> asks for work, you offer him alms, and he rebels, he shoots at you ... I
> glory in belonging to that proud race, inaccessible to dishonour!

Paris was now under an emergency dictatorship administered by
Cavaignac, the general who had suppressed the June revolt, and such a
bold statement immediately drew his attention to Proudhon. Two days
later, *Le Représentant du peuple* was suspended for an article in which, with a
view to easing the worsening economic crisis, Proudhon suggested that at
the next quarter day, the government should decree a third reduction in
all payments falling due. To make matters worse in the eyes of Cavaignac,
he came near to inciting mutiny by a direct call to the National Guard to
'ask for work, credit and bread from your pretended protectors'.

Proudhon was not the man to remain muzzled while there remained
any means of making his voice heard. With his newspaper silenced, he
made the Constituent Assembly his forum. He presented there a specific
motion that creditors should be asked to surrender a third of what was
owed them over the past three years, half to be returned to tenants,
debtors, etc., to re-establish their positions, and the rest to go to the state
as a fund to restore the standard of living which had existed before the
Revolution. It was in fact, though not in form, a proposal for interlocking
taxation and subsidy of a kind familiar enough in our own time, but the
members of the Finance Committee before whom it came for examination
were hostile to it, partly because even in its present form they regarded it
as an attack on property, and partly because they suspected that in

Proudhon's mind the suggestion had wider implications than were immediately apparent.

These implications became evident when Proudhon publicly defended his proposal in the Assembly on 31 July. For all his eloquence in print, he was no orator, and his speech was, as the British Ambassador remarked, 'irremediably dull' and very badly delivered. Yet it contained enough provocative material to raise the anger of those colleagues who had gone there with the idea of merely laughing at his extravagances. He defined his aim as the reduction of property to possession by the abolition of revenues, and he went on to say that the 'liquidation of the old society' would be 'stormy or amicable, according to the passions and the good or bad faith of the parties'. He put forward his proposal as a first step, remarking that the proprietors should be called upon 'to contribute, for their part, to the revolutionary work, proprietors being responsible for the consequences of their refusals'.

When his colleagues shouted for an explanation, Proudhon proceeded to make another of his historic definitions. 'It means that in the case of refusal we ourselves shall proceed to the liquidation without you.' When his hearers shouted again, 'Whom do you mean by *you?*' he replied: 'When I used these two pronouns, *you* and *we*, it is evident that I was identifying *myself* with the proletariat, and *you* with the bourgeois class.' 'It is the social war!' shouted the angry conservatives. They were not content with rejecting Proudhon's proposition. They also brought in a special resolution declaring that it 'is an odious attack on the principles of public morality, that it violates property, that it encourages scandal, it makes appeal to the most odious passions'. 691 votes were cast for the resolution and 2—including Proudhon's—against.

Proudhon now stood in virtual isolation among the February revolutionaries. He had not merely acknowledged the existence of a struggle between classes, but he had also for the first time suggested that in such a struggle the anarchists must take sides with the workers as a class and not merely as a vague entity called 'the people'. It is significant that when *Le Représentant du peuple* appeared again on 31 August, the heading on the front page had been enlarged by the words: 'What is the capitalist? Everything! What should he be? Nothing!'

Proudhon's speech to the National Assembly made his name anathema to the upper classes, but it increased his reputation greatly among the workers, and the circulation of his paper increased to 40,000 copies, a phenomenal figure for the relatively small Paris of the 1840s. But the authorities did not allow him to exploit his success undisturbed; a few days after its reappearance, *Le Représentant du peuple* was finally suppressed. Proudhon and his friends had foreseen the possibility. They immediately collected funds for a new paper, and in the middle of November *Le Peuple* began to appear.

Meanwhile, Proudhon was maturing his plans for the People's Bank. This was to be an institution for fostering the exchange of products among workers, based on labour cheques, and for providing credit with a nominal interest rate to cover the cost of administration. Proudhon believed it possible to create by these means a network of independent craftsmen and peasants and of associations of workers who would contract out of the capitalist system and eventually achieve what Proudhon always hoped—despite the frequent violence of his expression—would be a peaceful transformation of society.

But, though it was incorporated on 31 January 1849, and quickly gathered 27,000 members, the Bank never came into operation, owing to the hazards of Proudhon's journalistic career. In January *Le Peuple* carried two articles, one signed by Proudhon himself, accusing Louis-Napoleon, who had been elected President in December, of being the instrument and personification of reaction and of conspiring to enslave the people. When charges of sedition were brought against Proudhon, the Assembly enthusiastically waived his parliamentary immunity by a large majority, and he was sentenced to three years' imprisonment and a fine of three thousand francs. He appealed against the conviction and immediately fled, disguised in blue spectacles and a large muffler; over the Belgian frontier he assumed the name of Dupuis and tried to pass himself off as a vacationing magistrate. For a couple of weeks he wandered disconsolately through the country, and then returned secretly to Paris, where he liquidated the People's Bank for fear it should fall into the wrong hands, and continued to edit *Le Peuple* from hiding. Eventually he was seen by a police informer and arrested as he strolled on a June evening in the Place de Lafayette.

The three years of Proudhon's imprisonment in Sainte-Pélagie, in the Conciergerie, and in the fortress of Doullens, were, ironically, some of the best years of his life. French political prisoners in that happy age underwent a mild confinement. Proudhon was well-housed and well-fed; he could write, study, and receive his friends; he was even allowed, for the greater part of his term, to go out of prison once a week to look after his affairs. During this period he wrote three books, two of which were among his best, continued to edit his successive newspapers, and was even able to marry and start the propagation of a family. The restriction of movement was largely counterbalanced by the lack of distraction, and there is no

doubt that during these years Proudhon's life gained in richness and pro-
ductivity. In fact, when it was all ended and he was about to depart from
Sainte-Pélagie in the summer of 1852, he wrote with satisfaction:

> What have I lost? If I made the balance with exactitude, I would say,
> nothing. I know ten times more than I knew three years ago, and I
> know it ten times better; I know positively what I have gained, and
> truly I do not know what I have lost.

What Proudhon did lose—and the rest of his life he regretted it—was
his vocation as a journalist. *Le Peuple* came to an end in the collapse of the
insurrection against Louis-Napoleon on 13 June 1849. Proudhon did not
support the insurrection, which he realized was ill-timed and ill-planned,
but the friends he had left in charge of *Le Peuple* were led by their enthusiasm to take an active part, and as a result the paper was suspended and its
premises were wrecked by the National Guard.

But Proudhon was not willing without an effort to abandon his journalism, and on 30 September, his third paper, *Le Voix du peuple*, began its
career, generously financed by his friend and admirer Alexander Herzen.
Le Voix du peuple was even more popular than its predecessors, for imprisonment seemed merely to have given a new gloss to Proudhon's reputation; on the days when he wrote special articles, between fifty and sixty
thousand copies would sell, so quickly that, according to Herzen, 'often on
the following day copies were being sold for a franc instead of a sou'.

The career of *Le Voix du peuple* was as stormy as those of its forerunners.
It was constantly being suspended and fined, while Proudhon himself was
prosecuted for an article in which he accurately prophesied Louis-
Napoleon's *coup d'état* a year before it happened; he escaped a greatly
lengthened term of imprisonment only on technical grounds. *Le Voix du
peuple* was finally suppressed in May 1850. By this time Herzen's fund was
almost gone, and no other willing benefactor could be found.
Nevertheless, Proudhon soon began to publish a fourth paper, again called
Le Peuple, which, for lack of money, appeared only irregularly. He tried to
restrain his flights of indignation, but this did not prevent the first issue
from being seized as it came off the press, and *Le Peuple* was finally
destroyed by a new stamp duty on all political literature, which reduced
circulation sharply and left the paper with no resources to meet a last fine
of 6,000 francs, imposed on 14 October 1850 for alleged 'provocation to
civil war'. In this way, after more than two years, the first sustained experiment in anarchist journalism came to an end.

Proudhon regretted his forced withdrawal from journalism, but he did not allow it to prevent him from putting forward his ideas, and the time saved from periodicals he used for writing books. Of the three which he wrote during his imprisonment two at least remain important in anarchist history.

Les Confessions d'un révolutionnaire, which appeared in 1849, analyses the events of 1848 from an anarchistic point of view, and comes to the conclusion that the revolutionary tradition will not be fulfilled until the true principle of the revolution is accepted—'no more government of man by man, by means of the accumulation of capital'. *Les Confessions d'un révolutionnaire* is in fact most interesting for its unorthodox view of a particular historical event, for its sharp analysis of the various political trends of the time, and for the autobiographical passages which, despite the title, are brought in merely to reinforce Proudhon's theoretical arguments.

The General Idea of the Revolution in the 19th Century, which followed in July 1851, is considerably less brilliant in style than *Les Confessions*, but it is more important as a stage in the progress of anarchist thought, for here, more than in any other of his works, Proudhon presents the positive examination of society which he had promised five years before as a constructive supplement to *Economic Contradictions*.

The General Idea of the Revolution begins with a study of the revolutionary process, which Proudhon presents as a necessary phenomenon, a development that can be avoided no more than such natural events as death and birth and growth.

> A revolution is a force against which no power, divine or human, can prevail, and whose nature it is to grow by the very resistance it encounters ... The more you repress it, the more you increase its rebound and render its action irresistible, so that it is precisely the same for the triumph of an idea whether it is persecuted, harassed, beaten down from the start, or whether it grows and develops unobstructed. Like the Nemesis of the ancients, whom neither prayers nor threats could move, the revolution advances, with sombre and predestined tread, over the flowers strewn by its friends, through the blood of its defenders, over the bodies of its enemies.

Such a view of revolution fits into the anarchist conception of society as part of the world of nature, governed by the necessary forces which represent the realm of destiny within whose boundaries man has to work and achieve his freedom. Later, adopting Darwinian formulas, Kropotkin would express the idea more scientifically, presenting revolutions as leaps or mutations in an evolutionary process, but the general conception did not change.

Shifting focus to his own age, Proudhon argues that a revolution is necessary in the nineteenth century because the French Revolution of 1789 only half accomplished its task. The men who carried it out were concerned with political change only, and paid no attention to the economic changes demanded by the death of feudalism.

> The Republic should have established Society; it thought only of establishing Government ... Therefore, while the problem propounded in '89 seemed to be officially solved, fundamentally there was a change only in governmental metaphysics, in what Napoleon called *ideology* ... In place of this governmental, feudal and military rule, imitated from that of former kings, the new edifice of industrial institutions must be built.

That edifice can be built, Proudhon contends, by means of association, but he is careful to point out that by this he does not mean a rigid or Utopian organization. Association, considered as an end in itself, is dangerous to freedom, but considered as a means to a greater end, the liberation of individual men, it can be beneficial. There is already an anticipation of the syndicalist attitude in Proudhon's statement that the associations should be valued only in so far as they tend to establish 'the social republic'.

> The importance of their work lies not in their petty union interests, but in their denial of the rule of capitalists, usurers, and governments, which the first revolution left undisturbed. Afterwards, when they have conquered the political lie ... the groups of workers should take over the great departments of industry which are their natural inheritance.

> The great task of the associations will be to oppose to the idea of government the idea of contract.

> The idea of contract excludes that of government ... Between contracting parties there is necessarily a real personal interest for each; a man bargains with the aim of securing his liberty and his revenue at the same time. Between governing and governed, on the other hand,

no matter how the system of representation or delegation of the governmental function is arranged, there is *necessarily* an alienation of part of the liberty and means of the citizen.

It is in the generalization of this principle of contract, in the turning of society into a network of voluntary understandings between free individuals, that Proudhon sees the new order of economic as distinct from political organization. When that order is achieved, there will no longer be any need for government and, returning to his old serialist doctrine, Proudhon concludes that the end of the series beginning in authority is anarchy.

But he does not leave the argument in these general terms. Instead, he presents the nearest thing we have to a Proudhonian Utopia, a sketch of the arrangements of society as they may take shape when the idea of contract has triumphed. Already the elements of decentralization and federalism and direct workers' control which characterize later anarchist and syndicalist visions are there. One sees a clear progression from the Godwinian Utopia, brought about by the experience of those fifty years at the beginning of which Godwin lived in a mostly agrarian society and at the end of which Proudhon lived in a world that was becoming steadily industrial. This is the sketch of the free society as Proudhon presents it to us.

In place of laws, we will put contracts; no more laws voted by the majority or even unanimously. Each citizen, each town, each industrial union will make its own laws. In place of political powers we will put economic forces ... In place of standing armies, we will put industrial associations. In place of police we will put identity of interests. In place of political centralization, we will put economic centralization.

Law courts will be replaced by arbitration, national bureaucracies will be replaced by decentralized direct administration, and large industrial or transport undertakings will be managed by associations of workers; education will be controlled by parents and teachers, and academic training will be replaced by integrated education with 'instruction ... inseparable from apprenticeship, and scientific education ... inseparable from professional education'. In this way, Proudhon contends, a social unity will be attained, compared with which the so-called order of governmental societies will appear for what it is—'nothing but chaos, serving as a basis for endless tyranny'.

The General Idea of the Revolution can be regarded as the central work of Proudhon's career. Here the constructive hints of his earlier books are brought together into the semblance of a system, and here too are sketched the principal ideas his later works develop. Like all of Proudhon's books—and like the writing of most other anarchists—it is strongest on the attack. In contrast with his sharp critical insight into the errors of authoritarian revolutionary doctrines, there is a rather fuzzy optimism about Proudhon's faith in the power of reason and in man's propensity to detect and choose his own good. It is true that his main point—that the cure for social ills cannot be found on a political level and must be sought in the economic roots of society—has been reinforced historically by the consistent failure of politically dominated societies to establish social and economic justice. But even Proudhon's anarchist descendants soon ceased to claim that the solution could be quite so simple a matter of contractual arrangement as he suggests in his more hopeful flights.

Release from prison, which for most men means an enlargement of life, brought Proudhon into a world of unexpected frustrations. Within the walls of Sainte-Pélagie, in a select company of rebels, he had not realized how much the atmosphere of France had changed since the establishment of the Empire. He emerged to find himself marked by the extremity of his ideas. He even found it hard to earn a living; his name frightened away publishers, editors, employers, even prospective landlords. And when a Belgian publisher eventually brought out an innocuous pamphlet called *Philosophie du progrès* (in which Proudhon developed his idea of a universe 'in incessant metamorphosis') the police forbade its importation into France.

But the hard years seemed to be drawing to an end in 1858, when Proudhon succeeded in persuading a Paris publisher to bring out his most massive and his greatest work, *De la justice dans la révolution et dans l'église*. *De la justice* had begun as a reply to a scandalous personal attack by a dubious Catholic apologist who wrote under the name Eugène de Mirecourt, but it grew into a vast treatise comparing transcendental justice, the justice of the Church, with immanent justice, the true justice that finds its lodging in the human conscience and is the real moving force of the revolution.

De la justice is an extraordinary book, full of magnificent prose and curious learning, of original speculation and fascinatingly fresh passages of childhood recollections. If *The General Idea of the Revolution* provides the best summary of Proudhon's social proposals, *De la justice* is the best compendium of his individuality, a book rich in knowledge, in argument, above all in idiosyncrasy, full of apparent contradiction, but in the end projecting an image of personality that no biographer of Proudhon has been able to rival. Yet so far as the history of anarchist thought is concerned it remains a secondary book, since what it actually does is to take the social ideas Proudhon had already discussed and rearrange them in a larger philosophic frame. For immanent Justice, transmutted into terms of human action, is nothing else than Equality, and Equality—as Proudhon had already argued—is to be attained by the practice of mutualistic association and the economic reorganization of society.

De la justice, as the first work of importance to appear under Proudhon's signature since 1852, aroused a lively interest; six thousand copies were sold almost immediately, but less than a week after publication all the unsold copies were seized, and Proudhon was brought before the courts charged with a formidable series of offences against public morality, against religion, and against the state. For the second time he was unlucky in his judges, and received a sentence of three years' imprisonment and a fine of three thousand francs. Once again he appealed and, proudly proclaiming his reluctance to escape, departed for Belgium without delay.

This time he assumed the name Durfort and posed as a professor of mathematics. However, a reassuring interview with the Brussels police led him to use his own name again and establish his family in Belgium. He settled down to write *Le Guerre et la paix*, a provocative work on the sublimation of warlike impulses into creative social urges. He also became aware of a reawakening of interest in his ideas among Russian intellectuals and French working men. Tolstoy called, and a Russian officer brought greetings from Tomsk, where Bakunin was in exile; deputations of workers arrived from Rouen and Paris to ask his advice on their activities. His friends even began to talk of the appearance of a Proudhonian party. Proudhon, however, cautiously denied any such development, and a letter he wrote to Alfred Darimon echoes curiously back to Godwin in its emphasis on discussion and philosophic investigation in opposition to partisan activity; the anarchist frame of mind, even in the absence of an evident historical link, is surprisingly repetitive in its manifestations.

As for our concluding from this isolated fact the existence of a *Proudhonian* party, since you use the term, I believe that would be exposing ourselves to a great illusion [he protested]. The people can be of a Blanquist, Mazzinian, or Garibaldian party, that is to say of a party where one *believes*, where one conspires, where one fights; they are never of a party where one reasons and thinks. I have cause to believe, it is true, that since the *coup d'état* the public which from time to time shows me its goodwill has increased rather than diminished; there is hardly a week that does not give me proofs of this. But that élite of readers does not form a party; they are people who ask me for books, for ideas, for discussion, for philosophic investigation, and who, for the most part, would abandon me tomorrow with contempt if I spoke to them of creating a party and forming themselves, under my initiative, into a secret society.

In fact, Proudhon exaggerated the detachment of his position at this time. Far from being a mere man of theory, during the final period of his life he became more and more involved in social issues, and in his last four years he wrote at substantial length on such topical questions as literary copyright, realism in art as exemplified in Courbet's painting, federalism, abstention from voting, and, above all, the ability of the working class to conduct its own affairs.

There was a certain reciprocity in the situation; if Proudhon became more anxious than at any time since 1848 to take part in current events, it was largely because the world had become more interested in Proudhon. In the early 1860s the political atmosphere in France began to change rapidly; for the first time since 1848 the workers were showing their discontent, while Napoleon III, sensing the growing insecurity of his régime, tried to gain a wider basis of popular support by means of concessions to them. Open association again became possible, and the craft workers took advantage of the relaxation of controls to establish trade unions and producers' cooperatives. They remembered also how Proudhon almost alone among the leading socialists had taken the defence of the insurgents in June 1848, and the very isolation in which he had lived since the beginning of the Empire increased his prestige. Thus, whether Proudhon wished it or not, a movement based on his ideas of association and mutual credit began to emerge. But, though there were Proudhonians, and enough of them to dominate the French working-class movement by the middle of the 1860s, there was never a Proudhonian party. Until the rise of Marxism more than twenty years later, French socialism was to remain non-partisan in the strict sense, and here the influence of Proudhon was decisive.

Yet, although during his Belgian exile Proudhon became aware of his growing popularity among the French workers, it was not until he returned to France in the autumn of 1862 that the problems of working-class action began to dominate his mind. During the last months of his exile he was more concerned with the question of nationalism, which had been given a renewed topicality by Italy's rapid progress toward unification.

Nationalism was perhaps the most dynamic heritage of the French Revolution, and in that sense 1848 had carried on the tradition of 1789; national aims were equated with democratic aspirations, and in the eyes of most revolutionaries, whether Jacobins or socialists, the liberation of fatherlands was as important as the liberation of individuals or classes. Between 1848 and the Commune, Garibaldi and Mazzini became the great heroes of European democracy; even Bakunin, before his final anarchist phase, was a kind of Slav nationalist.

But Proudhon, despite his love of the French people and the French land, was never a true nationalist. His closest emotional loyalty was a regional one, to his native Franche-Comté, which he more than once remarked might be better off if it joined the Swiss Confederation. For him the unity of Frenchmen was not a political one, and in *The General Idea of the Revolution* he stated clearly his desire for the ending of national frontiers, with all the divisions they imply. He was one of the few men of 1848 to realize the reactionary aspects of nationalism, and a decade later he was even more distrustful of the uncritical support given by his fellow radicals to nationalist movements, and particularly to those in Poland and Italy. In *La Guerre et la paix*, whose main theme is that 'the end of militarism is the mission of the nineteenth century', he already touched on the question of nationalism, and as soon as the book was finished he began an epistolary campaign against the nationalists, which estranged him from his old friend Herzen, whom he reproached for lending himself, 'to all these [nationalist] intrigues, which represent neither political liberty nor economic right nor social reform'.

It was the situation in Italy that led him to give closer consideration to the problems of nationalism. Mazzini, Garibaldi, and the majority of the Italian revolutionaries wished to construct a centralized state out of the liberation that seemed within their grasp; most members of the Left in France supported them. Proudhon, with a prophetic eye, saw that a strong Italian state might lead both to internal Caesarism and to disruption in international politics. On the other hand, Italy as it was—split into many small political units—seemed to him the ideal country for the application of his own solution of a federal union of autonomous regions with no central government to impede social progress and no nationalist ambitions to endanger European peace and unity.

The articles he wrote on this question aroused the hostility of Belgian patriots, who demonstrated noisily outside his house, with the result that he finally took advantage of a Bonapartist political amnesty to return to France. Once back in Paris, he set to work on a book that would summarize his views on nationalism and put forward the federalist alternative. *Du principe fédératif,* which appeared in 1863, was one of his most chaotic works, written hastily at a time when his health was already failing; much of it was devoted to topical wrangles with nationalist critics, but basically his intention was to carry his idea of anarchy from the field of economic and industrial relations to world society in general. Federation, in fact, he saw as a stage on the way to final anarchy, which at this time he admitted might lie centuries ahead; at the basis of both he saw 'public order resting directly on the liberty and conscience of the citizen'. In his view the federal principle should operate from the simplest level of society. The organization of administration should begin locally and as near the direct control of the people as possible; individuals should start the process by federating into communes and associations. Above that primary level the confederal organization would become less an organ of administration than of coordination between local units. Thus the nation would be replaced by a geographical confederation of regions, and Europe would become a confederation of confederations, in which the interest of the smallest province would have as much expression as that of the largest, and in which all affairs would be settled by mutual agreement, contract, and arbitration. In terms of the evolution of anarchist ideas, *Du principe fédératif* is one of the most important of Proudhon's books, since it presents the first intensive libertarian development of the idea of federal organization as a practical alternative to political nationalism.

The rest of Proudhon's life was dominated by his awareness of the rising discontent of the French workers and by his desire to give that discontent an articulate expression. Already, when the Bonapartist government held elections in May 1863, he became the active centre of an abstentionist movement, and, if he did not yet go to the anarchist extremity of completely rejecting parliamentarianism and voting, he declared that universal suffrage was 'nothing' unless it were 'a corollary of the federal principle'.

Not all the workers who followed Proudhon in his general federalist and mutualist ideas agreed with his counsel of abstention from parliamentary action. Three mutualist workers stood unsuccessfully as candidates in 1863, and the reasoning behind their action was shown in 1864 when the group who had sponsored them issued the famous Manifesto of the Sixty, one of the key documents of French socialism. Except for one schoolmaster, the signatories were all manual workers; two of them, Henri Tolain and Charles Limousin, were to become leaders of the Proudhonian faction in the First International.

The Manifesto argued that, despite the theoretical equality of all

Frenchmen since 1789, the conditions of a capitalist world militate constantly against the workers. This situation is perpetuated by the existing parliamentary system, in which the deputies, instead of speaking for all their constituents, represent only interests in which they themselves are involved. Therefore it is necessary for the workers to be represented by men of their own class who will formulate 'with moderation, but with firmness, our hopes, desires, and rights'.

Though he disagreed with the Manifesto of the Sixty, Proudhon recognized its importance; he discussed it at great length with some of the signatories and also with working men who asked his opinion of it. To a group in Rouen he declared that some way must be found for the workers to be represented, but contended that this could not be done within society as it was constituted. Existing parties and political institutions were all designed to serve the propertied classes, and the workers must recognize this situation; unwillingly Proudhon granted the inevitability of the bitter social conflict that was to dominate France in the years after his death.

> I say to you with all the energy and sadness of my heart; separate yourselves from those who have cut themselves off from you ... It is by separation that you will win; no representatives, no candidates.

The salvation of the workers, in other words, is the task of the workers themselves. The anarchists who followed Proudhon were to hold consistently to this point of view.

These discussions of the Manifesto of the Sixty became the pretext for Proudhon's last book, *De la capacité politique des classes ouvrières*, on which he worked persistently through his last illness. 'Despite the gods, despite everything,' he cried, 'I will have the last word'; he considered the book so important that he dictated the last passages on his deathbed to Gustave Chaudey. He was right in the sense that, more than any other of his books, *De la capacité* influenced the development of the labour movement in France and indirectly, through syndicalism, the development of anarchism throughout Europe and the Americas. It gave, moreover, the final touch to the anarchist vision he had spent his life formulating.

In this book Proudhon elaborates his own statement of 1848, that 'the proletariat must emancipate itself', by celebrating the entry of the workers as an independent force in the field of politics. 'To possess political capacity,' he declares, 'is to have the *consciousness* of oneself as a member of the collectivity, to affirm the *idea* that results from this consciousness, and to pursue its *realization*. Whoever unites these three conditions is capable.'

He maintains that the Manifesto of the Sixty, despite its errors, shows the French proletariat beginning to fulfil these conditions. It is conscious that its life and needs make it a separate group with its own place in society and its own mission in social evolution. The *idea* emerging from this consciousness is that of mutuality, which, aiming at the organization of society on an egalitarian basis, gives the working class a progressive character. The *realization* comes through federalism. Federalism will guarantee the people true sovereignty, since power will rise from below and rest on 'natural groups' united in coordinating bodies to implement the general will. The sensitivity of this system will be assured by the immediate revocability of any delegation. The 'natural groups' will be identical with the working units of society, and so the political state will disappear and be replaced by a network of social and economic administration. Anarchy in its positive sense will be achieved.

Before this last testament was published Proudhon died, in January 1865; he had lived long enough to hear with joy the news of the founding of the First International, largely through the initiative of his own followers. A great procession followed his funeral to the cemetery of Passy, in which veterans of '48 mingled with thousands of anonymous Paris working men—the men who in a few years would be fighting in defence of the Commune. It was a symbolic meeting of two generations of revolutionaries, and it underlined Proudhon's peculiar importance as a transitional figure. He demonstrated in his life and his ideas the change in the libertarian attitude from the detached and idealistic point of view that Godwin represented to the close involvement in the social struggle that became more manifest in Bakunin and his successors. While Proudhon himself developed from the theorist of an agrarian world into the interpreter of an industrial society, the experiences of the working people in Latin countries were making them increasingly receptive to a doctrine that seemed to offer a way out of the disillusioning impasse of a political democracy governed by property owners. It was out of this *rapprochement* of the ideas of the revolutionary and the nascent wishes of a wide section of the working class that anarchism as a movement was finally to emerge in the late 1860s. Proudhon did not create the anarchist movement—though he shares credit with Godwin for creating anarchism—and he might have rejected many of its later manifestations, but without his preparatory work it could hardly have arisen under the captaincy of his most spectacular and most heretical disciple, Michael Bakunin.

6. The Destructive Urge

Of all the anarchists, Michael Bakunin most consistently lived and looked the part. With Godwin and Stirner and Proudhon there always seems a division between the logical or passionate extremes of thought and the realities of daily life. These men of terror, as their contemporaries saw them, would emerge from their studies and become transformed into the pedantic ex-clergyman, the brow-beaten teacher of young ladies, the former artisan—proud of his fine printing—who turns out to be a model family father. This does not mean that any of them was fundamentally inconsistent; both Godwin and Proudhon showed exemplary courage in defying authority when their consciences called them to do so, but their urge to rebellion seemed almost completely fulfilled by their literary activity, and in action their unconventionality rarely exceeded the milder degrees of eccentricity.

Bakunin, on the other hand, was monumentally eccentric, a rebel who in almost every act seemed to express the most forceful aspects of anarchy. He was the first of a long line of aristocrats to join the anarchist cause, and he never lost an inherited grace of manner which he combined with an expansive Russian *bonhomie* and an instinctive defiance of every bourgeois convention. Physically, he was gigantic, and the massive unkemptness of his appearance would impress an audience even before he began to win its sympathies with his persuasive oratory. All his appetites—with the sole exception of the sexual—were enormous; he talked the nights through, he read omnivorously, he drank brandy like wine, he smoked 1,600 cigars in a single month of imprisonment in Saxony, and he ate so voraciously that a sympathetic Austrian jail commandant felt moved to allot him double rations. He had virtually no sense of property or material security; for a whole generation he lived on the gifts and loans of friends and admirers, gave as generously as he received, and took literally no thought for the morrow. He was intelligent, learned, yet naïve; spontaneous, kind, yet cunning; loyal to the last degree, yet so imprudent that he constantly led his friends into unnecessary danger. Insurrectionary and conspirator, organizer and propagandist, he was an energumen of revolutionary enthusiasm.

He could inspire other men freely with his ideals and lead them willingly to action on the barricades or in the conference hall.

Yet there were times when all this vast and restless activity took on the appearance of a great game of prolonged childhood, and times also when Bakunin's extremities of act and speech produced passages of pure comedy that make him seem the caricature rather than the example of an anarchist. One catches glimpses of him parading the streets of a Swiss city unconvincingly disguised as an Anglican clergyman; naïvely posting ciphered letters with the code enclosed in the same envelope; genially bluffing chance acquaintances with tales of enormous and totally imaginary secret armies at his command. It is hard always to deny the justice of the portrait that E.H. Carr traced so ironically in the only English biography of Bakunin.

But Bakunin remains too solid a figure to be dismissed as a mere eccentric. If he was a fool, he was one of Blake's fools who attain wisdom by persisting in folly, and there was enough greatness in him—and also enough appropriateness to his time—to make him one of the most influential men in the general revolutionary tradition as well as in the particular history of anarchism. He became so by his failures as much as by his triumphs, and his failures were many.

He failed, to begin, where most of the great anarchists have succeeded—as a writer. Through he scribbled copiously, he did not leave a single completed book to transmit his ideas to posterity. He had, as he once admitted to Herzen, no sense of literary architecture, and also little staying power, so that whatever he wrote soon lost its original direction and was usually abandoned. His best essays are short pieces produced for special occasions, with all the weaknesses of topical literature. Nor are the ideas one can cull from his writings very original, except when he talks of the organization of revolutions; otherwise he says little that is not derived in some way from Hegel or Marx, from Comte or Proudhon.

His admirers, admitting the thinness of his literary and theoretical claims, have usually countered with the contention that Bakunin was really significant as a man of action. Yet even his actions, dramatic as they were, often seem singularly ineffectual. He was involved in more pointless plots and more forlorn hopes than most other revolutionaries in an age peculiarly given to such ventures. He arrived too late for the active phase of the only successful uprising of his life, the February Revolution of 1848 in Paris; the five other insurrections, spread over the map of Europe, in which he took a leading part, were all either heroic disasters or comic fiascos. The secret societies he loved to invent were stillborn or expired early from internal dissensions. And at the end of it all he died a lonely man, out of the struggle to which he had devoted his life and deserted by his own anarchist followers.

But in compensation for his weaknesses, Bakunin had the virtues of dedication and insight, and these led to his important achievements. He saw, more clearly than even Proudhon, that by the 1860s the time had come when anarchist theories could be used as the means for activating the discontent of working men and peasants in the Latin countries. This realization led him into the First International, and there he clearly perceived the authoritarian implications of Marxist socialism. It was in the conflict between Bakunin and Marx within the International that the irreconcilable differences between the libertarian and the authoritarian conceptions of socialism were first developed, and in this struggle the faction that Bakunin led gradually shaped itself into the nucleus of the historic anarchist movement. The years of his connection with the International are those to which Bakunin owes his lasting significance; without them he would have been merely the most colourful of a host of eccentric revolutionaries who filled the exile centres of Switzerland and England during the middle decades of the nineteenth century.

Like so many of the anarchists, Bakunin was by birth and upbringing a man of the country. He was born in 1814 on the estate of Premukhino in the Russian province of Tver, where his father, Alexander Bakunin, was a cautious liberal of the eighteent-century school, a man of scholarship, and an amateur poet; he had been in Paris during the French Revolution, and had taken his Doctorate of Philosophy at Padua. His wife, Varvara, was a member of the influential Muraviev family; three of her cousins, whom Michael Bakunin knew as a boy, were involved in the earliest of Russian revolutions, the Decembrist mutiny of the constitutionalists in 1825. The family was large; the ten children formed a closely knit and affectionate group, so that in his years of exile Bakunin would look back on the happiness of his childhood with the kind of romantic nostalgia which one finds so often in the memoirs of Russian aristocrats born in the early nineteenth century.

Life at Premukhino was almost Spartanly simple, but, since Alexander Bakunin was a disciple of Rousseau, the education of his children was well cared for, and in those early years Michael learned the languages—French and German, English and Italian—which were later so useful in his career as an international revolutionary. At that time it was almost obligatory for a Russian gentleman to spend at least part of his life either in the army or the bureaucracy, and Michael, as the eldest son, was sent to the Artillery

School in St. Petersburg. He was a reluctant student, but he finally received his commission and was sent to serve on garrison duty in the remote Lithuanian countryside. Boredom, resentment of discipline, and a suddenly awakened love of books made him discontented with military life, and the next year he went home, malingered convincingly, and managed to get himself discharged. A couple of months later he was in Moscow, where he met Nicholas Stankevich, the first of the men who were to help him on his path to revolution.

It was the period when the young intellectuals of Russia were beginning to respond to the influences that percolated through the barriers of censorship from western Europe. Literary romanticism, German metaphysics, French social thought—all found their converts in the circles of Moscow and St Petersburg literati. Around Stankevich gathered the disciples of Hegel; around Herzen those who were fascinated by the socialist doctrines of Fourier, Saint-Simon, and Proudhon. Bakunin followed Stankevich, and when the latter left Russia he became by sheer force of personality the leader of the Moscow Hegelians. In Russia his Hegelianism remained orthodox and authoritarian, and, in spite of his recurrent rebellions against family authority, he remained surprisingly loyal to the Tsarist régime. He was already on friendly, borrowing terms with Herzen, but there is no evidence that at this time he was in any way influenced by the socialistic ideas of the future editor of *The Bell*.

It is this indifference to radical ideas during his Moscow years that gives Bakunin's change of attitude after he left Russia in 1840 the dramatic quality of an emotional conversion. Already he had experienced an intense romantic malaise, a sense of spiritual claustrophobia that afflicted many Russians in his time, and by 1839 he felt that his very existence as a thinking being depended on gaining access to sources of knowledge cut off from him by the circumstances of Tsarist society. 'I cannot remain a moment longer,' he cried out in frustration to his sisters, and in his imagination Berlin became a philosophical Mecca. In the first of many such letters, he asked Herzen for a substantial loan to pay for his escape. 'I expect from this journey a rebirth and a spiritual baptism,' he told him. 'I sense so many deep and great possibilities within myself and up to now I have realized so little.' Herzen provided the loan and accompanied the borrower to the wharf on the Neva from which he sailed.

For almost two years in Germany Bakunin remained the enthusiastically searching student, exploring the intellectual circles and the bohemian society of Berlin; his closest companion was Ivan Turgenev, who later enshrined him in literature as the model for Rudin, the hero of his first novel. Bakunin still had academic ambitions and he saw himself as a future professor of philosophy at Moscow University.

But the change that heralded his expected rebirth was already taking place within him. He moved uneasily from philosopher to philosopher. He thought with increasing repugnance of leaving the mental freedom of Europe for the intellectual darkness of Russia. He began to find even Berlin irksome, and toward the end of 1841 he made a trip to Dresden which unexpectedly became a turning-point in his life, for there he met the unlikely man who began his conversion.

Arnold Ruge has already appeared as a rather pompous minor actor in the lives of Proudhon and Stirner. He was one of the leading Young Hegelians, who had turned Hegel's doctrine against the Master by their claims that the dialectical method could be used to prove that everything is in flux and that therefore revolution is more real than reaction. Bakunin immediately immersed himself in the writings of these unorthodox philosophers, and completed his conversion to the social revolutionary ideal by reading Lorenz von Stein's *Socialism and Communism in Contemporary France*, which appeared in 1841. The doctrines of Fourier and Proudhon, which Bakunin had ignored when Herzen was propagating them in Moscow, now seemed to offer, as he recollected in later years, 'a new world into which I plunged with all the ardour of a delirious thirst'.

He celebrated his conversion by writing and publishing in Ruge's *Deutsche Jahrbücher,* under the *nom de plume* Jules Elysard, his first and one of his most important essays, *Reaction in Germany.* For the most part it is a typical Young Hegelian attempt to present Hegel's doctrine as basically one of revolution, but there is a true Bakuninist feeling in the apocalyptic tone and the emphasis on destruction as the necessary prelude to creation. Revolution in the present is negative, Bakunin asserts, but when it triumphs it will automatically become positive; a tone of religious exaltation comes into his voice as he describes this desired end to the revolutionary process. 'There will be a qualitative transformation, a new living, life-giving revelation, a new heaven and a new earth, a young and mighty world in which all our present dissonances will be resolved into a harmonious whole.' He ends with the peroration that has become the most familiar of Bakunin quotations:

> Let us put our trust in the eternal spirit which destroys and annihilates only because it is the unsearchable and eternally creative source of all life. The urge to destroy is also a creative urge.

Bakunin does not yet appear as an anarchist, for he has no developed social vision to support his instinctive rebellion against whatever is established and seems permanent. Yet in *Reaction in Germany* he makes his first statement of perpetual revolt, and places an emphasis on the destructive element in the revolutionary process that will colour all his changing viewpoints until it becomes one of the leading elements in his own version of anarchism.

This was a time of successive influences. In Zürich a year later Bakunin met the German Wilhelm Weitling. Weitling, like Proudhon, was a self-taught working man, a tailor who had been involved in one of Blanqui's Parisian uprisings during the 1830s, and was now forming secret societies among Swiss working men who would listen to his preaching of a revolution carried out with merciless violence and leading paradoxically to an idyllic Utopian world. Weitling was the first militant revolutionary Bakunin had encountered, and it was his example that turned the young Russian from a theoretical into a practical rebel. More than that, Weitling had one phrase which seemed to answer the social problem so simply that it lodged in Bakunin's mind like a potent seed. 'The perfect society had no government, but only an administration, no laws, but only obligations, no punishments, but means of correction.' Weitling was in his own way a primitive anarchist, inconsistently mingling Proudhonism with a taste for conspiratorial organization which he had acquired from Blanqui. It was a combination Bakunin himself was to repeat on a far more dramatic scale than Weitling ever attained.

To some extent Bakunin seems to have become involved in Weitling's secret activities, and this initiation into practical revolutionism became also an invitation into exile. When Weitling was arrested and expelled from Switzerland Bakunin's name appeared compromisingly in his papers; it was mentioned publicly in a report on communist activities issued by the Zürich cantonal authorities. The Russian embassy notified St Petersburg, and Bakunin was summoned home to explain his conduct. He refused, and was condemned *in absentia* to indefinite exile with hard labour in Siberia.

His road now led almost inevitably to Paris, which was still, despite the Orléans regime, the Rome of revolutionary idealists. There he met many celebrated rebels; Marx and Lelewel, George Sand and Pierre Leroux, Cabet and Lamennais, and most important and congenial, Proudhon. With Proudhon, who differed from other French socialists in his Jurassic bluntness and his openness of mind, Bakunin talked the nights away, unravelling Hegelian intricacies over endless glasses of tea; and in these discus-

sions which lasted till the dawn his amorphous revolutionism received its
first shaping. 'Proudhon is the master of us all,' he was to declare long
afterward when the mantle of leading anarchist had fallen on his own
shoulders, and, despite the fact that he disagreed with Proudhon on vital
points of revolutionary action and rejected both his defence of individual
possession and his ideas of mutual banking, he never ceased to regard him
as an authentic revolutionary and the best of all socialist philosophers.

Yet in the years that followed immediately it was not the Proudhonian
doctrine, or even socialism in a general sense that dominated Bakunin's
activities. Rather it was a concern for the fate of his fellows Slavs, still subjected to the autocrats of Russia, Austria, and Turkey. His attention turned
first toward the Poles, who in the mid nineteenth century peculiarly sym-
bolized for the democrats of western Europe the plight of subjected
nationalities—and this in spite of the fact that the adherence of the Polish
nationalists to democratic principles was, to say the least, suspect. In 1846
there were small risings in the parts of Poland occupied by Prussia and
Austria; their suppression caused a wave of sympathy that carried Bakunin
on its crest. In November 1847 he made his first public speech at a Paris
banquet attended by 1,500 Polish refugees. He chose as his theme the
alliance of Poland and the 'real' Russia, as distinct from 'official' Russia,
and for the first time he enunciated the key theme of the middle period of
his life—the union in rebellion of the Slav peoples and the consequent
regeneration of Europe.

> The reconciliation of Russia and Poland is a great cause [he
> declared]. It means the liberation of sixty million souls, the libera-
> tion of all the Slav peoples who groan under a foreign yoke. It means,
> in a word, the fall, the irretrievable fall, of despotism in Europe.

A few days later, on the complaint of the Russian ambassador, Bakunin
was deported to Belgium. But little more than two months afterward he
returned, as the Citizen King fled in the opposite direction from the
February Revolution. Bakunin walked over the border and reached Paris
as soon as the disrupted railway system would allow him. He lodged
among the working-class National Guard who occupied the barracks in
the rue Tournon, and spent his days and a large part of his nights in a
fever of excitement and activity.

> I breathed through all my senses and through all my pores the intox-
> ication of the revolutionary atmosphere [he recollected later in the

forced tranquillity of a prison cell]. It was a holiday without beginning and without end. I saw everyone and I saw no one, for each
individual was lost in the same innumerable and wandering crowd. I
spoke to all I met without remembering either my own words or
those of others, for my attention was absorbed at every step by new
events and objects and by unexpected news.

But Bakunin's was an exaltation that fed on action—and there was no
action. In Paris the revolutionary wave was already beginning to ebb. Yet
hope was in the general European air. One kingdom had fallen; the rest
were threatened. Only the Russian Empire still reigned untroubled, and it
was natural that Bakunin should think of carrying the sacred fire to his
own country. Russia's weak spot was Poland, and it was here that Bakunin
decided to start his activities. He borrowed 2,000 francs from the French
Provisional Government, and set off on what was to become a sensational
odyssey.

His first destination was the Grand Duchy of Posen, in the Prussian-
dominated sector of Poland. The Prussian police intercepted him in
Berlin, and pointedly suggested he might do better in Breslau, where the
Polish refugees were gathering in the hope of provoking risings in
Austrian and Russian Poland. But Breslau was a disappointment. The
Poles were disorganized and divided; the only feeling that seemed to unite
them was a distrust of Bakunin, about whom the Tsarist agents were
spreading a rumour that he was one of their own spies. Then the news
reached him that the Czech National Committee was assembling a Slav
Congress. As he set off for Prague, his hopes of a revolutionary union of
the oppressed Slav peoples rose again, only to be submerged in the
intrigues of the actual assembly. The southern Slavs looked to Tsarist
Russia as their saviour from the Turks; many of the Czechs and Croats
nursed the hope of replacing the Germans as the master race of the
Hapsburg Empire. Only a tiny group of delegates showed any sympathy
for Bakunin's pan-Slavist revolutionism; imitating Weitling, he tried to
form them into a secret society.

But if Bakunin found few comrades in the Congress, he found many in
the uprising that broke out on its last day, when some Prague students and
workers raised the barricades in the name of Czech freedom. The Bakunin
legend credits him—doubtless apocryphally—with having started the rising by firing at Austrian troops from the windows of the Blue Star Hotel;
he was certainly in his element when the fighting actually began, giving
military advice to the insurgents and fighting in the ranks at the barri-

cades. The rebels held out for five days; at the end Bakunin slipped through the Austrian ranks and found his way to the Duchy of Anhalt, an island of liberalism in a Germany fast retreating into reaction after the first enthusiasm of 1848.

In Anhalt Bakunin wrote his *Appeal to the Slavs*, the major document of his nationalistic period. He called for the destruction of the Austrian Empire, for a great federation of all Slavs. He prophesied a messianic role for the Russian people, and saw his fatherland as the key to the worldwide destruction of oppression. Now, indeed, one sees a bitter irony in his half-fulfilled prophecy that 'the star of revolution will rise high and independent above Moscow from a sea of blood and fire, and will turn into a lodestar to lead a liberated humanity'.

Already for Bakunin nationalist revolutions had internationalist implications, and he went further on the path toward anarchism by declaring that such movements could only succeed if they incorporated the social revolution. In the most significant passage of the *Appeal* we find a strong influence of Proudhon, but it is a Proudhonianism impregnated with Bakunin's personal mystique of destruction.

> Two great questions were posed from the first days of spring [1848]; the social question and that of the independence of all nations, the emancipation of peoples internally and externally at once. It was not a few individuals, nor was it a party, but the admirable instinct of the masses which raised these two questions above all others and demanded their prompt solution. The whole world understood that liberty was only a lie where the great majority of the population is condemned to lead a poverty-stricken existence and where, deprived of education, of leisure and of bread, it is destined to serve as a stepping stone for the powerful and the rich. Thus the social revolution presented itself as a natural and necessary consequence of the political revolution. At the same time, it was felt that while there is a single persecuted nation in Europe the complete and decisive triumph of democracy will be possible nowhere ... We must first of all purify our atmosphere and transform completely the surroundings in which we live, for they corrupt our instincts and our wills, they constrict our hearts and our intelligences. Therefore the social question appears first of all as the overthrow of society.

Such ideas of the primacy of the social revolution, the indivisibility of liberty (with its implied rejection of Stirner's individualism), the need for

a complete breakdown of society in order to start anew, were to be incorporated into Bakunin's later anarchist doctrine of the 1860s, as were certain
other aspects of the *Appeal to the Slavs*, such as the emphasis on the revolutionary role of the peasants and the rejection of parliamentary democracy.
Here, however, we reach dubious ground, since in 1848 Bakunin had not
developed his later conceptions of libertarian organization; his rejection of
the bourgeois state at this time was not incompatible with the vision of a
revolutionary dictatorship which haunts the whole of his pan-Slavic period. As he afterward confessed, he thought during 1848 of a secret organization of conspirators which would continue after the revolution and would
constitute 'the revolutionary hierarchy'; as late as 1860 he was still talking
to Herzen of 'an iron dictatorship aiming at the emancipation of the
Slavs'.

However, it was not the liberation of the Slavs that provoked the most
epic passage of Bakunin's early manhood; it was, ironically, the defence of
the Germans, whom he regarded as conservators of the spirit of reaction.
In March 1849 the people of Dresden rose in support of the Frankfurt constitution for a federated democratic Germany, which had been rejected by
the King of Saxony. Bakunin happened to be in the city, engaged in
attempts to foment unrest in Bohemia. He had no sympathy for the bourgeois democratic aims of the Saxon insurgents; they were neither Slavs
nor social revolutionaries. But their enemies, the kings of Saxony and
Prussia, were his enemies too, and when Richard Wagner persuaded him
to visit the rebel headquarters he could not resist the impulse to take part
in the struggle, just because it was a struggle. He fought and organized
with disinterested enthusiasm, and he was captured after the defeat of the
revolution when he was retreating with a few other survivors to Chemnitz,
where he had hoped to carry on the rebellion.

Now began a long pilgrimage of agony. The Saxons kept him in prison
for a year and condemned him to death. After a tardy reprieve, they handed him over to the Austrians, who kept him another eleven months,
chained most of the time to a dungeon wall in the fortress of Olmütz;
again he was condemned to death, reprieved, and handed over, this time to
the Russians. In his own country there was not even the pretence of a trial;
he had been sentenced years ago, and he disappeared without formality
into the Peter-and-Paul fortress.

For six years Bakunin remained in prison. His teeth fell out from
scurvy; he became bloated and unkempt. His only contact with the outside
world happened on the rare occasions when members of his family were
allowed to visit him; solitude and inaction ate deeply into the spirit of this

active and gregarious man, but they neither broke his will nor destroyed his mind.

> Prison has been good for me [he said in one note which he passed secretly to his sister Tatiana]. It has given me leisure and the habit of reflection; it has, so to speak, consolidated my spirit. But it has changed none of my old sentiments; on the contrary, it has made them more ardent, more absolute than ever, and henceforward all that remains to me of life can be summed up in one word: liberty.

It is the sentiment of this secret letter, clearly springing from Bakunin's heart, that we must remember in considering the one piece of writing he was allowed to produce during his imprisonment, the celebrated *Confession* which he wrote at the request of the Tsar and which was found in the archives of the political police after the Russian Revolution. A confession from Bakunin to the Tsar, humbly begging forgiveness for his sins against the autocracy! It became the delight of Bakunin's enemies, and aroused consternation among his admirers.

Yet a glance at the circumstances and at the *Confession* itself goes very far to excuse Bakunin. It must be remembered that, unlike the Russian revolutionaries of later generations who performed acts of heroic resistance in the prisons and fortresses of Russia, Bakunin had no sense of belonging to a movement he must not betray. So far as he knew, he stood alone, the only revolutionary existing in Russia—and existing, moreover, unknown to anyone but his jailers and their masters. As for the *Confession*, it is by no means the abject document which the Tsar doubtless expected and which Bakunin perhaps intended to write as a cunning deception aimed at securing the transfer to Siberia which he desired. Much of it is a vivid description of his activities, impressions, and plans during the revolutionary years of 1848 and 1849. He asks to be pardoned for these, but he negates his apologies by passages in which he maintains that Russia is a land of greater oppression than any other in Europe and in which he defiantly refuses to name his accomplices in revolutionary activity. Nicholas read the *Confession* with great interest and sent it on to the Tsarevitch with the remark that it was worth reading and 'very curious and instructive'. But he understood, more clearly than those who have self-righteously condemned Bakunin, the defiant passages which revealed that the sinner had not repented in his heart. He decided to leave Bakunin rotting in his cell, and it was not until 1857, after extraordinary efforts on the part of the prisoner's highly placed relatives, that Alexander II finally agreed to offer him the alternative of exile.

The four years in Siberia were almost happy in comparison with those in prison. Bakunin was readily accepted in the societies of Tomsk and Irkutsk, where political exiles formed an unofficial intellectual aristocracy. He married a pretty, empty-headed Polish girl; he tried to persuade the Governor, his cousin Muraviev-Amurski, to become the dictator of a revolutionary Russia; and he never for a day allowed the idea of escape to pass out of his mind. To this end he gained employment as a merchant's agent; this allowed him to travel, and at last, in 1861, when the Governor who replaced Muraviev turned out to be another family connection, he got permission to make a journey down the Amur. A series of lucky coincidences and clever deceptions enabled him to board an American ship off Nikolayevsk; from that point he was free, returning via Japan, San Francisco, and New York to London, and bursting in on Herzen's Paddington home full of enthusiasm for the revolutionary cause. While his body had aged appallingly, prison and exile had preserved his spirit as the Siberian frost preserves the flesh of the mammoth; he had lived in a mental state of suspended animation, immune from the disillusionments that free men had suffered in the intervening years.

> The European reaction [said Herzen], did not exist for Bakunin; the bitter years from 1848 to 1858 did not exist for him either; of them he had but a brief, far-away, faint knowledge ... The events of 1848, on the contrary, were all about him, near to his heart ... they were all still ringing in his ears and hovering before his eyes.

His very theories had stood still in those twelve years of detachment, and he came back as fervent as on the day of his arrest for the Polish cause, and the federation of all Slavs, and the social revolution which would be the condition and the crown of both. It seemed natural at first that he should take his place beside Herzen in directing the propaganda for a liberal Russia which was being conducted through *The Bell.* But differences of personality and opinion soon divided them. Herzen in his own way was near to the anarchism which Bakunin was now approaching; he detested the state, despised Western democracies, and saw the salvation of Europe in the Russian peasant and his communal way of living. But he had not Bakunin's burning faith in violence and destruction, and temperamentally he was too pessimistic to expect anything more revolutionary in Russia than a constitutional government. He also distrusted the Poles and their particular brand of expansive nationalism. Consequently the partnership lasted uneasily for a few months, and then Bakunin withdrew to concentrate on his own grandiose plans.

'I am busy solely with the Polish, Russian, and pan-Slav cause,' he told one of his correspondents. He became aware that in the 1860s, unlike the 1840s, there were actually revolutionaries in Russia itself. The most active had formed secret societies like Land and Liberty, and with their representatives he established rather loose contacts. But his efforts to unite all the elements of Slav rebellion into a single pan-Slavist movement were unsuccessful, and were broken off by the Polish insurrection of 1863.

As an old hero of the barricades, Bakunin felt that he could not absent himself from the scene of action, and he doubtless had Garibaldi's successful invasion of Sicily in mind when he decided to join an expedition of two hundred Poles which had chartered a British ship to take them from Stockholm to Lithuania, where they hoped to raise the people and form a rebel force to attack the Russian army on the flank. The plan was quixotic enough in any case; given the personalities and the monstrous indiscretions of Bakunin and his Polish associates it became a ludicrous fiasco which ended when the British captain, fearful of Russian cruisers, landed the mutually accusatory legion back in Sweden. It brought an end to Bakunin's illusions about the Polish nationalists and a rapid fading of his pan-Slavist enthusiasms. At the end of 1863 he left London for Italy and the last phase of his career.

In Italy Bakunin found his second home. The easy-going, mercurial Italian temperament appealed to him, and he moved into a society where regional loyalties and a love of conspiracy congenially flourished. The waters in which he prepared to fish were troubled by growing discontent, not merely with the Savoy monarchy, but also with the republican nationalist movement that centred around Mazzini. The discontent was most demonstrative among the intellectuals, but it reflected the abiding, inarticulate resentment of the Italian poor, to whom political liberation had brought very little relief. The time had come when a social revolutionary appeal might draw a wide response from almost every class in Italy, and over the remaining years of the 1860s Bakunin was to exploit these opportunities, and to found in Italy the early organizations out of which the anarchist movement evolved.

He settled first in Florence, where letters of recommendation from Garibaldi gave him entry into republican circles. His house quickly became a gathering place for revolutionaries of all countries, from among whom he founded his first secret Brotherhood, which has remained a historically nebulous organization. Bakunin apparently conceived it as an order of disciplined militants devoted to propagating the social revolution;

an Italian teacher named Gubernatis, who belonged to it for a short period, estimated the membership at thirty. Even at this time Bakunin seems
to have had ambitions to create an international movement, for the great
French geographer Élisée Reclus attended one of the Florentine meetings
and later claimed that as early as the autumn of 1864 he and Bakunin were
making plans for an International Brotherhood.

What happened to the Florentine Brotherhood is not clearly known,
though Gubernatis claimed that it was dissolved before Bakunin left the
city for Naples in the early summer of 1865. In the south he found a more
responsive environment, and several of the Italians whose acquaintance he
made at this time—Giuseppe Fanelli, Saverio Friscia, and Alberto
Tucci—were eventually to become devoted Bakuninist propagandists.
Here his International Brotherhood was founded; by the summer of 1866 it
had recruited a following and achieved a certain complexity of organization, at least on paper. Its various documents, particularly the *Revolutionary
Catechism* which Bakunin wrote for its members, suggest that he and his
followers were taking the final steps toward an anarchist viewpoint. The
Brotherhood opposed authority, the state, and religion; it stood for federalism and communal autonomy; it accepted socialism on the grounds that
labour 'must be the unique base of human right and the economic organization of the state'; it declared that the social revolution could not be
achieved by peaceful means.

In the organization, however, the International Brotherhood planned a
hierarchical structure and laid a most unlibertarian emphasis on internal
discipline. At the summit of the hierarchy would stand the International
Family, an aristocracy of tried militants from all countries who would
make plans for revolution. The rank and file of the Brotherhood would
belong to the National Families, whose members would owe unconditional obedience to the national juntas.

To assess the actual scope of the Brotherhood one has to balance
Bakunin's optimism and love of mystification with the external evidence.
Writing to Herzen in July 1866, Bakunin boasted:

At present we have adherents in Sweden, Norway, Denmark,
England, Belgium, France, Spain, and Italy. We also have some
Polish friends and we even count some Russians among us. The
majority of the Mazzinian organization of southern Italy, of the
Falanga Sacra, have come over to us. In southern Italy, especially, the
lower classes are coming to us *en masse*, and it is not the raw material
we lack so much as the educated and intelligent men who act hon-
estly and who are capable of giving a form to this raw material.

In fact, most of the support Bakunin claimed appears to have been imaginary. One finds no evidence elsewhere of mass desertions from the Mazzinian ranks, and the only active sections of the International Brotherhood that can be identified are two small Sicilian groups and the Central Committee of Bakunin and his friends in Naples. As for the non-Italian adherents, apart from a few Russian and Polish refugees in Naples, Élisée Reclus remains the only one who can be identified with any certainty in 1866, though Emil Vogt and Caesar de Paepe were recruited in 1867.

Later on I intend to discuss how these scanty beginnings of the International Brotherhood led to the vigorous Italian anarchist movement of the 1870s. Here I am concerned with Bakunin's own career and in that connection the International Brotherhood is important because it prompted him, through the writing of such documents as the *Revolutionary Catechism*, to clarify the final stages of his progress toward genuine anarchism; it also gave him practical experience in building an organization, and brought him into contact with some of the men who became his active associates in the great struggle within the International.

It was not, however, the International that next attracted Bakunin's attention, but a Congress to be held in Geneva during September 1867 under the auspices of an international committee of liberals, to discuss 'the maintenance of liberty, justice, and peace' in a Europe menaced by conflict between Prussia and Imperial France. The non-revolutionary character of the enterprise was suggested by the very names of its sponsors, who included John Bright and John Stuart Mill, but to Bakunin it seemed to provide an excellent chance to bring his campaign out of the underground darkness of conspiratorial groups and into the open arena of public discussion.

Bakunin's exploits in 1848, his imprisonment, his escape from Siberia, had made him a legendary figure in western Europe, and his appearance at the Congress for Peace and Freedom—his first public appearance since the Prague conference eighteen years before—aroused the most active interest. He was elected to the executive committee, and as he walked up to take his place on the platform—a shambling, prematurely aged man, dressed carelessly and none too cleanly—Garibaldi strode forward to embrace him, and the six thousand delegates, shouting his name from row to row, rose spontaneously to applaud this seasoned hero of the cause of freedom.

The warmth of this welcome was soon tempered, since Bakunin's views on almost every subject were too extreme for the liberal majority of the

Congress. He developed the federalist viewpoint in an almost orthodoxly Proudhonian manner, but aroused considerable opposition because he could not resist a destructionist tone.

Universal peace will be impossible [he declared], so long as the present centralized states exist. We must desire their destruction in order that, on the ruins of these forced unions organized from above by right of authority and conquest, there may arise free unions organized from below by the free federations of communes into provinces, of provinces into nations, and of nations into the United States of Europe.

However, enough of the first-day glamour remained in the minds of the delegates to elect Bakunin to the central committee of the League which the Congress founded, and he dominated this smaller body as it prepared its reports for the second Congress in 1868. For the benefit of his colleagues he composed a vast thesis, which was later published under the title of *Federalism, Socialism and Anti-Theologism*. The section dealing with federalism was again based on Proudhon's ideas, and Proudhon also partly dominated the section on socialism, which emphasized the class structure of contemporary society and the irreconcilability of the interests of capitalists and workers. Bakunin defined his socialist attitude in the following terms:

What we demand is the proclamation anew of this great principle of the French Revolution: that every man must have the material and moral means to develop all his humanity, a principle which, according to us, is to be translated into the following problem: to organize society in such a fashion that every individual, man or woman, coming into life, shall find as nearly as possible equal means for the development of his or her different faculties and for their utilization by his or her labour; to organize a society which, rendering for every individual, whoever he may be, the exploitation of anybody else impossible, permits each to participate in social wealth—which, in reality, is never produced otherwise than by labour—*only in so far as he has contributed to produce it by his own labour.*

The final clause, which I have italicized, indicates that here too Bakunin stands with Proudhon. Unlike the anarchist communists of the 1880s, he believed not in the maxim, 'From each according to his means, to each according to his *needs*', but in the radically different formula, 'From each according to his means, to each according to his *deeds*'. The ancient curse of Adam—'In the sweat of thy face shalt thou eat bread'—still lay upon the world of Bakunin's vision; the saintly optimism of the Kropotkins and the Malatestas was needed to remove it.

Yet, while Bakunin was not in Kropotkinian terms a communist, he differed from Proudhon in taking association, which Proudhon had accepted unwillingly as a *means* of dealing with large-scale industry, and turning it into a central principle of economic organization. The group of workers, the collectivity, takes the place of the individual worker as the basic unit of social organization. With Bakunin the main stream of anarchism parts from individualism, even in its mitigated Proudhonian form; later, during the sessions of the International, the collectivist followers of Bakunin were to oppose the mutualist followers of Proudhon—the other heirs of anarchy—over the question of property and possession.

Bakunin did not convert the League's central committee to his full programme, but he did persuade them to accept a remarkably radical recommendation to the Berne Congress of September 1868, demanding economic equality and implicitly attacking authority in both Church and State. But the Congress itself rejected the recommendation by a majority which made it clear that Bakunin could achieve little through the League in the direction of promoting social revolution. At the end of the Congress he and seventeen of his associates formally withdrew from the organization; as well as his three close Italian supporters, Fanelli, Tucci, and Friscia, they included several other men who later played important parts in anarchist history, notably Élisée Reclus, the Russian Zhukovsky, and the Lyons weaver Albert Richard. They were a substantial proportion of the hundred delegates who represented the already moribund League, and from among them Bakunin recruited the nucleus of his next organization.

This was the celebrated International Alliance of Social Democracy. The Alliance did not at once supersede the International Brotherhood, which survived as a kind of shadow organization of Bakunin's intimates until its dissolution in 1869, but it did take over on an international scale the function of an open propaganda organization allotted to the National Families in the original plan of the Brotherhood. A loosening of the hierarchical principle appeared in the plan of organization; like later anarchist federations, the Alliance was to consist of more or less autonomous groups united in each country by National Bureaux. The programme also was more explicitly anarchistic than that of the International Brotherhood, and in some respects it showed the influence of the International

Workingmen's Association, of which Bakunin had become an individual member two months before he left the League for Peace and Freedom. Federalism was stressed more strongly than before—the programme called for the complete breakdown of national states and their replacement by a worldwide 'union of free associations, agricultural and industrial'—and the economic and social aims of the Alliance are summed up concisely in the following paragraph:

> It [the Alliance] desires above all the definitive and entire abolition of classes and the political, economic, and social equalization of the two sexes, and, to arrive at this end, it demands first of all the abolition of the right of inheritance, so that in the future each man's enjoyment shall be equal to his production, and so that, in conformity with the decision taken by the most recent congress of workers in Brussels, the land and the instruments of work, like all other capital, may be utilized only by agricultural and industrial workers.

Until the advent of the anarchist communists, this was to remain, broadly speaking, the programme of the anarchist movement.

How far Bakunin thought the Social-Democratic Alliance might have a life of its own, and how far he planned it as the Trojan horse that would allow him to lead an army of anarchists into the heart of the International, it is now difficult to determine. However, in view of the efforts that were made to establish organs of the Alliance in various countries, and its success in comparison with Bakunin's earlier organizations, it seems very unlikely that he regarded it merely as a temporary front organization. Fanelli went off to Spain in November 1868 and founded branches in Barcelona and Madrid. Other sections were formed in Lyons, Marseïlles, Naples and Sicily. The principal section, however, was in Geneva, where the Central Bureau also functioned, under the personal leadership of Bakunin. Thus the Alliance was spread extremely thinly over the Latin countries, but unlike the Brotherhoods, it did have a real life beyond Bakunin's immediate personal circle. All the evidence suggests that its formation was taken very seriously by Bakunin and his most important associates, and that they hoped for its continued existence as an anarchistic body enjoying a certain autonomy within the First International, and acting as a kind of radical ginger group, a dedicated legion of 'propagandists, apostles, and, finally, organizers', as Bakunin called them.

It was with this in mind that the Alliance formally sought admission as a body into the International. John Becker, a German socialist who had been a Garibaldian colonel, was chosen to transmit the request, perhaps because Marx, who had by now established control over the General Council of the International in London, was known to respect him. In the rather naïve hope of helping matters by personal contact, Bakunin—who had discussed the prospects of the International with Marx in London as early as 1864—now sent him a curious letter in which an evident devotion to the cause of the working class was combined with rather clumsy flattery.

> Since bidding a solemn and public farewell to the bourgeois at the Berne Congress [he said], I have known no other company, no other world, than that of the workers. My country is now the International, of which you are one of the principal founders. You see then, dear friend, that I am your disciple and proud to be one.

Marx was neither impressed nor convinced. As a former pan-Slavist, as an admirer of Proudhon, and as the propounder of a theory of spontaneous revolution based largely on the peasants and the *déclassé* elements in urban society, Bakunin was triply suspect to him, even though the central Marxist-Bakuninist conflicts over political action and the state had not yet defined themselves. And a man less intent on personal power than Marx might have been alarmed by the kind of organizational palatinate within the International demanded by the Alliance. Local branches of the Alliance were to become branches of the International, but also to retain their links with Bakunin's Central Bureau in Geneva, and the Alliance's delegates to the International were to hold their own separate gatherings at the same time and place as the larger body.

Before such a prospect the German Marxists, the French Blanquists, and the English trade-unionists on the General Council closed ranks, and the application of the Alliance was rejected on the grounds that a second international organization, either within or outside the International Workingmen's Association, could only encourage faction and intrigue. The decision was reasonable enough; the only irony was that it should be inspired by the one man in the international socialist movement who was Bakunin's superior in the fomenting of faction and intrigue.

Bakunin bowed to the decision of the General Council. The Alliance was publicly dissolved (though how far it continued to exist in secret is still an unsettled question), and the absorption of its branches, transformed into sections of the International, followed in the spring of 1869. Only the Geneva section retained the title of the Social-Democratic

Alliance, which it changed later to that of Section for Propaganda; it entered the International with one hundred and four members, and remained separate from the existing Geneva section of the International.

The dissolution of the Alliance made little real difference to the influence Bakunin was able to wield once he had established a foothold within the larger organization. The Spanish and Italian sections did not change their attitudes with their titles; within the International they remained devoted to Bakunin and his anti-political, collectivist anarchism. Bakunin's influence was also strong in southern France and Belgium, and in 1869 he gained a considerable following in the Fédération Romande, the group of thirty sections which made French-speaking Switzerland one of the most fruitful regions of Internationalist activity.

In the Fédération Romande his most faithful adherents were the watchmakers of the Jura villages, who combined their craft work with farming and came from the same mountain peasant stock as Proudhon. They were largely inspired by a young schoolmaster, James Guillaume, whom Bakunin had met at the first Congress of the League for Peace and Freedom in 1867. Within the Fédération Romande a split quickly developed between the Geneva working men, who had been led into the Marxist camp by a Russian refugee, Nicholas Utin, and the men of the Jura. The Bakuninist mountaineers eventually broke away and formed a separate Fédération Jurassienne, which throughout the 1870s became a centre of libertarian thought and the real heart of the anarchist movement during its early years.

Even before the foundation of the Jura Federation the first battle had been fought between Bakunin and the Marxists at the Basel Congress of the International in September 1869. This Congress marked a change in the power balance within the International. For the first four years of the organization's life the central conflict had been between the Proudhonian mutualists on the one hand and the heterogeneous body of their opponents—communists, Blanquists, English trade-unionists—over whom Marx had consolidated his influence through the General Council. The mutualists were anarchists of a kind, opposed to political revolutionism, and they combined a desire to keep all bourgeois elements out of the International with an insistent propaganda for mutual banking and cooperative societies as the basis for social reorganization; it was Proudhonism without Proudhon, for none of the mutualist leaders—Tolain, Fribourg, Limousin—had inherited the revolutionary vision or the personal dynamism of their master. Already, at the Brussels Congress of 1868, the mutualists had been defeated when they opposed collectivization, and at

the Basel Congress they were in a clear minority, since even some of the
French delegates were now opposed to their idea of individual 'possession.' Marx's struggle against the mutualists was virtually ended by 1869,
but he rejoiced only to face immediately one of the more formidable of
the Protean forms of anarchism.

The convinced Bakuninists were only a relatively small group among
the seventy-five delegates who attended the Basel Congress. Bakunin himself represented Naples; he was supported by seven Swiss, two Lyonnais,
two Spaniards, and one Italian, while the Paris bookbinder Eugène Varlin,
the Belgian de Paepe, and a few other delegates were sympathetic toward
him without being his actual disciples. It was by the force of his personality and the power of his oratory, rather than by numbers, that Bakunin
dominated the conference, and succeeded in defeating the plans of the
Marxists. As so often happens, the particular issue on which the defeat
took place had little real bearing on the fundamental differences between
the libertarian and the authoritarian socialists. It was a question of the
abolition of the right of inheritance, which Bakunin demanded as a first
step to social and economic equalization; the attitude of Marx, who did
not attend the conference, seemed more revolutionary, but was in fact
more reformist than Bakunin's, since he wished nothing less than the complete socialization of the means of production—but was willing to accept
higher death duties as a transitional measure. Bakunin won an apparent
victory, since his proposal gained thirty-two votes against twenty-three,
while Marx's gained only sixteen against thirty-seven, but in practice the
result was a draw, since abstentions counted as negative votes and thus
Bakunin's proposal, on which thirteen delegates abstained, failed to
receive the absolute majority necessary for inclusion in the programme of
the International.

From this point the struggle between Bakunin and Marx steadily and
inevitably deepened. In part it was a struggle for organizational control, in
which Bakunin marshalled the Internationalists of the Latin countries
against Marx and the General Council and sought to break their power.
But it was also a conflict of personalities and principles.

In some respects Marx and Bakunin were alike. Both had drunk deep of
the heady spring of Hegelianism, and their intoxications were lifelong.
Both were autocratic by nature, and lovers of intrigue. Both, despite their
faults, were sincerely devoted to the liberation of the oppressed and the
poor. But in other ways they differed widely. Bakunin had an expansive
generosity of spirit and an openness of mind which were both lacking in
Marx, who was vain, vindictive, and insufferably pedantic. In his daily life

Bakunin was a mixture of the bohemian and the aristocrat, whose ease of manner enabled him to cross all the barriers of class, while Marx remained the unregenerate bourgeois, incapable of establishing genuine personal contact with actual examples of the proletariat he hoped to convert. Undoubtedly, as a human being, Bakunin was the more admirable; the attractiveness of his personality and his power of intuitive insight gave him the advantage over Marx, despite the fact that in terms of learning and intellectual ability the latter was his superior.

The differences in personality projected themselves in differences of principle. Marx was an authoritarian, Bakunin a libertarian; Marx was a centralist, Bakunin a federalist; Marx advocated political action for the workers and planned to conquer the state; Bakunin opposed political action and sought to destroy the state. Marx stood for what we now call nationalization of the means of production; Bakunin stood for workers' control. The conflict really centred, as it has done ever since between anarchists and Marxists, on the question of the transitional period between existing and future social orders. The Marxists paid tribute to the anarchist ideal by agreeing that the ultimate end of socialism and communism must be the withering away of the state, but they contended that during the period of transition the state must remain in the form of a dictatorship of the proletariat. Bakunin, who had now abandoned his ideas of revolutionary dictatorship, demanded the abolition of the state at the earliest possible moment, even at the risk of temporary chaos, which he regarded as less dangerous than the evils from which no form of government could escape.

Where such divergences of aims and principles are united with such differences of personality, conflicts are inevitable, and it was not long before the rivalry within the International developed into an organizational war without quarter. But before we come to its final battles we must turn aside to consider two significant episodes in Bakunin's life shortly after his moral triumph at the Basel Congress. Each in its way was a moral defeat.

The first began with the arrival in Geneva during the early spring of 1869 of Sergei Nechayev, a student from Moscow University who had formed a revolutionary circle, talked blood and fire, and fled when he heard the police were on his track. Later Nechayev was to enter world literature as the original Peter Verkhovensky in *The Possessed*, and, though Dostoyevsky's portrait is a caricature which does insufficient justice to Nechayev's genuine courage, it does catch fairly accurately the young revolutionary's most evident characteristics—his nihilistic fanaticism, his lack of any personal warmth or compassion, his calculated amoralism, and his tendency to look at all men and women as tools to be used in the cause of revolution, magically identified, of course, with himself. Nechayev was no anarchist; rather he was a believer in revolutionary dictatorship who carried nihilism to that repulsive extreme where the end justifies every means, where the individual is negated along with everything else in society, and where the authoritarian will of the terrorist becomes the only justification for his actions. This, moreover, was no mere theoretical position; Nechayev actually used his theories to justify the murder, theft, and blackmail which he himself practised. He appears in the history of anarchism only by virtue of his malign influence on Bakunin.

The fascination that Nechayev wielded over Bakunin reminds one of other disastrous relationships between men of widely differing ages: Rimbaud and Verlaine, or Lord Alfred Douglas and Oscar Wilde. There certainly seems to have been a touch of submerged homosexuality; indeed, it is hard to find any other explanation for the temporary submissiveness of the usually autocratic Bakunin to this sinister youth. Overtly, however, the friendship was between two very self-conscious revolutionaries, each of whom tried to enhance his importance by extravagant bluffing. Nechayev told Bakunin—and seems to have convinced this veteran of Russian prisons—that he had escaped from the Peter-and-Paul fortress and was the delegate of a revolutionary committee which controlled a network of conspiracy extending throughout Russia. Bakunin in turn accepted Nechayev into the World Revolutionary Alliance (a phantasmic organization to which no other reference exists) as Agent No. 2771 of the Russian section. Having formed a tacit alliance of two vast but spurious *apparats*, Bakunin and Nechayev went into partnership in the preparation of literature for distribution in Russia. Nechayev was probably the more active of the two, but at least one of the seven pamphlets printed bore Bakunin's signature; it was entitled *Some Words to Our Young Brothers in Russia*. The more sensational pamphlets, *How the Revolutionary Question Presents Itself and Principles of Revolution*, were not signed at all; both extolled indiscriminate destruction in the name of revolution and preached the sanctification of the means by the end. 'We recognize no other activity but the work of extermination,' says *Principles of Revolution*, 'but we admit that the forms in which this activity will show itself will be extremely varied—poison, the knife, the rope, etc.'

Even more extreme was a manuscript in cipher, entitled *Revolutionary Catechism*, found in Nechayev's possession when he was finally arrested by the Swiss authorities in 1870. It set out the duties of the ideal revolutionary, who must lose his individuality and become a kind of monk of righteous extermination, a nineteenth-century descendant of the Hashishim.

> The revolutionary is a man under vow [says the *Catechism*]. He ought to occupy himself entirely with one exclusive interest, with one thought and one passion: the Revolution ... He has only one aim, one science: destruction ... Between him and society there is war to the death, incessant, irreconcilable ... He must make a list of those who are condemned to death, and expedite their sentence according to the order of their relative iniquities.

The *Revolutionary Catechism* and its related pamphlets occupy as controversial a position in Bakunin's later life as the *Confession* in his earlier manhood. The Marxists have done their best to father on him all these bloodthirsty documents; the anarchists have done their best to shift the blame on to Nechayev. And the lack of direct evidence makes it impossible even now to solve the problem. Bakunin probably helped to write at least some of the unsigned pamphlets, which contain eulogies of bandits like Stenka Razin that read remarkably like passages in his earlier writings. On the other hand, the references to 'poison, the knife, the rope' in *Principles of Revolution* suggest a pettier mind than his, which rejoiced in contemplating destruction in its more cataclysmic forms. The *Revolutionary Catechism* falls into a quite different category, since it was never printed and may well have been composed by Nechayev himself when he returned to Russia in August 1869 to set up his new revolutionary organization, the People's Justice. The title is the same as that of the document which Bakunin wrote for the International Brotherhood in 1865, but this is no evidence of his authorship.

Yet Bakunin allowed *Principles of Revolution* to be printed without any protest, which suggests at least his tacit approval. We have already observed his predilection for the more Gothic aspects of conspiracy. While all we know of his life suggests that in action he was the kindest of men, his imagination—shaped by the romanticism of the Russian 1840s—was always ready to be stirred by melodramatic dreams of blood and fire, and he was beset—like most professional revolutionaries—by the temptation to see his mission as a holy war in which evil must be destroyed to purify the world and make way for the heavenly kingdom. That he was not totally converted to Nechayev's tactics is shown by the disgust he displayed when Nechayev began to put them into action. Bakunin may have been as devoid of middle-class morality as Alfred Doolittle, but he retained an aristocratic concern for good manners; he would rebuke the young men of the Jura villages for using bad language in front of women, and there seems no doubt that, while in theory he may have found Nechayev's proposals delightfully horrific, in practice he saw them as merely caddish.

Nechayev, however, had all the single-mindedness of the earnest fanatic, and for him there was no division between idea and consequence. Having returned to Russia and set up his secret society, he proceeded cold-bloodedly to murder a student named Ivanov, whom he suspected of informing on him, and as callously left his associates to face the consequences of the crime. Back in Switzerland, he further compromised Bakunin by an act of stupid blackmail. In order to relieve his poverty, Bakunin had taken one of his rare decisions to earn money by actual work, but he chose a singularly unsympathetic task, the translation of *Das Kapital* for a Russian publisher. He received an advance of three hundred roubles, but found Marx's turgid prose heavier going than he had anticipated, and unthinkingly agreed that Nechayev should arrange to release him from his contract. Nechayev—apparently without Bakunin's knowledge—wrote a letter to Lyubavin, the publisher's agent in Switzerland, threatening him with the vengeance of the People's Justice if he troubled Bakunin any further. The letter found its way into the hands of Marx, who used it eventually for his own purposes. Meanwhile, having milked the Russians in Switzerland of every franc he could extract, Nechayev fled to London with a suitcase of confidential documents stolen from Bakunin. Disillusioned at last, Bakunin repudiated him and spend days writing letters of warning to his friends.

Throughout Bakunin's career runs the idea of action—particularly revolutionary action—as a purifying and regenerative force. It is so for society and for the individual; in many variations Bakunin echoes Proudhon's cry: '*Morbleu*, let us revolutionize! It is the only good thing, the only reality in life!' The revolutions in which he took part inspired him with an almost mystical exaltation, as is evident from his remarks in the *Confession* on his mood during 1848; the interludes of action that punctuated his later life seem to have been sought not only as means to ends, but also as experiences in themselves, capable of raising him from the everyday life, which 'corrupts our instinct and our will, and constricts our heart and our intelligence'. Revolutionary action, in other words, was a personal liberation, and even a kind of catharsis, a moral purging. It is in this light that we must observe the last revolutionary acts of his life. His own statements at the time of his participation in the Bologna rising of 1873 leave no doubt that he regarded this as a means of atonement for errors he had committed, and—though here we have no direct evidence—it seems likely that he welcomed the Lyons rising of September 1870 as a means of shedding the sense of humiliation he retained after his encounter with Nechayev. He had made a mistake. Now he would redeem it in action.

The Franco-Prussian War had already stirred his feelings deeply. His satisfaction at the defeats inflicted on Napoleon III was balanced by his fear of an Imperial Germany, but he also saw another possibility—that the national war might be transformed into a revolutionary war of the French people against both the invading Prussians and their own discredited rulers. It might even being the world revolution. To clarify his ideas, he wrote a letter of 30,000 words to an unknown Frenchman (said to be Gaspard Blanc, one of his followers in Lyons); James Guillaume printed it under the title *Letters to a Frenchman* after he had broken it into six sections and edited it so efficiently that it became the clearest and most consistent of Bakunin's works.

> France as a state is finished [Bakunin declared]. She can no longer save herself by regular administrative means. Now the natural France, the France of the people, must enter on the scene of history, must save its own freedom and that of all Europe by an immense, spontaneous, and entirely popular uprising, outside all official organization, all governmental centralization. In sweeping from its own territories the armies of the King of Prussia, France will at the same time set free all the peoples of Europe and accomplish the social revolution.

But Bakunin was not content merely to call upon the French people in a general way to unloose what he called 'an elemental, mighty, passionately energetic, anarchistic, destructive, unrestrained uprising'. He decided to do his best to foment it in the cities of the Rhône Valley, the region still unthreatened by the Prussian armies, and he wrote to his adherents in Lyons, calling upon them to act for the salvation of European socialism. When they invited him to join them he immediately accepted. 'I have made up my mind to shift my old bones thither, to play what will probably be my last game,' he told a friend of whom he asked a loan for the journey.

In Lyons the republic had been proclaimed immediately after the defeat of Sedan. A Committee of Public Safety was set up, and a number of factories were turned into national workshops, in imitation of the disastrous precedent of 1848. It was a parody recapitulation of French revolutionary history, and it carried so little conviction that by the time Bakunin arrived on 15 September the Committee of Public Safety had already handed over its power to an elected municipal council.

Bakunin and his adherents set out to give a more genuinely revolutionary turn to the situation. They began by creating a Committee for the Salvation of France; apart from Bakunin, and Ozerof and Lankiewicz, who had accompanied him, it included a strong local anarchist contingent (Richard, Blanc, and Pallix from Lyons, and Bastelica from Marseilles), but the majority of its members were moderates who recoiled before Bakunin's talk of violent insurrection.

However, the Bakuninists received unexpected support owing to the shortsightedness of the municipal councillors, who decided to reduce from three to two and a half francs a day the wages of the employees in the national workshops. At a great indignation meeting on 24 September, presided over by a plasterer named Eugène Saignes, resolutions were passed calling for a forced levy on the rich and for the democratization of the army by the election of officers. Bakunin and his Committee immediately wished themselves into power and followed up the meeting by a proclamation that declared the abolition of the state and its replacement by a federation of communes, the establishment of 'the justice of the people' in place of existing courts, and the suspension of taxes and mortgages. It ended by calling on other French towns to send their delegates to Lyons for an immediate Revolutionary Convention for the Saving of France.

It is a measure of the actual support Bakunin enjoyed in Lyons that the authorities did not consider such an obviously seditious proclamation worthy of action. When violence did break out, it was because the councillors, over-confident of their security, actually carried through their plan to reduce wages. The workers demonstrated on 28 September, and the members of the Committee for the Salvation of France, whom Bakunin had in vain tried to talk into armed action, took part in the manifestation. The municipal council was discreetly absent, and the Committee broke into the Hôtel de Ville with the assistance of the crowd and formed itself into a provisional administration. At last Lyons seemed to be in the power of Bakunin and his followers, and they settled down with some embarrassment to decide what they should do with the city.

Before they had reached any decision, the National Guard from the bourgeois quarters converged on the Hôtel de Ville, drove the crowd from its vicinity, and recaptured the building. The Committee fled, with the exception of Bakunin, who was imprisoned in the cellars of the Hôtel de Ville, and eventually rescued by the local anarchists. He escaped to

Marseilles, where he spent three weeks hiding with Bastelica until a friendly Italian ship's captain smuggled him to Genoa.

The venture that had begun with so much hope ended for Bakunin in disgust and despair. On 19 September he had written from Lyons to say that he expected 'an early triumph' for the revolution. At the end of it all, as he hid in Marseilles, he decided that France was lost and that alliance of Prussia and Russia would reign in Europe for decades. 'Good-bye to all our dreams of approaching liberation.'

But two other struggles awaited Bakunin before he was finally to lay down his arms in the exhaustion of premature old age. One was his polemic with Mazzini, which played a great part in the sudden growth of the Italian anarchist movement after 1870. The other was the last fight within the International, which had become inevitable as a result of his moral victory at the Basel Congress.

The annual Congress of the International had not taken place in 1870 owing to the outbreak of the Paris Commune, and in 1871 the General Council called only a special conference in London. One delegate was able to attend from Spain and none from Italy, while a technical excuse—that they had split away from the Fédération Romande—was used to avoid inviting Bakunin's Swiss supporters. Thus only a tiny minority of anarchists was present, and the General Council's resolutions passed almost unanimously. Most of them were clearly directed against Bakunin and his followers. The need for the workers to form political parties was provocatively affirmed. An ominous resolution warned sections or branches against 'designating themselves by separatist names ... or forming separatist bodies'. And, as an oblique thrust at Bakunin, the conference publicly disavowed the activities of Nechayev.

The intentions of the Marxists were so obvious that the Swiss Bakuninists immediately called a special conference in the small town of Sonvillier in the Jura. The only delegates who did not belong to the Jura Federation were two foreign refugees from Geneva, the Russian Nicholas Zhukovsky and the Frenchman Jules Guesde, later to become one of the leaders of French socialism, but at this time an ardent anarchist. Bakunin was not present. The main outcome of this conference was the famous Sonvillier Circular, which demanded an end to centralization within the International and its reconstitution as a 'free federation of autonomous groups'. Thus the central conflict between authoritarians and libertarians within the International was clearly defined on an organizational level, and the Circular gained support not only in Italy and Spain, but also in Belgium among the libertarian socialist followers of Caesar de Paepe.

One of the demands of the Sonvillier meeting was that a plenary congress of the International should be held without delay. The General Council found it impossible to deny this, but, by choosing another northern city, The Hague, as the place of meeting, it again created difficulties for the Latin representatives and prevented Bakunin from attending, since he did not dare cross either German or French territory.

The Hague Congress took place in September 1872. Marx not only attended in person, but also did his best to pack the gathering with his followers; as G.D.H. Cole has observed, at least five of the delegates forming the Marxist majority 'represented non-existent movements or nearly so'. Yet he was still faced by a formidable opposition, not merely from the Swiss and Spanish Bakuninists and the Dutch and Belgian libertarian socialists, but also from the British trade-unionists who, while they supported Bakunin in nothing else, were disturbed by the excessive tendency to centralization within the International and agreed that the powers of the General Council should be curbed. Indeed, Marx's victory would have been most doubtful if the Italian sections of the International, meeting in Rimini shortly beforehand, had not decided to boycott the Congress and break off relations immediately with the General Council. This left Marx with some forty supporters, including the French Blanquist refugees, against less than thirty opponents of various kinds.

The Congress began with what had now become a routine vote in favour of political action by the workers, and defeated a Bakuninist proposal to convert the General Council into a correspondence bureau. It then appointed a committee to investigate Marx's allegations that the Bakuninist Alliance was still clandestinely active. It was at this point that Marx astonished even his own followers by bringing forward a sensational proposal that the General Council should be moved from London to New York, where it would be safe from the Bakuninists and the Blanquists, whom he regarded as at best dangerous allies. The motion passed—mainly because the Bakuninists, no longer interested in the General Council, abstained; Marx, as it turned out, had killed the International in order to keep it out of other hands, for in New York the General Council languished and quickly died from sheer inaction.

The most scandalous proceedings of the Hague Congress were left until the end. Marx had submitted to the investigating committee not only evidence collected by his son-in-law Paul Lafargue on the continued functioning of the Alliance in Spain under Bakunin's instructions, but also Nechayev's letter to Lyubavin on the translation of *Das Kapital*. The committee submitted a vague report on the question of the Alliance, which it could not prove to be still in existence, but found that 'Bakunin has used fraudulent means for the purpose of appropriating all or part of another man's wealth—which constitutes fraud—and further, in order to avoid fulfilling his engagements, has by himself or through his agents had recourse to menaces'. Finally, it recommended the expulsion not only of Bakunin, but also of his Swiss followers, James Guillaume and Adhemar Schwitzguébel, the last two on the grounds that they still belonged to the Alliance, whose continued existence it had already declared itself unable to prove. The confusions in the report did not trouble the Marxist majority. They voted heavily for the expulsion of Bakunin and Guillaume; Schwitzguébel escaped by a narrow margin. On this undignified note the Congress ended; the International as a whole never met again.

How far the Alliance had in fact continued is just as hard to establish now as it was for the investigating committee of the Hague Congress. As we shall see, a Spanish Alliance of Social Democracy seems to have been formed in 1869 or 1870, while as late as 1877 a meeting of members of the Alliance, attended by Kropotkin, Malatesta, and Paul Brousse, took place in the Jura. Since the organization would hardly have been abandoned and then restarted, it does seem likely that Bakunin in fact maintained a secret organization of close followers after the open Alliance had been dissolved. Nevertheless, the existence of such a body was not proved at the Hague Congress, and the expulsion of Bakunin was based on conjecture. As for the question of *Das Kapital*, the Congress's decision on this point represents an extraordinary intrusion of bourgeois morality into an organization avowedly opposed to property in all its forms; furthermore, since the committee did not even attempt to establish that Bakunin was aware of Nechayev's letter, they really condemned him for that frequent peccadillo of writers—taking advances for works they do not complete.

At the time of the Hague Congress Bakunin was in Zürich, attempting to gain support among the Russian refugees in rivalry to the populist leader, Peter Lavrov. The Spanish delegates from The Hague and a group of Italians from Rimini joined him there, and, after a few days of discussion, they all went on to Saint-Imier in the Jura, where, in conjunction with Swiss and French delegates, they held a Congress of the anarchist rump of the International. The decisions reached at the Hague Congress were repudiated, and a free union of federations of the International was proclaimed.

With the anti-authoritarian International that stemmed from this meeting Bakunin had no direct connection. Indeed, from 1872 onward his activity narrowed with the rapid decline of his health. He maintained some

interest in the activities of the Russian revolutionaries in exile, and, after
settling in the Ticino in 1873, he re-established his links with the Italian
movement and particularly with Carlo Cafiero, a wealthy young aristocrat
who had recently abandoned his riches for the cause of the revolution.
There were times, indeed, when Bakunin's old fire flickered in resentment
or enthusiasm, but in general his outlook on his own life and on the world
was pessimistic. He saw immense difficulties ahead for the revolutionary
movement as a result of the defeat of the Commune and the rise of
Prussia, and he felt too old and too sick to face them. Besides, Marx's
calumnies had hurt him deeply, and there is no doubt of the sincerity with
which he wrote to the *Journal de Genève* on 26 September 1873, protesting
against the 'Marxist falsifications', and announcing his own retirement
from revolutionary life.

> Let other and younger men take up the work. For myself, I feel nei-
> ther the strength nor, perhaps, the confidence which are required to
> go on rolling Sisyphus's stone against the triumphant forces of reac-
> tion ... Henceforth I shall trouble no man's repose; and I ask, in my
> turn, to be left in peace.

But in the myth Sisyphus could not leave his stone, and in life Bakunin
could not leave his past. The revolutionary cause still clung to him, but
without glory—with, indeed, only added shame and bitterness. While the
young anarchist movement began to grow strong away from his tutelage,
he himself became involved in bitter financial wrangles over his irresponsible mismanagement of the fortune which Carlo Cafiero entrusted to him
for the revolutionary cause. The quarrel over the villa in Ticino which he
bought with this money to serve as a shelter for his old age and as a centre
for Italian conspirators caused an almost complete breach with his Swiss
and Italian followers. It also led him, in the hope of salving his uneasy
conscience, to join the Bologna anarchist insurrection of August 1874. On
his way into Italy he wrote a letter of farewell from the Pass of Splügen to
his censorious friends, explaining his acts, condemning himself for his
weakness. 'And now, my friends,' he ended, 'it only remains for me to die.'
   But even the glory of dying quixotically was denied him. The Bologna
rising did not fail; it never even began. The elaborate plans for storming
the city gates and barricading the streets miscarried, the few rebels who
reached the gathering-points outside the city dispersed for fear of the
alerted police, and within the city Bakunin waited in vain to take part in
the assault on the arsenal. His friends dissuaded him from suicide, and,

having shaved his abundant beard, disguised him as an aged priest and sent him off with a basket of eggs on his arm to Verona, whence he eventually reached Switzerland.

It was the last and most futile adventure of that veteran of the barricades. After two further years of physical decline and failing friendships, Bakunin died on 1 July 1876, in the hospital of Berne. The men who gathered around his grave, Reclus and Guillaume, Schwitzguébel and Zhukovsky, were already turning the anarchist movement—his last and only successful creation—into a network that within a decade would have spread over the world and would bring a terror into the minds of rulers that might have delighted the generous and Gothic mind of Michael Bakunin, the most dramatic and perhaps the greatest of those vanished aurochs of the political past, the romantic revolutionaries.

7. The Explorer

In the spring of 1872, when Bakunin was in Locarno nursing the humiliation of his failure at Lyons, another disaffected Russian aristocrat was travelling in Switzerland. He was a young but distinguished geographer of vaguely liberal inclinations; he was also a hereditary prince, and his name was Peter Kropotkin. Kropotkin spent much of his visit among the Russian refugees of Zürich and Geneva, listening to the arguments of the various revolutionary sects. Then he went for a short period into the Jura, where he met James Guillaume and joined the still undivided International as a supporter of the Bakuninist faction. Yet, though he was within easy distance of Locarno, Kropotkin did not meet Bakunin. The reasons for this omission are obscure, but the disinclination appears to have been on Bakunin's side; he may well have feared from this unknown Russian another experience like that which he had recently undergone with Nechayev. In the summer of the same year Kropotkin went back to Russia. He returned to Switzerland in 1877, a seasoned revolutionary propagandist who had served his time in the Peter-and-Paul fortress and had been the hero of a sensational escape. By this time Bakunin was dead, and Kropotkin quickly took his place as the leading exponent of anarchism.

There is an appropriateness in the fact that Bakunin and Kropotkin never met, for, despite their obvious similarities of background and belief, they were very different in character and in achievement. Kropotkin was a lifelong believer in the inevitability and desirability of revolution, yet he was never a practising revolutionary in the same sense as Bakunin. He did not fight at a single barricade, he preferred the open forum of discussion to the romantic darkness of conspiracy, and, though he might admit the necessity of violence, he was temperamentally opposed to its use. The destructive vision of blood and fire that so luridly illuminated Bakunin's thoughts did not attract him; it was the positive, constructive aspect of anarchism, the crystal vision of an earthly paradise regained, that appealed to him, and to its elaboration he brought a scientific training and an invincible optimism.

In contrast to Bakunin's bohemian energy, Kropotkin showed an extraordinary mildness of nature and outlook. No one has ever thought of describing Bakunin as a saint, but those who knew Kropotkin often spoke of him in terms of sanctification which in our own age have been reserved for men like Gandhi and Schweitzer. 'Personally Kropotkin was amiable to the point of saintliness,' Bernard Shaw once wrote to me, 'and with his red full beard and lovable expression might have been a shepherd from the Delectable Mountains.' Writers as varied as Oscar Wilde, Ford Madox Ford, and Herbert Read have given similar descriptions of Kropotkin.

To this secular saintliness he added a power of original thought that made him respected throughout the Western world as a scientist and a social philosopher, and while, like Bakunin, he lived out the best decades of his life in exile, it was an honoured rather than a hunted banishment. In the eyes of the English, who were his willing hosts for more than thirty years, he represented all that was good in the Russian fight for liberation from Tsarist autocracy, and in so far as anarchism came to be considered a serious and idealistic theory of social change rather than a creed of class violence and indiscriminate destruction, Kropotkin was principally responsible for the change.

Yet, though Bakunin and Kropotkin were so different in character and represented such different aspects of anarchism, the differences between them were not fundamental. The destruction of the unjust world of inequality and government was implicit in both their attitudes, as was the vision of a new, peaceful, fraternal world rising phoenix-like from the ashes of the old. The differences were of emphasis, dictated by historical circumstances as much as by personality. Bakunin was a man of the early nineteenth century, a conspiratorial romantic influenced by Carbonarist traditions and by German idealist philosophy; however emphatically he might declare himself a materialist and try to adapt his ideas to the scientific progressivism of the Darwinian age, it was still a semi-mystical vision of salvation through destruction from the Hegelian 1840s that dominated his development from a revolutionary nationalist into an anarchist international. Kropotkin, on the other hand, was born into the mid nineteenth century and absorbed its many-sided evolutionism into the very fabric of his thought, so that to him the conception of revolution as natural process was inevitably more sympathetic than the Bakuninist conception of revolution as apocalypse.

The visions of the two men, which we must thus regard as complementary rather than contradictory, reflect the change in historical circumstances from Bakunin's last phase, when the anarchist movement was just emerging out of the twilight of secret societies and minute insurrections, to Kropotkin's day, when it spread to almost every country in the Old and New Worlds and became for a time the most influential working-class

movement in the Latin world. Kropotkin played a notable part in that
expansion, but it was a different part from Bakunin's. Unlike Bakunin, he
had no passion for creating organizations, and other anarchists of his time,
such as Errico Malatesta and Fernand Pelloutier, were far more active in
marshalling mass followings and creating an anarchist élite of dedicated
militants and propagandists. Kropotkin was most important, even to the
libertarian cause, as a personality and a writer; all that was noble, all that
was 'sweetness and light' in anarchism seemed to be projected in the manifest goodness of his nature, while in writing he defined the ideal and related it to the scientific knowledge of his age with a simple clarity that even
Godwin did not equal. Such nobility and such simplicity had, if not their
faults, at least their limitations when Kropotkin came to look at the real
world through his spectacles of universal benevolence; Bakunin's insights,
even if they were not based on good scientific reasoning, were often more
shrewdly realistic than Kropotkin's optimistic rationalizations.

Kropotkin was born during the 1840s, when the men of the preceding
generation—Herzen and Turgenev and Bakunin—were already experi-
encing the intoxication of the Western ideas that finally detached them
from their native land. In the Moscow mansion and in the great Kaluga
country house where he spent his childhood there stirred only the slight-
est ripples of that great disturbance of minds. His family was rich and
powerful and ancient; his ancestors had been princes of Smolensk and
claimed to be descended from the ancient royal house of Rurik which
ruled Muscovy before the Romanovs. His father was a retired general, a
military martinet after the heart of the reigning Tsar Nicholas I.

Perhaps, in view of Alexander Kropotkin's character, it was fortunate
that he neglected his children and left them for the most part to the attention of the house serfs and, later, of a succession of tutors. It was from his
childhood contact with serfs, fellow sufferers from the capricious tyranny
of his parents, that Kropotkin, like Turgenev before him, first perceived a
common humanity between the rich and the humble, and learned, as he
himself remarked, 'what treasuries of goodness can be found in the hearts
of the Russian peasants'. A French tutor who had served in the Grand
Army of Napoleon introduced him to the Gallic conception of equality,
and a Russian tutor—one of those wandering students who appear so
often in nineteenth-century Russian novels—provided him with the books
that nurtured his opening mind, the stories of Gogol, the poems of
Pushkin and Nekrasov, the radical journalism of Chernyshevsky. It was
under the influence of his tutor, N.P. Smirnov, that Kropotkin first turned
to writing, editing at the age of twelve a handwritten literary review to

which he and his brother Alexander were the only contributors.

Meanwhile, as the son of a high-ranking officer, Kropotkin was expected to make his career in the service of the Emperor. By chance, when he was a child, he attracted the attention of Nicholas I at a reception given by the Moscow nobility to the visiting Tsar. Nicholas ordered that the boy should be enrolled in the Corps of Pages, the most exclusive military school in Tsarist Russia, from among whose students the personal attendants of the Imperial family were chosen. Kropotkin became the school's most brilliant student, and eventually Sergeant of the Corps, which meant that for a year he was the personal page of the new Tsar Alexander II. With such a position his future seemed assured; he could expect to become a young general, and by middle age the governor of a province.

But, when he left the Corps in 1862, Kropotkin's ideas had been through a series of changes that made it impossible for him to accept the career his teachers and his parents expected of him. His attitude toward both the court and the Tsar had always been ambivalent. He was superficially fascinated by the elegance and refinement of the setting in which he moved as a page. 'To be an actor in court ceremonies,' he commented long afterward, 'in attendance upon the chief personages, offered something more than the mere interest of curiosity for a boy of my age.' On the other hand, there was an innate puritanism in Kropotkin's character which made him shrink from the profligacy of court life, while he was disgusted by the intrigues for power and position which he witnessed from his position close to the Emperor. Toward the Tsar his attitude was equally divided. For having freed the serfs in 1861 he regarded Alexander as a hero, and he admired him also for his devotion to the duties of his office; at the same time he was disappointed with the retrogressive tendency which became evident in his policy shortly after the emancipation of the peasants and which was to end in the brutal suppression of the Polish rising in 1863.

Besides, there were two strong positive influences that drew Kropotkin away from any thought of an official career. His liberal instincts had matured, partly through his introduction to Herzen's first magazine, *The Polar Star*, and partly in resistance to the petty tyrannies of the officers of the Corps of Pages. At the same time his interest in the sciences was developing into a true passion.

It was the privilege of members of the Corps of Pages to pick their own regiments; commissions would be found for them regardless of vacancies. Most of the boys chose the Guards, but Kropotkin decided that he wanted three things more than honours and prestige: to escape from the mephitic atmosphere of St Petersburg; to follow his scientific studies; and to play his part in the great reforms which he still hoped would follow the emancipation of the serfs. He came to the conclusion that the one place which would give him all these things was Siberia. The eastern regions annexed by Bakunin's cousin, Muraviev-Amurski, were still largely unexplored, and offered opportunities in plenty for an apprentice scientist.

> Besides, I reasoned, there is in Siberia an immense field for the application of the great reforms which have been or are coming; the workers must be few there, and I shall find a field of action to my tastes.

He accordingly applied for a commission in the new and despised regiment of Mounted Cossacks of the Amur. The authorities were surprised, and his family was indignant, but the luck of attracting the Grand Duke Michael's attention by his resourcefulness in helping to put out a fire that threatened the Corps of Pages recruited this powerful man on his side and enabled him to overcome the opposition to his choice. 'Go—one can be useful anywhere,' said Alexander II to him; it was the last Kropotkin ever saw of his tragic monarch, already starting on the fatal path towards reaction that would lead to his death at the hands of the People's Will in 1881.

In Siberia Kropotkin found the atmosphere far more hopeful than in St Petersburg. Reform was still taken seriously there, and the Governor-General Korsakov, who had turned a blind eye to Bakunin's preparations for escape, welcomed Kropotkin with the remark that he very much liked to have men of liberal opinions about him. He appointed him aide-de-camp to the Governor of Transbaikalia, General Kukel, and Kukel in turn gave him the task of investigating the penal system in Siberia. Kropotkin attacked this task with energy and enthusiasm; he watched the chained processions of convicts tramping over the steppes and inspected the rotting lockups in which they slept on their great marches from European Russia; he visited the hard-labour prisons, which 'all answered literally to the well-known description of Dostoyevsky in his *Buried Alive*', and the gold mines, where the convicts worked in icy water up to their waists, and, most terrible of all, the salt mines where the Polish rebels died of tuberculosis and scurvy.

More than anything he had experienced before, these inspections aroused in Kropotkin a horror at the effects of autocratic government, but he still hoped that the tide of reform had really set in, and went ahead with his work on the prison report and with other projects of a similar kind. But he became disillusioned when he realized before very long how indifference in St Petersburg and corruption in Siberia conspired to frustrate his efforts. Yet, at the same time, he was impressed by what he saw of the success of cooperative colonization by the Doukhobors and other groups of peasant exiles in Siberia.

> I began [he says] to appreciate the difference between acting on the principle of command and discipline and acting on the principle of common understanding ... Although I did not then formulate my observations in terms of party struggles, I may say now that I lost in Siberia whatever faith in state discipline I had cherished before, I was prepared to become an anarchist.

But several years were to pass before Kropotkin's latent anarchism became evident. As he grew increasingly despondent about the possibility of achieving reforms, he turned first to science and welcomed the chance to make a series of exploratory journeys through eastern Siberia and the frontier regions of Manchuria. Here, in the company of Cossack soldiers and native hunters, he found a simple, uncorrupted life whose charm undoubtedly influenced the cult of the primitive which runs through the writings of his later life. He went usually unarmed, trusting to the natural peacefulness of simple people, and he was never in danger from human hostility; he went also without elaborate equipment, learning quickly how little is needed for life 'outside the enchanted circle of conventional civilization'.

It is on the fifty thousand miles of travel in the Far East which Kropotkin carried out during his service in Siberia that his reputation as a geographer is mostly based. Professor Avakumović and I have already described the journeys themselves.* Here it is enough to say that, besides exploring large areas of Siberian highlands hitherto untraversed by civilized travellers, Kropotkin also elaborated—on the basis of his observations—a theory of the structure of the Eastern Asian mountain chains and plateaus which revolutionized geographers' conceptions of Eurasian orography. He also made considerable contributions to our knowledge of the glacial age and of the great desiccation of Eastern Asia which led to the westward wanderings of the people of the steppes and, by a chain reaction, to the barbarian invasions of Europe and of the ancient kingdoms of the East. Among geographers Kropotkin is still remembered as a scientist who contributed much to our knowledge of the earth's structure and its history.

*George Woodcock and Ivan Avakumović, *The Anarchist Prince*, London, 1950.

But, like everything else that happened to him at this time, Kropotkin's explorations, by providing him with long periods of solitary thought, brought him nearer to the point where he would sacrifice even his scientific work to what seemed a higher cause. Many influences had been strengthening his tendency to social rebellion since he reached Siberia. He had mingled with the best of the political exiles, and had been influenced particularly by the poet M.L. Mikhailov, who was sent to Siberia in 1861 for his populist writings and died there of consumption in 1865. It was Mikhailov who introduced Kropotkin to anarchist ideas by encouraging him to read Proudhon; as a result of studying the poet's annotated copy of *Economic Contradictions*, which he bought after Mikhailov's death, Kropotkin began to regard himself as a socialist. He had taken the first step on the road to the mountains of the Jura.

In 1866 an incident occurred that crystallized all Kropotkin's half-formulated indignation against the autocracy he still served. A rebellion broke out among the Polish exiles who were building a road around Lake Baikal; they disarmed their guards, and set off southward with the quixotic plan of crossing the mountains into Mongolia and eventually reaching the Chinese coast, where they hoped to find transport to western Europe. They were intercepted by the Cossacks, and five of them were eventually executed. In disgust Kropotkin and his brother Alexander resigned from the Tsarist army. They returned to St Petersburg, where Peter enrolled as a student at the University and, since his father refused to send him any money, earned enough from casual secretarial work for the Russian Geographical Society to live in the Spartan way he had learned to appreciate during his explorations. A friend who knew him at this period describes him as established in 'a simple workers' lodging, a room where four people could hardly find space ... furnished with a table of white wood, a wicker armchair, and a great drawing bench on which he executed the charts of the rivers and mountains of our Siberian steppes'.

For several years Kropotkin's academic studies and geographical tasks took up most of his attention, but a guilty sense of the conditions of the poor gnawed at his conscience, until in 1871, when he was investigating the glacial deposits in Finland, he received a telegram inviting him to take up the secretaryship of the Russian Geographical Society. It was the kind of opportunity which only a few months before he would have accepted gladly. Now he felt that the offer forced him to make a choice over which he had too long wavered. Science, for all its remoter benefits to mankind, appeared almost a luxury at a time when he was so conscious of the urgent need to help his fellows.

What right had I to these higher joys when all round me was nothing but misery and struggle for a mouldy piece of bread; when whatsoever I should spend to enable me to live in that world of higher emotions must needs be taken from the very mouths of those who grew the wheat and had not bread enough for their children?

It is the cry one hears from many a guilty nobleman of Kropotkin's generation, and it led him to decide that, for the time being at least, his duty lay elsewhere than in scientific research. His break with science was in fact not so complete as it seemed at this time, but from now onward social idealism was to remain the dominant factor in his life, and science was to become the servant rather than the equal of his revolutionary aims.

At first he did not know how his decision would lead him to act. He was moved initially by a rather vague urge to 'go to the people', as so many young Russians were doing during the 1870s, and to try to educate them as the first step to a better life. Already, as a youth in the Corps of Pages, he had taken part in a plan to provide schools staffed by volunteer teachers for the newly liberated serfs, but his efforts and those of his friends had been brought to an end by the suspicion with which the Tsarist authorities regarded any effort to enlighten the people. Now he realized that anything so public as the foundation of a school would merely invite suppression, but he went nevertheless to the family estate in Tambov, ready, in the true populist spirit, to do anything 'no matter how small it might be, if only it would help to raise the intellectual level and the well-being of the peasants'. He found, less painfully than those other *narodniks* who were attacked and even handed over to the police by the villagers they had gone to help, that the time for a *rapprochement* between Russian peasants and intellectuals had not yet come. He decided therefore to visit western Europe, where, in an atmosphere of intellectual freedom, he might be able to order his ideas and see more clearly the course he should take.

It was natural that he should go first to Switzerland, which had become the Mecca of radical Russians in the same way as the spas and gambling towns of Germany had attracted their more conventional compatriots. Kropotkin settled first in Zürich, where several hundred Russians, both men and women, were studying at the University or devoting themselves to expatriate politics on the side of Bakunin or of his populist rival, Peter Lavrov. Alexander Kropotkin was a friend and supporter of Lavrov, but this did not affect Peter's intention to consider carefully the many socialist and revolutionary trends he encountered during those exciting weeks of discussion among the Russians of Zürich. He met Bakunin's disciple Michael Sazhin, better known as Armand Ross, and he assembled all the

books on socialism he could find and all the pamphlets and fugitive newspapers that were being published by the sections of the International
throughout Europe. In the process he became convinced that among the
workers of western Europe there existed the very consciousness of their
own identity and their own power which he hoped to awaken among the
peasants of his own country.

> The more I read the more I saw that there was before me a new
> world, unknown to me, and totally unknown to the learned makers
> of sociological theories—a world that I could know only by living in
> the Workingmen's Association and by meeting the workers in their
> everyday life.

He left Zürich for Geneva, a more active centre of the International,
and there he became aware of the divisions that had arisen within the
Association. For five weeks he mingled with the Geneva Marxist group.
But the political calculations that moved Nicholas Utin, the leading
Russian Marxist in Geneva, soon irked him, and he then sought out
Zhukovsky, at this time the leading Bakuninist in the city. It was
Zhukovsky who sent him on the trip into the Jura that became Kropotkin's
road to Damascus.

The first man he met in the Jura was James Guillaume, working in his
little printing shop in Neuchâtel; from there he went on to Sonvillier,
where he sought out Schwitzguébel, and made the acquaintance of the
mountain watchmakers, talking with them in their little family workshops
and attending the meetings in the villages when the peasant craftsmen
came tramping down the hills to discuss the anarchist doctrine that
seemed to offer them a chance of establishing social justice while retaining
their treasured independence.

It is hard to imagine a situation more likely to appeal to Kropotkin. The
enthusiasm that pervaded the Jura villages during the early 1870s
confirmed all the hopes he had conceived when he read the pamphlets of
the International in Zürich. The anarchist theories he heard expounded
by Guillaume and Schwitzguébel and discussed fervently by the watchmakers 'appealed strongly to my mind,' he tells us,

> But the egalitarian relations which I found in the Jura mountains; the
> independence of thought and expression which I saw developing in
> the workers and their unlimited devotion to the cause appealed
> even more strongly to my feelings; and when I came away from the

mountains, after a week's stay with the watchmakers, my views upon socialism were settled; I was an anarchist.

In its rapidity and its emotional nature, Kropotkin's experience had all the elements of a conversion; it set the pattern of his thought for the rest of his life.

It was only with difficulty that Guillaume dissuaded Kropotkin from staying in Switzerland and himself adopting the craftsman's life. His duty, Guillaume austerely reminded him, lay in Russia, and Kropotkin agreed. Soon after his return to St Petersburg he took up active propaganda as a member of the Chaikovsky Circle, the most celebrated of the *narodnik* groups of the 1870s.

The Chaikovsky Circle has little place in the history of anarchism except as the setting in which Kropotkin began to develop his ideas of action and organization. Its members at this time had no thought of terrorist activity or of conspiring to overthrow the Tsar by force; they set out to be propagandists, to write and publish pamphlets, to import illegal literature from western Europe, and to carry on the great task of educating the people. Most of them were moderate constitutionalists with a leaning toward social democracy; Kropotkin was the only anarchist among them, and his ideas had little influence on the Circle as a whole. Indeed, when a quarrel broke out between the followers of Bakunin and those of Lavrov over the control of the Russian library in Zürich, the Chaikovsky Circle took the side of the Lavrovists.

Nevertheless, it was at this time that Kropotkin wrote his first anarchist essay. This was a pamphlet entitled *Should We Occupy Ourselves with Examining the Ideals of a Future Society?* One secret report of the Tsarist police asserts that the pamphlet was actually published, but no printed copy exists, and only a manuscript was produced when it was quoted as evidence in the famous Trial of the Hundred and Ninety-three, which marked the end of the peaceful phase of the Russian populism in 1878.

What this pamphlet shows is that, despite his active association with a group who did not share his attitude, Kropotkin was already working out the anarchism he was later to propagate. In some ways his attitude at this time was nearer to both Proudhon and Bakunin than it became in his mature years. The influence of Proudhon appears in a suggestion that labour cheques should be substituted for money, and in the recommendation that consumers' and producers' cooperatives should be founded even under the Tsarist system, at least as a form of propaganda. His advocacy of the possession of the land and factories by workers' associations seems, however, much nearer to Bakuninist collectivism than to mutualism, and there is as yet no trace of the communistic form of distribution which afterward became so particularly associated with the name of Kropotkin.

At the same time he explicitly opposes Nechayevism and the idea of revolution by conspiratorial means. Revolutionaries cannot make revolutions, he claims; they can only link and guide the efforts that originate among the dissatisfied people themselves. He rejects the state, contends that manual work should be regarded as a universal duty, and launches an argument characteristic of his later years when he advocates a form of education in which intellectual training will be combined with apprenticeship to a craft.

For two years Kropotkin took part in the activities of the Chaikovsky Circle, using his geographical work as a cover for the agitation which he carried on, disguised as the peasant Borodin, in the working-class quarters of St Petersburg. In 1874 he was arrested and imprisoned in the Peter-and-Paul fortress. After two years his health broke down, and he was transferred to the prison block of the St Petersburg military hospital. It was from here—and not from the fortress as has so often been said—that he made his celebrated escape, described with great vividness in his *Memoirs of a Revolutionist.* In August 1876 he reached England, and early the following year he travelled on to Switzerland and picked up the connections made more than four years ago with the members of the Jura Federation.

This time he was quickly accepted into the inner circles of the anarchism movement, doubtless on the strength of his activities in Russia. He began to write for the *Bulletin* of the Jura Federation and for other more fugitive anarchist sheets, and in August 1877 he attended what may well have been the last meeting of the secret Alliance, and was elected secretary of an international correspondence bureau which it was proposed to set up in Switzerland. Later in the same year he went as delegate for the Russian *émigré* groups to the last Congress of the Saint-Imier International at Verviers in Belgium, and then continued to the International Socialist Congress in Ghent with the futile hope of reuniting the socialist movement. But he fled precipitately, under the impression that the Belgian police intended to arrest him, and returned to England, where for a time he contented himself with studying in the British Museum. It was now that he began to develop a conception of anarchism as a moral philosophy rather than as a mere programme of social change.

I gradually began to realize that anarchism represents more than a mere mode of action and a mere conception of a free society; that it is part of a philosophy, natural and social, which must be developed in a quite different way from the metaphysical or dialectical methods which have been employed in sciences dealing with men. I saw it must be treated by the same methods as natural sciences ... on the solid basis of induction applied to human institutions.

But such speculations had to wait, for Kropotkin felt the urge toward agitational activity much too strongly to settle down to the kind of libertarian scholarship that dominated his later years, and before 1877 was out he had left the Reading Room of the British Museum to collaborate with Andrea Costa and Jules Guesde in founding the small groups that were to form the nucleus of an anarchist movement in Paris. In April Costa was arrested, and Kropotkin fled to Switzerland where, except for short trips abroad, he remained until 1880.

Now began his most active period as an agitator and a publicist. He was disappointed to find on his return that the enthusiasm of the Jura watchmakers which had inspired him so much in 1872 was almost spent; Guillaume had withdrawn into an inactivity that was to last for twenty years, the Jura Federation was withering away, and its *Bulletin*, long the semi-official organ of pure Bakuninism, had ceased to appear. In Geneva, on the other hand, anarchist activity had revived, largely through the presence of a number of energetic Russian and French exiles, and with one of the latter, the young doctor Paul Brousse, Kropotkin collaborated in editing *L'Avant-garde*, which was printed principally to be smuggled over the border in the hope of fostering the growth of anarchism in France.

At the end of 1878 *L'Avant-garde* was suppressed by the Swiss authorities and Brousse was imprisoned; to fill the gap left by the paper's disappearance, Kropotkin now founded *Le Révolté*, destined to become the most influential anarchist paper since the disappearance of Proudhon's *Le Peuple* in 1850. At first he did almost all the writing himself, besides spending a great deal of his time on lecture tours in an effort to reactivate the International in the small towns around Lake Leman and in the Jura. He was becoming conscious—possibly under the influence of the Italian anarchists, who were already propounding the theory of 'propaganda by deed'—that the time had come for the anarchist movement to pass beyond theoretical discussion.

What practical things can one do? [he wrote to his friend Paul Robin]. Unfortunately the International has been until now and is at present particularly only a study association. It has no practical field of activity. Where can this be found?

The search for practical fields of activity dominated his work for *Le Révolté*, which he endeavoured to make 'moderate in tone but revolutionary in substance', and in which he set out to discuss in a simple way the historical and economic questions which he felt should interest the more intelligent workers. He wrote in a vivid journalistic manner, clear yet without the least trace of condescension, and the vigour of *Le Révolté*, in comparison with the dull sheets so far published by the anarchists, quickly made it popular among the radically minded workers not only in Switzerland but also in southern France, where it helped to stimulate the revival of anarchism, which had languished since the failure of Bakunin's Lyons revolt in 1870.

Kropotkin continued to edit *Le Révolté* until, after attending the London International Anarchist Congress of July 1881, he was expelled from Switzerland because of pressure exerted by the Russian ambassador, and settled in the little French town of Thonon on the southern shore of Lake Leman. Even then he continued to write regularly for the paper.

Kropotkin's early articles in *Le Révolté* were concerned mostly with current issues, treated with an optimism that saw in every strike or bread riot a hopeful omen of the disintegration of the great national states which he saw as the particular enemies of peace and social justice. For many years, indeed, he expected a Europe-wide revolution in the immediate future; in this he was not exceptional, for his expectations were shared not only by most of his fellow anarchists, but also by many of his Marxist opponents.

Soon he began to write less topical articles, criticizing contemporary society and its institutions from the point of view of a libertarian sociologist, and attempting to pose concrete anarchist alternatives. Two of his earlier books, *Paroles d'un révolté* and *The Conquest of Bread*, were actually composed of articles contributed to *Le Révolté* and its Parisian successor, *La Révolte*, as were many of his pamphlets which in later years circulated across the world. Some of these, such as *An Appeal to the Young, Revolutionary Government*, and *The Spirit of Revolt*, have retained much of their appeal and are still printed and distributed by anarchist groups in Europe and Latin America.

It is from these articles that one can date Kropotkin's influence as the last of the great anarchist theoreticians; even his later books, such as *Mutual Aid, Fields, Factories and Workshops*, and the posthumously published *Ethics*, were largely designed to provide scientific and philosophic support for the general conceptions that emerged from his period of militant journalism and agitation during the 1880s. For this reason it is appropriate to pause in the biographical narrative and consider the more important aspects of his developing ideas.

The desire to link theory with practice is evident in almost all Kropotkin's contributions to *Le Révolté*. He is considering the revolution, not in the apocalyptic form of a vast inferno of destruction which so often haunted Bakunin, but as a concrete event in which the rebellious workers must be aware of the consequences of their actions, so that revolt will not end in the establishment of new organs of power that will halt the natural development of a free society. His theme is the same as Proudhon's in 1848. Revolution cannot be made with words alone; a knowledge of the necessary action and a will toward it must also exist.

> If on the morrow of the revolution [he says in *The Spirit of Revolt*], the masses of the people have only phrases at their service, if they do not recognize, by clear and blinding facts, that the situation has been transformed to their advantage, if the overthrow ends only in a change of persons and formulae, nothing will have been achieved … In order that the revolution should be something more than a word, in order that the reaction would not lead us back tomorrow to the situation of yesterday, the conquest of today must be worth the trouble of defending; the poor of yesterday must not be the poor today.

In other words, the revolution must immediately ensure two things: first, the frustration of any attempt to create that self-defeating anomaly, a 'revolutionary government', and secondly, a substantial advance toward social equality. Gradualism is fatal, for all aspects of social and economic life are so closely interconnected that nothing less than a complete and immediate transformation of society will provide an effective guarantee against a retrogression of the kind that has followed every past revolution.

> When these days shall come—and it is for you to hasten their coming—when a whole region, when great towns with their suburbs shall shake off their rulers, our work is clear; all equipment must return to the community, the social means held by individuals must be restored to their true owners, everybody, so that each may have his full share in consumption, that production may continue in everything that is necessary and useful, and that social life, far from being interrupted, may be resumed with the greatest energy.

When Kropotkin says that everything must return to the community, he does not mean this in a vague and general way; he means specifically that it must be taken over by the *commune*. This is a term familiar enough to the French, whom he was primarily addressing; it describes the local unit of administration that is nearest to the people and their concerns, but it also carries the revolutionary connotations of the Paris communes of 1793 and 1871. But Kropotkin extends the idea; for him the commune is not an agency of local government, or even an expression of political federalism, as the two great Communes were. It is a voluntary association that unites all social interests, represented by the groups of individuals directly concerned with them; by union with other communes it produces a network of cooperation that replaces the state.

Economically the commune will find expression in the free availability of goods and services to all who need them, and here, in this emphasis on *need* rather than *work* as the criterion of distribution, we come to the point that differentiates Kropotkin from Bakunin the collectivist and Proudhon the mutualist, both of whom envisaged systems of distribution directly related to the individual worker's labour time. Kropotkin, in other words, is an anarchist communist; for him the wage system, in any of its forms, even if it is administered by Banks of the People or by workers' associations through labour cheques, is merely another form of compulsion. In a voluntary society it has no longer any place.

The whole theory of anarchist communism is developed particularly in *The Conquest of Bread*, which was published in Paris as late as 1892, though the articles that composed it had been written during the preceding decade. However, it must be emphasized that anarchist communism was not new even when Kropotkin was writing about it in the pages of *Le Révolté* and *La Révolte*. He was its great apostle and popularizer, but it is doubtful if he was its actual inventor.

The feature that distinguishes anarchist communism from other libertarian doctrines is the idea of free distribution, which is older than anarchism itself. Sir Thomas More advocated it in the sixteenth and Winstanley in the seventeenth century; it was a feature of Campanella's City of the Sun, and even in the phalansteries imagined by Fourier the rare individuals who could not be charmed into finding work attractive would still have their right as human beings to receive the means of living from the community.

Indeed, it seems likely that Fourier's idea was one of the sources of anarchist communism. Proudhon had condemned the Phalansterians because of the regimentation that seemed to be involved in their socialist communities but Élisée Reclus was an active Phalansterian before he associated with Bakunin in the early days of the International Brotherhood, and it seems likely that he brought certain of Fourier's ideas with him when he became one of the leaders of French anarchism in the 1870s.

The earliest publication that links anarchism and communism in any way is a small pamphlet by François Dumartheray, a Geneva artisan who later helped Kropotkin to produce *Le Révolté*. It is entitled *Aux travailleurs manuels partisans de l'action politique*, and was published in Geneva during 1876. At this time Kropotkin had only just left Russia, and he did not reach Geneva until February 1877, so that Dumartheray can hardly have been influenced by him. Élisée Reclus, on the other hand, was in Geneva at the time, and may very well have converted Dumartheray, who does not appear to have been a man of highly original mind.

In any event, whether the idea originated with Reclus or with Dumartheray himself, once afoot it spread rapidly. Cherkesov, the Georgian prince who was active among the anarchists in Switzerland during the 1870s, said that by 1877, within a year of Bakunin's death, everybody in Swiss libertarian circles had accepted the idea of anarchist communism without being willing to use the name. The Italians, in contact with trends in Switzerland through Cafiero, Malatesta, and other militants who occasionally found it wise to cross the border into Ticino, were also advancing by 1877 in the same direction. The final step of accepting the title anarchist communist was taken both in Switzerland and in Italy during 1880, when, as Kropotkin told Guillaume long afterward, he, Reclus, and Cafiero persuaded the Congress of the Jura Federation to accept free communism as its economic doctrine. The remaining active section of the anarchist movement at this time, in Spain, did not take the same decision, and remained until 1939 under the influence of Bakunin's collectivist ideas.

The Jura Congress of 1880 was in fact the first occasion on which Kropotkin publicly discussed anarchist communism. Under his revolutionary pseudonym of Levashov, he presented a report entitled *The Anarchist Idea from the Point of View of Its Practical Realization*, later published in *Le Révolté*, which from this point became the organ of the anarchist-communist viewpoint. The report stressed the need for the revolution, when it came, to be based on the local communes, which would carry out all the necessary expropriations and collectivize the means of production. It did not specifically mention the communist method of distribution, but in the speech that accompanied it Kropotkin made quite clear that he regarded communism—in the sense of free distribution and the abolition of any form of wage system—as the result that should follow immediately from the collectivization of the means of production.

In *The Conquest of Bread*, whose component articles were actually written in the mid 1880s, a few years after those collected in *Paroles d'un révolté*, Kropotkin brings a more reflective attitude to his presentation of anarchist communism. A corresponding shift in emphasis occurs. The discussion of revolutionary tactics is not absent, but it is no longer preponderant, and Kropotkin's attention is diverted largely to a discussion of the scientific and historical reasons that may lead us to accept the possibility of a life of 'well-being for all'. It is not a Utopia, in the sense of projecting the image of an ideal world presented to the last detail, for, like all the anarchists, Kropotkin accepted the view that society, especially after the social revolution, will never cease growing and changing, and that any exhaustive plans for its future are absurd and harmful attempts by those who live in an unhappy present to dictate how others may live in a happier future. What he really does is to take a series of the major social problems that afflict us now and consider tentatively how they may be worked out in a world where production is for use and not for profit and where science is devoted to considering means by which the needs of all may be reconciled and satisfied.

The Conquest of Bread really sets out from the assumption, deriving from Proudhon, that the heritage of humanity is a collective one in which it is impossible to measure the contribution of any individual; this being so, that heritage must be enjoyed collectively.

> All things are for all men, since all men have need of them, since all men have worked in the measure of their strength to produce them, and since it is not possible to evaluate everyone's part in the production of the world's wealth ... If the man and the woman bear their fair share of the work, they have a right to their fair share of all that is produced by all, and that share is enough to secure their well-being.

It follows that inequality and private property must both be abolished, but in the place of capitalist individualism there should appear not restrictive state ownership as contemplated by the authoritarian socialists but a system of voluntary cooperation, which, as Kropotkin points out, has been found practical by governments themselves in such matters as international postal and railway agreements. There is no logical reason, he suggests, why such voluntary agreements should not be extended to embrace all the functions of a complicated society.

The injustices and economic crises of capitalism proceed, Kropotkin argues, not from overproduction, but from underconsumption, and from the diversion of labour into unproductive tasks. If luxuries were no longer produced, if all the energy misdirected into bureaucratic and military activities were diverted to socially useful tasks, then there would be no problem in providing plenty for all. In fact, taking a line of thought already followed by Godwin, he suggests that if all men worked with their hands as well as their brains, 'five hours a day from the age of twenty or twenty-five to forty-five or fifty', it would assure the physical comfort of all. Having himself experienced the joy of creative activity as a scientist, he realizes that leisure is as necessary as bread for the burgeoning of the human spirit.

> Man is not a being whose exclusive purpose in life is eating, drinking, and providing shelter for himself. As soon as his material wants are satisfied, other needs, which, generally speaking, may be described as of an artistic nature, will thrust themselves forward. These needs are of the greatest variety; they vary in each and every individual, and the more society is civilized, the more will individuality be developed, and the more will desires be varied.

Accordingly, just as man's working life will be organized by cooperative working associations, so his leisure will be enriched by a vast proliferation of mutual-interest societies, like the present learned societies, but reaching out into a great population of fervent amateurs. All artists and scientists will in fact become amateurs in both senses of that ambivalent word, since all of them, Kropotkin is confident, will wish to carry on their manual work and through it broaden the experience they bring to artistic or intellectual pursuits.

From Fourier, Kropotkin takes up the argument for 'attractive work', which to him, as to his later friend William Morris, becomes one of the clues to the success of a free society. In a capitalist world there is no doubt that the majority of people find their work distasteful and would be glad to escape from it. But this does not mean, Kropotkin argues, that man is naturally idle; on the contrary, he prefers to be occupied and finds satisfaction in work that is done freely and under pleasant circumstances. Division of labour and bad factory conditions lie at the base of the boredom and frustration that workers now endure; if these can be replaced by pleasant and healthy surroundings, and by varied work which gives the producer a sense of the usefulness of his task, then work will lose its disagreeable character, and its attractiveness will be reinforced by the moral satisfaction of knowing oneself a free man working for the general good. Kropotkin suggests that here is a sufficient answer to those who bring up the argument that in an anarchist-communist world, where each man can take freely from the store-house whatever he needs, there will no longer be any incentive for men to work. The best incentive is not the threat of war, but the consciousness of useful achievement.

Here he shows a characteristic anarchist reliance on man's natural leaning toward social responsibility. Society, unlike government, is a natural phenomenon, and so—he suggests—when all artificial restrictions have been removed, we may expect men to act socially, since that is in accordance with their natures. He fails to take into account the fact that when men have been conditioned into dependence the fear of responsibility becomes a psychological disease that does not in fact disappear as soon as its causes are removed.

Indeed, he himself reluctantly admits that some asocial individuals may resist the attractions work can provide in a free society. And here he claims that society has a right to exert moral pressure, so that into the Eden of freedom conjured up in *The Conquest of Bread* there enters the serpent of public opinion which Orwell detected as one of the inhabitants of the anarchist paradise. One listens unquietly to the exhortation which at this point Kropotkin addresses to the useless man.

> If you are absolutely incapable of producing anything useful, or if you refuse to do it, then live like an isolated man or like an invalid. If we are rich enough to give you the necessities of life we shall be delighted to give them to you ... You are a man, and you have a right to live. But as you wish to live under special conditions, and leave the ranks, it is more than probable that you will suffer for it in your daily relations with other citizens. You will be looked upon as a ghost of bourgeois society, unless friends of yours, discovering you to be a talent, kindly free you from all moral obligations by doing all the necessary work for you.

A free society where the outsiders, those who are not 'in the ranks', are subjected to the moral condemnation of their neighbours may seem self-contradictory. Yet Godwin propounded the same idea a hundred years before Kropotkin, and it is not out of keeping with the strain of puritanism which disturbingly recurs throughout the libertarian tradition; like all theoretical extremists, the anarchist suffers acutely from the temptations of self-righteousness.

The discussion of Kropotkin's anarchist-communist ideas has taken us ahead of the actual course of his life, and I return to the point at which he settled in the French Savoy after having been expelled from Switzerland.

He stayed only a few weeks at Thonon, and then went on to England, addressing anarchist groups in the Lyons region on his way north. He seems to have contemplated settling in England, but he found few signs there of the socialist upsurge that began later in the decade, and after almost a year in London he found its apathetic atmosphere unendurable. In October 1882 he returned to Thonon, where at least he was near his old Geneva comrades.

He arrived inopportunely. During his months in England there had been a surge of unrest in central France, climaxed by a series of riots and dynamite explosions at Monceau-les-Mines in the Massif Central. These events were linked in the minds of the French authorities with the growth of anarchism in southern France. Kropotkin had lost touch with the French movement during his residence in England, but his connection with *Le Révolté*, the principal libertarian periodical, and his international reputation as a revolutionary theoretician, as well as the fact that his return to France happened to coincide with a new outbreak of violence, were causes enough for the police to consider him too dangerous to remain at liberty. When a round-up of anarchists was carried out at the end of 1882, his arrest marked the culmination of the campaign. On 3 January 1883 he and fifty-three other anarchists appeared before the Lyons Police Correctional Court; fourteen men who had gone into hiding were also included in the indictment. Since there was no evidence to suggest that any of the prisoners had been implicated in the recent acts of violence, the prosecution invoked a law against the International that had been passed after the Commune, and charged that the accused were active in a forbidden organization.

The defendants did their best to turn the event into an opportunity to expound their views. Kropotkin drafted the statement of principles to which they all subscribed. It denounced governments and capitalism; demanded equality 'as a primordial condition of freedom' and 'the substitution, in human relationships, of a free contract, perpetually revisable, for administration and legal tutelage, for imposed discipline'; and ended in ironic defiance: 'scoundrels that we are, we demand bread for all; for all equally independence and justice'. He also made his own speech, telling how and why he became a revolutionary and calling on his judges not to perpetuate class hatred, but to join with all just men in establishing a society where the absence of want would remove the causes of strife.

His eloquence had no influence on the court; it was not even intended for that purpose. Even though the prosecutor was forced to admit that the International no longer existed, the prisoners were still found guilty of belonging to it. Kropotkin and three other leading anarchist propagandists were each condemned to five years' imprisonment. They were sent to the prison of Clairvaux in the old Abbey of St Bernard, where they were given the privileged treatment of political prisoners. Kropotkin's time was filled with the many occupations of a resourceful and versatile man. He conducted classes among his fellow prisoners in languages, cosmography, physics, and geometry; he experimented with intensive cultivation in the prison garden; he wrote articles on Russia for the *Nineteenth Century* and on geography for *La Revue socialiste*, as well as contributions to the *Encyclopaedia Britannica* and to Élisée Reclus's monumental *Géographie universelle*.

The variety of highly respectable publications that were ready to accept Kropotkin's work from a French prison illustrates not merely the extent of his recognition as a serious scholar, but also the widespread disapproval of his trial and imprisonment. Georges Clemenceau brought a motion for amnesty before the Chamber of Deputies; it gathered more than a hundred votes. Moderate French papers like the *Journal des économistes* condemned the sentence, the French Academy of Sciences offered to send Kropotkin any books he needed, and Ernest Renan put his library at the prisoner's disposal. When Victor Hugo submitted to the President of France a petition from British men of learning and letters, it bore some of the most distinguished names of Victorian England: Swinburne and Morris, Watts-Dunton and Burne-Jones, Leslie Stephen and Frederic Harrison, Sidney Colvin and Patrick Geddes, John Morley and James Runciman and Alfred Russell Wallace, as well as fifteen professors of the major universities and the leading officials of the British Museum.

None of these manifestations of sympathy and protest had any immediate effect, and Kropotkin went through a period of grave illness from malaria—endemic in the Clairvaux region—and recurrent scurvy. After this, and after the French Premier, De Freycinet, had admitted Russian pressure by declaring that 'diplomatic reasons stood in the way of Kropotkin's release', popular indignation finally forced the President to pardon him and the other anarchist prisoners.

After serving three years of his sentence, Kropotkin was released on 15 January 1886; in March 1886 he landed in England for the fourth time. It was to become his home for more than thirty years, and his arrival there marked the end of his active life as an explorer and a revolutionary, which had lasted a quarter of a century from the time of his arrival in Siberia. It is true that he participated in the English anarchist movement, helping to found the periodical *Freedom* and the Freedom Group, which has remained the only durable anarchist organization in Britain; he also went on occasional lecture tours in England and even, on two occasions, in North America, and he took part in the foundation of a number of Russian exile periodicals. But these activities were sporadic, and he never again assumed the role of militant leader which he had occupied during his editorship of *Le Révolté*. Rather he tended to retire into the life of the scholarly theoretician, combining a consideration of the wider, sociological aspects of anarchism with a return to his former scientific interests. For long periods he lived in the seclusion of distant suburbs, where he cultivated gardens that were the envy of his neighbours and kept open house at week-ends to a succession of visitors, including not only fellow geographers and anarchist comrades, but also English radicals and intellectuals of many types, from Bernard Shaw to Tom Mann, from Frank Harris to Ford Madox Ford. To the anarchists he became the great prophetic savant of the movement, to be asked for advice and articles, to be welcomed when he made a rare appearance at a public meeting or at a reunion in one of the revolutionary clubs which then dotted Soho and Whitechapel. To the educated British public he was an honoured symbol of Russian resistance to autocracy. His articles in *The Times* and in scientific periodicals were read with respect, while his autobiography, *Memoirs of a Revolutionist*, and his discussion of cooperation as a factor in evolution, *Mutual Aid*, were quickly accepted as classics in their own fields.

At the same time Kropotkin's own attitude was slowly modified. More and more he stressed the evolutionary aspect of social change, relating it to peaceful developments in society rather than to abrupt revolutionary upheavals; less and less he advocated violent methods, and as early as 1891 he suggested in one of his speeches that anarchism might come 'by the ripening of public opinion and with the least possible amount of disturbance'. He suffered genuine anxiety over the actions of anarchist assassins during this period; he did not wish to condemn them, since he felt their impulses were honest and understandable, but he could not approve of their methods.

There were several reasons for these changes in Kropotkin's attitude. Failing health demanded a more tranquil existence, and this brought to the surface his natural benignity. He turned toward evolution because it was in his gentle nature to prefer it, but also because of the renewal of his scientific interests, which led him to react against the apocalyptic romanticism of Bakunin. He recognized that his earlier agitational activities had not brought the rapid results he had expected, and perceiving the constant setbacks experienced by the revolutionary movement, he became steadily less confident of victory in the comparatively near future. But perhaps the most important single influence on his changing views was his contact with the English socialist movement. He was the close friend of William Morris,* he knew and esteemed many of the Fabians and some of the founders of the Independent Labour Party, such as Keir Hardie, and though he and H.M. Hyndman, the Marxist leader of the Social Democratic Federation, were in constant disagreement, there remained a great deal of personal respect between them. Kropotkin was impressed by the mutual tolerance that existed between the various sections of the British labour movement. He recognized that British socialism had a greater libertarian element than its continental Marxist counterparts, and he was influenced, perhaps only half consciously, by the hope of proceeding toward the ideal goal gradually and reasonably, which permeated the English labour tradition. To a great extent these aspects of English socialism derived from the submerged influence of William Godwin and his disciples; significantly, it was at this time that Kropotkin himself discovered Godwin and recognized him as an ancestor.

These changes in attitude did not mean that Kropotkin in any way abandoned his earlier ideals. To the end of his life he remained convinced of the evils of capitalism and government, of the need for a change that would transform the whole of society and create a free communism in place of a system dominated politically by the state and economically by the wage system. However friendly he may have been to the English socialists, he never compromised on the basic issues that divided him from them. But he did present a very different aspect of anarchism from that suggested by the violent acts of the propagandists of the deed who were beginning to operate in Latin Europe; and if in France and England anarchism appeared to many non-anarchists, such as the Fabian Edward Pease, 'a consistent and almost sublime doctrine', this was, as Pease further remarks, because of the 'outstanding ability and unimpeachable character' of Kropotkin and his associates. Kropotkin's benign presence as a platform speaker, the sweet reasonableness which in his writings replaced the fulminations of Bakunin and the wilful paradoxolatry of Proudhon, and the talent for amiability that made him as easily at home in the country houses of aristocrats as in the terrace cottages of Durham miners, all contributed to this transformation of the image of anarchism. It began to appear not as a creed in which radical criticism was the most important element, as with

---

*It is significant that he never supported the group of violent anarchists who made life within the Socialist League so difficult for Morris.

Proudhon, or where the destruction of the old society was considered the one urgent task—with the new world taking care of itself—as with Bakunin, but rather as a doctrine which, without being Utopian in the restrictive manner of Cabet and the later Phalansterians, nevertheless presented a concrete and feasible alternative to existing society.

Kropotkin's major contributions to general anarchist theory end with the publication in 1902 of *Mutual Aid*, and in 1903 of a long pamphlet entitled *The State*. His later books, *Ideals and Realities in Russian Literature*, *The Great French Revolution*, and the posthumously published *Ethics*, are peripheral works, irradiated by a libertarian spirit, but not directly aimed at presenting the anarchist-communist case.

Mutual Aid was Kropotkin's contribution to a controversy that had its remoter origins in the work which marked the real beginning of theoretical anarchism, Godwin's *Political Justice*. Godwin's conception of universal benevolence was not dissimilar to Kropotkin's idea of mutual aid, and on it he based his contentions that if men behaved rationally, did their due share of socially useful work, eliminated wasteful activities, and exploited scientific discoveries for the general benefit, all could enjoy well-being and still have leisure for developing their spiritual selves. The resemblance of these arguments to those developed in *The Conquest of Bread* is evident.

In reply to Godwin, T.R. Malthus brought forward in 1798 his celebrated theory that there is a natural tendency for population to increase in a higher ratio than the available supply of food, and that the balance is only preserved by such phenomena as disease, famine, war, and the general struggle for life in which the weak are eliminated. Godwin's suggestions, if put into practice, would merely upset the natural limitation of population, and would thus be self-defeating, since population would again increase more rapidly than available supplies of food, and famine would restore the natural balance; hence all talk of a fundamental improvement in human conditions is merely chimerical.

Hazlitt and Godwin both replied to Malthus, but his doctrine remained an enduring presence in Victorian thought, and it received new support in the biological field when Darwin emphasized competition and the 'struggle for existence' as dominant elements in the process by which natural selection preserves favourable variations and eliminates unfavourable ones. Though in his later years Darwin acknowledged that cooperation within species should not be ignored as a factor in evolution, the idea of conflict remained a much stronger element in his conception of the evolutionary process, and it was emphasized by the neo-Darwinians, such as Thomas Henry Huxley with his view of the animal world as a perpetual 'gladiator's show' and of the life of primitive man as a 'continuous free fight'. Strife, according to Huxley, was not merely desirable as a condition of progress; it was also inevitable.

Superficially this attitude may seem to have much in common with those aspects of anarchist thought which stress the idea of struggle as necessary for the attainment of a free society. But the anarchists maintain that struggle is necessary only in order to eliminate the negatively competitive aspects of existing society. If competition exists at all in the future they envisage, it will be transformed into socially useful emulation. But the continued existence of the kind of perpetual struggle posed by the neo-Darwinians would be fatal to a cooperative society. Thus it became necessary for libertarian thinkers to provide an effective reply to the arguments of Malthus and Huxley; Kropotkin undertook this in *Mutual Aid*.

His interest in the cooperative aspects of evolution dated from the years of his Siberian explorations. Observing the animal life of the wild regions he traversed, he had discovered less evidence of struggle than of cooperation between individuals of the same species. His conversion to anarchism sharpened his interest in animal sociability, and in April 1882 he contributed an article to *Le Révolté* in which he discussed Darwinism and foreshadowed his own theory of mutual aid by contending that 'solidarity and communal work—these strengthen the species in the fight for the maintenance of their existence against adverse powers of nature'. A little later, while in prison at Clairvaux, he was impressed by a lecture the scientist Kessler had given in Moscow, arguing the importance of cooperation as a factor in evolution. But it was Huxley's paper on *The Struggle for Existence and Its Bearing upon Man*, published in 1888, that prompted Kropotkin to attempt a reply, and in 1890 he began to publish in the *Nineteenth-Century* the series of essays that eventually formed *Mutual Aid*.

He begins this book by suggesting that throughout the animal world, from the insects up to the highest mammals, 'species that live solitarily or in small families are relatively few, and their numbers are limited'. Often they belong to dwindling species or live as they do because of artificial conditions created by human destruction of the balance of nature. Mutual aid, in fact, appears to be the rule among the more successful species, as Kropotkin shows by an impressive series of observations made by himself and other scientists, and he suggests that it is in fact the most important element in their evolution.

Life in societies enables the feeblest animals, the feeblest birds, and the feeblest mammals to resist, or to protect themselves from the most terrible birds and beasts of prey; it permits longevity; it enables the species to rear its progeny with the least waste of energy and to maintain its numbers albeit a very slow birth-rate; it enables the gregarious animals to migrate in search of new abodes. Therefore, while fully admitting that force, swiftness, protective colours, cunningness, and endurance to hunger and cold, which are mentioned by Darwin and Wallace, are so many qualities making the individual or the species the fittest under certain circumstances, we maintain that under *any* circumstances sociability is the greatest advantage in the struggle for life. Those species which willingly abandon it are doomed to decay; while those animals which know best how to combine have the greatest chance of survival and of further evolution, although they may be inferior to others in *each* of the faculties enumerated by Darwin and Wallace, except the intellectual faculty.

The intellectual faculty, Kropotkin suggests, is 'eminently social', since it is nurtured by language, imitation, and accumulated experience. Moreover, the very fact of living in society tends to develop—in however rudimentary a form—'that collective sense of justice growing to become a habit' which is the very essence of social life.

The struggle for existence is indeed important, but as a struggle against adverse circumstances rather than between individuals of the same species. Where it does exist within a species, it is injurious rather than otherwise, since it dissipates the advantages gained by sociability. Far from thriving on competition, Kropotkin suggests, natural selection seeks out the means by which it can be avoided.

Such considerations apply equally to men. Kropotkin counters Huxley's Rousseauish vision of primeval man engaged in a continual free fight for existence with observations of actual primitive societies which suggest that man may always have lived in tribes or clans in which the law as we know it is replaced by customs and taboos ensuring cooperation and mutual aid. Man is and always has been, Kropotkin contends, a social species. He sees mutual aid reaching its apogee in the rich communal life of the medieval cities, and shows that even the appearance of coercive institutions such as the state has not eliminated voluntary cooperation, which remains the most important factor in the intercourse of men and women, considered as individuals. The urge to sociability is the foundation of every creed of social ethics, and if it did not condition almost all our daily acts toward our fellow men, the most highly organized state could not prevent the disintegration of society.

I have necessarily oversimplified a complex and well-argued book which, with the exception of *Memoirs of a Revolutionist*, remains Kropotkin's most effective work. Despite the colouring optimism, his evidence is well presented and the facts are well argued; very little that biology and sociology has since discovered about the behaviour of men and animals substantially disproves Kropotkin's conclusions.

Mutual Aid creates, of course, no departure in libertarian thought. It represents rather the classic statement of the idea common to most anarchists, that society is a natural phenomenon, existing anterior to the appearance of man, and that man is naturally adapted to observe its laws without the need for artificial regulations. The major flaw of *Mutual Aid* is that it does not acknowledge the tyrannies of custom and habit as it does those of government and regulation. Once again, Kropotkin shows that he is willing to accept moral compulsion, whether it is the rule of custom in a primitive tribe or that of public opinion in an anarchist society, without admitting how far this force also negates the freedom of the individual. A taboo-ridden native of the primitive Congo had in reality far less freedom of action than a citizen of the England in which Kropotkin himself lived with such slight interference. A stateless society, in other words, may be very far from a free society so far as the personal lives of its members are concerned. This possibility Kropotkin was never willing to consider seriously.

The later years of Kropotkin's life declined into ill health, and in 1914 the First World War abruptly separated him from the majority of his fellow anarchists. Following the anti-militarist tradition, the anarchist movement as a whole opposed the war, though a number of its leaders, including Cherkesov and Grave, supported Kropotkin's stand in favour of the Allies.

Kropotkin's own attitude showed a return to the tradition of the *narodniks* among whom he had first become a revolutionary. The earlier Russian radicals saw Germany, and particularly Prussia, as an enemy of their own ideals. They felt that the worst elements of Tsarism were derived from Prussian autocracy, grafted on by the German empress, Catherine the Great, and by Nicholas I, who admired Junker military methods so much that he introduced them into his own administration. In his pan-Slavist days Bakunin abandoned his earlier worship of Germany as the homeland of philosophy, and his distrust grew into hatred during the Franco-Prussian War. Since that time, in Kropotkin's view, the German Empire had been consolidated and even German socialism had taken on a universally authoritarian character. He believed that Germany and the Germans desired war in order to dominate Europe, and that such a domination would set back the cause of freedom immeasurably. In these circumstances he fell into the habit of identifying—against his own theories—states with peoples, and where Bakunin had talked of a popular war against the Prussians, a war that would destroy all states, Kropotkin argued himself into the position in which he supported England and France, as states, against the German state.

The break with the anarchists was probably the most unhappy event of Kropotkin's life. It looked as though he was drawing near the lonely and melancholy end of an active career when the news arrived in March 1917 that the Russian people had revolted and the autocracy had come to an end. Kropotkin was delighted. His own people had freed themselves from tyranny, and his last days might after all be dedicated to the service of his native land. In the summer of 1917 he left England and arrived at the Finland station in Petrograd, where he was welcomed by Kerensky, a regiment of Guards, and military bands playing the 'Marseillaise'. Absent were the Russian anarchists, most of whom opposed the war.

Forty years abroad had put Kropotkin out of touch with Russian realities. He did not realize how far the February Revolution had been motivated by the war-weariness of a people involved in a conflict they hardly understood, and he immediately began—as if it were the most urgent task of all—exhorting the Russians to pursue the war against Germany with a vigour the Germanophile Tsar had been unable to summon up. He refused any part in the government, yet because of his support for continuation of the war his name became associated with the discredited régime of Kerensky, while from the Left—whether anarchist, social revolutionary, or Bolshevik—he was cut off because the supporters of all these trends opposed the war and accepted Lenin's policy of revolutionary defeatism. Consequently, Kropotkin sank rapidly into insignificance in the changing political scene, and all the influence for moderation that he might have wielded in Russia was wasted.

The events of the October Revolution followed in some ways the pattern anticipated by the anarchist theoreticians, including Kropotkin himself. The peasants seized the land and the workers the factories, so that the decrees by which the Bolsheviks made these facts legal merely recognized accomplished situations. Most of the anarchists actually took part in the October rising, seeking within it the possibilities of a genuine libertarian revolution. Yet Kropotkin was prophetically right when he said to Atabekian, one of the few old comrades with whom he maintained contact at this time, 'this buries the Revolution'.

In the long run the Bolshevik seizure of power reunited Kropotkin with
the Russian anarchists, since it effectively removed the main cause of their
differences, the issue of the war. Moreover, the movement as a whole was
soon forced to oppose the Bolshevik régime not only because of its dictatorial nature, but also because the anarchists were among the first dissidents to endure the persecutions of the Cheka. Kropotkin was too internationally celebrated to be subjected to any direct persecution, but he
protested as much as he could against the course of events. He met Lenin
on more than one occasion to criticize his policies, and in November 1920
he wrote a letter to him courageously attacking the practice of taking
hostages. But perhaps the most important document of this final period
was the 'Letter to the Workers of the World' which he handed to Margaret
Bondfield on her visit to Russia.

In this letter, which was published widely in the western European
press, Kropotkin sharply dissociated himself from those who thought of
destroying the Bolsheviks by external force, and called on all progressive
elements in Western countries to bring an end to the blockade and the war
of intervention, which would merely reinforce the dictatorship and make
more difficult the task of those Russians who were working for a genuine
social reconstruction. He next put forward his own anarchist vision of a
Russia based on the federal union of free communes, cities, and regions.
Then he exhorted the people of other lands to learn from the errors of the
Russian Revolution. Some aspects of that revolution he praised, particularly its great steps toward economic equality and the original idea of
Soviets as institutions that would lead to the direct participation of the
producers in the administration of their own fields of work. But he
remarked that, once they came under the control of a political dictatorship, the Soviets were reduced to the passive role of instruments of
authority.

> The immense constructive work that is required from a Social
> Revolution [he argued] cannot be accomplished by a central govern-
> ment, even if it had to guide it in its work something more substan-
> tial than a few socialist and anarchist booklets. It requires the knowl-
> edge, the brains, and the willing collaboration of a mass of local and
> specialized forces, which alone can cope with the diversity of eco-
> nomic problems in their local aspects. To sweep away that collabora-
> tion and to trust to the genius of party dictators is to destroy all the
> independent nuclei, such as trade unions and the local distributive
> cooperative organizations, turning them into the bureaucratic organs

of the party, as is being done now. But this is the way *not* to accomplish the Revolution; the way to render its realization impossible.

Yet Kropotkin retained enough optimism to foresee an eventual worldwide revival of socialism, and he called on the workers to set up a new International, divorced from political parties and based on freely organized trade unions aiming at liberation of production from 'its present enslavement to capital'.

These were courageous words at the time of the Civil War and the deepening Bolshevik Terror, and Kropotkin's last years were among his noblest in their stoical dedication to his fundamental ideals. But his words had no influence on events, either in the outside world or in Russia itself. Even for the anarchists he could do nothing, since most of them were either in prison or exile, or fighting their own battle in Makhno's revolutionary army of the Ukraine. Conscious of his loneliness, of the failure of his present hopes for Russia, but still mentally active and working constantly on his last book, *Ethics*, Kropotkin declined slowly into feebleness and died on 8 February 1921. A procession five miles long followed his coffin through the streets of Moscow; it was the last great demonstration of the lovers of freedom against the Bolsheviks, and the black banners of the anarchist groups bore in scarlet letters the message, 'Where there is authority there is no freedom.' In such dramatic fashion did the last of the great anarchist theoreticians pass into history.

Kropotkin himself might have claimed—though he would have done so in all humility—that his contribution to the anarchist tradition was the application of the scientific approach to its practical problems. But his irrepressible optimism, his exaggerated respect for the nineteenth-century cult of evolution, his irrational faith in the men of the people, deprived him of true scientific objectivity. His approach, as he sometimes recognized, was as much intuitive as intellectual, and his compassionate emotion always overcame his cold reasoning. I would suggest that his real contribution was rather the humanization of anarchism, the constant relating of theory to details of actual living, which gave the doctrine a concreteness and a relevance to everyday existence that it rarely shows in the writings of Godwin, Proudhon, or Bakunin. But his concreteness of approach was irradiated by the quality of personality; Kropotkin believed fervently in human solidarity because everything in his nature attracted him to the idea. He was a man of unimpeachable honesty, kind and conscious of the needs of others, generous and hospitable, courageous and uncomfortably devoted to sincerity. His well-balanced goodness, indeed, seems almost too bland and blameless in our modern age, when the assumption is easily made that genius must spring from frustration and saintliness from some deep Dostoyevskian stain; yet that goodness was real, and to it we owe the particular benignity of Kropotkin's view of human nature and, less directly, that complexly organized yet simple-hearted vision of an earthly and agnostic City of God with which he crowned the rambling edifice of anarchist thought.

8. The Prophet

STEFAN Zweig once described Tolstoy as 'the most passionate anarchist and anti-collectivist of our times'. One may dispute the extremity of this statement, but a consideration of Tolstoy's thought and teaching during the last thirty years of his life, and of the tendencies lightly concealed in the great novels written before the period of his conversion, leaves little doubt of its general truth. Tolstoy did not call himself an anarchist, because he applied the name to those who wished to change society by violent means; he preferred to think of himself as a literal Christian. Nevertheless, he was not entirely unpleased when, in 1900, the German scholar Paul Eltzbacher wrote a pioneer survey of the various trends of anarchist thought and included Tolstoy's ideas among them, demonstrating that, while he repudiated violence, his basic doctrine—and particularly his categorical rejection of the state and of property—fitted clearly into the general anarchist pattern.

Tolstoy's links with anarchists of other types were few but important. In 1857 he read some unspecified work of Proudhon (probably *What Is Property?*), and the notes he was stimulated to write at this time suggest that the French anarchist had already influenced him profoundly. 'Nationalism is the one single bar to the growth of freedom,' he commented. And even more significantly he added: 'All governments are in equal measure good and evil. The best ideal is anarchy.' Early in 1862, on a trip to western Europe, he went out of his way to visit Proudhon in Brussels. They talked of education—much on Tolstoy's mind at this period—and Tolstoy later recollected that Proudhon was 'the only man who understood in our time the significance of public education and of the printing press'. They also talked of Proudhon's book, *Le Guerre et la paix*, which was on the point of completion when Tolstoy called; there is little doubt that Tolstoy took much more than the title of his greatest novel from this treatise on the roots and evolution of war in the social psyche rather than in the decisions of political and military leaders.

Bakunin's pan-destructionism clearly did not appeal to Tolstoy, yet these two rebellious but autocratic *barins* had more in common than either of them might have cared to admit. For Tolstoy was an iconoclast and a destroyer in his own way, longing to see an end—even if it must be achieved by moral and pacific means—to the whole artificial world of high society and high politics. But for Kropotkin, whom he never met, Tolstoy had the greatest personal respect. Romain Rolland has even suggested that, in this prince who had given up his wealth and his social position for the cause of the people, Tolstoy saw a living example of the renunciations he had achieved only in his thought and his writings. Certainly Tolstoy admired Kropotkin's *Memoirs of a Revolutionist*, and, like Lewis Mumford in our own day, he recognized the great originality and practicality of *Fields, Factories and Workshops*, which he thought might become a manual for the reform of Russian agriculture. His disciple Vladimir Chertkov, exiled in England, served as an intermediary through whom Tolstoy and Kropotkin established contact, and one exchange of messages is particularly interesting. Tolstoy rather shrewdly came to the conclusion that Kropotkin's defence of violence was reluctant and contrary to his real nature.

> His arguments in favour of violence [he remarked to Chertkov] do not seem to me the expression of his opinions, but only of his fidelity to the banner under which he has served so honestly all his life.

Kropotkin, who in turn had the greatest respect for Tolstoy and described him as 'the most touchingly loved man in the world', was evidently troubled by this opinion, and he remarked to Chertkov:

> In order to understand how much I sympathize with the ideas of Tolstoy, it is sufficient to say that I have written a whole volume to demonstrate that life is created, not by the struggle for existence, but by mutual aid.

What Kropotkin meant by 'mutual aid' was not very far from what Tolstoy meant by 'love', and when we examine the development of Tolstoy's social thought and compare it with that of the other anarchists we realize how firmly his doctrine fits into the libertarian tradition.

Tolstoy's anarchism, like his rational Christianity, was developed by a series of climactic experiences. His years as an officer in the Caucasus, in contact with mountain tribesmen and Cossacks living in their traditional manner, taught him the virtues of simple societies close to nature and far from urban corruption; the lessons he drew from his experience were very close to those which Kropotkin drew from similar encounters in Siberia.

His presence at the siege of Sebastopol, during the Crimean War, prepared him for his later pacifism. But perhaps the decisive experience in Tolstoy's life was a public execution by guillotine which he witnessed in Paris during 1857. The cold, inhuman efficiency of the operation aroused in him a horror far greater than any of the scenes of war had done, and the guillotine became for him a frightful symbol of the state that used it. From that day he began to speak politically—or anti-politically—in the voice of an anarchist:

> The modern state [he wrote to his friend Botkin] is nothing but a conspiracy to exploit, but most of all to demoralize its citizens ... I understand moral and religious laws, not compulsory for everyone, but leading forward and promising a more harmonious future; I feel the laws of art, which always bring happiness. But political laws seem to me such prodigious lies, that I fail to see how one among them can be better or worse than any of the others ... Henceforth I shall never serve any government anywhere.

During the rest of his life Tolstoy elaborated this doctrine in many forms and at much greater length, but the core of it remained the same, and one can draw from the writings of his last decade statements that resemble closely what he had said forty years before when the memory of the guillotine haunted his dreams and outraged his humanity.

> I regard all governments [he said at the very end of his life], not only the Russian government, as intricate institutions, sanctified by tradition and custom, for the purpose of committing by force and with impunity the most revolting crimes. And I think that the efforts of those who wish to improve our social life should be directed towards the liberation of themselves from *national* governments, whose evil, and above all, whose futility, is in our time becoming more and more apparent.

To recognize the continuity of the anarchistic strain in Tolstoy from his early manhood down to his death is important, since there is a persistent view of Tolstoy which sees him as two different and even mutually antagonistic beings. The period of terrible doubts and spiritual agonies which accompanied the completion of *Anna Karenina* and which was largely recorded in its final chapters, the period which Tolstoy regarded as his time of conversion, is seen as a great watershed dividing his life. On one side lies the land of vibrant sunlight and dew-drenched forests that belongs to the great novels. On the other side lies the desert of spiritual effort in which Tolstoy, like a latter-day John the Baptist, seeks the locusts of moralism and the wild honey of spiritual joy. On one side stands the artist and on the other side the combined saint and anarchist, and one picks one's own particular Tolstoy according to one's taste.

It seems to me that this view, which I once held and defended, is a false one; that it ignores the many threads which unite the later and earlier Tolstoy. The features we see change, as a man's features change with age, but the face is always the same, played over by longings for justice and love, and held always by the lure of the natural world in all its beauty. The artist and the anarchist both live in that face, as they lived together throughout Tolstoy's life.

For there was, to begin, no time when Tolstoy really abandoned the art of literature. Even at his most propagandist moments he was never free of the desire to seek artistic expression, and to the end of his life his mind was full of plans and ideas for novels and stories and plays, as his diaries for the 1880s and 1890s attest; many were started and abandoned, but some at least came to fruition. As late as 1904 Tolstoy finished one of his finest novellas, *Hadji Murad*, in an acute state of mingled delight at his achievement and guilt at his self-indulgence. The best of his later works—stories like *Master and Man* and *The Death of Ivan Ilyich*—show no real falling off in his peculiar power to render life into art and yet retain its freshness untarnished. What does happen is a failure of the power to carry through longer works on a consistently high artistic level, for the one novel Tolstoy wrote during this period, *Resurrection*, though it is superb in parts, does not succeed as a whole. It has often been suggested that the failure of *Resurrection* is due to the preponderance of Tolstoy's moralism at this time; I would suggest that, though the moralism does preponderate, the primary failure is an artistic one, a failure of form and feeling due to emotional catastrophes. I have analysed that failure elsewhere; here I wish to emphasize the fact that until the very end Tolstoy never lost interest in literature as such, and within a decade of his death he was writing works that would be a credit to any writer in his seventies.

Tolstoy's conversion did not, then, destroy him as an artist. Nor did it bring him into being as a Christian anarchist reformer of the world, for it was no new thing for Tolstoy to turn away from literary work to other absorbing activities. Most of his mature life he distrusted any suggestion that literature was an end in itself. He disagreed strongly with Turgenev on this point, and a good twenty years before his conversion, in the 1850s, he was arguing that a man's main activities in life should be outside literature. At times, even in this earlier period, he talked of giving up writing altogether. He did not do so, any more than he did in later life, but for long periods his efforts to become a good farmer, or to improve the conditions of his peasants, or to relieve the victims of famine, or to evolve a progressive system of education, seemed to him more urgent than writing. In such efforts he displayed a concern for action and a practical ability that mirrored the extreme concreteness of his literary vision. Even in the midst of his work on *Anna Karenina* during the mid 1870s he became so involved in his educational experiments that he temporarily abandoned the novel, and impatiently remarked to one of his relatives: 'I cannot tear myself away from living creatures to bother about imaginary ones.' His teaching, incidentally, was highly libertarian in character, and the kind of free collaboration between teachers and pupils which he tried to attain in practice resembled closely the methods advocated by William Godwin in that pioneer work of anarchistic educational theory, *The Enquirer.*

It must be remembered that Tolstoy's consistent reluctance to accept an all-consuming literary discipline and his inclination to regard the actual profession of man of letters as a kind of prostitution, did not spring entirely from moral scruples. It originated largely from an aristocratic view of literature as one of the accomplishments of a gentleman. The sense of *noblesse oblige* was strong in Tolstoy. Even his radicalism, like that of the two other great Russian anarchists, Bakunin and Kropotkin, was based on a traditional relationship between aristocrat and peasant. All three of them wished to invert the relationship, but it remained none the less an important element in their thought and action.

What I have been seeking to show is that in Tolstoy the tension between the writer and the reformer was always present and usually stimulated both sides of his life; it only became destructive at the very end, when his artistic impulses were in decay. In his most fertile years as a novelist, his literary talents and his sense of moral purpose supported each other instead of falling into conflict. His earlier novels—*War and Peace, Anna Karenina,* even *The Cossacks*—have the effortless didacticism which so often characterizes great literature, and they present his views on the subjects that concern him passionately with as little violation of artistic proportion as one finds in Milton's justification of the ways of God to Man in *Paradise Lost.* None of these works is deliberately propagandist in the same way as *Resurrection,* and it would be stretching too many points to call them anarchist novels in any full sense. Yet they reveal, as powerfully as any of Tolstoy's tractarian writings, a whole series of attitudes which we have seen to be characteristically anarchistic.

There is, to begin, the naturalism—moral as well as literary—which pervades all these works, with a sense that man is best, or at least better, if he rejects the more artificial manifestations of civilization and lives in an organic relationship with the world of nature, himself a natural being. Such an existence is related to the concept of 'real life' of which Tolstoy makes so much in *War and Peace.*

> Life meanwhile—real life, with its essential interests of health and sickness, toil and rest, and its intellectual interest in thought, science, poetry, music, love, friendship, hatred, and passions—went on as usual, independently of and apart from political friendship or enmity with Napoleon Bonaparte and from all schemes of reconstruction.

Tolstoy, in all his early novels, sees life as being more 'real' the closer it is lived to nature. Olenin, the hero of *The Cossacks*, dwells as an officer in a village of half-savage peasants in the wilds of the Caucasus, and his life seems to him at this point infinitely more meaningful than that of his former friends in St Petersburg.

> O, how paltry and pitiable you all seem to me [he writes to one of them in a letter which he does not send off because he fears it will not be understood]. You do not know what happiness is, you do not know what life is. One must taste life in all its natural beauty; must see and understand what I have every day before my eyes—the eternal, inaccessible snow on the mountain-peaks and a woman endowed with all the dignity and pristine beauty in which the first woman must have come from the hand of the Creator—and then it will be quite clear which of us, you or I, is ruining himself, which of us is living truly, which falsely ... Happiness is being with Nature, seeing Nature, and discoursing with her.

What is expressed almost naïvely in *The Cossacks* is elaborated with far more artistry and depth in *War and Peace* and *Anna Karenina.* A life closer to nature, Tolstoy suggests time and again, brings us nearer to truth than a life bound by elaborate bonds of law and fashion. This is indicated with a deliberate social emphasis in *Anna Karenina.* There the division is maintained throughout the novel between town and country, between artificial urban civilization, which always tends toward evil, and natural rural life, which always tends toward good if it is left to follow its own courses. Anna Karenina, dominated by the city and corrupted by its unnatural standards, is morally and at last physically destroyed. Levin, a man of the country, goes through many trials of love and faith, but finally succeeds in his marriage and at the end of a long process of spiritual travail gains enlightenment.

But, as Levin realizes, it is the peasant—the man of the people—who is nearest to nature and, by the simplicity of his life, nearest to truth. Already in *War and Peace* this theme of the natural man is introduced in the character of Platon Karataev, the peasant soldier whom Pierre meets among his fellow prisoners when he is arrested by the French in Moscow. Karataev is for Pierre 'an unfathomable, rounded, eternal personification of the spirit of simplicity and truth', and he is so because he lives naturally and without conscious intellectualism. 'His words and actions flow from him as evenly, inevitably, and spontaneously as fragrance exhales from a flower.' Similarly, Levin's conversion in *Anna Karenina* is precipitated when he hears of a peasant, also named Platon, who lives 'for his soul, rightly, in God's way'.

Linked with this search for the natural life is the urge toward universal brotherhood which runs through all the novels and which projects a dream Tolstoy had shared with his brothers early in childhood, when they believed that their own close circle could be extended indefinitely into the fraternity of all mankind. In *The Cossacks* Olenin longs for comradeship with the primitive inhabitants of the Caucasus; the same vision haunts Pierre in *War and Peace*, and is linked with Tolstoy's Christianity in *Anna Karenina* when Levin tells himself: 'I do not so much unite myself as am united, whether I will or no, with other men in one body of believers.'

If so many of the general attitudes of Tolstoy's novels—the naturalism, the populism, the dream of universal brotherhood, the distrust of the myth of progress—parallel those of the anarchist tradition, one finds also many specific libertarian ideas suggested in them. The rough egalitarianism of the Cossacks is contrasted to the hierarchical structure of the Russian army; the cult of leadership is deliberately attacked in *War and Peace*; the moral flaws of a centralized political system and the fallacies of patriotism are exposed in *Anna Karenina*.

When we turn from the suggestions in Tolstoy's novels to the explicit statements in his tractarian works, we find that his anarchism is the external aspect, expressed in behaviour, of his Christianity. The lack of any real conflict between the two is due to the fact that his is a religion without mysticism, a religion without even faith, for, like Winstanley, he bases his beliefs on reason and submits them to the test of truth. Christ is for him the teacher, not God incarnate; his doctrine is 'reason itself', and what distinguishes man in the animal world is his power to live by that reason.

Here is a humanized religion; we seek the Kingdom of God not without but within ourselves. And for this reason Tolstoy presents an attitude that belongs clearly in the realm of anarchist thought; his idea of the immanent Kingdom of God is related to Proudhon's idea of an immanent justice, and his conception of religion as dependent on reason draws him into close relationship with both Godwin and Winstanley. And even in his religious phase he does not reject the natural world; he envisages life after death, if it exists, as taking place in a realm that is little else than nature transfigured. This he made clear in the moving letter he wrote to his wife during the 1890s when he happened to ride one evening through the woods that had once belonged to his friend Turgenev, now long dead.

In Tolstoy's world of reason and nature, time slows down, as it does in the long summer afternoon of freedom dreamed by William Morris. Progress is rejected as an ideal; freedom, brotherhood, and the cultivation of man's moral nature are more important, and to these progress must be subordinated. It is true that Tolstoy, like Morris, protests against an interpretation of his doctrines which presents him as the opponent of all progress; in *The Slavery of Our Time* he claims only to oppose progress that is achieved at the expense of human liberty and human lives.

> Truly enlightened people [he says] will always agree to go back to riding on horses and using pack-horses, or even to tilling the earth with sticks and with their own hands, rather than to travel on railways which regularly crush a number of people, as is done in Chicago, merely because the proprietors of the railway find it more profitable to compensate the families of those killed, than to build the line so that it will not kill people. The motto for truly enlightened people is not *fiat cultura, pereat justicia,* but *fiat justicia, pereat cultura.*
>
> But culture, useful culture, will not be destroyed ... It is not for nothing that mankind, in their slavery, have achieved such great progress in technical matters. If only it is understood that we must not sacrifice the lives of our brother-men for our own pleasure, it will be possible to apply technical improvements without destroying men's lives.

Despite such protests, however, Tolstoy did not look toward a more abundant life in physical terms. For him, as for the peasant anarchist of Andalusia, the moral ideal was the simple and ascetic life, where a man would rely as little as possible on the labour of others. The resemblance to

Proudhon is significant; Tolstoy must have read with approval that philosopher's lyrical praises of the glories of dignified poverty. It is the hatred of luxury, the desire that culture should serve men rather than be served by them, that explains his apparently eccentric rejection of the works of art that appeal to 'the Happy Few'; for him true art became that which communicated its message to all men and gave them hope.

Central to Tolstoy's doctrine is his rejection of the state, but equally important is his denial of property. Indeed, he sees the two as interdependent. Property is a domination by some men over others, and the state exists to guarantee the perpetuation of property relationships. Therefore both must be abolished, so that men may live freely and without domination, in the state of community and mutual peace which is the true Kingdom of God on Earth. To the objection that the positive functions of society cannot exist without government, Tolstoy replies in terms reminiscent of Kropotkin's arguments in *Mutual Aid* and *The Conquest of Bread*:

Why think that non-official people could not arrange their life for themselves, as well as government people can arrange it not for themselves but for others?

We see, on the contrary, that in the most diverse matters people in our times arrange their own lives incomparably better than those who govern them arrange things for them. Without the least help from government, and often in spite of the interference of government, people organize all sorts of social undertakings—workmen's unions, cooperative societies, railway companies, *artels*, and syndicates. If collections for public works are needed, why should we suppose that free people could not, without violence, voluntarily collect the necessary means and carry out anything that is now carried out by means of taxes, if only the undertakings in question are really useful for everybody? Why suppose that there cannot be tribunals without violence? Trial, by people trusted by the disputants, has always existed and will exist, and needs no violence ... And in the same way there is no reason to suppose that people could not, by common agreement, decide how the land is to be apportioned for use.

Tolstoy is as reluctant as other anarchists to create Utopias, to sketch out the plan of the society that might exist if men were no longer subject to governments.

The details of a new order of life cannot be known to us. We must shape them ourselves. Life consists solely in the search for the unknown and in our work of harmonizing our actions with the new truth.

Yet he does envisage a society where the state and law and property will all be abolished, and where cooperative production will take their place; the distribution of the product of work in such a society will follow a communistic principle, so that men will receive all they need, but—for their own sakes as well as the sakes of others—no superfluity.

To attain this society Tolstoy—like Godwin and to a great extent like Proudhon—advocates a moral rather than a political revolution. A political revolution, he suggests, fights the state and property from without; a moral revolution works within the evil society and wears at its very foundations. Tolstoy does make a distinction between the violence of a government, which is wholly evil because it is deliberate and works by the perversion of reason, and the violence of an angry people, which is only partly evil because it arises from ignorance. Yet the only effective way he sees of changing society is by reason, and, ultimately, by persuasion and example. The man who wishes to abolish the state must cease to cooperate with it, refuse military service, police service, jury service, the payment of taxes. The refusal to obey, in other words, is Tolstoy's great weapon.

I think I have said enough to show that in its essentials Tolstoy's social teaching is a true anarchism, condemning the authoritarian order of existing society, proposing a new libertarian order, and suggesting the means by which it may be attained. Since his religion is a natural and rational one, and seeks its Kingdom in the reign of justice and love on this earth, it does not transcend his anarchist doctrine but is complementary to it.

Tolstoy's influence has been vast and many-sided. Thousands of Russians and non-Russians became his passionate disciples, and founded Tolstoyan colonies, based on communal economies and ascetic living, both in Russia and abroad. I have never encountered a comprehensive record of these communities, but all I have been able to trace failed in a relatively short period, either from the personal incompatibility of the participants or from the lack of practical agricultural experience. Nevertheless, an active Tolstoyan movement continued to exist in Russia until the early 1920s, when it was suppressed by the Bolsheviks. Outside Russia, Tolstoy certainly influenced the anarchist pacifists in Holland, Britain, and the United States. Many British pacifists during the Second World War participated in neo-Tolstoyan communities, few of which survived the end of hostilities. Perhaps the most impressive example of Tolstoyan influence in the contemporary Western world has been—ironically in view of Tolstoy's distrust of organized churches—the Roman Catholic group associated in the United States with the *Catholic Worker* and particularly with that saintly representative of Christian anarchism in our time, Dorothy Day.

But the most important single Tolstoyan convert was undoubtedly Mahatma Gandhi. Gandhi's achievement of awakening the Indian people and leading them through an almost bloodless national revolution against foreign rule lies only on the periphery of our subject, but at this point it is worth remembering that Gandhi was influenced by several of the great libertarian thinkers. His non-violent technique was developed largely under the influence of Thoreau as well as of Tolstoy, and he was encouraged in his idea of a country of village communes by an assiduous reading of Kropotkin.

In Russia itself Tolstoy's influence went far beyond the narrower circles of his disciples, who often embarrassed him by the odd extremity of their behaviour. It was rather as the passionately unofficial and unorthodox conscience of Russia than as the leader of a movement that Tolstoy stood out during the last decades of his life. Taking advantage of the worldwide prestige that made him, almost alone among Russians, exempt from persecution of a direct kind, he time and again denounced the Tsarist government for its offences against rational morality and Christian teachings. He spoke without fear, and he never let himself be silenced. Rebels of every kind felt that they were not alone in the great police state of Russia while Tolstoy was there to speak as his sense of justice moved him, and his relentless criticism undoubtedly played its part in undermining the foundations of the Romanov empire during the fateful years from 1905 to 1917. Here again he was teaching a lesson dear to anarchists: that the moral strength of a single man who insists on being free is greater than that of a multitude of silent slaves.

PART TWO: THE MOVEMENT

9. International Endeavours

Humanity is one, subjected to the same condition, and all men are equal. But all men are different, and in his inner heart every man is in fact an island. Anarchists have been especially conscious of this duality of universal man and particular man, and much of their thought has been devoted to seeking a balance the claims of general human solidarity and those of the free individual. In particular they have sought to reconcile internationalist ideals—the idea of a world without frontiers or barriers of race—with a stubborn insistence on local autonomy and personal spontaneity. And even among themselves they have not often been able to achieve this reconciliation. For more than a century they have tried to create an effective world organization of anarchists; their efforts have been frustrated by an intolerance of any form of centralism and a tendency to retreat into the local group, which are both encouraged by the nature of anarchist activity. Since the anarchists do not seek electoral victories, there is no need to create elaborate organizations similar to those of political parties, nor is there any need to frame general programmes of action; most anarchist groups have in fact been dedicated to individually motivated propaganda—either of the word or the deed—and in activity of this kind the lightest of contacts between towns and regions and countries is usually sufficient. Significantly, only in the marginal field of anarcho-syndicalism, which is based on mass trade-union formations rather than on small propaganda groups, have local and individual interests been sufficiently subordinated to allow the creation of a durable and relatively efficient form of libertarian international organization.

Since this largely unsuccessful search for an effective international organization raises so clearly the central libertarian problem of a reconciliation of human solidarity with personal freedom, it seems appropriate to consider anarchism as an international movement before discussing its record in individual countries. The approach is further justified by the fact that the anarchist movement made its earliest appearance within the First International and the cosmopolitan brotherhoods founded by Bakunin, and only later separated into the national movements in which it was developed.

The history of anarchist internationalism falls into five periods. From the participation of the Proudhon mutualists in the discussions that led to the foundation of the First International, down to the break with the Marxists after the Hague Congress of 1872, the anarchists—whether they followed Proudhon or Bakunin—were seeking to fulfil their international-ist aspirations in collaboration with socialists of other kinds. From 1872 to the famous 'Black International' Congress of 1881, they tried to create a purely anarchist International, and this urge continued weakly through a series of abortive congresses during the 1880s and the early 1890s. In the third period, from 1889 to 1896, the anarchists concentrated on an attempt to gain a footing in the Socialist Second International. Their final ejection from the London Socialist Congress of 1896 initiated a further period, reaching its climax at the Amsterdam Congress of 1907, during which an organization restricted to convinced anarchists was once again sought; this period came to an end with the outbreak of the First World War in 1914. The period from 1919 to 1939 was dominated by the relative success of the anarcho-syndicalists who, after several false starts, finally created at Berlin in 1922 their own organization of libertarian trade unions, the International Workingmen's Association, which still survives in Stockholm nearly sixty years after its foundation. Finally, after World War II, links were reopened between individual anarchists and the remnants of groups and movements in various countries, and this led to a series of international congresses, which began largely as reunions of the survivors of pre-war anarchism but over the years have expanded to include newcomers from student radical groups, from peace movements, and from environmental movements, so that such gatherings, like their predecessors, have in fact reflected the changing character of anarchist preoccupations and the changing types of people who become involved in anarchist activities.

During the 1840s, as I have shown, Proudhon was already speculating on the prospects of an international association of producers, and it is thus appropriate that his followers should have played a decisive part in the negotiations that led to the foundation of the First International. These negotiations began when Napoleon III, as part of his policy of courting the French workers, encouraged a delegation of artisans to visit the London International Exhibition of 1862. Among them were several of the mutual-ists who later signed the Manifesto of the Sixty, and who on this occasion started conversations with English trade-unionists and with the German expatriates clustered around Karl Marx. In the following year, 1863, three of the same group—Tolain, Limousin, and Perrachon—went again to England at the invitation of the London Trades Council. Their ostensible purpose was to take part in a meeting in support of Polish freedom, held at

St James's Hall on 22 July, but once again there were conversations on the possibilities of international organization. Finally, in September 1864, a delegation of French socialists arrived in London with the aim of cooperating in the actual foundation of an association. All the delegates were Parisian artisans. Three of them, Tolain, Limousin, and Fribourg, were more or less orthodox Proudhonians; the fourth, Eugène Varlin, was a near-anarchist of another kind, who, while rejecting authoritarian socialism, held collectivist views similar to those of Bakunin. The French delegates attended the great meeting held at St Martin's Hall on 28 September, and it was they who put forward the resolution proposing the foundation of the International Workingmen's Association.

Tolain, Limousin, and Fribourg were chosen as French correspondents for the International, and the bureau they set up in Paris was the real centre of anarchist organization in that country; in this sense it will be discussed more fully when I deal with the movement in France. So far as the International as a whole was concerned, the task of implementing the St Martin's Hall resolution was left to a Central Committee of twenty-one members, entrusted with the task of drawing up rules and a constitution, and, since London seemed the safest place for such a body to operate, the control fell into the hands of English trade-unionists and foreign refugees, including Marx and his German followers, a few French Blanquists, and the Mazzinian Major Wolff. This situation, which continued after the Central Committee was replaced by the General Council at the Geneva Congress of 1866, meant that the anarchists, whether of Proudhonian or Bakuninist persuasion, never had any foothold in the executive centre of the International, and were restricted to deploying their strength at the various congresses, so that they could only influence comparatively general fields of policy.

The consequences of this division of control did not become immediately evident. The Geneva Congress—the first plenary gathering of the International—was preceded by an interim conference in London, at which reports of the working-class movements in various countries were exchanged, and a few general resolutions on such uncontroversial subjects as the Polish question and the lamentable influence of the Russian autocracy on European affairs were passed. The general atmosphere of this gathering was cordial, though Marx went out of his way to slander Proudhon privately to Tolain and Fribourg in the hope of leading these two influential delegates into his own camp. He was unsuccessful; the French remained determinedly anti-authoritarian, as did the only Belgian delegate, Caesar de Paepe.

At the Geneva Congress the line of division between libertarians and

authoritarians within the International was already beginning to show
sharply. The French delegates, who constituted almost a third of the
Congress, were mostly Proudhonians, though collectivists like Benoît
Malon and Eugène Varlin were present, as also were Albert Richard of
Marseilles—soon to become a devoted Bakuninist—and, among the Swiss
representatives, James Guillaume and Adhemar Schwitzguébel, the later
leaders of anarchism in the Jura. But Bakunin was not yet a member of the
International, and it was the mutualists who at this point maintained the
struggle against the authoritarians in favour of a strictly working-class
programme based on association and mutual credit, in the spirit of
Proudhon's suggestions in *De la capacité politique des classes ouvrières.*

In accordance with this attitude, the mutualists sought to restrict the
membership of the International to actual manual workers; they were
defeated as a result of strong opposition from the British trade-unionists.
They were also defeated when they opposed a Marxist resolution which,
under the guise of approving legislation to protect labour, subtly introduced the concept of the 'workers' state', since it claimed that 'by com-
pelling the adoption of such laws, the working class will not consolidate
the ruling powers, but, on the contrary, will be turning that power which is
at present used against it into its own instrument'. On the other hand, they
gained one minor victory by persuading the Congress to pass a resolution
for the establishment of a mutual credit bank, as well as securing approval
for the promotion of producers' cooperative societies as a vital part of the
general struggle for workers' freedom.

A pronounced shift soon became apparent in the balance of power
within the International. At Lausanne in 1867 the mutualists were percep-
tibly weaker, largely because of the spread of the collectivist viewpoint in
France. This resulted in Tolain and his followers compromising over resolutions calling for state intervention in education and—more important—
for the public ownership of the means of transport and exchange. The
deliberately ambiguous wording of the latter resolution made it acceptable both to those who wished for state ownership and to those who preferred control by associations of workers. Yet the mutualists once again
won a small success by obtaining the postponement of the question of
public ownership of the land, to which they preferred peasant possession,
until the next congress.

The mutualists were still a force to be reckoned with at the Brussels
Congress of September 1868, yet this gathering in the end marked a clear
shift toward a policy of economic collectivism. The Proudhonian opposition to socialization of the land was now unavailing, since the Belgian col-

lectivists, led by Caesar de Paepe, controlled more than half the votes, and a resolution calling for public ownership of mines, transport, and land was passed by a large majority. On the other hand, the mutualists gained a last triumph when Belgian support enabled them once again to pass a resolution approving the foundation of mutual credit banks.

The Brussels Congress established a socialized economy as the future aim of the European working-class movement. It did not determine the vital question whether that socialization should be carried out by authoritarian or libertarian means, but it seems clear that the spirit of the gathering tended in the latter direction, and the stage was now set for the second wave of Proudhon's followers, those who accepted collectivism but retained all the Master's hatred of authority, to appear on the scene. They presented themselves at the Basel Congress of 1869 under the leadership of Bakunin. Bakunin, like Proudhon, had long dreamed of an international organization for the emancipation of the working class, and I have traced the attempts he made during the period before he entered the International, theoretically as an individual member but really as the leader of movements in Italy, Spain, the Jura, and southern France, all of which were formed largely under his influence.

It is unnecessary to repeat the accounts of the Geneva and the Hague Congresses of the International in which the issues between Marx and Bakunin were fought out and the organization itself split apart into the dying Marxist rump centred around the New York General Council and the anti-authoritarian majority centred around the Bakuninist Jura Federation. But it is desirable to consider some of the factors underlying the final emergence of a predominantly anarchist International in 1872.

The conflict between Bakunin and Marx was the dramatic encounter of two historically important individuals, and for this reason one is tempted to interpret events in the epic terms of personal combat. But such an interpretation cannot explain entirely either the considerable following which Bakunin gathered during his struggle with Marx or the fact that such a substantial proportion of the International—certainly representing the greater part of its actual membership—finally entered the Bakuninist camp.

In fact, the schism was not merely between convinced Marxists and convinced Bakuninists. When the delegates of the Jura Federation and a few Geneva expatriates met at Sonvillier in November 1871, at the conference that marks the real beginning of the attempt to form an anarchist International, the circular they issued received the support of the Bakuninist federations of Spain and Italy but also of the Belgian followers of Caesar de Paepe, who stood half-way between anarchism and social democracy, while it aroused interest in Holland and England. The appeal it made was not due to the anarchist viewpoint of those who framed it, but to the fact that it echoed a growing discontent, even among Marx's former followers, with the way in which he sought to bring the centralized authority of the General Council under his own control. Whether the threat was regarded as one of personal dictatorship or of organizational rigidity, it was repugnant not only to the anarchists but also to men reared in the democratic traditions of labour movements in Britain and in the Low Countries. This was why they responded favourably to the key paragraph of the Sonvillier Circular, which stated with a moderation rare in nineteenth-century socialist polemics the libertarian ideal of a decentralized working-class organization.

We do not wish to charge the General Council with bad intentions. The persons who compose it are the victims of a fatal necessity. They wanted, in all good faith, and in order that their particular doctrines might triumph, to introduce the authoritarian spirit into the International; circumstances have seemed to favour such a tendency, and we regard it as perfectly natural that this school, whose ideal is *the conquest of political power by the working class*, should believe that the International, after the recent course of events, must change its erstwhile organization and be transformed into a hierarchical organization guided and governed by an executive. But though we may recognize that such tendencies and facts exist, we must nevertheless fight against them in the name of the social revolution for which we are working, and whose programme is expressed in the words, 'Emancipation of the workers by the workers themselves', independently of all guiding authority, even though such authority should have been consented to and appointed by the workers themselves. We demand that the principle of the autonomy of the sections should be upheld in the International just as it has been heretofore recognized as the basis of our Association; we demand that the General Council, whose functions have been tempered by the administrative resolutions of the Basel Congress, should return to its normal function, which is to act as a correspondence and statistical bureau ... The International, that germ of human society of the future, must be ... a faithful representation of our principles of freedom and of federation; it must reject any principle which may tend towards authoritarianism and dictatorship.

The men of Sonvillier considered that they were maintaining the original aims of the International, and it was in this spirit that, after the great
schism of the Hague, the Saint-Imier Congress came together in 1872.
There were delegates from Spain, Italy, and the Jura; they included many
of the great names of anarchist history—Bakunin, Cafiero, Malatesta,
Costa, Fanelli, Guillaume, Schwitzguébel. Two Communard refugees,
Camet and Pindy, represented France, and another, Gustave Lefrançais,
represented two sections in the United States. The Saint-Imier Congress
was concerned mostly with the establishment of the new International, or
rather, as its members contended, with the reformation of the old. For the
Bakuninists always regarded their International as the true heir of the
organization set up in 1864, and counted their congresses from the First
(Geneva) Congress of 1866.

There was some justification for this point of view, since it soon became
clear that the Marxist rump, with its headquarters in New York, had
retained hardly any support among the rank-and-file membership of the
International. Its one attempt at a Congress, at Geneva in 1873, was, as the
Bolshevik historian Stekloff admitted, 'a pitiful affair', attended almost
entirely by Swiss and German exiles in Switzerland. 'The game was up,' as
Marx exclaimed when he heard of it.

The Saint-Imier International, on the other hand, gathered at its 1873
Congress (also in Geneva) a fair number of delegates, not only from Spain,
Italy, and the Jura, but also from France, Holland, Belgium, and Britain,
including—the most surprising catch of all—Marx's former lieutenant
Eccarius. How many actual adherents of the International these delegates
represented is as hard to suggest as it is to estimate the numerical support
of the International at any period of its existence. Stekloff quotes estimates
that place the adherents of the united organization in 1870 as high as five or
even seven million, but he rightly dismisses these figures as 'pure inven-
tion'; fairly reliable estimates of the membership of the Spanish
Federation, one of the largest, place it at 60,000 in 1872, and on this basis
one can assume that the total membership of the International before the
Hague Congress was probably less than a million, and that even at its
height in 1873 the Saint-Imier International had considerably fewer adherents, many of whom must have been no more than inactive card-carriers.
Nevertheless, one can safely assume that from 1872 to 1877 the Bakuninists
commanded a following far greater than the Marxists.

The diminished International did not immediately begin to take on a
specifically anarchist character. The Congress at Saint-Imier was concerned mostly with questions of organization, and its decisions were

acceptable to a range of anti-Marxists as far apart as conservative English trade-unionists and extreme anarchist insurrectionists. It proclaimed the autonomy of sections and federations, and denied the legislative compe-tence of congresses, which should confine themselves to expressing 'the aspirations, the needs, and the ideas of the proletariat in various localities or countries, so that they may be harmonized or unified'. It set up 'a friendly pact for solidarity and mutual defence' directed against the threat of centralism.

Only one resolution at Saint-Imier was specifically anarchist, and that repudiated the emphasis laid on political action at preceding congresses since the Lausanne gathering of 1867. 'The aspirations of the proletariat,' it maintained in characteristically Bakuninist tones, 'can have no other aim than the creation of an absolutely free economic organization and federa-tion based on work and equality and wholly independent of any political government, and ... such an organization can only come into being through the spontaneous action of the proletariat itself, through its trade societies, and through self-governing communes.' And it clearly attacked the Marxist vision of a working-class state by declaring that 'no political organization can be anything but the organization of rule in the interests of a class to the detriment of the masses, and ... the proletariat, should it seize power, would become a ruling, an exploiting class'. On the basis of these contentions, the Congress passes an anti-political resolution, declar-ing that 'the destruction of every kind of political power is the first task of the proletariat'.

The anarchist intent of such a resolution is clear, yet there was enough moderation in its expression to make it acceptable both to the Belgian and Dutch collectivists and to the English trade-unionists, who retained the distrust of political methods they had inherited from the Owenite past The Belgian Federation, which had a considerable mass following in the Walloon mining and weaving towns, declared in favour of the Saint-Imier International in December 1872, and, in January 1873, the Marxist General Council in New York issued a statement suspending the Jura Federation, which provided a convenient excuse for the Italian, Spanish, Belgian, and Dutch federations officially to sever connections with it. At the end of January the British Federation held its congress, where some of Marx's old supporters in the General Council, notably Hales, Eccarius, and Hermann Jung, denounced the dictatorial attempts of their former leader. In the end the delegates resolved that the Hague Congress had been illegally consti-tuted, and that its resolutions conflicted with the rules of the Association. However, with British caution, they did not specifically adhere to the

Saint-Imier International, yet sent their delegates to its Geneva Congress in 1873.

This was the largest congress of the anti-authoritarian International, though only thirty-two delegates from seven countries actually attended. Hales and Eccarius came from England, Farga-Pellicer from Spain, Pindy and Brousse from France, Costa from Italy, and Guillaume and Schwitzguébel from Switzerland. It was a controversial gathering, in which the differences between anarchists and non-anarchists were quickly made clear. The first important discussion concerned the question of the General Council. There was no doubt about its abolition; this was voted in enthusiastic unanimity. But when the question arose of establishing some other body for centralized administration, there were sharp divergences of opinion. Ironically, it was Paul Brousse and Andrea Costa, later to become leaders of socialist political parties in France and Italy, who maintained the extreme anarchist attitude of opposing any continuing central organization whatever. The English trade-unionist, John Hales, flatly attacked their point of view, and his comments immediately revealed the wide divergences within the anti-Marxist ranks.

Anarchism [he declared] is tantamount to individualism, and individualism is the foundation of the extant form of society, the form we desire to overthrow. Anarchism is incompatible with collectivism … Anarchism is the law of death; collectivism is the law of life.

The Belgian and Jura delegates formed a bridge between the two extremes, and procured a compromise decision to establish a federal bureau which would have no executive authority and would be concerned only with collecting statistics and maintaining an international correspondence. To avoid any chance of control being established by a local group, as had happened in the case of the General Council in London, it was decided that the operation of the federal bureau should be shifted each year to the country where the next International Congress would be held. But since the International was proscribed in France after the Paris Commune and led a stormy life in Spain and Italy during the 1870s, subsequent congresses were in fact held only in Switzerland and Belgium, and this meant that in reality the fate of the anti-authoritarian International was bound up very closely with developments within the Belgian and Jura federations.

Disagreements arose also over the question of the general strike, which the Belgians, anticipating the anarcho-syndicalists of a later decade, defended as the principal means of inaugurating the social revolution. The Dutch and the Italians supported their argument, but the British opposed, on the grounds that the necessary preparations for a general strike would make it impractical in a critical situation. The Jura delegation again followed the middle course, declaring, in the words of James Guillaume, that a general strike was 'the only kind of strike competent to bring about the complete emancipation of the workers', but that the partial strike should not be despised as an effective weapon during the pre-revolutionary stages of the struggle. No effective general view emerged from all this discussion, and the delegates contented themselves with a weak compromise resolution:

> The Congress, considering that in the present state of the organization of the International no complete solution of the question of the general strike is possible, urgently recommends the workers to undertake international trade-union organization and to engage in active socialist propaganda.

Thus the first two congresses of the Saint-Imier International were singularly barren in original thought or discussion, and showed a tendency toward middle-of-the-road compromise which disappointed the sections of the movement anxious for spectacular action. The results began to appear when the next congress met in Brussels during September 1874. On this occasion a German delegation attended for the first time; its two members were Lassalleans, a fact which at least speaks for the lack of partisan rigidity in the reformed International. On the other hand, the Italian anarchists refused to participate. They had formed an Italian Social Revolutionary Committee which, having organized the abortive Bologna rising, was now driven underground by governmental persecutions. Their message to the Congress pointed out that since circumstances had forced them into conspiratorial ways of action, it was patently absurd for them to take part in an open congress; in their present mood they understandably seemed to prefer the excitement of insurrectionary dreams to the dull discussions that had occupied the congresses since 1872.

At Brussels it became clear that the only real bond between the national groups was their opposition to the centralizing tactics of Marx and the now defunct General Council, and that the old division between libertarians and authoritarians had in fact been carried over into the new organization. There was no agreement on such important questions as political action, the dictatorship of the proletariat, the destiny of the state, and the possibility of a transitional period before the attainment of a society based on communal organization. The German delegates and Eccarius, representing Britain, stood for state socialism; the delegates from Spain and the Jura, with some of the Belgians, maintained a purist anarchism. De Paepe, the leading figure among the Belgians, took an intermediate position which prefigured his later shift toward state socialism; it was his report on 'the organization of the public services' that brought the issue into the open and occupied most of the discussion during the Brussels Congress.

De Paepe submitted a plan derived largely from Proudhon's federalism; it envisaged a society organized in a network of communes, federations of communes, and finally a worldwide federation of federations. The communes would deal with all matters of local interest, the world federation with general coordination between regional organizations and with such matters of world interest as scientific exploration and 'the irrigation of the Sahara'. During his report de Paepe used the word 'state' somewhat ambiguously to define his idea of supra-communal organization:

Against the liberal conception of the police state we pose the notion of the state which is not based on armed force, but whose function is to educate the younger members of the population and to centralize such public activities as can be better performed by the state than by the Commune.

Such vagueness of phraseology might have passed unnoticed had not de Paepe at one point expressed a conditional support of the idea of a transitional 'collective dictatorship'. In a passage which the anarchists regarded as particularly offensive he argued:

In view of the political trend of the working class in certain lands, and notably in Britain and Germany, a political trend whose impetus is constitutional today but may be revolutionary tomorrow, one which does not aim at overthrowing the extant state organized from above downwards, but at seizing the state and utilizing its gigantic centralized power for the purpose of emancipating the proletariat ... we may well ask ourselves whether the reconstitution of society upon the foundation of the industrial group, the organization of the state from below upwards, instead of being the starting-point and the signal of the social revolution, might not prove to be its more or less remote result ... We are led to inquire whether, before the grouping of the workers by industry is adequately advanced, circumstances

may not compel the proletariat of the large towns to establish a collective dictatorship over the rest of the population, and this for a
sufficiently long period to sweep away whatever obstacles there may
be to the emancipation of the working class. Should this happen, it
seems obvious that one of the first things which such a collective dictatorship would have to do would be to lay hands on all the public
services, to expropriate for the public benefit the railway companies,
the great engineering works—to declare that all their possessions,
machinery, buildings, and land, had become state property, had
passed into public ownership.

The Jura delegates protested in the name of anarchism, and even some
of the Belgians opposed de Paepe; Verrycken in particular maintained that
to put the workers in the saddle of authority instead of the bourgeoisie
would represent no gain of any kind. But de Paepe stood his ground, and
in doing so he underlined what the discussion was making clear in any
case: that the schism within the old International had not silenced the
basic dialogue on revolutionary strategy. 'The alternatives of workers'
state and anarchy still confront one another,' he insisted. It was in tacit
recognition of this difference, which the Marxists had left as an apple of
discord in the very centre of the Saint-Imier International, that the
Congress decided to take no vote at all on the question of public services
in a future society. It was referred back for discussion in the following year.
   On political action, which again raised its controversial head, there was
more unanimity. Only Eccarius and the Lassalleans argued that the workers should engage in constitutional and parliamentary activity. The
Belgians united with the Jurassians and the Spaniards in denying completely the usefulness of working-class participation in parliamentary
activities. Yet again the decision was based on compromise. 'It must be left
to each federation and to the social democratic party in each country to
decide upon its own line of political behaviour.' In its fervent attempts to
reach decisions that offended nobody the Brussels Congress had merely
accentuated the divisions within the International and hastened the decay
that was already appearing.
   It is true that geographically and in other ways the International still
seemed to be growing during 1875 and 1876. Its influence was reviving
strongly in France and around Lake Leman, and it claimed new groups of
adherents in Latin America, Portugal, Alexandria, and Greece. But it was
losing to parliamentary socialism such influential ex-Communards as
Jules Guesde and Benoît Malon, while its strength in the countries

bordering the North Sea was dwindling sharply. No congress at all met in 1875. There was talk of organizing one in Paris during the spring of 1876, but this did not materialize, and the next plenary gathering took place at Berne toward the end of October 1876, more than two years after the Brussels Congress.

To Berne the Italians returned, with Malatesta and Cafiero at their head, while the Spaniards, French and Swiss were reasonably represented; there was even for the first time a German Swiss delegate. But no one came from Britain, and the Belgians and Dutch between them sent only a single delegate, de Paepe, who brought cold comfort to the Congress by stressing the extent to which the workers in the Low Countries were being influenced by German and English examples and retreating into a north European social-democratic pattern which began to differentiate itself sharply from the anarchistic pattern of the Alpine and Mediterranean regions.

The Italians enlivened the proceedings with passionate speeches in favour of 'propaganda by deed', but on the whole the congress was a more than usually lifeless gathering. The more aggressive authoritarians had dropped away, while de Paepe was willing to make terminological compromises with the Bakuninists which did not really mean an abandonment of the position on the workers' state he had defended at Brussels.

By now it was becoming apparent that the International as at present constituted had little practical reason for existence, and de Paepe emphasized the situation by proposing that in the following year a Universal Socialist Congress should be called in the hope of reuniting the European labour movement. The Spaniards opposed the proposal, but abstained from voting, as did the Italians, who stood beside them on the extreme anarchist left. De Paepe cast the Belgian and Dutch votes for the proposal and was supported by the French and Jura delegates, who occupied the moderate anarchist centre.

The Universal Socialist Congress actually took place at Ghent from 9 to 16 September 1877. Immediately beforehand the Saint-Imier International held its own Congress, from 6 to 8 September, in the industrial town of Verviers, where the Walloon weavers were strongly anarchist It was to be the last Congress of the International; it was also the only one that could be called completely anarchist in both composition and decisions.

Many of the important anarchist leaders were present. Kropotkin, under the name of Levashov, represented the expatriate Russian groups. Paul Brousse led the French delegation and Gonzales Morago the Spanish.

Guillaume represented the French-speaking and Werner the German-speaking Swiss. Andrea Costa carried mandates from groups in Greece and Alexandria, as well as from the Italians. And Costa's handsome mistress, Anna Kulichov, later to play an important part in founding the Italian Socialist Party, was present in a somewhat shadowy role as a delegate with a consultative voice. In addition, anarchist groups in Germany, Mexico, Uruguay, and Argentina were represented. The most significant absentee was de Paepe, who after pointedly avoiding the meeting at Verviers, took part in the Universal Socialist Congress at Ghent two days later.

The decisions of the Verviers Congress were the most unequivocally anarchist the International had ever adopted. Much of the discussion centred around the distribution of the product of labour, and, although no definite conclusion was reached, it was clear that the general feeling was turning toward the anarchist-communist idea of sharing the pool of goods on the basis of need. The task of collectivizing property—the delegates decided—must be undertaken by groups of workers without intervention from above. All political parties—even if they called themselves socialist—must be combated, since all of them were reactionary in their reliance on power and in their failure to recognize that the true divisions in society run not on political but on economic lines. Finally, on the question of trade unions, the delegates at Verviers adopted a resolution that strikingly anticipated the demands of the anarcho-syndicalists twenty years later. Trade unions were inadequate where they aimed merely at increasing wages or reducing hours; they should work toward the destruction of the wage system and the taking over of the control of production.

The Verviers Congress at least gave a deceptive appearance of vigour and unity. The Ghent Congress, far from producing socialist solidarity, merely betrayed the hopes of its Belgian sponsors by emphasizing the differences between the anarchists and their rivals. Only eleven anarchists went on from Verviers to Ghent, while most of the remaining thirty-one delegates were authoritarians, ranging from Wilhelm Liebknecht to de Paepe and his followers. Only one issue brought universal agreement; unanimously—with Andrea Costa alone abstaining—the Congress proclaimed the desirability of founding an international federation of trade unions and passed a resolution calling on all workers who had not already done so to organize themselves industrially. But on such issues as state ownership of the means of production and working-class political activity the anarchists voted in a compact minority against the rest of the Congress.

The divisions between the delegates were too deep and obvious to be ignored by the most optimistic advocates of socialist unity, and this was recognized when the key resolution for a pact of solidarity between the participating movements was defeated. There was to be no new comprehensive International, and the irreconcilability of the two factions was underlined when the social democrats held a secret meeting the same evening to which the anarchists were not invited. There a limited solidarity pact was in fact worked out, and arrangements were made for establishing a central headquarters in Ghent.

Before dispersing, the Congress as a whole had second thoughts on the question of solidarity, and decided at least to establish a Correspondence and Statistics Office for Working-class Socialists, to be situated permanently at Verviers. In fact, neither this office nor the social-democratic headquarters in Ghent was established, and the Universal Socialist Congress did little more than establish, in the minds of continental socialists at least, the idea that it was impossible to work with the anarchists.

Meanwhile, the Saint-Imier International itself disintegrated rapidly, and this happened at a time when the Spanish and Italian movements were vigorous, when the movement in France was reawakening and when a great extension was being given to anarchist ideas by the establishment of federations in several Latin American countries. The International's collapse stemmed mainly from the fact that since the schism in 1872 it had swung on the axis of Belgium and the Jura, the two regions where political conditions allowed sustained and open activity. The numerically large movements in Spain and Italy and the active nuclei in France all suffered from governmental persecutions which made it difficult for them even to maintain their own organizations and which encouraged the kind of separatism shown in the refusal of the Italians to be represented at the Brussels Congress of 1874. Any change in the situation in Belgium or the Jura was therefore bound to affect the International as a whole. And we have seen already how de Paepe with the majority of the Belgian socialists had moved away toward social democracy. By the end of 1876 the Association was dependent on the Jura Federation for its continued existence.

But in the Jura also the situation had been changing from the days of early anarchist enthusiasm which Kropotkin had witnessed in 1872. Economic conditions had worsened, and peasant craftsmen were much more dependent on the watch manufacturers than a few years before. This led to greater caution, and the diminished vitality of the Jura Federation was shown when its *Bulletin*, which for a period had been the leading anarchist journal, ceased publication in March 1878. Even some of the most active militants fell away from the movement. James Guillaume, the close disciple of Bakunin, who had been the most active inspirer of the Jura Federation and one of the key members of the Saint-Imier International, was disillusioned by the failure of the various congresses to achieve any positive results; he departed to Paris in the spring of 1878 and there retired into political inactivity, to emerge after more than two decades as an advocate of syndicalism. Of the important native leaders only Schwitzguébel remained active, and the last congresses in the Jura, held in 1879 and 1880, were dominated by foreign leaders, Kropotkin, Reclus and Cafiero, who used the occasion to hammer out their theories away from the danger of hostile police forces. Soon afterward the once influential Jura Federation faded from the scene as an active organization.

Even before then the Saint-Imier International had slipped quietly into inactivity. It was never formally dissolved, but no congress was called after 1877. However, the idea of international organization was not lost, and in 1880 the Belgian anarchist groups, which had reorganized themselves after the defection of de Paepe and still maintained some strength among the Walloon miners, held a congress in Brussels where the idea of reconstituting the International was discussed. The Belgians made contact with anarchists in other countries, and gained support for their plan of a congress aimed at constituting a wholly libertarian organization. London was chosen as the place of meeting, and a committee was established there, with Gustave Brocher as chairman and Malatesta as an active member.

When the Congress met on 14 July 1881, in the club rooms of a tavern in Charrington Street, some forty-five delegates appeared, claiming to represent sixty federations and fifty-nine individual groups, with a total membership of 50,000. Many of the organizations had only a phantom existence, and it is likely that the estimated membership was exaggerated. Nevertheless, it was a gathering formidable enough to cause alarm in European government circles; the British ambassador in Paris, for instance, reported that the French Minister of Foreign Affairs had expressed concern that the British government should have allowed such a gathering to take place upon its soil. Despite the absence of such stalwarts of former congresses as Guillaume, Cafiero (who was ill in Italy), and Costa and Brousse, who had gone over to parliamentary socialism, its delegates included a fair array of the celebrated names of anarchism. Malatesta and Merlino, Kropotkin and Nicholas Chaikovsky, Louise Michel and Émile Pouget, represented their various countries; among the English delegates were Joseph Lane and Frank Kitz, later to play important parts in the anarchist faction of the Socialist League; Dr Edward Nathan-Ganz represented the Mexican Federation of Workers, and an

elderly New England lady, Miss M.P. Le Comte, came on behalf of the
Boston Revolutionists. Among the French delegates was at least one police
spy, Serreaux, who edited the 'anarchist' journal *Le Révolution sociale* with
money provided by the Paris Prefect of Police, and some of the other delegates were suspected of being *agents provocateurs*; Kropotkin later claimed
that there were at least five of these as well as Serreaux, but this seems an
exaggeration.

The variety of attitudes that characterized anarchists in the later nineteenth century was already evident at the London Congress. Some
thought in terms of conspiratorial activity; others, like Kropotkin, held
that a revolutionary movement must always spring from a broad upsurge
among the people. The idea of propaganda by deed, and the various
aspects of revolutionary violence, came in for copious discussion. There
seems to have been agreement on the general inevitability of violence (for
the pacifist current had not yet entered the anarchist movement), but its
more extreme forms aroused considerable argument. The terrorist phase
of anarchism had not yet begun, but the Congress was held shortly after
the assassination of Alexander II by the People's Will, and this event had
its influence on the discussions. The advocates of extreme violence were
impelled by various motives. Serreaux, the police agent, was naturally
among the most voluble on this subject. On the other hand, there is no
reason to doubt the sincerity of Dr Nathan-Ganz from Mexico, who was
obsessed with the idea of 'chemistry' as a weapon in the class struggle and
with the need for para-military organization. He even suggested a 'military academy' for anarchists, and kept on interrupting the proceedings to
draw attention to the need for 'education in chemistry'.

Kropotkin sought to bring a more realistic tone to the assembly. In particular, speaking as a scientist, he deprecated the light talk he heard about
the use of chemistry. Yet, despite the moderating influence of such men,
there is no doubt that increasing governmental hostility in many countries
was tempting the anarchists to think in terms of underground organization
and spectacular deeds, and in this sense the 1881 Congress opened a period,
extending into the 1890s, when anarchists in general turned away from the
idea of direct-actionists. In the minds of most of the delegates there was
indecision as to whether they wished to create an open organization like
the defunct International or a clandestine organization like Bakunin's
International Brotherhood. Even Kropotkin, at least in private conversation, advocated parallel public and secret movements.

In the end it was resolved to form a new open International, to set up a
permanent correspondence bureau, and to call a congress in London the
following year, while a blanket policy resolution looked forward to a

period of great revolutionary struggles and called for the development of unconstitutional methods, the establishment of wide-spread secret presses, the encouragement of propaganda by deed (with a friendly nod to 'the technical and chemical sciences'), and agitation among the backward rural workers, where the anarchists rightly realized they could make a more effective appeal than the authoritarian socialists.

In practical terms, the congress achieved very little. The 'Black International' it founded was long to remain a terrifying spectre in the minds of governments, but it was no more than a spectre, and its phantom presence seems to have influenced the working-class movement only in the United States. As an organization it never functioned; the correspondence bureau did not come into active existence, and the proposed London Congress of 1882 did not meet.

It was not, indeed, until 1907 that the next real international congress of anarchists took place. During the intervening quarter of a century there were a few gatherings that are sometimes mentioned as international congresses, but all of them were either abortive or limited in scope. A congress of the latter kind was held in Geneva in 1882. Apart from a single Italian delegate, those who attended were all either from France or the Jura; great stress was laid on the absolute autonomy of groups 'in the application of the means that seem to us most efficacious', and the spirit of the gathering was indicated when the delegate from Cette drew unanimous applause by ending his speech with the words, 'We are united because we are divided.'

In fact, this was a time when anarchists inclined toward extreme separatism. A proposal to hold an international congress in Barcelona during 1884 failed because it met indifference in most countries and positive hostility in France. In 1887 a similar proposal for a congress in Paris came to nothing, but in 1889, on the occasion of the International Exhibition in that city, a small conference did in fact take place in the Faubourg du Temple, attended by a dozen delegates from England, Germany, Spain, and Italy, together with representatives of the French groups. This conference appears to have been run on the strictest anarchist principles; no resolutions were passed, no votes were taken, no plans for organization were considered, and the meetings seem to have been devoted merely to a prolix exchange of views on matters of topical importance. In 1892 the French police reported that a group of Paris anarchists was planning the establishment of an international correspondence bureau, but no evidence of this appears elsewhere, and the whole plan may have been created in the mind of an agent short of interesting facts to report. The following year the anarchists of Chicago announced a forthcoming congress, and the editors of *La Révolte* in Paris called on the European movements to take part in it; however, no delegates crossed the Atlantic, and the congress itself was evidently a very slight affair. According to Emma Goldman, it was banned by the Chicago police and took place secretly in a room of the town hall, into which the dozen delegates were smuggled by a friendly clerk.

These rather pitiful efforts are the only specifically anarchist international congresses I have been able to trace from 1881 to the end of the nineteenth century. Their meagreness is at least in part due to the fact that between 1889 and 1896 there was a persistent effort on the part of the anarchists to infiltrate the congresses of the Second International, which the social democrats were then in the process of establishing.

The Second International came into being in 1889, when two rival socialist congresses were held in Paris. One of them was organized by the followers of Jules Guesde; to this came the Marxists from the rest of Europe. The other was organized by the possibilist followers of Paul Brousse, now striving with his former fellow anarchist Guesde for control of parliamentary socialism in France. The anarchists, with admirable impartiality, infiltrated both gatherings. To the Guesdists went Sébastien Faure, Domela Nieuwenhuis (leader of the resurrected anarchist movement in Holland), and the Englishman Frank Kitz; to the possibilist gathering went the Italian Saverio Merlino and the French carpenter-orator Joseph Tortelier, celebrated as an advocate of the general strike. In both gatherings the anarchists vigorously put their point of view; the wider rivalry between the two congresses perhaps explains why no concerted attempt was made to expel them.

When the socialists united in the Brussels Congress of 1891, however, the presence of the anarchists became one of the major issues. They were deliberately not invited, but they appeared, and were dealt with in a very confused manner. Dr Merlino, the Italian who had already distinguished himself by spirited interruptions in 1889, rather surprisingly gained admittance, but on the second day was deported by the Belgian police; the anarchists afterward accused the Marxists of informing on him. The congress itself expelled the Spanish anarchists on the second day, but the Belgian anarchists had been kept out from the beginning. Finally, Domela Nieuwenhuis was allowed to remain, and tried in vain to bring up for discussion such thorny questions as parliamentarism and universal suffrage. Nieuwenhuis, who really began the pacifist trend in the anarchist movement (for Tolstoy and his followers always remained outside organized anarchism and were somewhat hostile to it), also brought forward a strong resolution in favour of a general strike in the event of war, but was defeated by the Marxist majority.

At the Zürich Congress of the Second International in 1893 the anarchists appeared in force, seeking admission on the ground that they too were socialists and heirs of the First International. The German Marxist Bebel led the attack against them. Bebel was addicted to the verbal abuse frequent among the followers of Marx, and he shouted, amid the indignant cries of his opponents: 'They have neither programme nor principles, if it is not the common aim of combating the social democrats whom they consider greater enemies than the bourgeoisie. We can have no relationship with them.' The anarchists were expelled by force, loudly protesting. The old Garibaldian Amilcare Cipriani spoke out against the brutal intolerance of the Marxists and then resigned his mandate. Next a French resolution was passed, declaring that only those socialists who admitted the necessity of political action should be admitted in future to the congresses of the Second International. After their expulsion the anarchists, to the number of sixty, held their own impromptu congress, and later a public meeting attended by a few hundred people, but it was little more than a manifestation of mutual solidarity. *La Révolte* commented, in words that might have been used of almost any other anarchist international gathering:

> There was much speaking and much peroration, but we do not see that this gathering has produced any practical result. A congress is not improvised in twenty-four hours; and then, what is the good of crying from the rooftops that one will do this, that and the other thing? That kind of expenditure of spittle should be left to the social democrats.

The last battle over admission to the Second International was fought at London in 1896; it was also the bitterest. This time the anarchists were strongly entrenched in the French and Dutch delegations, and many of their leaders had come to London with the intention of holding a parallel congress in the event of their expected expulsion from that of the Second International. They included Kropotkin, Malatesta, Nieuwenhuis, Landauer, Pietro Gori, Louise Michel, Élisée Reclus, and Jean Grave, as well as a strong syndicalist group from France headed by the anarchist leaders of the revolutionary wing of the Confédération Générale du Travail (CGT), such as Pelloutier, Tortelier, Pouget, and Delesalle.

The dispute over the anarchists made the London Congress the most stormy of all the gatherings of the Second International. Apart from the French syndicalists, who were admitted by an inconsistent ruling which exempted trade-union delegates from admitting the need for political action, there were more than thirty anarchist delegates. The German chairman, Paul Singer, tried to close the question of admissions without allowing the anarchists to speak. Keir Hardie, leader of the Independent Labour Party, who was deputy chairman that day, protested that both sides should be given a full hearing before the vote was taken. Gustav Landauer, Malatesta, and Nieuwenhuis all spoke at length, and the last effectively summarized their contentions when he said:

This Congress has been called as a general Socialist Congress. The invitations said nothing about anarchists and social democrats. They spoke only of socialists and trade unions. Nobody can deny that people like Kropotkin and Reclus and the whole anarchist-communist movement stand on the socialist basis. If they are excluded, the purpose of the Congress has been misrepresented.

The decision on the admission of the anarchists was delayed by a quarrel within the French delegation over this very issue, which took most of the Congress's second day. By a majority of fifty-seven to fifty-five the French had voted in private caucus against exclusion of the anarchists. But, rather than accept a majority decision so distasteful to themselves, the French Marxists, led by Millerand, decided to withdraw, and asked Congress to authorize two French delegations, each with its own vote. Such a proposal was contrary to the general procedure of the Second International, which gave each country a single vote, and was supported by the German Marxists only because it happened to serve their interests. Both Bernard Shaw and the Belgian socialist Vandervelde attacked the motion, and it was only carried because the Germans had the support of a number of tiny delegations such as those of Poland, Bulgaria, and Romania.

The anarchists were finally expelled on the second day, on a motion that again specifically exempted trade-union delegates: all the delegations eventually voted for expulsion except the French syndicalist faction and the Dutch. However, many anarchists were left as trade-union delegates to carry on the dispute during the verification of mandates, so that in the end little time was left for debating the issues that the Congress had met to discuss. Despite the exclusion of the anarchists, anarchism had in fact dominated the London Congress of the Second International.

What the anarchists themselves lost in being expelled they gained in publicity and in the sympathy of the more liberal-minded socialists. They had planned an evening meeting in the Holborn Town Hall on 28 July, and their expulsion on that day made the gathering a great success. As well as all the anarchist leaders, Keir Hardie and Tom Mann appeared on the platform to make speeches asserting the rights of minorities, and William Morris, now nearing his death, sent a message to say that only sickness prevented him from adding his own voice to the chorus of protest. But the real triumph of the anarchists remained their success in turning the Congress of the Second International into a battleground over the issue of libertarian versus authoritarian socialism. Not only did they effectively present themselves as champions of minority rights; they also provoked the German Marxists into demonstrating a dictatorial intolerance which was a factor in preventing the British labour movement from following the Marxist direction indicated by such leaders as H.M. Hyndman.

Clearly, after the London Congress, there could be no further question of unity between the two opposing wings of the socialist movement. The social democrats recognized it by passing a resolution which, in directing policy for issuing invitations to future congresses, for the first time specifically stated, 'Anarchists will be excluded.' The anarchists recognized it by making no further attempts to invade the Second International.

Yet it was not until 1907, after plans for a congress in Paris had been frustrated by the police in 1900, that they finally assembled to plan anew their own International. During the intervening period, perhaps in reaction to the organizational complexity of the syndicalist wing of the movement, the purist anarchists had tended to stress the pattern of individual militant groups acting autonomously, to such an extent that in France (admittedly an extreme example) there was not even any kind of national federation during the early years of the twentieth century. This fact did not mean that national and international links were lacking, but they were not of the organizational kind. Anarchist literature passed freely from country to country, and the works of men like Bakunin, Kropotkin, and Malatesta were translated into many languages. In addition to this exchange of ideas and propaganda there was also a constant intercourse between anarchist militants, owing largely to the fact that the life of the dedicated revolutionary often forced him to go into temporary exile or even seek an entirely new home abroad. Errico Malatesta agitated and conspired not only in Italy, but also in France, England, Spain, the Levant, the United States, and Argentina, and there were many like him. In this way, anarchist groups frequently had the opportunity to entertain foreign intellectuals and orators and to hear their opinions, while ties of personal friendship or shared experience created a kind of shadow circle of leaders, even less substantial than the mysterious international organization that loomed in the background of Henry James's mind when he wrote *The Princess Casamassima*, but perhaps as influential in its own way. Anarchism was international in theory and to a great extent in practice even if it was only sporadically so in organizational terms.

Though the majority of anarchists in 1907 were to be found in the Latin countries, the initiative from the Amsterdam Congress was taken by the Belgian and Dutch groups. It met from 24 to 31 August, and was the largest gathering of its kind until recent years, attended by eighty delegates from almost every European country, as well as from the United States, Latin America, and Japan. Its proceedings were dominated by Malatesta, not merely because of his prestige as an associate of Bakunin and a veteran of insurrection and conspiracy in many lands, but also because of his dynamic personality and flowery eloquence. The other delegates included many younger men and women who had brought fresh vigour into the movement in recent years, such as Emma Goldman, Rudolf Rocker, the Italian intellectual Luigi Fabbri, the Russian Alexander Schapiro, Tom Keell (editor of *Freedom*), the Dutch syndicalist Christian Cornelissen, and Pierre Monatte, a young and capable militant from the revolutionary wing of the French CGT.

Owing to the mental calibre of those who attended it, this was one of the livliest anarchist congresses, and it took place in an atmosphere of confidence, largely because of the impetus given to the spread of anarchistic teachings through the extension of revolutionary syndicalism from France to Spain, Italy, Latin America, and the Germanic countries of the north, where vigorous anarcho-syndicalist minorities existed in Germany, Sweden, and Holland.

The syndicalist issue was dramatized by a great debate between Malatesta and Monatte which emphasized the presence of two clearly identifiable currents of anarchist opinion at this period. Monatte saw the revolutionary trade union as the means and end of revolutionary action. Through unions the workers could carry on their struggle against capitalism and precipitate its final end by the millennial general strike; then the union could become the basic structure of the new society, where the solidarity of the workers would find concrete form through individual organization.

Despite his idealistic devotion to the anarchist cause, Malatesta had too practical a mind to ignore the weapon which syndicalist forms of action

might place in its hands. But he insisted that syndicalism could be regarded only as a means, and an imperfect means at that, since it was based on a
rigid class conception of society, which ignored the fact that the interests
of the workers varied so much that 'sometimes workers are economically
and morally much nearer to the bourgeoisie than to the proletariat'.
Furthermore, immersion in union affairs and a simple faith in the general
strike was not only unrealistic; it also led revolutionary militants to
neglect other means of struggle, and particularly to ignore the fact that
the great revolutionary task would not be for the workers to stop working
but, as Kropotkin had pointed out, for them to 'continue working on their
own account'. The extreme syndicalists, in Malatesta's view, were seeking
an illusory economic solidarity instead of a real moral solidarity; they
placed the interests of a single class above the true anarchist ideal of a revolution which sought 'the complete liberation of all humanity, at present
enslaved, from the triple economic, political, and moral point of view'.

The two other issues, anti-militarism and the organization of the anarchist movement, occupied the attention of the Congress. Its delegates
identified the struggle against war with the struggle against an authoritarian society, and the resolution that eventually emerged combined both
concepts.

> The anarchists urge their comrades and all men aspiring to liberty,
> to struggle according to circumstances and their own temperaments,
> and by all means—individual revolt, isolated or collective refusal of
> service, passive and active disobedience and the military strike—for
> the radical destruction of the instruments of domination. They
> express the hope that all the peoples concerned will reply to any
> declaration of war by insurrection and consider that anarchists
> should give the example.

It was a bold-sounding but vague resolution, and, as one of the delegates was quick to suggest, it did not provide what was really needed, 'a
concrete programme of propaganda and anti-militarist action'. But, given
the anarchist emphasis on autonomous action and distrust of any kind of
centralized decision that might be interpreted as binding on groups and
individuals, a concrete programme was the very thing an International
Congress could not provide.

Organization at this time was a crucial issue in the anarchist movement.
Many militants, particularly among the French, had stayed away from the
Congress because of their opposition to any organization more elaborate

than the loose local group, and yet there was still a considerable debate on the question of how far organization should be carried. Eventually the Congress came to the conclusion—rejected by many critics within the movement—that 'the ideas of anarchy and organization, far from being incompatible, as has sometimes been pretended, in fact complement and illuminate each other'. As a practical manifestation of this belief, the assembled anarchists decided to establish yet another International, and to set up a bureau, of which Malatesta, Rocker, and Schapiro were members, charged with 'creating international anarchist archives' and maintaining relationships with the anarchists of various countries. The bureau was to work in London, and to arrange a further International Congress in 1909.

In fact a familiar pattern was repeated. The 1909 Congress never took place, and the new International led a brief, sickly existence. Its Bureau started to publish a monthly bulletin of information, but this ceased to appear early in 1909 with the twelfth number, after complaining that 'apathy has overcome all those who clamoured most loudly at the Congress on the need for the Anarchist International'. By 1911 the Bureau—and the International with it—had ceased its activities.

By 1914 the pendulum had again swung away from indifference, and a project for a new International Congress in London was set on foot by the Jewish groups of the East End, but war broke out before it could take place. With the war came not only the isolation of national movements by hostile frontiers and their persecution by belligerent governments in the interests of security, but also the schism over the question of supporting the Allies which I have already discussed in relation to Kropotkin. For these various reasons the anarchist movements, except in neutral Spain, emerged from the war greatly weakened, and the Amsterdam Congress remained their last important international meeting until after the Second World War.

Yet a moderately successful and, for the first time, a durable anti-authoritarian International did emerge during the early 1920s from the anarcho-syndicalist wing of the movement. In the early period of syndicalism the anarchists, in France and Italy especially, were mingled with reformist trade-unionists in the same federations. These bodies first sought unity within the Trade Union International, founded in Amsterdam in 1905. Here for some years the anarcho-syndicalists formed a perpetually uneasy left wing, and by 1911 the desire to break away from the reformist majority of the Amsterdam International reached the point where they began to consider seriously forming an independent organization. The idea had in fact been circulating since the anarchist Congress of

1907, when Christian Cornelissen founded a *Bulletin international du mouve-ment syndicaliste*, which served as a means of exchanging opinions and information between the revolutionary syndicalist factions in the various European and American countries.

At the end of 1913 an International Congress in London was attended by delegates from twelve countries in Europe and South America. The war intervened before the organization it sought to found could get under way, and by 1918 the syndicalist urge toward international organization was temporarily diverted by the Russian Revolution. After October 1917 the Bolsheviks assiduously wooed the anarcho-syndicalists in those countries where they represented a majority of the revolutionary movements, and at the founding congress of the Comintern, in July 1920, there appeared rep-resentatives from almost all the anarcho-syndicalist organizations of Europe, as well as the American IWW.

It was clear from the start of this congress that the syndicalists were unhappy with the rigidly partisan form which the Bolsheviks intended to impose on the Comintern, and the Russian leaders therefore decided that it might be easier to accommodate them in a separate organization of rev-olutionary trade unions. With this intent, after a year of preparation, a congress met in Moscow during July 1921 to found the Red International of Labour Unions, better known as the Profintern. The anarcho-syndicalists, who had held a brief international meeting in Berlin during December 1920 to discuss their attitude to the Profintern, agreed to take part in it provided it became completely independent of political parties and aimed at reconstructing society by means of the 'economic organization of the producing classes'. This effort to create a syndicalist policy for a commu-nist body was frustrated by the fact that the Profintern Congress was effectively dominated by the Bolshevik-controlled Central Alliance of Russian Trade Unions.

The immediate result was a split in the anarcho-syndicalist ranks. The smaller organizations of northern Europe—Germany, Sweden, Holland, Norway—seceded immediately, but the larger Spanish, Italian, and French organizations remained for a while in the hope of forming an effective minority. On the initiative of the German Freie Arbeiter Union, the seceding groups held a conference in Düsseldorf during October 1921 and decided to call a general Revolutionary Syndicalist Congress in Berlin late in the following year. In the meantime, the Italian and Spanish organi-zations left the Profintern during 1922, and the anarchist wing of the French CGTU split away, leaving the larger part of that organization in the communist camp. Thus, though many individual syndicalists were converted to communism, most of the western European anarcho-syndicalist organizations had broken their links with Moscow by the time the Berlin Congress met on 22 December 1922.

This congress was attended by delegates from twelve countries, representing organizations claiming rather more than a million members. The most important were the Unione Sindicale Italiana, with 500,000 members; the Federación Obrera Regional Argentina, with 200,000 members; the Portuguese Confederação General de Trabalho, with 150,000 members; and the German Freie Arbeiter Union, with 120,000 members. There were smaller organizations from Chile, Denmark, Norway, Mexico, Holland, and Sweden, whose Sveriges Arbetares Central, then claiming more than 30,000 members, has remained the most durable of all syndicalist unions. The French Comité de Défense Syndicaliste Révolutionnaire represented 100,000 anarcho-syndicalists who had broken away from the Profintern, and 30,000 Paris building workers sent a separate delegation. Finally, there were the representatives of the exiled Russian anarcho-syndicalists.

The major decision of the congress was to set up an International of Revolutionary Syndicalists and to emphasize its continuity with the anarchist past by taking the old name of International Workingmen's Association. The delegates also adopted a lengthy document called 'The Principles of Revolutionary Syndicalism', whose ten paragraphs restated succinctly the basic principles of revolutionary unionism, rejected nationalism, militarism, and political activity, and, by stating the goal of syndicalist endeavour to be free communism, at least bowed dutifully to the other current of anarchist thought and its dead leader, Kropotkin.

During the 1920s the new International expanded considerably. The Spanish CNT entered with almost a million members in 1923, and small federations in Poland, Bulgaria and Japan also joined. In Latin America a Continental Workingmen's Association was founded in 1928, made up of syndicalist unions in Argentina, Mexico, Brazil, Costa Rica, Paraguay, Bolivia, Guatemala, and Uruguay, with its headquarters first in Buenos Aires and later in Montevideo. This organization entered the International Workingmen's Association as its American division.

At its height, the International Workingmen's Association counted more than three million members, but it must be remembered that by no means all of them were convinced anarchists, and that the memberships of some of the constituent organizations, such as the Spanish CNT, fluctuated greatly according to economic and political circumstances. Furthermore, the spread of dictatorship during the years between the wars soon began to wear away at the syndicalist movement. It was the largest organizations that became the earliest victims. The Unione Sindicale Italiana collapsed with the advent of fascism; it was followed into extinction by the Portuguese, Argentinian, and German movements, and eventually, in 1939, the largest union of all, the CNT, was reduced to a remnant of exiles by Franco's victory in the Civil War.

These political misadventures made the life of the International Workingmen's Association precarious in the extreme. From its foundation in 1922 the centre remained for a decade in Berlin, where the principal organizational work was carried out by Germans, Swedes, and Dutch, led by Rudolf Rocker, for many years the leading figure in the IWMA. When the threat of Nazi dictatorship grew strong in 1932, the International Bureau was moved to Amsterdam and it remained there until 1936. In that year syndicalism assumed a dramatic role with the outbreak of the Spanish Civil War, and the Bureau moved to Madrid, where, at the centre of the conflict, it played an important part in putting the anarchist case to labour movements in other countries. Indeed, because it attracted so many foreign volunteers willing to fight beside or otherwise assist the Spanish anarchists, Barcelona seemed for a great part of the Spanish Civil War to provide a kind of unofficial cohesion within the international movement without any congress actually taking place. Finally, in 1939, the Bureau made its last move to Stockholm, where it has remained ever since, sheltered and supported by the still active Sveriges Arbetares Central. Since 1976, the IWMA has enjoyed a new lease of life with the revival, even though in a much reduced form, of what was always its most important constituent group, the CNT in Spain.

The reason the anarcho-syndicalist International has survived, even as a shadow of its earlier self, while the international organizations of purist anarchists have all led short, ineffectual lives—or have even failed to survive the congresses that founded them—can be found at least partly in the nature of syndicalist organizations. Their most militant members may be devoted libertarians, but most of the rank and file will be workers seeking the best kind of life they can find here and now, and for this reason even the revolutionary syndicate has to share with ordinary trade unions a stability and even—though this may be overtly denied—a centralization of structure which is never encountered among purely anarchist groups devoted to propaganda by word or deed.

The anarchist purist, whether he is an intellectual, a direct-actionist, or a secular prophet, is an individualist working with other individuals; the syndicalist militant—even when he calls himself an anarcho-syndicalist—

is an organizer working with the masses. In his own way he develops an organizational outlook, and this makes him more capable of carrying out fairly elaborate plans and of keeping a complex association working over a long period. There were men of this kind, as we shall see, in both the French CGT and the Spanish CNT. In the case of the International Workingmen's Association, the German, Swedish, and Dutch intellectuals who ran the organization were men who combined libertarian ideals with a respect for efficiency derived from their own Germanic cultures.

As for the anarchists as distinct from the anarcho-syndicalists, the period after the Second World War tended to repeat in organizational terms the pattern of earlier times. National federations did emerge and even survived in some countries like France and Italy, though the Anarchist Federation of Great Britain broke apart in 1944, falling into the hands of extreme syndicalists, under whose control it died, and later attempts to re-create a British national organization were only fitfully successful. Not even the will to create a durable organization was evident in the various international congresses, in Berne, in Paris, in Carrara, in Venice, that had taken place during the post-war era.

The congress in Berne was held in 1946 to mark the seventieth anniversary of Michael Bakunin's death in that city. Travel in Europe was still difficult so shortly after the end of the war, and the only participants from outside Switzerland were George Woodcock, who came from England, and two delegates from southern France, who had crossed the frontier illegally. Italians and Germans, Poles and other French were there, but they represented only themselves, since they had spent the war as refugees in Switzerland. For the rest, the congress consisted of delegates from various areas of Switzerland, speaking all the Swiss languages, so that the flavour rather than the reality of internationalism was given, particularly at the polyglot ceremony over Bakunin's grave. But no lasting links were made at this congress or at the later gatherings in the 1950s, which still consisted largely of representatives of revived traditional movements.

The atmosphere was entirely different at the International Congress which was held at Carrara in August 1968, towards the end of the radical 1960s, and in the wake of the Paris uprising of May and June that year. Some of the more dramatic student leaders like Daniel Cohn-Bendit made an appearance, and the congress reflected the revival of anarchism in new forms that had occurred during the decade. It also reflected a recognition on the part of many of the younger people present that the field of protest had broadened out into so many fronts where anarchists became involved with people who did not entirely share their viewpoints—environmentalism, feminism, opposition to nuclear war—that it was impossible to sustain the traditional orthodoxies that had grown up in the nineteenth century. One British delegate represented the shift in viewpoint when he argued that 'our aim is not the struggle for anarchism as an abstract ideal but as a revolutionary movement with the most libertarian character possible. That is why we prefer to work with large numbers of revolutionaries some of whom might not bear our anarchist label rather than with certain anarchists for whom the only thing that made them anarchists was the use of the label itself.'

It is a remarkable feature of anarchism as a movement that it can endure and thrive on the very disagreements that make it virtually impossible to organize, and the Carrara Congress, which failed to create a new International, illustrated the fruitful flexibility that has enabled the more doctrinaire anarchists, who still think in old-fashioned ways of revolutions, and the pragmatists, who seek ways by which a measure of anarchy can be realized in contemporary society, to continue in contact and to work together.

It would be hard to find more striking evidence of the international revival of anarchism than the largest of all libertarian congresses, held in Venice during the summer of 1984 and attended by no less than three thousand people from many countries. Some went as delegates but more as individuals. The congress, which was publicly welcomed by the Venice municipality, revealed that though anarchism had re-emerged nowhere in the world as a mass movement, it had reasserted its right to consideration and respect as a viable socio-political policy with a great deal to contribute to a troubled world in the way of crucial and constructive thought. By 1984 nobody even thought of creating an International; it was tacitly recognized that such outdated organizational ideas should be left to the authoritarian socialists who needed rigid structures to keep united; the anarchists could always come together like migrating birds when the need occurred to them.

Looking back over the history of the anarchist Internationals, it seems evident that logically pure anarchism goes against its own nature when it attempts to create elaborate international or even national organizations, which need a measure of rigidity and centralization to survive. The loose and flexible affinity group is the natural unit of anarchism. Nor does it seem to need anything more elaborate to become international in character, since anarchist ideas were able to spread far over the earth—in the days when they were historically appropriate—by an invisible network of personal contacts and intellectual influences. The anarchist Internationals all failed, principally because they were unnecessary.

But syndicalism, even in its revolutionary form, needs relatively stable organizations and succeeds in creating them precisely because it moves in a world that is only partly governed by anarchist ideals, because it has to consider and make compromises with the day-to-day situation of labour, because it has to maintain the allegiance of masses of working men who are only remotely conscious of the final aim of anarchism. The relative success and the eventual durability of the second International Workingmen's Association is therefore no true triumph of anarchism; it is rather a monument to a period when some anarchists learned to compromise deeply with the actualities of a pre-anarchist world.

10. Anarchism in France

IN England, with Winstanley and Godwin, anarchism first appeared as a recognizable social doctrine. In Spain it attained its largest numerical support. In Russia it produced, with Kropotkin, Bakunin, and Tolstoy, its most distinguished group of theoreticians. Yet for many reasons it is France that deserves pride of place among the countries that have contributed to the anarchist tradition. This is not merely because it is the country of Proudhon, from whom most varieties of anarchism draw their ultimate inspiration, or because Proudhon's mutualist disciples in the First International created the prototype of an organized anarchist movement. It is also because in France the various implications of anarchism were explored with a passion and a logical extremity rare elsewhere. In France the only form of anarchism that gained real mass support—anarcho-syndicalism—was first developed; in France the contradictory trend of extreme individualism was carried to its grim conclusions by a series of dedicated assassins; yet in France anarchism, as a doctrine of almost spiritual intensity, also caught the imagination of poets and painters to such an extent that its links with symbolism and post-impressionism form one of the most interesting aspects of that *fin-de-siècle* world in which it reached its fertile and sensational apogee.

As I have shown, the early stirrings of French anarchism can be found among the Enragés of 1793 and among the mutualist working men of Lyons with whom Proudhon mingled during the 1840s. In 1848 anarchism was peculiarly associated with Proudhon, and in a sense Proudhon and the disciples who helped him with *Le Représentant du peuple* and the People's Bank—Darimon, Duchêne, Langlois, Ramón de la Sagra—established the primitive form of the anarchist functional group, dedicated not to political partisanship but to the tasks of propaganda and economic organization.

Of Proudhon's own significance and of the way in which he consistently personified the anarchist viewpoint during the dark Bonapartist days from 1849 to his death in 1865, I have already written sufficiently, but before I begin to discuss the broadening of anarchism into a distinct movement through the activities of his followers, it is desirable to consider three lesser-known men who during this early period made independent contributions to the anarchist tradition in France.

Most of the revolutionaries who turned toward anarchism as a consequence of 1848 did so by virtue of hindsight, but one man at least, independently of Proudhon, made his defence of the libertarian attitude during the Year of Revolutions itself. 'Anarchy is order: government is civil war.' It was under this slogan, as wilfully paradoxical as any of Proudhon's, that Anselme Bellegarrigue made his brief, obscure appearance in anarchist history. Bellegarrigue appears to have been a man of some education, but little is known of his life before the very eve of 1848; he arrived back in Paris on 23 February from a journey in the United States, where he had met President Polk on a Mississippi steamer and had developed an admiration for the more individualistic aspects of American democracy. According to his own account, he was as little impressed as Proudhon by the revolution that broke out on his first morning back in Paris. A young National Guardsman outside the Hôtel de Ville boasted to him that this time the workers would not be robbed of their victory. 'They have robbed you already of your victory,' replied Bellegarrigue. 'Have you not named a government?'

Bellegarrigue appears to have left Paris very soon, for later in the year he published from Toulouse the first of his works that has survived, a pamphlet entitled *Au fait! Au fait! Interprétation de l'idée démocratique*, the epigraph, in English, reads: 'A people is always governed too much.' During 1849 Bellegarrigue was writing articles attacking the Republic in a Toulouse newspaper, *La Civilisation*, but by early 1850 he had moved to the little village of Mézy, close to Paris, where, with a number of friends who had formed an Association of Free Thinkers, he attempted to set up a community devoted to libertarian propaganda and natural living. Their apparently harmless activities soon attracted the attention of the police; one of their members, Jules Cledat, was arrested, and the community then dispersed.

Bellegarrigue returned to Paris, where he now planned a monthly journal devoted to his ideas. The first number of *L'Anarchie: journal de l'ordre* appeared in April 1850; it was the first periodical actually to adopt the anarchist label, and Bellegarrigue combined the functions of editor, manager, and sole contributor. Owing to lack of funds, only two issues of *L'Anarchie* appeared, and though Bellegarrigue later planned an *Almanach de l'anarchie* this does not seem to have been published. Shortly afterward this elusive libertarian pioneer disappeared into the depths of Latin America, where he is said to have been a teacher in Honduras and even—

briefly—some kind of government official in El Salvador, before he died—
as he was born—at a time and place unknown.

Bellegarrigue stood near to Stirner at the individualist end of the anarchist spectrum. He dissociated himself from all the political revolutionaries of 1848, and even Proudhon, whom he resembled in many of his ideas
and from whom he derived more than he was inclined to admit, he treated
with little respect, granting merely that 'sometimes he steps out of the old
routine to cast a few illuminations on general interests'.

At times Bellegarrigue spoke in the words of solipsistic egoism. 'I deny
everything; I affirm only myself ... I am, that is a positive fact. All the rest
is abstract and falls into Mathematical X, into the unknown ... There can
be on earth no interest superior to mine, no interest to which I owe even
the partial sacrifice of my interests.' Yet in apparent contradiction,
Bellegarrigue adhered to the central anarchist tradition in his idea of society as necessary and natural and as having 'a primordial existence which
resists all destructions and all disorganizations'. The expression of society
Bellegarrigue finds in the commune, which is not an artificial construction
but a 'fundamental organism' and which, provided rulers do not interfere,
can be relied on to reconcile the interests of the individuals who compose
it. It is in all men's interests to observe 'the rules of providential harmony',
and for this reason all governments, armies, and bureaucracies must be
suppressed. This task must be carried out neither by political parties,
which will always seek to dominate, nor by violent revolution, which
needs leaders like any other military operation. The people, once enlightened, must act for itself.

> It will make its own revolution, by the sole strength of right, the
> force of inertia, *the refusal to cooperate*. From the refusal to cooperate
> stems the abrogation of the laws that legalize murder, and the
> proclamation of equity.

This conception of revolution by civil disobedience suggests that in
America Bellegarrigue may have made contact with at least the ideas of
Thoreau, and there is much that anticipates American individualist anarchism in Bellegarrigue's stress on possession as a guarantee of freedom,
though this of course he shared with Proudhon. His picture of the progression of the free individual places him clearly outside the collectivist or
communist trend in anarchism.

> He works and therefore he speculates; he speculates and therefore
> he gains; he gains and therefore he possesses; he possesses and there-

fore he is free. *By possession he sets himself up in an opposition of principle to the state, for the logic of the state rigorously excludes individual possession.*

A different current of anarchism is represented by the two other men of the 1850s who merit our attention. Unlike Proudhon and Bellegarrigue, both Ernest Coeurderoy and Joseph Déjacque were physically involved in the revolution of 1848. As young men in their twenties, they took active parts in the February rising, and Déjacque at least fought on the barricades of the workers' insurrection during June 1848. He was imprisoned, but released in time to take part, like Coeurderoy, in the insurrection of 13 June 1849, when the republicans of the Mountain rose belatedly against the Presidency of Louis-Napoleon. Coeurderoy fled to Switzerland and was condemned in his absence to transportation. Déjacque escaped with a slight sentence, but two years later he also fled, to avoid heavy punishment for having written revolutionary verses; he was condemned in his absence to two years' imprisonment.

Coeurderoy spent the rest of his life in exile, travelling restlessly from country to country—Spain, Belgium, Italy, Switzerland—and dying in poverty near Geneva in 1862. Déjacque travelled farther; he reached New York in 1854 and spent seven years in that city and in New Orleans. In 1861 he returned to France, and he appears to have died some time during the 1860s, though the accounts of his death are vague and contradictory; according to one, he died mad in 1864, according to another he committed suicide in 1867, and according to a third he found consolation in religion and died peacefully at an unspecified time. The very doubt that attends his passing out of life suggests the obscurity in which his final years were lived. Not merely are there remarkable parallels between the lives of Coeurderoy and Déjacque, but their writings also reveal the same kind of sombre desperation, a desperation that must have been widespread among the disillusioned exiles of the Second Empire.

Coeurderoy, who was a physician and an intellectual, is best known for a philosophizing autobiography entitled *Jours d'exil*, which he published in Brussels during 1854, but he also wrote during the same decade a number of polemical works, including *Révolution dans l'homme et dans la société*, the bitterly ironical *Hurrah! ou la révolution par les Cosaques*, and a *Letter to Alexander Herzen*, whose ideas influenced him considerably.

The progression of Coeurderoy seems to have led him from Jacobinism, through Blanquism, to a final rejection in exile of all the political and authoritarian revolutionary groups. He signalized his break with them by publishing in 1852 a pamphlet attacking, among other venerated expatriates, Mazzini, Ledru-Rollin, Cabet, and Pierre Leroux. He significantly omitted Proudhon from those he so emphatically rejected.

Coeurderoy was not a very clear or specific writer. His style was romantically lush and he was given to wordy passages of rhapsodical prophecy. At the same time, he harboured a passion for destruction as extraordinary as Bakunin's. He believed that a new barbarism might be necessary before society could be regenerated. He longed to set the torch to the old world, beginning with his own father's house.

> Disorder is salvation, it is order [he cried]. What do you fear from the uprising of all the peoples, from the unleashing of all the instincts, from the clash of all the doctrines? ... Anarchist revolutionaries, we can take hope only in the human deluge, we can take hope only in chaos, we have no recourse but a general war.

The idea of the liberating general war, of the universal uprising of the peoples, haunted Coeurderoy; nowhere else does the apocalyptic strain in anarchism reach quite the same intensity as in the prophetic passages of *Hurrah! ou la révolution par les Cosaques*, where destructionism and Satanism are combined in a startling vision of man rising upward and asserting his dignity through the paradoxically revivifying processes of war:

> Forward! Forward! War is Redemption! God desires it, the God of the criminals, of the oppressed, of the rebels, of the poor, of all those who are tormented, the Satanic God whose body is of brimstone, whose wings are of fire and whose sandals are of bronze! The God of courage and of insurrection who unleashes the furies in our hearts— our God! No more isolated conspiracies, no more chattering parties, no more secret societies! All that is nothing and can achieve nothing! Stand up, Man, stand up, people, stand up, all who are not satisfied! Stand up for right, well-being, and life! Stand up, and in a few days you will be millions. Forward in great human oceans, in great masses of brass and iron, to the vast music of ideas! Money will no longer avail against a world that rises up! Forward from pole to pole, forward, all peoples from the rising to the setting of the sun! Let the globe tremble under your feet. Forward! War is life! The war against evil is a good war!

It is the vision of the world revolution in the image of Armageddon, yet beneath all its violence of phrase lurk ideas advocated more soberly by Kropotkin and even Proudhon: that political methods are unavailing, that the liberation of the people is their own task, that no power could stand against a humanity resolved and united in the war against injustice and social evil.

Coeurderoy set himself against conspiracy and the secret society, features of his own Blanquist past, and in this sense his advocacy of violence does not really anticipate the attitude of those who came forward in the 1870s as propagandists of the deed. He did not see the deed as an isolated provocative or preparatory act; he saw it as an apocalyptic fact, part of a cumulative and irresistible process of liberation through destruction.

In Déjacque, on the other hand, we meet the true ancestor of the theorists of propaganda by deed, and of the ascetic assassins of the 1890s. But we meet also a man to whom the paradox of a natural order arising out of disorder was as provocative as it had been for Proudhon. Like Proudhon, Déjacque was a manual worker—an upholsterer—and like him he had an original mind, a natural power of writing, and a considerable self-taught erudition. He called himself a 'social poet', and published two volumes of heavily didactic verse—*Lazaréennes* and *Les Pyrénées nivelées*. In New York, from 1858 to 1861, he edited an anarchist paper entitled *Le Libertaire, journal du mouvement social*,*—in whose pages he printed as a serial his vision of the anarchist Utopia, entitled *L'Humanisphère*. And he expounded his 'war on civilization by criminal means' in a treatise entitled *La Question révolutionnaire*, which was written in 1852 among the peaceful gardens of Jersey and read to a unanimously disapproving audience at the Society of the Universal Republic in New York before eventually being published in that city during 1854.

Déjacque's advocacy of violence was so extreme as to embarrass even the anarchists in a later generation, for when Jean Grave came to reprint *L'Humanisphère* in 1899 he eliminated many passages that might have been interpreted as incitements to criminal acts. Unlike Coeurderoy, Déjacque retained the idea of conspiratorial and secret action as a means of destroying the old society in order to make way for the new. He envisaged a campaign for the final abolition of religion and property, the family and the state, which would be carried out by small anarchist groups, each containing three or four direct-actionists who would be willing to use steel and poison and fire to hasten the destruction of the old order. Clearly, despite his avowed admiration for Proudhon, Déjacque went far beyond him, attacking institutions—like the family—which Proudhon considered sacred nuclei of a free society, and recommending means which Proud-

---

*Sébastien Faure, who founded *Le Libertaire* in 1895, is often credited with having invented the word *libertarian* as a convenient synonym for anarchist. However, Déjacque's use of the word as early as 1858 suggests that it may have had a long currency before Faure adopted it.

hon, though he never declared himself a pacifist, would have considered
repugnant because of their amorality. In his conviction that all moral con-
straints must be relaxed in the cause of the revolution, Déjacque anticipated Nechayev, but he did not accept Nechayev's concept of hierarchical
discipline as necessary for the revolutionary movement.

Déjacque balanced a passion for destruction with an equally strong passion for order, which he developed in *L'Humanisphère*. For reasons I have
already discussed, anarchists rarely construct Utopias, but Déjacque's
humanispherical world, which he imagined might have evolved by the
year 2858, stands in the true Utopian tradition and in some remarkable
ways anticipates the vision of the future which H.G. Wells projected in
Men Like Gods.

> Man holding up in his hands the sceptre of science [says Déjacque]
> has henceforward the power which formerly one attributed to the
> gods, in the good old times of the hallucinations of ignorance, and
> according to his will he makes rain and good weather and commands
> the seasons.

As a result of these godlike powers, humanispherical man makes the
desert blossom and brings eternal spring to the poles; he has channelled
the heat of volcanoes and domesticated the beasts of prey, so that lions are
children's pets. In this kind of futurist fantasy one soon begins to see the
influence of Fourier, and when we come to Déjacque's actual proposals for
social organization the Phalansterian influence is evident; it is Fourier
modified by his opposite, Proudhon.

In Déjacque's world of the future, the great metropolises of the nineteenth century will disappear, and on their sites will rise enormous monumental meeting halls, called cyclideons, each capable of holding million
people, and conceived by Déjacque as 'altars of the social cult, anarchic
churches of Utopian humanity'. There, in the total liberty of discussion,
'the free and great voice of the public' will be heard; there the solemn cer-
emonials of the libertarian world and its vast universal exhibitions—an
idea which haunted nineteenth-century anarchists as much as it did mid-
Victorian liberal princes—will take place in grandiloquent splendour.

At the same time the actual working lives of the people will be centralized into humanispheres, which bear a strong resemblance to Fourier's
phalansteries, without their hierarchical organization. Each will contain
five or six thousand people, housed in a great building of twelve wings
radiating like enormous starfish. Though the physical form of the humanispherical community is so rigidly set by its author, the life within it will be

conducted on the principles of complete freedom, so that members will be allowed to exchange apartments and to change their work whenever they desire, since labour will be organized on Fourier's principle of attraction. The family will be abolished, love will be free, and children will be lodged separately and cared for by those whose instincts of maternity or paternity are well developed. Workshops and stores will be integrated into the star pattern of the humanisphere, and in the centre will be the assembly hall, the place for dealing with 'questions of social organization', in which the seemingly rigid physical pattern of the humanisphere will be counterbalanced by its intellectual liberty.

In this parliament of anarchy, each is his own representative and the peer of his associates. Oh, it is very different from what happens among the civilized; one does not perorate, one does not debate, one does not vote, one does not legislate, but all, young and old, men and women, confer in common on the needs of the humanisphere. It is each individual's own initiative that grants or refuses him speech, according as he believes it useful to speak or otherwise ... Neither the majority nor the minority ever makes the law. If a proposition can gather enough workers to put it into operation, whether they be in the majority or the minority, it is carried out, so long as it accords with the will of those who support it. And usually it happens that the majority rallies to the minority, or the minority to the majority ... each yielding to the attraction of finding himself united with the rest.

Natural solidarity, in other words, becomes the uniting and activating force of the humanisphere, as it is in the world seen by all anarchists. It is true that an administrative bureau will exist in each humanisphere, but 'its only authority is the *book of statistics*'. Just as each individual will be his own master in every respect, so each humanisphere will be autonomous, and the only relation existing between the various communities will be economic, based on the exchange of products. But this exchange will be free in nature, deriving from universal benevolence and keeping no account of obligations.

Exchange takes place naturally and not arbitrarily. Thus one human sphere may give more one day and receive less; it matters little, since tomorrow it will doubtless receive more and give less.

Here, mingled with so much that derives obviously from Fourier and from Proudhon, we have a clear anticipation of the ideas of economic organization elaborated by Kropotkin in *The Conquest of Bread*; since Jean Grave republished *L'Humanisphère* it is possible that his friend Kropotkin was aware of Déjacque's ideas.

I have dwelt at some length on Bellegarrigue, Coeurderoy, and Déjacque in order to show the variety of thought among French anarchists even during that early period of the 1850s. But none of these men exercised any appreciable influence, either direct or deferred, and when anarchism began to gain importance in France during the 1860s it was at first mutualist in character, deriving almost entirely from the ideas Proudhon elaborated during his last months in *De la capacité politique des classes ouvrières*. Although some of the mutualist leaders, such as Tolain and Limousin, departed from Proudhon's abstentionist attitude toward politics by appearing as candidates in elections, the movement was generally non-political in character and sought to permeate the workers' associations of various kinds that were beginning to emerge as a result of Napoleon III's policy of trying to woo the support of the lower classes. Mutualism not only became a dominant influence in many of these organizations, particularly where they had a cooperative orientation; its advocates also began, in various directions, to revive libertarian journalism.

Some of the most active propagandists were friends of Proudhon, like Darimon, who advocated popular banking in *La Presse*, and Langlois, who wrote in *Rive gauche*, the organ of the younger republican intellectuals. But more typical of the current trend was the desire of the Proudhonian working men to establish their own journals; in June 1865 *La Tribune ouvrière* appeared, announced by its editors as 'a kind of thermometer of the intellectual development of the labouring classes'. In the four numbers of *La Tribune ouvrière* the most active contributors were the craftsmen already involved in the creation of the International, particularly Tolain and Limousin. They avoided direct political attacks on the government, and concentrated a great deal on criticizing bourgeois conceptions of art and science from the point of view laid down by Proudhon in *Du Principe de l'art*, but their evident anti-clericalism was distasteful to the government and their review was soon suppressed. Its editors then attempted to publish a journal in Brussels for importation into France. However, the first number of *La Presse ouvrière* was seized by the customs officers, and, though one issue of its successor, *La Fourmi*, was allowed to pass the frontier, the police issued a warning that any further numbers would be seized. Opposed as they were to clandestine activity, the mutualists accepted the situation and began to contribute articles to a friendly republican paper, *L'Avenir national.*

Workers' association and mutual credit were the panaceas which the mutualists put forward in *L'Avenir national*, as they did in the avowedly Proudhonian and socialist paper, *Le Courrier français*, which the poet Vermorel established shortly afterward. Vermorel himself was a thorny, uncompromising journalist, and in the pages of *Le Courrier français* some of the Proudhonian fire of 1848 and 1849 returned to Parisian journalism. Duchêne and Tolain, Jules Guesde and Paul Lafargue, all wrote in its pages, whose vigorous criticism of government and financiers alike upheld Vermorel's claim to have raised once again the banner of socialism and to have provided its first avowed and authentic organ since the disappearance of *Le Peuple*. Its fate was not unlike that of Proudhon's papers. Crippled by persecutions, fines, and libel suits, it came to an end in 1868.

In the meantime, however, a considerable working-class movement, largely dominated by Proudhonian ideas, was coming into existence as a result of the activities of the International. The beginnings of the Association in France had been slow. Tolain, Fribourg, and Limousin were named as French correspondents at the inaugural London Congress of 1864, but it was only nine months later, on 8 July 1865, that they opened the Paris bureau of the International. Support was at first scanty, largely because the Blanquists, fearing that the International would draw away much of their own following among the Paris workers, accused the organization of being a tool of the Bonapartists, a suggestion given at least a certain colour by Jerome Bonaparte's interest in the workers' delegation to the London Exhibition of 1862. Eventually, in an effort to dissipate suspicion, the members of the commission called 150 militant Parisian workers to a secret meeting. Here they insisted on the working-class character of their organization, on their desire to recruit as many republicans as possible, on their intention to avoid political action. Their effort was successful; a new and enlarged commission, including some of the former critics, was appointed, and the International began to spread into the provinces, so that by September 1865 the French delegates to the London Conference could report correspondents in Lyons, Marseilles, Rouen, Nantes, and a number of smaller cities.

Nevertheless, the actual membership of the International in France long remained scanty. At the time of the Geneva Congress in 1866 it appears to have been less than 500. Yet, barely four years later, on the eve of the Franco-Prussian War, the International was claiming a membership of 245,000 in France. There are several reasons for this rapid growth. The

workers who were organizing themselves in trade associations long
remained aloof from the International, largely because at first its leaders
were thought to disapprove of strikes. Then, early in 1867, the bronzework-
ers went on strike, and the International decided to support them. Tolain
crossed to London to collect funds, and his success so impressed the
employers that they agreed to the strikers' demands. As a result one workers' association after another came into the International, which continued
during this period of labour unrest to assist workers whenever they came
out on strike.

As soon as the International began to show activity of this kind, the tolerance which the Imperial government at first extended came to an end.
The excuse for the first official proceedings against the organization was
the participation of its members in republican demonstrations during
November 1867. On 30 December Tolain and his colleagues of the Paris
commission were arraigned on charges of belonging to an unauthorized
organization with more than twenty members. In March 1868 they were
fined, and the Association was dissolved. It continued to grow in semi-
secrecy. Before the condemnation of the first commission, a second commission had already been elected, on 8 March 1868; Eugène Varlin and
Benoît Malon were its leading members. Within a few months, they too
were arrested because Varlin had organized the collection of funds to support a strike of building workers in Geneva; this time the convicted men
were imprisoned for three months each, and the International was once
again dissolved. It still operated, however, and even prospered from a third
trial, so that at the beginning of the Franco-Prussian War the legally non-
existent French federation was numerically the strongest in the whole
International.

The accession of Varlin and Malon to positions of influence was indica-
tive of deep changes in the orientation of the French International, beginning in the early days of 1868. It remained inspired by anarchistic ideas,
but the recruitment of large bodies of organized workers shifted the
emphasis from mutualism to collectivism. In addition, the influence of
Bakunin and his Alliance was now beginning to operate in France. Élie
and Élisée Reclus had been closely associated with Bakunin since 1864.
During the immediately following years a number of prominent French
militants joined his Alliance, including Benoît Malon, Albert Richard of
Lyons, and Bastelica of Marseilles, while Varlin, as a result of his activities
in Geneva, established enduring contacts with the Jura Federation.
Through these men, and many lesser-known militants, particularly in the
south, the ideas of Bakunin began to permeate a working-class movement

which by 1869 was already beginning to establish Federated Chambers of trade associations closely anticipating the Bourses de Travail developed by the anarcho-syndicalists twenty years later. A considerable ideological influence on these events in France was wielded by *L'Égalité*, which was published in Geneva but primarily intended for distribution in France. This journal had been started originally as an organ of the Bakuninist Alliance, but later it became the first mouthpiece of the libertarian trend within the International, and among its contributors were the men who by 1868 were shaping the attitudes of the movement in France—Reclus, Malon, Varlin, and Richard.

At the same time, by no means all the French collectivists within the International were personal disciples of Bakunin. Varlin, despite his links with the Jura and Geneva anarchists, seems to have moved independently toward his collectivist position. Pure Bakuninism was influential only in the Rhône Valley, and it was the presence of groups of personal adherents in the towns in the Midi that led Bakunin, in September 1870, to play his only direct part in the history of French anarchism, when he travelled to Lyons to take part in the communalist rising that was also the first French insurrection in which anarchists played a notable part. I have already described that rather comic fiasco, whose main significance in the present context is its illustration of the unpreparedness of the Bakuninists in the Midi for any serious action. Perhaps the most surprising aspect of the Lyons rising is that it did not discredit anarchism in the Rhône Valley; indeed, the fact that the anarchists were the only people who even attempted serious revolutionary action in the region at this period may have told in their favour. Certainly, when the doctrine re-emerged in France after the proscriptions that followed the Paris Commune, it was in Lyons that it made its first successful appeal.

Meanwhile, in the Paris commune of 1871, the internationalists played a considerable and courageous part. During the Franco-Prussian War their attitude had been confused; Tolain and his associates had published a statement vaguely proclaiming the international solidarity of the workers, and early in August 1870, some of the Internationalists in Paris had hatched an abortive plot to capture the Palais-Bourbon and proclaim the Social Republic, but the anti-militarism that in later decades became a predominant anarchist attitude did not appear in any clear form. Even during the Commune the French sections of the International were not wholly united in their support, for Tolain and some of the other mutualists remained aloof. Nevertheless, a notable contribution to the activities of the Commune and particularly to the organization of public services was

made by members of various anarchist factions, including the mutualists
Courbet, Longuet, and Vermorel, the libertarian collectivists Varlin,
Malon, and Lefrançais, and the Bakuninists Élie and Élisée Reclus and
Louise Michel. Yet the Commune really stands on its own as an episode in
revolutionary history. Neither the Blanquists nor the anarchists, much less
the Marxists, can claim it as their own. In a larger sense it may be true that
the Commune fought under the banner of Proudhonian federalism; there
were sentences in its Manifesto to the French People of 19 April 1871 that
might have been written by Proudhon himself:

> The absolute autonomy of the Commune extended to all the locali-
> ties of France, assuring to each its integral rights and to every
> Frenchman the full exercise of his aptitudes, as a man, a citizen, and
> a worker. The autonomy of the commune will have for its limits only
> the equal autonomy of all other communities adhering to the con-
> tract; their associations must assure the liberty of France.

Yet even the mutualists and collectivists within the Commune made little effort to put their ideas into practice during the period in which they
shared control of Paris; they were content with doing their best to carry on
existing services and with a few reformist measures for the improvement
of working conditions. The most that can be said is that they often showed
that working men can be efficient administrators.

In terms of anarchist history the after-effects of the Commune were
perhaps more important than the rising itself. The immediate result of its
defeat was the suppression of all socialist activities and the passing of a
specific law in March 1872 banning the International as a subversive organization. This meant that for more than a decade all socialist or anarchist
activity in France was illegal and had to be carried on secretly. The other
important result was a mass flight of all the leading Internationalists who
were not—like Varlin—summarily shot by the Versailles troops or—like
Louise Michel—transported to the penal settlements. Many of these
expatriates settled just over the border in the French-speaking cantons of
Switzerland; there they formed an important element in the Saint-Imier
International and sought to create a base from which propaganda could be
directed into France.

In France itself it was in the south-eastern region, nearest to
Switzerland and therefore most open to the influence of the Jura
Federation and the Communard exiles, that anarchist activity first began
to appear after the months of repression that followed the Commune. The

earliest organizations were small secret groups which toward the end of 1872 began to re-establish connections with the Bakuninists over the frontier, to hold secret meetings in Lyons and Saint-Étienne, and to import literature from Geneva. In the autumn of 1872 a small secret congress of local militants was held in Saint-Étienne. Its participants all adhered to the Saint-Imier International, and its resolutions, in favour of autonomous groups and abstention from parliamentary activities, were anarchistic in tone. Shortly afterward a group of Bakuninist refugees from southern France established a propaganda committee in Barcelona and in the beginning of June 1873 published the first number of *La Solidarité révolutionnaire*, which ran for ten issues and had a considerable influence on the nascent groups of the Midi and particularly on the first important post-Commune anarchist congress in France, held on the night of 15 August in the unlit basement of a Lyons tavern.

The thirty delegates were all collectivists, for, though the mutualists re-emerged later in the 1870s and even retained some influence in the trade unions until the later 1880s, the two libertarian currents were from this time sharply distinct. While the collectivists became steadily more extreme in their revolutionism, the mutualists, following the example of Tolain, who had now made his compromises and entered the ranks of respectability as a Senator of the Third Republic, became steadily more reformist, so that it was no longer possible to regard them as representing even an approximately anarchistic point of view.

The Lyons Congress was concerned largely with organizational questions, and it showed that the anti-authoritarians—who did not yet openly call themselves anarchists—were planning the re-creation of a national movement. Some groups in the region had already accepted Bakunin's advice—transmitted through a Saint-Étienne worker named Gillet—to reorganize in the traditional conspiratorial pattern of groups of five, but it is doubtful if this kind of segmentation was ever thoroughly carried out, and there was a compensating urge toward a more sweeping form of federal organization. This the secret congress in Lyons attempted to achieve. The autonomy of groups was reaffirmed, but at the same time a regional council for eastern France was created, and similar councils were planned for the north, the centre, and the south. The regional council of the east actually came into being, largely through the energy of Gillet, and sent its delegates to the Geneva Congress of the Saint-Imier International.

The hopes of re-establishing the International in France were thwarted toward the end of 1873 by a series of arrests of active propagandists which led to the Lyons Plot trial of April 1874. Twenty-nine Bakuninists were accused of plotting against the state, and there seems no doubt that some at least of them, such as Gillet and Camille Camet, an old associate of Bakunin in the Lyons Commune, had tried to create an insurrectional organization to take advantage of the confusion that might follow a widely expected attempt to restore the monarchy. However, the evidence was insufficient to support the prosecution's case, and the accused were finally condemned for affiliating themselves with the forbidden International and for concealing weapons; Camet at the time of his arrest was well-armed with a loaded revolver, a knife, and a dagger. All but three of the accused were imprisoned, and the International ceased to function in France even as a secret organization.

It was several years before an identifiable anarchist movement appeared again on French soil; when it did the anti-authoritarians were no longer the dominant force in French socialism. Politically oriented movements had arisen in the meantime, and ironically their most important leaders were drawn from the anarchist ranks. The first to split away was Jules Guesde, who in November 1877 founded a socialist weekly which bore the old Bakuninist title, *L'Égalité*, but tended toward the Marxism that was to dominate the Parti Ouvrier which Guesde founded in 1882. The anti-authoritarian rival of *L'Égalité* was Paul Brousse's *L'Avant-garde*, which began to appear during August 1877 at Chaux-de-Fonds in the Swiss Jura. At this period Brousse was one of the most uncompromising of the French anarchists in exile; the first issue of his paper appeared under the slogan, 'Collectivism; Anarchy; Free Federation', and demanded the complete destruction of the state and its replacement by a society based on contract and 'the free formation of human groups around each need, each interest, and the free federation of these groups'. However, after the suppression of *L'Avant-garde* at the end of 1878 and his own brief imprisonment, Brousse quickly shifted ground until he too entered the socialist ranks and became the leader of a dissident faction within the Parti Ouvrier which advocated the most unanarchistic doctrine of possibilism and sought a way to socialism through factory legislation and municipal government.

But before this extraordinary volte-face Brousse had been one of the most active promoters of the revival of French anarchism. He returned to France secretly in the early part of 1877 to re-establish contacts with the Lyons militants, and started a series of gatherings in the Swiss frontier village of Perly. Some fifty Frenchmen crossed the border clandestinely for the first of these meetings; later, at a special congress at Chaux-de-Fonds, in August 1877, the delegates of twelve groups gathered to refound the French Federation of the International, with a programme accepting the principle of propaganda by deed already upheld by the Italian and Spanish federations. The International itself was by now moribund, but the gatherings of 1877 at least indicated a resurgence of anarchist sentiment in the Rhône Valley. The next year, largely owing to the activities of Kropotkin and Andrea Costa, the first Parisian groups began to appear, though their growth suffered a setback when Costa and a number of his associates were arrested.

It was not until 1881 that the anarchist movement separated itself clearly from the general socialist trend in France. Until that time the Guesdists, the mutualists, and the collectivist anarchists—now turning toward anarchist communism—all participated in the series of National Labour Congresses which were held during the latter half of the 1870s in the hope of creating a unified workers' movement; only the Blanquists, headed by Édouard Vaillant, kept aloof. The first and second of these congresses, in Paris (1876) and Lyons (1878), were largely dominated by mutualist moderates. By the time the third Congress was held at Marseilles in 1879 a considerable change was evident in the general political climate of France; the revolutionary tendencies of the early Third Republic were diminishing, and various left-wing movements began to emerge into the open. At the 1879 Congress the new atmosphere was reflected in the triumph of collectivism over mutualism; the socialists and the anarchists voted together in favour of the public ownership of the means of production. They disagreed, however, on the question of parliamentary activity, and the Guesdist victory on this point preluded the breaking of the uneasy unity between the various factions.

Later in 1879 the Chamber of Deputies voted a general amnesty for those who had taken part in the Commune. The exiles returned from the countries where they had taken refuge; the prisoners came back from New Caledonia and were welcomed by enthusiastic crowds at the stations. The influx of dedicated militants invigorated the various socialist factions; it also sharpened their differences of viewpoint. At regional congresses in Marseilles and Lyons, during July 1880, the anarchist majorities carried resolutions rejecting political activity, while in Paris the authoritarian socialists were victorious. The real splintering of the movement began at the National Labour Congress of 1880 in Le Havre, where the mutualists split away completely to form their own short-lived Union des Chambres Syndicalistes. The anarchists remained, but the irreconcilable differences over tactics which emerged during the Le Havre Congress made further collaboration between them and the socialists difficult. The final crisis occurred in May 1881 over a relatively minor point of procedure at the

Regional Congress of the Centre in Paris. The nine participating anarchist organizations asked that delegates should identify their groups without revealing personal names. The Guesdist majority refused to accept this condition, and the anarchists withdrew to hold their own Revolutionary-Socialist Congress from 25 to 29 May; it was attended by some 200 militants who voted in favour of propaganda by deed and the abolition of property—even collective property—and against participation in political action. Similar schisms followed in the provinces, and the separate identity of the anarchist movement in France was further emphasized by the participation of many groups and of a number of important French anarchist leaders in the 'Black International' Congress of 1881.

The year 1881 can thus be taken as that in which a separate and avowedly anarchist movement began its independent career in France. The actual strength of this movement in its early stages is hard to estimate. In terms of groups and members alike it appears to have been far smaller than its repute in France during the 1880s might suggest. The anarchists themselves often made extravagant claims; in 1882, for instance, the delegates who attended the International Congress in Geneva spoke of 3,000 militants in the city of Lyons alone and another 2,000 in the surrounding region. For other reasons, the conservative newspapers also tended to exaggerate anarchist strength; in 1883 L'Univers estimated that there were 5,000 active members of the movement in Paris. However, the evidence recently gleaned by Jean Maitron from confidential police reports and more sober anarchist estimates* suggests that in 1882 there were about forty groups in the whole country, with an active membership of approximately 2,500. Lyons and Paris were the most active centres, with 500 militants each; there were strong groups in Bordeaux, Marseilles, and Saint-Étienne. During the next decade the growth in numerical strength was not great; a police estimate at the end of 1894 gave a total of just over 4,500 activists, but this appears to have been based partly on the subscription lists of anarchist journals, and subscribers were not necessarily active anarchists; the poet Stéphane Mallarmé subscribed regularly to libertarian papers, but the most elastic imagination does not allow one to consider him an anarchist militant.

On the basis of these figures it seems reasonable to assume that during the 1880s there were about fifty anarchist groups in France with an active membership averaging 3,000 and a fringe of sympathizers whose strength is suggested by the fact that at the end of the decade the two leading Paris

---

*Histoire du mouvement anarchiste en France (1880-1914), Paris, 1955.

anarchist journals, *Le Révolté* and *Le Père peinard*, sold between them more than 10,000 copies each week.

Between the groups there were few organizational links. After a number of futile attempts at regional, national, and international organization in 1881 and 1882, the trend toward group autonomy became progressively stronger, and no national organization of French anarchists came into active existence until the eve of the First World War. But organizational disunity does not necessarily mean an absence of either solidarity or communication; in practice there was a real unity of feeling in the French movement and a constant intellectual intercourse between groups and individuals, encouraged by the emergence of journals that circulated nationally and by the presence of a number of prominent propagandists who enjoyed the prestige, if not the power, commonly accorded to political leaders. Élisée Reclus, the internationally famous geographer; Louise Michel, the heroine of the Commune and veteran of the penal settlements; Jean Grave, the shoemaker turned tireless editor and propagandist; Sébastien Faure, the former Jesuit seminarist who became a leading libertarian philosopher and educationalist; Émile Pouget, editor of the fearless *Père peinard* and later a devoted interpreter of anarcho-syndicalism; these men and women were national figures in the France of the *fin-de-siècle*, and their activity as writers and touring lecturers gave the anarchist movement far more importance, in the eyes of workers and intellectuals alike, than its numerical strength might lead one to expect.

Moreover, it must be remembered that the French anarchists deliberately restricted their groups to men and women willing to take part in regular propaganda by speech, writing, or the deed. After the collapse of the International they no longer tried to establish the large card-carrying memberships at which political parties usually aim. Their real influence—as against their numerical strength—was to be shown before the end of the century by their ability to dominate for at least a decade the largest working-class movement of pre-1914 France, the revolutionary-syndicalist movement that reached its height in the golden days of the CGT. They attained this position of influence not because of their numbers, but because of their passionate devotion to ideals that seemed to coincide with the longings and the experience of the French workers in that age when the insolent display of wealth went hand-in-hand with dire poverty, when arrogant corruption and naked repression tempted the minds of the poor to desperate dreams of an idyllic equality attained through social revolution.

But before the syndicalist phase of French anarchism began to open, there was a clearly defined period of somewhat different character that

began with the separation of the anarchists from the main socialist movement in 1881 and ended with the Trial of the Thirty in 1894. It was above all
a period of dramatic gestures and the cult of romantic violence, and it
came to a climax in the series of sensational terroristic acts that marked
the beginning of the 1890s. By no means all anarchists at this period were
terrorists; in fact only a tiny minority were implicated in acts of violence.
But the idea of violence wielded an extraordinary fascination even over
those whose gentler spirits shrank from its practice.

Several influences contributed to this attitude. In 1877 Paul Brousse,
whose part in the resurrection of anarchism after the Commune we have
already noted, became converted to the idea of propaganda by deed
already evolved by the Italian Internationalists, and in the following year
Andrea Costa—one of the leading exponents of this trend in Italy—propagated his point of view in Paris. The Bakuninist tendencies of the anarchists in the Rhône Valley made them naturally sympathetic to the idea of
conspiratorial violence, and the passionate discussions of the London
International Congress of 1881 on the questions of insurrection and terrorism encouraged the tendency. Separation from other currents of the
socialist movement undoubtedly removed certain moderating influences,
and at the same time encouraged the development of those very features
of theory and tactics which differentiated the anarchists from the Marxists
and mutualists. Finally, there was the sinister influence of the Paris Prefect
of Police, Louis Andrieux, and his creature Serreaux, a Belgian *agent provocateur* whose real name was Égide Spilleux.

Serreaux made contact with the Paris groups during 1880 and drew
attention to himself by his eloquent defence of violence. Shortly after his
appearance, he began to talk of founding an anarchist journal, and offered
3,000 francs for the bond demanded by law and a subsidy of 1,500 francs a
month for six months so as to assure the establishment of the paper. The
money really came from Andrieux, but Serreaux claimed that it was the
gift of an elderly London lady who was sympathetic to the anarchist cause.
He took care to find an accomplice who would act the part of the benevolent heiress, and she maintained the role well enough to hoodwink one of
the leading French anarchists, Émile Gautier, who went over to visit her.
Jean Grave and Éliseé Reclus, whom Serreaux first approached, were both
suspicious of his story, as were Kropotkin and Malatesta, but the desire to
have a magazine of their own lulled the misgivings of most of the Paris
comrades, and on 12 September 1880 a weekly journal was launched under
the title of *La Révolution sociale*.

La Révolution sociale was the first anarchist journal to appear in France
since the suppression of the Commune, and the movement as a whole was

enthusiastic, as was the real founder, Andrieux, who in his memoirs remarked: 'To give the anarchists a journal was to set up a telephone line between the conspiratorial centre and the office of the Prefect of Police.' But the role of Serreaux was not merely to spy; it was also to provoke, and the columns of La Révolution sociale, to which Gautier, Merlino, Cafiero, and Louise Michel all contributed, maintained a violent tone as well as—with calculated indiscretion—publishing names and even addresses of anarchist groups and their leading members. The suspicions of the more astute comrades were soon aroused, but La Révolution sociale continued for more than a year, and came to an end in September 1881 only because Andrieux left the Prefecture.

Not until 1885 did a regular anarchist periodical again appear in Paris, when Le Révolté, which Jean Grave had gone to Geneva to edit in 1883, was transferred to the French capital, where it continued to appear—changing its title in 1887 to La Révolte—until the wave of police repressions that led to its disappearance in March 1894.

In the interval between 1881 and 1885 the centre of anarchist journalism shifted to the militant city of Lyons, with its close links with the anarchists of Geneva and northern Italy and its traditional loyalty to the Bakuninist tradition. There, early in 1882, appeared the first number of Le Droit social. Its publishers were men of extraordinary enthusiasm and tenacity, and of an outspoken militancy which continually involved their paper in trouble with the authorities. Le Droit social disappeared under the burden of fines in July 1882; less than three weeks later its successor, L'Étendard révolutionnaire, was being published, and for more than two years the succession of papers with different titles but the same policy and the same contributors continued, until, on 22 June 1884, the last number of Le Droit anarchique appeared. It was the ninth in the succession of Lyonnais anarchist papers; the seventh had been called, with defiant humour, L'Hydre anarchiste. The editors of this eventful dynasty of Lyons papers claimed that on an average 7,000 copies were distributed, and, even making allowances for the customary exaggerations, there is no doubt that—with the Geneva Le Révolté as their only rival—Le Droit social and its successors played an extremely important part in shaping French anarchism during the early 1880s.

There remains one anarchist paper of the decade which to my mind reflects more eloquently than any of those I have mentioned the spirit of the period of propaganda by deed. This is Le Père peinard, whose first number appeared on 24 February 1889 under the very lively editorship of Émile Pouget. It represented a new direction in anarchist journalism. In the hands of Kropotkin and Grave Le Révolté had spoken in the language of the educated, simplified and pruned of academic affectation, but uncorrupted by the vernacular. Pouget revolted against middle-class language as well as against middle-class morality and middle-class politics, and deliberately encouraged his writers to use the *argot* of the outer boulevards. Moreover, in his exhortations to his readers—'*les bons bougres*'—he lost no opportunity to recommend decisive and dramatic action. The result was a humorous, unpredictable, scurrilous, irascible paper which is still entertaining for its vigour and eccentricity, while Grave's solemn lucubrations in *Le Révolté* exact an effort from even the most earnest modern researcher.

The violent spirit of the times was manifested in many other ways. It appeared in the names adopted by anarchist groups—La Panthère of Paris, La Haine of Bordeaux, Les Terribles of La Ciotat. It appeared in the songs written by the anarchist *chansonniers*, of which 'La Dynamite' by Marie Constant, one of the numerous revolutionary shoemakers of the time, was among the most popular:

> *Nos pères ont jadis dansé*
> *Au son du canon du passé;*
> *Maintenant la danse tragique*
> *Veut une plus forte musique:*
> *Dynamitons, dynamitons.*

There were many who did not merely talk of dynamite. Indeed, given the amount of violent oral and written propaganda that began to emanate from anarchist sources in France after the London Congress of 1881, and the enthusiasm aroused by the populist assassination of the Tsar Alexander II in 1881, it is surprising that the wave of terrorism mounted so slowly to its peak at the beginning of 1890s.

The first widely publicized act of violence during this period was an attempt to blow up a statue of Thiers at Saint-Germain in June 1881; since the Prefect Andrieux admitted a previous knowledge of the plan and did nothing to prevent it, this act may well have been planned by him and Serreaux and it cannot therefore be regarded as a genuine anarchist deed of propaganda. A few months later the first assassination was attempted by a French anarchist. Émile Florian, a young unemployed weaver, tramped from Reims to Paris with the intention of shooting the republican leader Gambetta. Failing to get near his intended victim, Florian decided to kill the first bourgeois he met, and on 20 October he shot and slightly wounded a certain Dr Meymar, afterward trying to kill himself. His attempt is important only because it established a pattern; all the terrorist acts by

French anarchists were to be acts of individuals or at most of minute circles of three or four people, prompted by personal and not by group decisions. In this sense the practice of terrorism in France differed markedly from that in Russia, where almost all the political assassinations were performed by groups organized in the Social Revolutionary Party.

The first actual assassination did not take place until the spring of 1884, when a gardener named Louis Chavès, a convinced advocate of propaganda by deed who had been sacked from his work at a convent in Marseilles, decided to take his revenge by what seemed to him a pioneer act of propaganda. He accepted his own extinction as inevitable, and wrote to *L'Hydre anarchiste* a letter of explanation which he calculated would arrive after his death.

> You start with one to reach a hundred, as the saying goes. So I would like the glory of being the first to start. It is not with words or paper that we shall change existing conditions. The last advice I have for true anarchists, for active anarchists, is to arm themselves according to my example with a good revolver, a good dagger, and a box of matches ...

He then returned to the convent and killed the Mother Superior. When the police came to arrest him, he shot at them without warning and died from their bullets.

Chavès became a nine days' wonder for the anarchist papers, which praised his heroism and held up his act as an example. One paper even opened a subscription for a revolver to avenge him, but nobody came forward to use it, and almost eight years were to elapse before another anarchist assassin succeeded in his attempt.

It was direct action of a different kind that in the meantime led to some of the most dramatic incidents in the history of French anarchism. The series of events began in the mining town of Monceau-les-Mines, which was dominated by a particularly ruthless company with whose management the local representatives of Church and state cooperated willingly. An organization known as the Black Band began to send warning letters to managers and government officials; in August 1882 the members of the Band proceeded to a series of anti-religious acts, first overthrowing roadside crosses and then, on the night of 15 August, gathering in considerable numbers to pillage and burn a chapel and a religious school in a near-by village, after which they sounded the tocsin and began to march on Monceau, but dispersed before reaching the town. The authorities acted quickly, and arrested twenty-three men, who were brought to trial in an atmosphere of excitement and apprehension; the court was guarded by companies of infantry and gendarmes. The evidence produced at the trial suggests that the Black Band, whose membership was estimated at 800, was a working-class terrorist organization of the primitive kind that appears when the desperation of half-educated and half-starved workers is confronted by ruthless and unimaginative repression. Its members met at night in the forests, and neophytes were initiated in elaborate ceremonies accompanied by macabre oaths.

In spite of the prosecution's efforts to implicate the anarchists in the Monceau-les-Mines incidents, no facts were offered which suggested that they had any hand in them. On the contrary, the Lyons anarchists were surprised and admiring when they heard of the miners' exploits and immediately sent their representatives into the region. There is no doubt, however, that members of local anarchist groups took part in a later series of dynamitings directed at churches and managers' houses during 1883 and 1884, though it was also shown at the trials connected with these explosions that at least one of them was engineered by a police agent with the object of implicating suspected terrorists.

The events at Monceau-les-Mines might soon have been forgotten if the French government had not conceived the idea that the first series of outrages were signs of a widely laid insurrectional plot on the part of the already extinct Saint-Imier International. Acting on this assumption, the police began in the middle of October a series of arrests in Paris and south-eastern France, and on 8 January 1883 sixty-five prominent anarchists were brought to trial at Lyons; as well as Peter Kropotkin and Émile Gautier, almost all the leading militants of eastern France were among them.

The atmosphere in which the Lyons trial took place was made particularly tense by the explosion, shortly after the arrests began, of a bomb placed in the restaurant of the Théâtre Bellecour at Lyons, a place already denounced in Le Droit social as a rendezvous of 'the fine flower of the bourgeoisie' which should be destroyed as the first act of the revolution; only an employee of the restaurant was killed. The crime was never satisfactorily solved, although at the end of 1883 an anarchist journalist named Cyvoct was condemned on highly circumstantial evidence to penal servitude on Devil's Island. The anarchists consistently denied any connection with the affair and proclaimed Cyvoct's innocence. Remembering how eager they were to hail as heroes other terrorists of the period, one is tempted to accept their denials and to suspect that, like at least one of the dynamitings at Monceau-les-Mines, the outrage may indeed have been police-inspired. It could not have happened at a more convenient time—during the actual trial of the members of the Black Band and at the beginning of the widespread arrests of anarchist leaders.

I have already discussed in my chapter on Kropotkin the main features of the Lyons trial. Accused of belonging to the forbidden International, Kropotkin, Gautier, and some of the other defendants proved effectively that the International no longer existed, but this did not prevent their being given sentences which showed clearly the French government's intention to behead the anarchist movement before it grew too strong. Kropotkin and Gautier, the two intellectuals of national importance, and Bernard and Bordat, the leaders of the strong Lyons movement, were sentenced to five years each. Liégon, Ricard, and Martin, the most active militants in Villefrance, Saint-Étienne, and Vienne respectively, were sentenced to four years each.

The same governmental eagerness to manipulate justice for the sake of political expediency was evident in the other celebrated anarchist trial of 1883, that of Louise Michel and Émile Pouget. During the 1880s, before the anarchists began to enter the organized labour movement in large numbers, they tended to concentrate on the more depressed groups in society, and particularly, in Paris, on the unemployed, whom they encouraged to protest against their condition by illegal actions. On 9 March 1883 an open-air meeting of the unemployed near the Invalides was broken up by the police, and about 500 of the demonstrators, led by Louise Michel and Pouget, who was carrying a black flag, marched off in the direction of the Boulevard Saint-Germain. In the rue des Canettes the demonstrators, shouting 'Bread, work or lead!', pillaged a baker's shop. Two other shops were similarly plundered and the bread they contained distributed to the marchers. Then, having allowed the procession to get as far as the Place Maubert, the police attacked them. Pouget chivalrously put up a fight to allow Louise Michel to escape, but she was arrested and in due course appeared in court. The case was complicated by the fact that leaflets were found in Pouget's room addressed to 'soldiers who have decided to aid the Revolution', calling on them to burn their barracks, kill their officers, and join the insurgent people in their fight against the police. The leaflets had been printed in Geneva, but Pouget had assumed the task of distributing them in France. Louise Michel was, with very little proof, accused of inciting the pillage of the bakers' shops. She was sentenced to six years' solitary confinement and Pouget to eight years.

At this point the French government must have congratulated itself on the stretching of justice which had put away for a long period the most active and intelligent anarchists in France. But public opinion was disturbed by the trial and the sentences, and eventually forced the granting of an amnesty which freed Louise Michel and Pouget as well as the condemned of the Lyons trial. Far from harming the anarchist movement, the Lyons and Paris trials increased its prestige among both the workers and large sections of the educated classes.

Indeed, by the end of the 1880s the place of anarchism among the complex pattern of urges toward liberation from social, moral, and artistic bonds which characterized the *fin-de-siècle* in France, was recognized by both intellectuals and artists. The first group of anarchist students was formed in Paris in 1890, and from that year onward many writers and painters began to identify themselves with anarchism, which became something of a fashion in literary-artistic circles, as it was to become in London, New York, and San Francisco in the 1940s. The visiting celebrity Oscar Wilde, answering a questionnaire which the Symbolist review *L'Hermitage* submitted to various writers in 1893, remarked that once he had been politically a supporter of tyrants, but that now he was an anarchist. He spoke for very many of his French colleagues, as one can see from the anarchist journals and the near-anarchist literary reviews.

Among the painters, Camille Pissaro and his son Lucien were both intimately involved in the anarchist movement, and regularly contributed drawings and lithographs to *Le Père peinard* and to *Les Temps nouveaux*, the journal Jean Grave founded in 1895 after *La Révolte* had ceased publication. Grave, in fact, attracted to his pages many of the important experimental painters and the more vigorous caricaturists of the 1890s; not only the two Pissaros, but also Paul Signac, Van Dongen, Felix Vallotton, Steinlen, Caran d'Ache, and Van Rysselberghe provided illustrations for *Les Temps nouveaux*, while a few years later Vlaminck and other Fauve painters found anarchism a congenial doctrine.

As for the writers, many of the characteristic figures of the nineties hovered like splendid and fascinated insects around the dangerous flame of anarchism. Octave Mirbeau, Richepin, Laurent Tailhade, Bernard Lazare, and Paul Adam all contributed to *Les Temps nouveaux*, while the Symbolist poet Stuart Merrill was one of the 'angels' who helped the journal out of its periodical financial crises. In 1892 another leading Symbolist, Francis Vielé-Griffin, turned his review, *Les Entretiens politiques et littéraires*, into an organ of literary anarchism; his contributors included Paul Valéry, Henri de Regnier, Remy de Gourmont, and Stéphane Mallarmé. The most violently anarchist review, *L'Endehors*, a kind of intellectual *Père peinard* run by a flamboyant eccentric who called himself Xo d'Axa but whose real name was Galland, published the work of such writers as Émile Verhaeren and Saint-Pol Roux. In one way or another almost every important Symbolist writer was linked with anarchism in its literary aspects.

What attracted the writers and painters to anarchism was clearly not the prosaic daily activity of the groups. It was perhaps not even principally the idea of anarchy itself, but rather a spirit of daring and inquiry which Mallarmé expressed sensitively when he gave evidence on behalf of an anarchist friend at the Trial of the Thirty in 1894, and described him as 'a fine spirit, curious about everything that is new'. It was the anarchist cultivation of independence of mind and of freedom of action and experience for its own sake that appealed to the artists and intellectuals. Significantly, when the terrorists carried out their sensational series of attempts and assassinations during 1892 and 1893, the libertarian intelligentsia, far from deserting anarchism, saw in these acts of isolated protest great expressions of individuality. They also saw, with their *fin-de-siècle* thirst for the varieties of experience, a terrible but intriguing sensationalism in the lives of the assassins. Perhaps most of all, they recognized the element of perverted mysticism which formed part of the terrorist attitude, and which Paul Adam identified when he referred to Ravachol, the most formidable of all the assassins, as '*le Rénovateur du Sacrifice Essentiel*'.

The series of terrorist acts which Ravachol initiated in March 1892 form the most dramatic and controversial passage in the history of French anarchism. It lasted for only a brief period—from March 1892 to June 1894—but during that time there were eleven dynamite explosions in Paris in which nine people were killed; the Serbian minister was severely wounded by an anarchist shoemaker, and the President of the Republic was killed by the dagger of an assassin. As a result of these acts, four of the assassins were executed, repressive laws were passed against revolutionary groups, and the anarchist movement faced and survived its worst crisis, to emerge changed and renewed at the end.

As I have shown, the terrorism of the 1890s had been prepared by a decade in which French anarchists had talked much of violence without showing any great inclination to turn their talk into action. So long after the event, it is not easy to decide why in 1892 a number of young men should appear at the same time, resolved to act violently and willing to sacrifice themselves for what they conceived to be justice. Unlike their medieval namesakes, these assassins belonged to no order and worked in no disciplined group. They acted on their own initiatives, carrying individualism to a Stirnerite extreme. Society looked upon them as criminals;

they regarded themselves as judges and executioners. Many of their fellow anarchists applauded them, even raised them to the status of martyrs, but for the most part declined to imitate them. And in this reluctance to imitate they were right from their anarchist point of view, since killing is the supreme form of power, and the terrorist who kills on his own responsibility is surely the most irresponsible of tyrants. The act of assassination in fact completes a circle that unites anarchism with its opposite. One may perhaps be moved by the sincere intentions of these men and the darkness of their fates, but their deeds remain as negative as any other murder. Nevertheless, their shadows walk darkly beside any historian of anarchism; he cannot dismiss them as intruders on the road. By the right of tragedy alone they demand their place.

The terroristic acts of 1892 and 1894 follow a curious chain of cause and effect which began in an apparently insignificant incident on the outskirts of Paris. On 1 May 1891 a group of anarchists attempted to hold a demonstration in the suburb of Levallois. The police dispersed them and set off in pursuit of the leaders, whom they caught in a Clichy wineshop. The anarchists were armed, and a gun-fight followed in which one of them was wounded. The wounded man and two others were caught and brought to trial, where the prosecutor Bulot demanded the death penalty; the jury acquitted the wounded man and, on the instigation of the President of the Court, Benoît, sentenced the two others to long terms of imprisonment.

This case, which aroused comparatively little comment in the anarchist press, stirred deeply the anger of a dyer named Koenigstein, who went under the name of Ravachol. Ravachol had been converted to anarchism as a youth and, largely through his extreme poverty, had slipped into the margin of the criminal underworld. It was a time when the justification of robbery was being lengthily debated in anarchist circles. Men of high principle and exemplary life, like Élisée Reclus and Sébastien Faure, were so carried away by their convictions on the immorality of property that they were ready to condone any kind of theft on purely theoretical grounds; others, like Jean Grave, saw in the practice of crime a corruption that would make men unfitted for the high ideals of a free society. Ravachol was one of those who put the theories of Reclus and Faure into practice, and his life is perhaps an object lesson in the truth of Grave's arguments. He began with petty thefts, and went on to liquor smuggling and counterfeiting, in neither of which he was very successful. During this time he evolved a primitive philosophy which naïvely combined a defence of violence in the present with an idyllic vision of future brotherhood. He expressed it thus in one of the songs he would chant to the accompaniment of his own accordion:

Pour établir l'Égalité
Il faut le coeur plein de colère,
Réduire les bourgeois en poussière;
Alors au lieu d'avoir la guerre,
Nous aurons la Fraternité.

Soon he decided to leave the unprofitable ways of petty crime for large-scale robbery, and during the early summer of 1891 he committed two unsavoury crimes which only came to light some time afterward and which in no way fall into the category of propaganda by deed. One was the rifling of the tomb of the Comtesse de la Richetaillée at Terrenoire in search of rings and jewels; he found nothing of value, and a month later he was involved in the one murder that was conclusively proved against him. The victim was Jacques Brunel, a nonagenarian miser known as the Hermit of Chambles, who had lived on alms for fifty years and was reputed to have accumulated a considerable fortune. Rumour, which in such cases often lies, was true of the Hermit; when Ravachol and his accomplices killed the old man they took 15,000 francs away with them. In the following year, brought to trial for the murder, Ravachol declared that his motives were not wholly selfish:

> If I killed, it was first of all to satisfy my personal needs, then to come to the aid of the anarchist cause, for we work for the happiness of the people.

How much he gave to the cause is not known, but it is certain that he used part of his gains to maintain the families of the men imprisoned in connection with the Clichy affair. Meanwhile, four of his accomplices in the murder of the Hermit of Chambles were rounded up and imprisoned for their parts in the affair. Ravachol was arrested, but escaped, and the police showed a singular lack of interest in tracking him down. This led to rumours that he was an informer, and a writer in *Le Révolté* described him as 'nothing more than a new edition of the agent Serreaux who formerly published *La Révolution sociale* of sad memory for Monsieur Andrieux'.

A desire to remove this stigma may have been one of the motives that now led Ravachol into a series of crimes which could not be interpreted either as acts of a police agent or as being committed for personal gain. The victims he chose were those who had played the most prominent part in the prosecution of the men involved in the Clichy incident. On 11 March 1881 he blew up the house of President Benoît. Sixteen days later, on 27 March, he blew up the house of the prosecutor, Bulot. Nobody was harmed in either explosion. Two days later Ravachol was arrested, after a dramatic struggle, in a restaurant where one of the waiters had recognized him and informed the police.

On 26 April, in a heavily guarded courtroom, Ravachol was sentenced to hard labour for life. Two months later he appeared at Montbrison to face trial for killing the Hermit of Chambles. He was now being tried for his life, but in the court he showed a calmness which astonished all those who saw him. He greeted the sentence of death with a shout of '*Vive l'Anarchie!*' and walked to the guillotine singing an anti-clerical song.

Ravachol was in the tradition of the heroic brigand. His courage was undeniable. Even his idealism and his sense of mission seem to have been sincerely held. He really believed that his terrible acts would lead to a world where such horrors need never again be done by men to men. He saw himself as the novelist Octave Mirbeau described him—'the peal of thunder to which succeeds the joy of sunlight and of peaceful skies'. Poverty and the experience of injustice done to himself and others had bitten deeply into his mind, and he acted for ends which he thought were just. But he forgot how far the means can warp the end, how the contempt for individual lives—even for the life of a worthless old man like the Hermit of Chambles—can lead to contempt for life as a whole. He was tragically mistaken, and he paid stoically for his mistakes.

As Ravachol stood before his judges at Montbrison, he said these words: 'I have made a sacrifice of my person. If I still fight, it is for the anarchist idea. Whether I am condemned matters little to me. I know that I shall be avenged.' The process of vengeance had begun when he spoke these words. Four days after his first dynamiting, a bomb exploded mysteriously outside the Lobau barracks in Paris. Then, the day before he was sentenced on his first trial, another bomb, placed in the restaurant where he had been arrested, killed the proprietor and a customer. Not until 1894 was the perpetrator of these acts arrested in London and brought to trial in France. He was Théodule Meunier, a cabinet-maker, and he represented a quite different type of terrorist from Ravachol. A young man of exemplary life, an excellent and sober worker, he was also, as his former comrade Charles Malato described him, 'the most remarkable type of revolutionary illuminist, an ascetic and a visionary, as passionate in his search for the ideal society as Saint-Just, and as merciless in seeking his way towards it'. The natural violence that surged in Ravachol was not a part of Meunier's nature, but the cold rationality that impelled him was just as destructive. Meunier escaped the guillotine, but during the long years he endured in the penal colony he never repented the killing of innocent persons to which his act had led. 'I only did what I had to do,' he told Jean Grave more than twenty years later. 'If I could start over again, I would do the same thing.'

After the execution of Ravachol there was a lull of several months in the terrorist campaign. Then, on 8 November 1892, a bomb was placed in a mining company's offices in the avenue de l'Opéra. Four policemen were killed when it exploded in the police station of the rue des Bons-Enfants. The assassin was not immediately discovered, and more than another year went by before the terrorist fever suddenly reached its climax in a whole series of sensational acts.

They began on 13 November 1893, when another honest, sober, and fanatical workman, Léauthier, inspired by the thought that 'I shall not be striking an innocent if I strike the first bourgeois I meet', attacked the Serbian Minister with a cobbler's knife and gravely wounded him. And four weeks later, on 9 December, Auguste Vaillant threw a bomb from the gallery of the Chamber of Deputies and struck fear in the hearts of the French rulers.

Unlike Meunier and Léauthier, Vaillant was an amiable bohemian, bred in poverty, shifting restlessly from occupation to occupation, becoming converted to socialism and then to anarchism, and finally emigrating to the Argentine, where for three years he tried to work a concession of land in Chaco province. He failed and returned to France in March 1893. There he tried to get the kind of work that would bring comfort to his companion and his daughter, and was distressed by the poverty in which they were forced to live. This preyed so much on his mind that at last he decided to commit a symbolic deed that would be 'the cry of a whole class which demands its rights and will soon add acts to words'. The obvious mental torture that led him to plan and carry out his attempt makes him one of the more sympathetic of the terrorists; here at least was a mind working in passion, moved by devotion and pity for human beings who were near his heart, and confusedly believing that one great gesture might awaken men from the nightmare of injustice.

But the fear his attempt aroused left no room for pity or for understanding. Nobody had died from this act, but he was condemned to death; it was the first time since the beginning of the century that such a sentence had been passed on a man who had not actually killed another. But, despite a petition circulated by one of the wounded deputies, the President, Sadi Carnot, refused to sign a pardon.

Vaillant went to the scaffold as courageously as Ravachol, crying out: 'Long live Anarchy! My death shall be avenged!' And avenged it was, terribly and repeatedly. A week after his execution a bomb was thrown into the Café Terminus at the Gare St-Lazare. Twenty people were wounded; one of them died.

The bomb-thrower, who was arrested immediately, was a young man named Émile Henry, the son of a famous Communard; later he confessed with pride that he had planted the bomb which exploded in the police station of the rue des Bons-Enfants. Henry was perhaps the most remarkable—and certainly the most ferocious—of the French terrorists. He had an extraordinary intelligence and considerable literary ability, but he had sacrificed the possibility of a good career to devote himself to anarchist propaganda. At first he had opposed the theory of propaganda by deed, but Ravachol's execution had a great effect on him and afterward he turned full circle to become a defender of the violent acts which 'waken the masses ... and show them the vulnerable side of the bourgeoisie'. With the implacable logic that replaces passion in a cold mind, Henry followed his new course to its extremity, and that extremity led him to the indiscriminate attack on people certainly innocent of the injustices he hated. His only regret, he said afterward, was that the explosion had not claimed more victims.

Henry's crime sent a shudder of fear through France, and it shocked the anarchists themselves into a realization of the destination to which their decade of violent dreams had brought them. 'The act of Henry,' said the militant Charles Malato, 'has struck anarchy most of all.' The event had a similar sobering effect on the literary anarchists. Laurent Tailhade had seen 'a beautiful gesture' in Vaillant's attempt; Victor Barracund had seen Ravachol as 'a kind of violent Christ'; but there were few who, after Henry's horrifying act, did not echo the admirable words with which Octave Mirbeau dissociated essential anarchism from the deeds that were done in its name:

> A mortal enemy of anarchy could have acted no better than this Émile Henry when he threw his inexplicable bomb into the midst of peaceful and anonymous persons come to a café to drink a glass of beer before going home to bed ... Émile Henry says, affirms, claims that he is an anarchist. It is possible. It is a fashion nowadays among criminals to use it for their justification when they have carried out a good coup ... Every party has its criminals and its fools, because every party has its men.

The lesson was not lost. From the explosion in the Café Terminus one can date the beginning of a new trend in French anarchism towards the assumption of more realistic responsibilities in the world of its time. But the era of terror had not quite closed. A group of three explosions shortly after the arrest of Henry ended when a Belgian anarchist, Pauwels, blew himself up in the Madeleine. On 4 April an explosion in a restaurant—the last of the bomb outrages—ironically injured the admirer of Vaillant, Laurent Tailhade. But the final vengeance for which Vaillant had called was still to come, and it brought a dramatic finale to the years of violence. On 24 June President Carnot arrived in Lyons on a state visit. On the same day the Italian anarchist Santo Caserio arrived from Cette; at nine o'clock in the evening he mingled with the crowd that pressed around the President and stabbed him in the liver, shouting, '*Vive la Révolution! Vive l'Anarchie!*' in what had become a ritual manner. Carnot died from his wound. It was an act of primitive justice. Carnot had shown no mercy to Vaillant, and Caserio, the blood revenger, showed no mercy for him. But for those who seek something beyond the law of vendetta it was merely the last of a series of heroic and useless sacrificial acts which neither furthered the cause of anarchism nor lessened the weight of injustice borne by nineteenth-century man.

To this realization the anarchists came, assisted by the struggle for life which the movement had to undergo as the indirect result of the terrorist campaign. In the panic following Vaillant's attempt, the Chamber of Deputies passed a series of measures which gained infamy in French polit-ical history as *les lois scélérates.* The first made it a crime not merely to incite to criminal acts, but even to apologize for them. The second con-cerned 'associations of malefactors', and defined them by intent rather than by action. Finally, after the death of Carnot, a third law forbade acts of anarchist propaganda 'by any means whatever'.

A rigorous use of these laws could at the least have driven the anarchist movement completely underground. And this was what the government hoped to do. Its first target was the anarchist press. On 21 February 1894 *Le Père peinard* was forced out of publication. Less than three weeks later *La Révolte* ceased to appear. Many anarchist intellectuals were arrested, and on 6 August some of the best known were brought before the courts in the Trial of the Thirty.

The prosecution arranged the Trial of the Thirty with a self-defeating Machiavellianism. Among the defendants it placed a celebrated gang of 'illegalist anarchists' led by a Mexican named Ortiz; in plainer terms, they were professional burglars who handed part of their profits to the cause. By putting nineteen well-known anarchist theoreticians in the dock beside these latter-day Robin Hoods, the prosecution hoped to confuse the issue before the jury, and to present men like Jean Grave and Sébastien Faure,

Paul Reclus and Émile Pouget, as the actual accomplices of criminals. The trial lasted for a week, and, despite the evident bias of the judges, the links which the prosecution sought to establish were easily disproved. In the end only Ortiz and two of his companions were imprisoned. The verdict acquitting the actual anarchist leaders spelled the end, not only of the terrorist epoch, but also of the reaction it had produced.

The essential vitality of French anarchism and the toughness of its roots in the nineteenth-century political terrain were shown by the rapidity with which the movement climbed out of the depths of 1894, when its press was destroyed, its leaders were standing trial, and its structure of autonomous groups was almost completely dispersed, toward the highest point of its influence, which came in the last years of the nineteenth and the early years of the twentieth century. The period from 1881 to 1894 had been a time of isolation, when the anarchists wandered in a wilderness of marginal social groups and sought the way to a millennium in desperate acts on the one hand and idyllic visions on the other. The period from 1894 to 1914 saw a fruitful equilibrium between the visionary and the practical, accompanied by a tendency to experiment, not only in ways of embarrassing the existing system of authority, but also in means of training men and women for a fuller, freer life, and even in organizations that might be regarded as fragmentary sketches of the future. Anarcho-syndicalism, as well as the movement to establish anarchist-communist colonies in the French countryside (which resulted in the creation of many communities that lasted into the 1930s), and the movement of libertarian education (which led to the formation of some famous progressive schools, including Faure's La Ruche, and the Universités Populaires with their evening courses for adults), all showed anarchism seeking constructive solutions.

It is, of course, true that there were other fields of activity in which only resistance to established authority was involved. This was so particularly with the Ligue Antimilitariste and other war-resisting organizations in which the anarchists formed the most active element. Finally, the end of the terrorist era and the imprisonment of the celebrated Ortiz did not bring an end to illegalist activities. On the fringe of the movement, and particularly in the individualist faction which became relatively strong after 1900 and began to publish its own sectarian paper, L'Anarchie (1905-14), there were groups and individuals who lived largely by crime. Among them were some of the most original as well as some of the most tragic figures in anarchist history. The gang led by Marius Jacob operated successfully for five years, from 1900 to 1905, carrying out hundreds of robberies and priding itself on robbing only the unproductive.* But there was also the much more sinister Bonnot gang of neo-Stirnerite individuals, who in 1913 embarked on a career of large-scale banditry; most of its members died in gun-battles with the police. But these were exceptions, running contrary to the generally constructivist tendencies of anarchism during the two decades after 1894.

Since I have no space to deal fully with all these variations of French anarchist activity in its most fertile age, I will restrict myself to something about the organization and press of the movement, and rather more about anarcho-syndicalism and its relationship to the anarchist movement in the narrower sense. For, from the 1890s onward we are in fact concerned with two parallel and interconnecting forms of libertarian doctrine—or perhaps even with three if one considers the individualists, who bitterly opposed the syndicalist trend and even rejected the anarchist communism that had preceded it. The anarchist movement itself remained an organization of propagandists—of the word now rather than of the deed—adhering for the most part to Kropotkin's free communist doctrine, and organized, as before, in autonomous groups. The distrust of organizational unity persisted almost to the eve of the First World War. It was only in 1908, under the stimulus of the Amsterdam International Congress of 1907, that the trend began to change, and the first efforts at regional organization were made in northern and central France. Later, in 1911, a Communist-Anarchist Alliance was created, weakly supported by individual members, but from this eventually emerged a National Congress, held in Paris during August 1913, which created a nation-wide Fédération Communiste Révolutionnaire Anarchiste. The FCRA's short life was terminated by the outbreak of the First World War, but its successors, under various names, have maintained a precarious peacetime existence in France down to the present.

The numerical strength of the movement during the twentieth century is hard to determine owing to the lack of any attempt to keep records of membership. Sixty groups took part in the Congress of August 1913, but since there was opposition to the Congress, other groups certainly existed. So far as individuals are concerned, one anarchist leader of the time, A. Hamon, estimated the adherents of anarchism at the turn of the century at 60,000 'or perhaps 100,000', a statement whose very vagueness makes it suspect. Jean Maitron, in criticizing Hamon, produced figures which

*Once Jacob was burgling a house when he realized that it belonged to the writer Pierre Loti; he left without taking anything.

suggested that in the Paris groups there were just over 500 militants, as
there had been twenty years before, and from such evidence he contends
that the movement in France was no larger in the 1900s than it had been in
the 1880s. However, when one takes into account the multiple forms of
anarchist activity which had developed outside the actual propaganda
groups, and when one remembers the number of convinced anarchists
who worked within the syndicates, it seems certain that the active adherents of various kinds were considerably more numerous than the 3,000
French militants of the 1880s, though even the smaller of Hamon's figures
seems far too generous.

Anarchist influence was exerted most powerfully during the decades
after 1894 through its press and through active participation in the trade
unions. The anarchist press rose enriched from the persecutions of 1894.
Pouget, who had fled to England to avoid the Trial of the Thirty, continued to publish *Le Père peinard* in exile; after his return to France in 1895 he
founded *La Sociale*, but the next year he resumed the former title, and *Le
Père peinard* continued until 1900, when Pouget abandoned it in order to
edit the daily paper of the Confédération Générale du Travail, which
revived the old Proudhonian title of *La Voix du peuple*. Meanwhile Jean
Grave, conscious that a new era had begun in anarchist activities, came
back to journalism with the appropriately titled *Temps nouveaux*, which was
not merely a replacement of *La Révolte*, since it took a fresh direction by
supporting from the beginning the developing trend of anarcho-syndicalism. Finally, in December 1895, Sébastien Faure established the most
durable of all the nationally distributed anarchist papers, *Le Libertaire*,
which continued to appear, with interruptions caused by two world wars,
until the late 1950s.

During this period there were also efforts to create anarchist dailies but,
with the exception of *La Voix du peuple*, which was a trade-union journal
and only partly anarchist in its orientation, none of them was lastingly
successful. The most important was *Le Journal du peuple*, founded by
Sébastien Faure during the heyday of the Dreyfus agitation; it printed
articles by left-wing socialists as well as by anarchists, and followed a
sharply anti-clerical line, but it was never a financial success and disappeared after ten months of publication in December 1899. Two years later
Faure founded in Lyons a second anarchist daily, *Le Quotidien*, which ran
for almost 300 numbers, until it also failed for lack of adequate support.
Clearly, outside the trade unions, the following of the anarchists was not
wide enough to support anything more frequent than weekly periodicals;
even these were always in debt and had to be subsidized by supporting
groups.

It was through the increasing participation of French anarchists in the trade-union movement during the 1890s that the doctrine of anarcho-syndicalism developed; during the following years it spread beyond France and largely replaced anarchist communism as the dominant libertarian attitude, not only in the Latin countries, but also in Germany, Holland, and Scandinavia.

Neither the basic approach of anarcho-syndicalism nor the forms of action advocated by its supporters was entirely new. In England of the 1830s, under the theoretical influence of Robert Owen, the Grand National Consolidated Trades Union had not merely set out to press the demands of the workers for better conditions under capitalism; it had also envisaged the establishment of a socialized society by means of a movement divorced from political activity. And the method which the Owenite unionists favoured for bringing an end to capitalism and ushering in the new world was the Grand National Holiday of the Working Class—an early version of the general strike, conceived and advocated by the English restaurant-keeper William Benbow in 1833. Even in France the syndicalist emphasis on the need for working men to achieve their own liberation dated back to Proudhon's *De la capacité politique des classes ouvrières*; Varlin and the French Bakuninists had also recognized before the Paris Commune the role of the trade unions in the social struggle, and the general strike had been supported by the non-Marxist collectivists within the International, particularly as a means of war-resistance. What was original in anarcho-syndicalism was its adaptation of these elements from the past to the circumstances of the industrial world of the late nineteenth century, and its creation of a theory that made the trade union the centre of the class struggle and also the nucleus of the new society. The emphasis on the syndicate rather than the commune as the basic social unit, and on industrial action as opposed to conspiratorial or insurrectional action, were the two points on which the anarcho-syndicalists principally differed from the anarchist communists and the collectivists.

The trade-union movement began to re-form in France after the legislation of 1884 which allowed working-class associations for the defence of economic interest. Almost immediately the anarchists began to enter the new unions; among the first of them was the carpenter Joseph Tortelier, a celebrated orator and a great advocate of the general strike as the means to the social revolution.

It was some time, however, before a clearly revolutionary trend began to appear in the unions. Their first general organization, the Fédération Nationale des Syndicats, was created in 1886; it was a reformist body controlled by the socialists of Guesde's Parti Ouvrier. Two years later an anarchist tendency began to emerge. Encouraged by the government of Waldeck-Rousseau, which hoped to gain social peace by courting the workers, the unions of Paris founded in 1888 a Bourse de Travail, or labour exchange, to compete with the *bureaux de placement* operated in the interests of the employers. It was hoped that the activities of the Bourses de Travail might moderate the militancy of the workers; the reverse happened. The local groupings of unions formed by the Bourses appealed to anarchist decentralism and offered a means of opposing the centralizing tendencies of the Guesdists with the Fédération Nationale des Syndicats. Moreover, the anarchists hoped that the Bourses would result in union control of the supply of labour and thus establish a useful instrument of economic power.

The movement spread rapidly, Bourses de Travail were set up in many provincial towns, and the anarchists quickly established control over the most important. By 1892 there were enough to form a Fédération des Bourses de Travail, which also the anarchists effectively infiltrated; in 1894 Fernand Pelloutier became assistant secretary of the federation, and in 1895 he rose to the position of general secretary, while another anarchist, Paul Delesalle, was made his assistant. Pelloutier was a brilliant young journalist who had started as a Radical and moved on to the Guesdists; disillusioned by his experience of political parties, he decided that industrial action, culminating in the general strike, was the best protection for the workers in existing conditions and also their best way toward the eventual social revolution. It is an exaggeration to say—as G.D.H. Cole has said—that 'Pelloutier founded syndicalism', but it is at least true that his idealistic and pure-hearted enthusiasm made him its first and most important leader. The anarchists in general brought with them into the Bourses de Travail their hatred of the state and their extreme anti-militarism, represented particularly by Georges Yvetot, who succeeded Pelloutier in the secretaryship of the federation after the latter's premature death in 1901.

Meanwhile the anarchists had also begun to penetrate the rival Fédération Nationale des Syndicats. In alliance with the Blanquists and the revolutionary socialist group led by Jean Allemane, they managed to unseat the Guesdists from their control of the FNS. Collaboration between the two organizations now became possible, and at a joint Congress of Nantes in 1894 a large majority of the delegates resolved that 'the ultimate revolutionary means is the general strike', and established a special committee, controlled by the revolutionary factions, to transmit this millennial idea to the workers.

An actual amalgamation of the two federations did not take place immediately (though it had already been urged at a joint congress in 1893) largely because the militants of the Bourses de Travail were reluctant to abandon their decentralized form of organization. As a consequence, it was not until 1902 that the syndicalist movement in France was finally united. A first step toward unification was made in 1895 when the Fédération Nationale des Syndicats transformed itself into the Confédération Générale de Travail; by providing a structure of two sections—one of national syndicates and the other of local federations—it hoped to attract the Bourses de Travail into affiliation, but Pelloutier and his followers entered the Confederation for a few months and withdrew. Meanwhile, in 1898, the CGT planned a dress rehearsal of the general strike, in support of a projected walkout of the railwaymen who, as public servants, were excepted from the provisions of the Trade Union Act which legalized strikes; the railwaymen, however, were intimidated by the threats of the government, and the great experimental general strike ended in a fiasco which discredited the moderates within the CGT, who had allowed the plans for the strike to reach the authorities. This enabled the anarchists to strengthen their influence within the Confederation, and by 1902 the attitudes of the two organizations were sufficiently close for a union to be achieved. In the enlarged CGT, a former Blanquist, Victor Griffuelhes, became secretary-general, but the anarchists Yvetot and Delesalle headed the section of Bourses de Travail while Pouget headed the section of national federations and also edited *La Voix du peuple*.

In the years from 1902 to 1908 the anarchists reached the peak of their influence among the French workers. The CGT, of course, was never a completely anarchist organization. A large minority of its members remained reformist in attitude, while among the revolutionary majority the anarchists competed with Blanquists, Allemanists, and a new generation of 'pure' syndicalists, of whom Pierre Monatte was typical, who saw in the militant trade union the only means and the only end of revolutionary activity. Nor did the CGT as a whole represent a majority among the workers of France; the anarcho-syndicalist theoreticians rather welcomed this fact, since they felt that a relatively small organization of dedicated militants could activate the indifferent masses in a critical situation, and in the meantime would not lose their potency by immersion in a mass of inactive card-carriers. The Bakuninist conception of a revolutionary élite played a considerable part in anarcho-syndicalist theory.

During the first decade of the twentieth century the CGT set the pace for labour action, and turned this into a tense period of strikes, sabotage, police violence, and syndicalist attempts to undermine the morale of the armed forces. Perhaps not very much was achieved materially in the improvements of working conditions, but this did not seem important to the anarcho-syndicalists; they wished to create an atmosphere of struggle, in which class enmities would sharpen and the workers would learn from experience the need for a revolutionary solution to the social problem.

In this context of intense strife the revolutionary syndicalists worked out their theories. Beginning with the conception of a society divided between producers and parasites, they saw the syndicates as a union of struggle on the part of the producers, a union strengthened by the fact that it bound men by their most fundamental bonds—the bonds of common work and common economic interests. In the industrial struggle alone the worker actually confronts his nearest enemy, the capitalist; in that struggle alone can he practise 'direct action', action not perverted by intermediaries. In the eyes of the revolutionary syndicalist action can be violent or otherwise. It can take the form of sabotage, of boycott, of the strike. Its highest form is the general strike, which the anarcho-syndicalists regard as the means of overthrowing not merely capitalism, but also the state, and of ushering in the libertarian millennium. This was a teaching that reinforced the anarchist's traditional rejection of political action, since the syndicate seemed to provide a practical alternative to the political party; it also left undiminished his hatred of the state, the church, and the army, all of which stood in the background as supporters of the direct enemy, the capitalist.

Such a doctrine attracted not only the militant workers, but also the intellectuals they distrusted. Among these the most imaginative was Georges Sorel. Sorel, whose ideas were most fully developed in his *Reflections on Violence*, had no direct connection with the syndicalist movement, and he was repudiated by its theoreticians, Pelloutier, Pouget, Pataud, and Yvetot. He was an engineer by profession who had become interested in Marx and then in Bergson, and who tried to combine the ideas of these very different philosophers with the practical experience of the syndicalist movement in order to create his own theory of social development. According to this theory, the class struggle was valuable because it contributed to the health and vigour of society, and should be pursued with violence because—says Sorel in words that seem to foreshadow writers like Malraux and Sartre—violent action provides extreme moments 'when we make an effort to create a new man within ourselves' and 'take possession of ourselves'. These moments, for Sorel, are the true freedom; he looks for no world that goes beyond them. And so, while he praises the conception of the general strike, he does so not because he thinks it will ever achieve its millenarian aim, but because the idea of its success is an invaluable 'social myth' for sustaining the enthusiasm of the

workers and maintaining their willingness to take part in the struggle—
which is everlasting. There are elements of Sorel that certainly remind
one of Proudhon, whom he admired, but he never claimed to be an anarchist, and his place in anarchist history is peripheral. For his ideas could
have led him to the right as easily as to the left; indeed, he later became
involved in monarchist and anti-Semitic movements, and eventually
found a niche among the prophets of Italian Fascism.

The influence of anarcho-syndicalism reached its height in France
round about 1906, with the celebrated Charter of Amiens, which
announced the complete autonomy of the syndicalist movement and
denied all political allegiances, whether to the Right or to the Left. It
began to decline round about 1908. This was partly due to a series of disastrous strikes which led to the imprisonment of the principal revolutionary-syndicalist leaders—Griffuelhes, Pouget, Yvetot, and others—and to
their replacement by the 'pure' syndicalist group led by Léon Jouhaux,
which moved steadily towards the right. As a result, the national unions,
which always had an inclination toward the reformism of the British trade-
union movement, gradually attained more power within the
Confederation; the anarchists remained well entrenched within the
Bourses de Travail, but their influence over the policy of the CGT as a
whole declined rapidly from 1909 to 1914, their grasp on key positions
weakened, and the organization ceased to bear their peculiar stamp.

During the anarcho-syndicalist heyday, the strictly anarchist propaganda groups continued their work, and the relationship between these two
currents of the movement was often strained. From the start the individualists were opposed to any participation in trade unions. At the opposite
extreme, Jean Grave and *Temps nouveaux* were in general sympathetic to
the syndicalists. In *Le Libertaire* Sébastien Faure maintained for several
years an opposition based on a purist conception of anarchist communism,
but later shifted to benevolent neutrality. As time went on and the younger
syndicalists began to think in terms of a revolution only through industrial
activity, many of the anarchists outside the syndicates became disturbed
by the vision of a future dominated by monolithic syndicates, and the
debate between Malatesta and Pierre Monatte at the Amsterdam
International Congress of 1907 underlined a difference of viewpoint that
increased as a type of revolutionary syndicalism began to evolve whose
exponents found it no longer necessary to declare in any way their allegiance to anarchism.

For anarchist communism and anarcho-syndicalism alike, in France, the
First World War precipitated a decline that had already begun several

years before. The loudly proclaimed anti-militarism of both anarchists and syndicalists produced no spectacular effects when the testing of war came upon them. Most of the anarchists of military age went to the colours without resistance, and many of their leaders, including Jean Grave, Charles Malato, and Paul Reclus, declared their support of the Allies. It is true that Sébastien Faure and E. Armand, the leading individualist, stood their ground in opposition, but the disunity within the movement hastened its decline. The anarchist papers ceased to appear; the anarchist groups were dissolved; no effective underground movement came into existence.

When the war was over, the Russian Revolution, with the concreteness of its achievement, became an equally disintegrative influence. Within the CGT it created vast divisions of opinion. The communists and the revolutionary syndicalists at first entered into alliance and formed a Centre Syndicaliste Révolutionnaire within the Confederation, of which the anarchists, led by Pierre Besnard, gained temporary control. In 1921 the Centre split away to form a rival organization, the CGT Unitaire. Again the anarcho-syndicalists at first seemed to have the upper hand, and they succeeded in provoking, in various parts of France, a strike movement whose failure discredited them and enabled the communists to seize control of the CGTU at its Saint-Étienne Congress in 1922. Shortly afterward the CGTU joined the Profintern, and a further split ensued, as the anarchists broke away to form a Federal Union of Autonomous Syndicates, which allied itself to the International Workingmen's Association recently founded in Berlin, and in 1925 became the CGT Syndicaliste Révolutionnaire. The CGTSR survived until 1939, but it was never more than a small sectarian movement, and from 1923 onward anarcho-syndicalism played an insignificant part in French working-class activity.

The decline in the anarchist movement itself was in militancy rather than in numbers. Anarchist journals and groups revived after 1918, but the revolutionary glamour which anarchism in its various forms had almost monopolized in the years from 1880 to 1910 faded in the light of the Russian Revolution, and many of the younger activists deserted to the Communist Party, while no new leaders of stature emerged, and many of the survivors of the pre-war élite were discredited by their support of the war. French anarchism took no new directions. It merely followed with diminished vigour the paths laid down in the fruitful years after 1894. With the decline in importance of the artisan class which had contributed so greatly to its ranks in the past, it seemed out of tune with the mood of French workers, yet it was kept alive largely by the fascination which the logic of extreme doctrines holds for certain types of Frenchmen of all classes.

Yet, if the native libertarian movement became a kind of living fossil during the years between 1918 and 1939, Paris and parts of southern France remained notable anarchist centres because of the willingness of most French governments during the 1920s and the 1930s to give asylum to political refugees. Wave by wave, as the totalitarian nightmare struck Europe, the foreign anarchists converged on France. First they came from Russia, then from Italy and Germany and finally from Spain, until, by 1939, there were probably more foreign than native anarchists on French soil. Nestor Makhno and Alexander Berkman died there; Camillo Berneri, the last of the great Italian anarchists, lived there until his sense of duty called him to a death in Spain. But these were only transients, waiting—usually in vain—for the day when fortune would call them back to the struggle in their own countries. They had very little influence on the French movement, and their presence did nothing to halt the decline that had come from the withering of its roots in popular life.

During World War II there were undoubtedly individual anarchists who played an active role in the resistance movement, but there was no organized presence like that of the communists, and therefore when the war ended the revived French Anarchist Federation, with its paper named after Faure's *Le Libertaire*, failed to offer the kind of image of social regeneration which the communist appropriated as a result of their well-publicized wartime activities, by which they were able to wipe out the inconvenient memory of the *rapprochement* early in the war between Stalin and Hitler. Thus the revived anarchist movement tended to take on an archaicist flavour, particularly as it no longer retained any appreciable influence in the trade-union movement, and its ideological ossification was paralleled by a tendency towards organizational rigidity against which younger anarchists began to rebel, particularly when an undifferentiated malaise spread among the youth in France as broadly as elsewhere in the Western world, and groups of young anarchists detached from the main movement began to emerge and to publish magazines of their own like *Noir et rouge*.

Against the organization-bound somnolence of 'official' post-war anarchism in France one has to place the events of the near-revolution that was precipitated by the student uprising in May of 1968 and was taken up by younger workers not only in Paris but also in much of the rest of the country. Here, in the ideas of spontaneous insurrection and of workers' control that circulated and were given practical expression at this time one can see the enduring influence of the teachings Proudhon developed from the Lyons mutualists of the 1840s and passed on to the libertarians of the International and to the anarcho-syndicalists.

During the uprising of 1968, over which the leaders of the French Anarchist Federation admitted that they had no influence as an organization and which they had not even foreseen, this tradition surged impressively out of the past when the workers not merely went on strike but occupied their factories; in France, despite so long and so stifling a control of the trade unions by the communist apparat, the memories of the past when the anarchists led them in fighting syndicalist organizations are not very deeply buried, and the French working-class militant is still likely to be inspired—whatever his party affiliation—by a belief in the worker's competence to control his own affairs, in the workplace as elsewhere, that derives far less from anything Marx ever wrote than from Proudhon's *De la capacité politique des classes ouvrières*.

The events of 1968 in France show admirably the way in which anarchist ideas and anarchist tactics can emerge spontaneously in a situation where the actors for the most part do not regard themselves as anarchists and have little knowledge of anarchist history or of the classic libertarian writings. The ageing intellectuals who publicly represented anarchism in France played no part in inspiring the event and the traditional movement played no real part. Certain dissident student groups of anarchists and other fractional libertarian movements were active, and there were anarchist elements among the Situationists (where the traditional alliance between anarchism and surrealism was perpetuated) and among the leaders of the March 22 movement which developed at Nanterre. Nevertheless, it was not always easy to determine how far their ideas on workers' councils, for example, were derived from German Left communist theories, which certainly influenced the Situationists, and how far from surviving anarcho-syndicalist traditions.

The spectacle of the black flag of anarchism flying beside the red flag of socialism over the Sorbonne and the Bourse was in fact truly symbolic of the eclectic attitude towards revolutionary doctrines that inspired most of the student and worker rebels outside the sectarian groupuscules of Maoists and Trotskyists, which were almost completely out of touch with the spirit of the movement. This feeling of solidarity between various strands of the anti-authoritarian left was expressed in an editorial in *Noir et rouge* a few months after the uprising (November 1968), which remarked that 'the real cleavage is not between "Marxism" or what is described as such, and anarchism, but rather between the libertarian spirit and idea, and the Leninist, Bolshevik, bureaucratic, conception of organization', and went on: 'We are not afraid to say ... that we feel closer to "Marxists" in the Council Communist movement of the past or to ... many friends in the March 22 movement than we do to official "anarchists" who have a semi-Leninist conception of party organization.'

The importance of the anarchist contribution to the events in May 1968 was recognized by sociologists who later studied the events. In *Le Mouvement de mai* Alain Touraine remarked that 'the union of the red flag and the black flag was the symbol of the May movements', and Edgar Morin, in *Mai 1968: La Brêche* said that 'it was a time of intellectual revival for anarchism, tinged with libertarian Marxism and situationism'. Other commentators noted how close the anarchists were to the spirit of what was happening, and Morin remarked on the open-mindedness that distinguished the young anarchists:

> They are not prisoners of dogmatic scholasticism, as is the case with many militants in the official Marxist, Trotskyist or Maoist parties. They are less captives to the limitations of rigid thought.

And indeed it was among the uncelebrated rank and file of the movement of May 1968, rather than among the demagogic romantics like Daniel Cohn-Bendit, that the anarchist spirit often appeared in its purest form. One remembers the laconic poster of the Jeunesse Anarchiste Communiste bearing the single word 'Create!' And that other anonymous poster which seemed to give expression to all that was good and idealistic in the youth movements of the 1960s. 'The society of alienation must disappear from history. We are inventing a new and original world. Imagination is seizing power!' Note the wording. Not men seizing power, or parties seizing power, or even students seizing power, but *imagination!* This, surely, is the only seizure of power that could take place without corruption!

The movement of May 1968 was an impressive experiment in free organization, and perhaps the nearest thing to a truly anarchist revolution that history has yet seen. But as a revolution it eventually failed, largely because of its betrayal by the communists who entered the movement late in order to salvage their own influence over the working class. In the years that followed, the rebellious urges it had expressed tended to die down or to be diverted into the political channels that led to the eventual election of Mitterrand and a socialist régime remote in spirit from the rebels of 1968.

But when the excitement was all over, anarchism retained much of the consideration among the young which its activists had earned during the May days. Somewhat revived by events, the French Anarchist Federation continued, absorbing the Alliance Syndicaliste and publishing *Le Monde libertaire* as a successor to the defunct *Le Libertaire*. But other libertarian groups have flourished, coming together occasionally in alliances over specific issues, but otherwise pursuing their autonomous courses. Some are propaganda groups; some are devoted to specific worker or student areas of interest. They have included the Union des Travailleurs Communistes Libertaires, the Co-ordination Libertaire Étudiante, and the Organisation Communiste Libertaire, and Contre-Pouvoir, formerly the Tribune Anarchiste Communiste. Such groups publish a variety of periodicals expressing various anarchist viewpoints, including *L'Entraide, Courant Alternatif, Lutter, and Agora*. In recent years the various anarchist formations have been especially disposed to unite where issues of surviving French imperialism are concerned, and in 1985 they established in Paris the Co-ordination Libertaire contre les Impérialisms, with the specific intent of rallying support in France for the cause of the native Kanak peoples of New Caledonia who are seeking liberation from what is one of the last surviving colonial régimes. This is a cause that echoes back to the great militant days of French anarchism, for in 1878 Louise Michel, an exile in New Caledonia, supported the Kanaks who rose that year in rebellion, and later she organized a literacy campaign among them and became so much accepted as their champion that twenty thousand tribespeople gathered on the quay at Noumea to bid farewell when she went home from exile.

As a critical movement, a left-wing conscience touching the nerve of the Left installed in the Élysée Palace, the anarchists sustain their special role in the French political spectrum.

ii. Anarchism in Italy

THE tendency of anarchist movements to take on local characteristics has been particularly evident in Italy, where the revolutionary attitude developed during the Risorgimento was one of the shaping influences on the libertarian movement. The first anarchist militants in the country were former Mazzinians or Garibaldians; under the Savoy monarchy anarchism continued for long periods the same kind of clandestine life as the republican movements of the earlier nineteenth century, and the traditions of conspiracy, insurrection, and dramatic deeds developed by the Carbonari helped to determine anarchist ways of action. Even the loose organization of the movement resembled that which the Carbonari assumed under persecution, and the typical libertarian heroes, such as Errico Malatesta and Carlo Cafiero, lived in the flamboyant manner of Garibaldi and Pisacane.

But if the movement of national liberation influenced Italian anarchism—and through it, as we shall see, anarchist methods in other countries—the ideas of foreign anarchists in their turn influenced the general development of revolutionary movements in Italy. Even before the arrival of Bakunin in 1864 the ideas of Proudhon were already having their effect on Italian republican thought, particularly through the writings and preachings of that Don Quixote of the Risorgimento, Carlo Pisacane, Duke of San Giovanni.

Pisacane had played a distinguished part as a young man in the Revolution of 1848, when he was Chief of Staff in Mazzini's Army of the Roman Republic. In 1857 he anticipated Garibaldi's Sicilian adventure, but with more tragic results, by sailing from Genoa with a small army of republicans in the steamship *Cagliari* and landing on the coast of Calabria. The local insurgents he had expected did not rally to him, and he was defeated by the Bourbon forces, himself dying upon the battlefield.

Pisacane became one of the hero-martyrs of the Risorgimento, but it was only after his death, with the publication in Paris of his collected essays (under the title *Saggi*), that his libertarian ideas became known widely. During the years of exile between 1848 and the fatal Calabrian adventure he had read deeply in Proudhon and Fourier, and had entered into polemical discussions with Mazzini on the nature of the forthcoming

Italian revolution. Pisacane's attitude was not unlike that of Bakunin during his pan-Slavist phase; he looked for a national revolution by means of a social revolution. The peasants must be aroused before the nation could be free, and this could only be done by offering them economic liberation, liberation from the yoke of their immediate tyrants, the landlords. For this reason Pisacane became a Proudhonian socialist. He demanded, like Proudhon, that every man have 'the fruit of his own labour guaranteed' and that 'all other property be not only abolished but denounced as theft'. Pisacane in fact went beyond Proudhon in the direction of collectivism, since he wanted industrial plants to become collective property and the land to be cultivated by the communes in such a way that the people should share equally in the produce of agriculture.

Not only did Pisacane accept Proudhon's basic economic theory, he also adopted his ideas on government, and saw the ultimate aim of the revolution not as the centralized state of the Jacobins and the Blanquists, but as 'the only just and secure form of government; the anarchy of Proudhon'. He demanded the simplification of social institutions, and further declared that 'society, constituted in its real and necessary relationships, excludes every idea of government'. But perhaps the most striking link between Italian anarchism and the earlier traditions of the Risorgimento is to be found in Pisacane's advocacy of what later became known as the propaganda of the deed.

> The propaganda of the idea is a chimera [he wrote]. Ideas result from deeds, not the latter from the former, and the people will not be free when they are educated, but will be educated when they are free. The only work a citizen can do for the good of the country is that of cooperating with the material revolution; therefore, conspiracies, plots, attempts, etc., are that series of deeds by which Italy proceeds towards her goal.

It would be easy to write the history of anarchism in Italy as a record of the effort to carry out these injunctions.

Pisacane left no movement behind him. Nevertheless, he had a great influence on the younger republicans, both through his personal associates and posthumously through his writings, and that influence helped to prepare the friendly reception Bakunin encountered when he reached Florence in 1864. It is significant that among both the Florentine Brotherhood and the International Brotherhood later founded in Naples there were several old comrades of Pisacane.

The influence of Proudhon also permeated Italy in the more direct form of mutualism; the first socialist journal founded in Italy, *Il Proletario*, edited by the Florentine Nicolo lo Savio, was Proudhonian in inspiration. However, as in France, the mutualists in Italy tended toward moderation and conservatism, and their part in the development of anarchism there is negligible. The Italian anarchist movement virtually begins with Bakunin's arrival.

I have shown already how in Florence Bakunin finally abandoned his early pan-Slavism and adopted anarchism as his revolutionary doctrine; as a consequence, the birth of anarchism in Italy coincided with the birth of the international anarchist movement in its rudimentary prototype, the Florentine Brotherhood. I have also told what little is known of that short-lived organization, and I have described its successor, the International Brotherhood, as an event in Bakunin's life and in the international development of anarchism. Here I shall discuss the International Brotherhood in so far as it can be regarded as an Italian movement.

In the constitutional documents drawn up by Bakunin and his immediate associates, the Italian section of the Brotherhood was variously called La Società per la Rivoluzione Democratica Sociale and La Società dei Legionari della Rivoluzione Sociale Italiana. There is no reason to suppose that these were separate organizations; Bakunin's passion for high-sounding titles is enough to explain the duplication. The high command of the society seems to have coincided roughly with Bakunin's Central Committee of the International Brotherhood in Naples. Several members of this caucus of initiated militants were later to play considerable parts in anarchist history. Giuseppe Fanelli, a veteran of 1848, was actually a deputy of the Italian parliament, but he fell so far under Bakunin's spell that later he went on a strange but successful mission to convert the Spanish masses to anarchism. Saverio Friscia, a Sicilian homoeopathic physician, was also a member of the Chamber of Deputies, but more important to the International Brotherhood as a thirty-third degree Freemason with great influence in the lodges of southern Italy.* Carlo Gambuzzi, a Neapolitan lawyer, was to become a close personal friend of Bakunin and the lover of his wife Antonia, as well as remaining for many years as active leader of the Italian anarchist movement. The last important member of this early élite was Alberto Tucci, another young Neapolitan lawyer.

The size of the movement which these men led is hard to estimate, largely because of the pretentiousness of its paper organization. An Italian

---

*Bakunin himself, like Proudhon, was a Freemason; a study has yet to be made of the links between Continental Freemasonry and the early anarchist movement.

Central Committee was created, and the whole country was optimistically divided into regions, in each of which the members would be controlled by a general staff appointed by the Central Committee; at this stage the Bakuninists, while accepting generally anarchistic ideas of organization for society after the revolution, had not yet shaken free from the authoritarian forms of conspiratorial tradition within their own organization. However, it seems clear that the only parts of Italy where branches of the Brotherhood became active were the city of Naples and the towns of Palermo and Sciacca in Sicily; no reliable figures for the membership of any of these groups exist, but they were probably small. In addition, a few of Bakunin's old associates in Florence may have adhered as individual members to the Brotherhood, but there is no trace of a Florence branch. Even the sections that existed seem to have languished as soon as Bakunin left Naples for Geneva in August 1867, and it is safe to assume that the International Brotherhood, which was not formally dissolved until 1869, became in Italy, as elsewhere, a skeleton organization of Bakunin's immediate associates.

During these early years the association between Bakunin and his Italian followers was close. Fanelli, Friscia, and Tucci all accompanied him into the League for Peace and Freedom and later resigned with him to become founding members of the International Alliance of Social Democracy. Fanelli, Gambuzzi, Tucci, and Friscia, with Raffaele Mileti of Calabria and Giuseppe Manzoni of Florence, formed the nucleus of the National Committee of the Alliance. Again, it is difficult to say what strength the Alliance attained in Italy, since early in 1869 the organization was dissolved, and its branches automatically became sections of the International Workingmen's Association. The Italian militants had opposed this move, but it was from this time—the early months of 1869— that an influential anarchist movement began to arise in Italy.

At first it was restricted to the Mezzogiorno, and the most active branch was in Naples, under the leadership of Gambuzzi and the tailor Stefano Caporosso. Many local artisans joined it, and at the Basel Congress of the International, in September 1869, Caporosso reported a membership of 600. Two months later, the Naples section founded the first Italian anarchist journal, L'Eguaglianza, edited by the ex-priest Michelangelo Statuti, whose ideas seem to have anticipated those developed later by Georges Sorel, since he maintained that strikes were useful only because they developed the spirit of solidarity among the workers.

After three months L'Eguaglianza was suppressed by the police, but the Neopolitan section continued to flourish. Indeed, after intervening in a leather-workers' strike it expanded so rapidly that early in 1870 the local police reported a membership of 4,000. Other branches appeared in the Campania and Sicily, but it was still some time before the movement spread to the rest of Italy. In fact, police persecutions, the imprisonment of Gambuzzi and Caporosso, and the discovery of *agents provocateurs* among the members of the Naples section resulted in a decline even in the south.

In the middle of 1871, however, a new group of militants appeared, different in character from those veterans of earlier struggles who had first gathered around Bakunin. The leaders among them, Carlo Cafiero, Errico Malatesta, and Carmelo Palladino, were all young men in their early twenties, the educated sons of southern Italian landowners; all of them came from regions where peasant poverty was endemic (Cafiero and Palladino from Apulia and Malatesta from Capua in the Campania); they were in fact the Italian equivalents of the conscience-stricken Russian noblemen who in the same decade felt the burning urge to 'go to the people'. Their sense of injustice done to the poor and the defenceless made them intolerant of the pietistic liberalism of Mazzini, and—with Garibaldi ageing and reluctant to become involved again in the struggle—Bakunin was the leader to whom they turned, though Cafiero flirted briefly with Engels and Marx. The triumvirate of Cafiero, Malatesta, and Palladino reconstructed the section of the International in the Mezzogiorno, but their work proceeded slowly, hampered by further police persecution, and might have come to little if Mazzini had not decided on a course of action that played into the hands of Bakunin and gave him the opportunity to intervene massively in Italian left-wing politics.

In his old age Mazzini had become steadily more conservative and more distrustful of the activist elements within the Italian republican movement. He was disturbed by the growing influence of socialism in Europe, and he had already denounced the Paris Commune for its godlessness and its denial of true nationalism. Now he turned against the International, and attacked it similarly in *La Roma del popolo*. Many of his followers, who had admired the heroism of the Communards and knew that some of the best of them were Internationalists, were repelled by his attitude, and one of the left-wing republican journals, *Il Gazzetino Rosso* of Milan, published on 24 July 1871 a sharp reply from Bakunin, entitled *The Reply of an Internationalist to Giuiseppe Mazzini*; Bakunin accused the veteran leader of 'turning his back on the cause of the proletariat' at a time when it had suffered the horrors of the last days of the Commune. Immediately after completing this article, Bakunin, who realized that at this moment the influence of anarchism in Italy was in the balance, set to work on a much longer essay entitled *Mazzini's Political Theology and the International*, which appeared in the autumn of 1871.

The immediate effect of these polemics was a spread of Internationalist organization, which now began to break out of the Mezzogiorno and into its later strongholds in Tuscany, Romagna, and the Marches. On 18 October Cafiero gave Engels a list of towns in which Internationalist activity had begun; they included, besides the old southern centres, Florence, Parma, Ravenna, Pisa, Turin, Milan, Rome, and Bologna. How many of these towns had active sections at this time it is hard to tell, but when the Jura Federation issued its Sonvillier Circular against the General Council in November 1871, branches in Bologna, Milan, and Turin supported it along with those in southern Italy.

About this time, however, a rapid change began. Bakunin had circulated at a Mazzinian congress of workers in November 1871 a fresh pamphlet entitled *Circular to My Italian Friends*, which induced some of the delegates to withdraw from the congress rather than condone Mazzini's attitude. In the following month, a movement of Fascio Operaio (Workers' Unions) appeared in central Italy; this movement was from the beginning socialistically inclined, and in February 1872 a gathering of its members from Ravenna, Lugo, and Forli allied themselves to the International, adopting the anarchist demand for autonomous communes. In the following month the fourteen Romagna sections of Fascio called together in Bologna the first anarchist gathering that was really national in scope, since there were also delegates from Naples, Turin, Genoa, Mantua, and Mirandola. The congress was dominated by a group of young Romagnols, headed by Andrea Costa, a student of philology who had been led into the International by his enthusiasm for the Paris Commune, and who was to join Malatesta and Cafiero among the moving spirits of Italian anarchism during the greater part of the 1870s.

The Bologna Congress destroyed any hope the Marxists may have had of establishing their influence, for the present at least, in the nascent Italian socialist movement. On the question of political action which divided Marx and Bakunin its delegates voted against participation in elections and stated pointedly that 'any authoritarian government is the work of the privileged to the detriment of the disinherited classes'. They also declared in favour of a general insurrection aimed at the solution of the social problem. Organizationally, the Congress resulted in the foundation of a Federation of the Bologna Region, which shelved any decisions in the Marx-Bakunin struggle by deciding to remain autonomous and to treat the General Council and the Jura Federation equally as corresponding bureaux. Marx and Engels, who believed that whoever was not with them was against them, decided that the Italians had 'unmasked themselves as pure Bakuninists'; as time quickly showed, they were not wrong.

The Romagna now became the centre of anarchist militancy, largely because of Costa's energetic organizational work. In the rest of Italy many sections of the International were formed, but there was little regional coordination, except in Umbria, and it was only the initiative of the Romagnols and of Fanelli in Naples, anxiously prodded by Bakunin—who wished to consolidate his forces for the struggle in the International—that brought the anarchists of the country together in a national congress. This congress, which met at Rimini on 4 August 1872, was of historic importance, since it not merely established the anti-authoritarian tendency of socialism in Italy for almost a decade, but also decided indirectly the fate of the International as a whole.

Twenty-one sections were represented, and their distribution showed the geographical shifts that were taking place in anarchist influence. The once-dominant Mezzogiorno sent delegates for only two sections; in this region of poverty-stricken peasants anarchism had been unable to make any advances outside the larger towns. Except for one Roman section, the rest of the delegates came from the north-central provinces—Romagna, Tuscany, Umbria, and Emilia. Milan, whose delegate, Vincenzo Pezza, was ill owing to recent imprisonment, sent a message couched in fervently anti-Marxist terms. Both generations of militants were represented among the delegates—Fanelli and Friscia from the old republican Left, and Costa, Cafiero, and Malatesta from the younger generation.

The Congress established the Italian Federation of the International as a simple network of autonomous sections, whose only common organs would be correspondence and statistical bureaux. The customary anarchist resolutions against political action were passed unanimously, and then, in its third day, the Congress moved on to the question of its relations to the General Council and its attitude to the Hague Congress. Bakunin and his followers in the Spanish and Jura Federation had urged the Italians to send as many delegates as possible to The Hague, but, led by the fiery oratory of Cafiero and Costa, the Italians passed a drastic comprehensive resolution in which they broke off 'all solidarity with the General Council in London', refused to acknowledge the Hague Congress, and called upon all Internationalists who shared their opposition to authoritarian methods to send representatives to a separate anti-authoritarian congress in Neuchâtel. Thus the Italian Federation, the last to be founded in the life of the old International, was the first to begin the breakaway which all the anarchists knew in their hearts was inevitable.

The Italians kept to their resolution not to support the Hague Congress. Carlo Cafiero went there, but only as an observer; when he returned through Switzerland he met four other delegates from Italy and participated in the Congress of Saint-Imier which confirmed the breach with the Marxist sections of the International.

The militancy displayed by the Italian anarchists at the Rimini Congress did not diminish during the following months. They not only severed their connections with the Marxists; they also refused any alliances with the left-wing republicans, and daily drew nearer to a consistently Bakuninist attitude. This implied not merely an insistence on libertarian forms of social and economic organization; it meant also the decision that, as one clandestine journal declared, 'today propaganda is no longer enough; now we must organize ourselves for the struggle'. Clearly, the insurrectional struggle was meant. As its attitude became more extreme, the anarchist movement in Italy also grew stronger, and when the second national congress took place in Bologna in March 1873, its fifty-three delegates represented 150 sections, seven times as many as had been represented seven months before at the first congress.

This rapid growth of the Federation was observed by the Italian government with concern; the Minister of the Interior sent instructions to the provincial authorities to destroy the International in their regions. The police raided the Bologna Congress and arrested Cafiero, Costa, and Malatesta, but the remaining delegates merely shifted the meeting place and carried on their deliberations, with suitably defiant resolutions attacking the persecution to which they had been subjected. Apart from the reaffirmation of general principles, the most important resolution adopted by the 1873 Congress was one calling for propaganda work among the peasants, in the hope of tapping that great reservoir of 'fourteen million peasants in Lombardy and the southern provinces who are in agony because of fever and hunger and anxiously await the hour of emancipation'. The attempt to carry out this hope and spur the peasants to action was to have a great influence on future anarchist activity.

In nineteenth-century Italy there was nothing discreditable or even fearful about police persecution. The sufferings of the heroes of the Risorgimento had made it almost a badge of worth and the efforts of the government to stamp out the International merely brought new recruits to its sections, so that by the early months of 1874, which was to be one of the dramatic years of Italian anarchism, the police and the anarchists—preparing separate estimates—came to roughly the same conclusion; that the membership of the International had grown to more than 30,000. Moreover, owing largely to the activities of Costa, who was in constant contact with Bakunin, this small army of anarchists was at last united by an organizational network which operated through ten regional federations, extending into every district of Italy and even into Sardinia.

It was at this time that the Italian anarchists decided to shift the centre of their activities from the congress halls to the open field of revolutionary struggle. Not until 1876 did Cafiero and Malatesta actually emerge as missionaries of the Propaganda by Deed, carrying it as a new gospel to the rest of the international anarchist movement. In that year Malatesta declared in the *Bulletin* of the Jura Federation: 'The Italian Federation believes that the *insurrectionary deed*, destined to affirm socialist principles by acts, is the most efficacious means of propaganda.' Picked up by theoreticians in France and Spain, this Italian viewpoint dominated European anarchist activities during the 1880s. But as a matter of practical tactics it emerged from the circumstances of the Italian movement as early as 1873.

The anarchists had now gained a considerable popular support, but—remembering Italian revolutionary traditions—they realized that they could only sustain their position if they dramatically rivalled the feats of the Garibaldians and the Mazzinians. 'Violent action,' said Andrea Costa in recollection of these days, 'was considered ... a necessity ... to pose the problem, to show the new ideal above the old ones.' The winter of 1873–4 was one of distress and unrest, and its strikes and hunger demonstrations gave the anarchists an opportunity to demonstrate their direct-actionism on a small scale. But this was not enough; a deliberately planned programme of action was needed, and for this purpose the militant leaders of the Federation revived Bakunin's old idea of a secret inner organization to initiate insurrectionary action. Accordingly, toward the end of 1873 they established, as a shadow group within the International, an Italian Committee for the Social Revolution, which acted entirely by clandestine means. Its purpose was to provoke a group of well-planned risings in carefully selected parts of Italy, which it was hoped might set going by chain reaction a whole series of regional insurrections in which the sections of the International would guide the mass uprisings toward a general social revolution.

The Committee for the Social Revolution planned an elaborate action for the summer of 1874. On the night of 7–8 August, the anarchists of the Romagna would seize Bologna, and the news of their success would be the signal for risings in Rome, Florence, Palermo, and Leghorn, and also in the country districts of Apulia and Sicily, after which it was hoped that the conflagration might spread across Italy and the 'social liquidation' be accomplished. It was a fearsome project, but the performance of the Internationalists was far from equal to their intentions. Through inform-ers, the police gained a fair knowledge of their plans, and before the day of the great rising they arrested Andrea Costa, the key organizer of the insur-rection. The conspiracy had been scotched: it had not been destroyed, and on the morning of 7 August a proclamation of the Italian Committee for the Social Revolution appeared in towns and cities throughout Italy, call-ing on the workers 'to fight to the death for the abolition of every privilege and the complete emancipation of mankind'.

The plans for the Bologna insurrection were elaborate. A thousand Bolognese would gather at two points outside the city, where they would be joined by 3,000 insurgents from other cities of the Romagna. The united force would march in two columns into the city, where Bakunin was wait-ing to join them; one column would attack the arsenal—two sergeants had already promised to throw open the gates—and then distribute the arms to the other insurgents, who in the meantime would have raised barricades out of materials already collected at key points.

The Bolognese rebels gathered in considerable numbers, but of the forces from other cities who had promised to gather at Imola, less than 200 arrived out of the expected 3,000. These set off for Bologna, but they were intercepted on the way by carabinieri and troops, and those who escaped arrest fled into the hills. The Bolognese, having waited in vain for the sup-porting column, buried their arms in the fields and dispersed. The project-ed risings in other Italian cities were frustrated by the action of the alerted police, and only in Apulia did Malatesta quixotically raise the standard of revolt even when his hopes were clearly doomed to disappointment. There is a wry humour in his own description of the event which shows the quality of this man who was soon to become the real leader of Italian anarchism and to remain so for half a century.

Several hundred confederates had promised to be at Castel del Monte. I arrived there, but of all those who had sworn to come, we found we were only six in number. It does not matter, the case of arms is opened; it is full of old muzzle-loaders; *non fa niente*, we arm ourselves and declare war on the Italian army. We fought the cam-paign for several days, seeking to involve the peasants on our side, but without getting any response. The second day, we had a fight with eight carabinieri, who fired on us and imagined that we were very numerous. Three days later we saw that we were surrounded by soldiers; there was but one thing to do. We buried the guns and decided to disperse. I hid myself in a hay wagon and thus succeeded in getting out of the danger zone.

Malatesta was actually arrested at Pesaro on his way north toward Switzerland, and joined the other anarchist leaders in prison. The final result of the great plan for social liquidation was that the International in Italy was crippled for many months. Most of its active militants were behind bars or in exile, its sections were dispersed, and its press was suppressed. On the other hand, the insurgents won a great deal of popular sympathy, not because they were anarchists, but because they had defied the government of Victor Emmanuel, and the consistent acquittal by respectable juries of these men who were obviously guilty before the law, became a cumulative popular gesture against a régime that had done little to remove economic and social evils. By June 1876 all the insurgents had been found 'not guilty' and set free; their main suffering had been from the law's delay, which kept some of them almost two years in prison without trial.

Reinvigorated by the propaganda success of the trials, with their interminable revolutionary orations—Andrea Costa alone stayed in the witness box for three days—and by the return of the most active militants to public life, the International began in 1876 to rebuild its organization. Regional federations were reconstructed and held conferences in Bologna, in Florence, in Jesi, unmolested by the police. The anarchist press revived with the appearance of *Il Nuovo Risveglio* in Leghorn and *Il Martello* in Fabriano. Finally, a national congress was called for late October in Florence. This time the police again moved into action, fearing—or pretending to fear—that the real aim of the congress would be to plan another series of uprisings. Andrea Costa and other delegates were arrested at the station as they arrived in Florence, while the congress meeting hall was occupied by the police. But almost fifty delegates still remained at liberty, and the congress finally took place in a wood among the foothills of the Apennines, with the rain falling steadily throughout the day.

Cafiero and Malatesta dominated the congress, and under their influence the delegates adopted an intransigently insurrectional and antipolitical programme. More important, theoretically at least, was a resolution which showed the Italians moving away from Bakuninist collectivism toward anarchist communism.

Each must do for society all that his abilities will allow him to do, and he has the right to demand from society the satisfaction of all his needs, in the measure conceded by the state of production and social capacities.

But, whatever their thoughts on such economic questions, the dreams of the revolutionary deed which would act like the stone precipitating an avalanche still haunted the minds of the anarchist leaders. Despite the failure of the Apulian rising in 1874, Cafiero and Malatesta remained convinced that there was combustible material in the hearts of the southern Italian peasants, and in the summer of 1877, after elaborate preparations, they set up their headquarters in the mountain village of San Lupo, near Benevento in the Campania. They had recruited the Russian revolutionary Stepniak, and also a mountain guide named Salvatore Farina, who turned out in the end to be a police spy. His activities led to the arrival of the carabinieri before the conspirators' plans had matured, and, after a brisk gun battle in which one of the police was mortally wounded, twenty-six anarchists loaded their equipment on mules and set off into the Apennines. Two days later, on the morning of 8 August—it was a Sunday—the little troop descended into the village of Letino carrying their red-and-black flags. In the presence of the assembled peasants, Cafiero deposed King Victor Emmanuel, and his companions solemnly burned the local tax records. The villagers applauded the latter act, and Father Fortini, the priest of Letino, welcomed the anarchists as 'true apostles sent by the Lord to preach His divine law'. The muskets of the militia were distributed, and Cafiero exhorted the people to make use of them and assure their own liberty. Then, guided by Father Fortini, the anarchist band set off for the next village of Gallo, where Father Tamburini came out to welcome them, and went from house to house, shouting to the people, 'Fear nothing. They are honest folk. There has been a change in the government and the burning of the register.' In Gallo the insurgents not only burned the tax records, but also appropriated the cash in the collector's safe and smashed the meter that assessed the tax on flour at the local mill. All this delighted the peasants; it was good practical action that might save them a few lire in taxes owing to the confusion that would result. But neither the men of Letino nor the men of Gallo were inclined to take up arms for the cause. They remarked very reasonably that, while they were grateful to the insurgents for what they had done, their parishes could not defend themselves against the whole of Italy. 'Tomorrow the soldiers will come and everybody will be shot.' Their prophecies were partly correct. A battalion and a half of infantry, two squadrons of cavalry, and two companies of Bersaglieri were deployed against the tiny band of insurgents, who took once again to the mountains. They were drenched with rain, walked into snowdrifts, and eventually got lost in the fog. Finally they took refuge in a peasant house, and there they were surrounded and captured, too exhausted to make any effective resistance. Their comic little attempt was prophetic of the fate of anarchist efforts to reach the Italian peasantry; unlike the landworkers of southern Spain, those of southern Italy were impervious to libertarian messianism, and anarchism in Italy was to remain for the most part a movement of the smaller cities.

The Benevento rising set going another cycle of governmental repression—imprisonment, bannings of papers and organizations, followed by the customary acquittals of international prisoners by juries hostile to the Savoy monarchy. By the end of the year the legally suppressed International was reorganizing itself and in April 1878 a secret congress in Pisa decided on a 'general insurrection' on a national scale, 'without heeding the sacrifices, since the day is not far distant when the armed proletariat will bring about the downfall of whatever remains of the bourgeoisie, throne, and altar'. A series of local congresses dutifully approved the plan, but the failures of Bologna and Apulia and Benevento had sapped the enthusiasm of even the most militant insurrectionists, and the plans for a countryside revolution never got beyond the talking stage.

Instead, perhaps as a result of collective frustration, individual acts of violence began. On 17 November 1878, as the new King Umberto was driving through the streets of Naples, a cook named Giovanni Passanante jumped on his carriage and tried to stab him with a knife engraved with the words, 'Long live the international republic'. There was no evidence linking Passanante with any anarchist group, but popular opinion—perhaps not unjustifiably—saw a connection between his act and the exhortations which had appeared recently in the libertarian papers to destroy 'all kings, emperors, presidents of republics, priests of all religions', as 'true enemies of the people'. On the day immediately following Passanante's attempt a bomb was thrown into a monarchist parade in Florence and four people were killed; two days later another bomb exploded in the midst of a crowd in Pisa, without any fatal result. There is a strong possibility that the bomb in Florence may have been thrown by an *agent provocateur*; it is certain that the Pisan bomb was thrown by an anarchist.

These acts became the excuse for an even greater persecution of the International. By the end of 1878 every anarchist militant of standing, whether or not suspected of complicity in the terrorist acts, was either in prison or in exile, and the government attempted to persuade the courts to consider the International an association of malefactors, which would automatically justify the detention of its members. This attempt failed, since the courts realized that the International itself could not be held responsible for the acts of individuals who—like Passanante—might not even belong to it, but the result of the relentless pressure which the police maintained during the winter of 1878 and the spring of 1879 was the final break-up of the International as an organization.

Its failure to revive was due largely to the fact that the dynamic young leaders who had guided the movement through the years between 1871 and 1877 were no longer active in Italy. Cafiero and Malatesta were both in exile, the former presiding over the group of expatriates who gathered in Lugano, and the latter ranging through Europe and the Levant in search of revolutionary adventure. Even more serious than their absence was the defection of Costa. In 1877 Costa went to the last congress of Saint-Imier International at Verviers, and there he followed, in collaboration with Paul Brousse, a consistently extremist line. Shortly afterward, in Paris, he was arrested and imprisoned for two years for activities in connection with the revival of the anarchist movement there. In 1879, while still in prison, he announced his abandonment of anarchism, and wrote a letter, which the moderate socialist Bignami published in *Il Plebe* of Milan, announcing that he now believed in political action. Though it is impossible to trace the mental evolution by which Costa reached his changed viewpoint, it is significant that already in 1877 he had turned so far against insurrectionism that he tried to persuade Cafiero and Malatesta to give up their plans for the Benevento rising. Costa was to turn his great eloquence and his popularity in the Romagna to the cause of parliamentary socialism; in 1882 he was elected to the Chamber of Deputies, and during the following years he played a leading part in creating the Socialist Party in Italy.

All of Costa's close associates among the anarchist élite denounced him. But one at least of them, Cafiero, eventually followed him into apostasy; in March 1882 he unexpectedly issued a statement in Milan calling upon the Italian anarchists to adopt social democracy, and shortly afterward he supported the candidacies of parliamentary socialists. However, his former friends found a charitable explanation for Cafiero's defection when, in the spring of 1883, he was found wandering naked in the hills outside Florence; he never recovered his sanity, and died in 1892 in a mental home, haunted by the thought that the windows of his room might be giving him more than his just share of sunlight.

Costa's decision was the result of personal convictions, but it coincided with a general shift toward parliamentary socialism among the workers in Italy; from 1878 onward the anarchists became a dwindling minority. It is true that in December 1880, when a socialist congress of delegates from fifteen northern Italian cities met in the Ticinese town of Chiasso, the anarchist refugees from Lugano secured a victory for their point of view. Cafiero, as chairman of the congress, advocated eloquently the policy of political abstention, and the anarchists received a new and formidable recruit in the person of Amilcare Cipriani, an ever-young veteran of the Risorgimento who had fought with Garibaldi at Aspromonte and had just returned from New Caledonia, where he had been transported for his part in the Paris Commune. It was Cipriani who drafted a declaration to which the great majority of the congress adhered, declaring that only an armed insurrection offered any hope for the Italian working class. But this declaration was principally the work of exiles who were already beginning to lose sight of the realities of Italy in the dawning 1880s, and its ineffectuality was shown by its scanty outcome in real action.

The exiles in Lugano actually set up a new Revolutionary Committee and—if the police reports can be trusted—planned an uprising in the Romagna for the next spring in which Italian anarchists would be assisted by a legion of Russian political exiles and French ex-Communards, led by Cipriani. It is certain that Cafiero and Cipriani crossed the border and went secretly to Rome in January 1881, but Cipriani was arrested in Rimini and Cafiero returned over the border.

By this time anarchist activity in Italy had in fact declined to the sporadic functioning of local groups, with little regional and no national organization remaining. At the International Congress of 1881 only two Italian delegates were present, Malatesta and Saverio Merlino, a young lawyer who had been Malatesta's schoolfellow and had been brought into the movement through his interest in the case of the Benevento insurgents. Malatesta represented one regional federation, that of Tuscany, and about sixteen individual groups, mostly in the Mezzogiorno, Piedmont, and the Romagna, were also represented. But neither Malatesta nor Merlino held mandates from groups in such former anarchist strongholds as Bologna, Rome, or Milan. On the other hand, Malatesta represented expatriate groups in Constantinople, Marseilles, Geneva and Alexandria.

Here already emerges a pattern that was to characterize Italian anarchism for at least a quarter of a century. There were many individual anarchists in Italy during this period, and they continued to form local groups, but, partly through police persecution and partly through a distrust of organization, they rarely formed federations like those of the 1870s. A deceptive appearance of rich activity was given by the number of anarchist journals which appeared. For the six years from 1883 to 1889, for instance, Max Nettlau, that indefatigable bibliographer, lists thirteen cities in which such papers were published; all of these journals, however, were ephemeral, some surviving only for a single issue and the longest-lived lasting no more than a few months. To a great extent anarchism in Italy was now maintained by the phenomenal activity of a few individuals, among whom Merlino and Malatesta were particularly prominent during the 1880s and 1890s. The groups that existed were constantly disappearing and changing their membership not only because of governmental suppression, but also because the anarchists shared the urge of so many other Italians at this period to emigrate where there was the chance of a better living.

What distinguished the Italians from anarchists of other countries is the extent to which, in emigrating, they became the missionaries of their ideas. Men and women like Malatesta, Merlino, Pietro Gori, Camillo Berneri and his daughter, Marie Louise Berneri, exerted a continuing influence on international anarchist thought and activity down to the middle of the present century. Throughout the Levant the first anarchist groups were Italian, while in Latin America and the United States, the Italian immigrants played a very great part in spreading anarchist ideas during the 1890s, and published more expatriate journals than all the other national groups put together.

Furthermore, though the Italian anarchist leaders, and particularly Malatesta, were opposed to deeds of individual terrorism, Italian assassins acquired a dubious fame during the later years of the nineteenth century for the relentlessness with which they acted as self-appointed executioners of heads of state in many parts of Europe. Caserio's assassination of the French president, Sadi Carnot, in 1894, was only the first of a series of spectacular political murders carried out by Italians. In 1897 Michele Angiolillo travelled to Spain and shot the reactionary prime minister, Antonio Canovas. In 1898 Luigi Luccheni carried out one of the most abominable of all political assassinations by stabbing the tragic and gentle Empress Elizabeth of Austria in Geneva. And in 1900 King Umberto of Italy, who had already escaped two attempts, was finally shot by Gaetano Bresci as he was attending a country fête in Mosca. Caserio, Angiolillo, and Luccheni all appear to have been obsessional fanatics who acted on their own initiative from a desire to strike at the symbolic figureheads of the system of injustice and authority they detested; Bresci, on the other hand, seems to have been the chosen agent of an anarchist group in Paterson, New Jersey.

But though the acts of these assassins helped to give anarchism its bad name and provided excuses for continued persecution of the movement in general by the Italian government, they were by no means typical of the movement during the 1880s and 1890s. There were other Italian anarchists who travelled abroad in the hope of setting up Utopian colonies which would show by experiment the possibility of living in voluntary communism. The most famous was the Cecilia Colony in Brazil. A number of anarchists left Italy in February 1890 to take up land granted to them by the Brazilian government in accordance with its policy of encouraging immigration. A successful beginning was made during the first year, and by the spring of 1891 some 200 people were living and working in the colony. But it lasted only four years; by the middle of 1894 the last of its members had departed. Its failure was due to a number of causes; undoubtedly the unsuitability of the land allocated to the colonists was one of them, but even more important were the increasingly bitter differences of opinion which arose over every conceivable point of action and organization, and which in the end divided the community—as so many other communities have been divided—into irreconcilable factions.

The majority of the Italian anarchists, however, were neither individualist assassins nor community-minded Utopians; at this period, whether in Italy or abroad, they combined agitation with precarious economic existence, and the career of Malatesta during these years, while exceptional in its dramatic adventurousness, seems almost to epitomize the character of the movement after the collapse of the International at the end of the 1880s.

Malatesta, who—despite the legends that quickly crystallized around him—was in no way connected with the Tyrant of Rimini, came of the southern Italian landowning class. As a medical student at the University of Naples, he joined in the student republican movement and was expelled for taking part in demonstrations. Soon afterward he became an anarchist, and from his conversion he decided to subordinate all his other interests to the revolutionary cause. He learned the electrician's trade, and when his parents left him property in Capua he got rid of it immediately by giving the houses to the tenants.

Malatesta's activities in Italy during the 1870s, which we have already described, were punctuated by his earliest expeditions abroad. After being acquitted in connection with the Apulian uprising in 1874, he wandered for two years around the Mediterranean, conspiring in Spain and trying vainly to reach Bosnia in order to take part in the revolt against the Turks which broke out in 1875. He was back in Italy to lead the Benevento insurrection of 1877, but after his acquittal in connection with this affair he set off again on his wanderings, which took him from Alexandria through Syria and Turkey to Greece, hunted by the police and founding Italian anarchist groups in almost every country he entered. After a brief interlude in Romania he travelled for a while in the French-speaking countries, and in Paris challenged the renegade anarchist Jules Guesde—already a leading parliamentary socialist—to a duel which never took place. Finally, he reached London in time for the International Congress of 1881. There he encountered Cafiero, and collaborated with him in the short-lived *Insurrezione*, probably the first expatriate Italian anarchist journal to appear outside Switzerland.

Malatesta did not return to Italy until 1883, when he and Merlino tried to reorganize the International so as to counter the growing influence of Costa and his political propaganda. Under their influence the groups in Rome, Florence, and Naples were strengthened, and Malatesta founded a journal, *La Questione Sociale*, devoted particularly to attacking the Socialist Party. Shortly afterward he and Merlino were arrested; they were tried at Rome in February 1884 and received sentences of three years' imprisonment for belonging to a forbidden organization, while fifty-eight Florentines who signed a statement in support of them were given thirty months each. The sentences were appealed, and eventually, a year later, reduced. In the meantime the prisoners were free, and carried on their propaganda activities until the cholera epidemic of 1886 broke out in Naples. Then Malatesta and his friends immediately set out for the stricken city, where they worked with a complete disregard for their own safety until the end of the epidemic. The Italian government is said to have offered Malatesta a medal, but it did not think of wiping out his sentence, and accordingly he and many of his Florentine comrades escaped to Argentina before the time came for surrendering themselves to the court. The Malatesta legend tells how, being watched constantly by the police, he had himself nailed into a case which was supposed to contain a sewing machine, and in this way was carried on board the ship of a friendly captain.

In Buenos Aires Malatesta found the beginnings of a movement inspired by Ettore Mattei, an emigrant from Leghorn who in 1884 founded the Circolo Comunista-anarchico. Malatesta opened a mechanical workshop and restarted *La Questione Sociale*; with a missionary intent typical of him, he made it a bilingual Spanish-Italian journal. When funds ran short, Malatesta and a group of his comrades set off on a prospecting expedition in the wilds of Patagonia. They actually found gold in one of the rivers, but were almost immediately dispossessed by a company which had bribed the government officials to transfer the concession.

Malatesta returned to Europe in the summer of 1889. He settled in Nice, whence he hoped to influence affairs in his own country by publishing a magazine, *Associazone*, to be distributed clandestinely in Italy. The French police soon began to pry into his activities, and he left for the more tolerant atmosphere of London, where he rented a house in Fulham, installed a printing press, and resumed publication of *Associazone*, the journal expired when Malatesta fell ill of pneumonia and one of his comrades ran away with the editorial funds.

Meanwhile, in Italy there had been new outbreaks of unrest, particularly through the May Day celebrations of 1890. These disturbances, some of them incited by republicans and anarchists, and others evidently spontaneous popular reactions against economic distress, helped to bring about a perceptible revival of anarchist influence, and in January 1891 some eighty-six delegates, claiming to represent several hundred groups from all parts of Italy, assembled at Capolago in the Ticino. Malatesta and Cipriani were the leading speakers of this gathering, which decided to found an Anarchist-Socialist-Revolutionary Party to unite all the scattered libertarian organizations and points of view into an insurrectionary movement opposed to government of any kind, either on the Right or on the Left. The division between the two left-wing trends was finally established when the socialists, meeting shortly afterward, in Genoa, decided to form a new united party from which the anarchists would be formally excluded.

After the Congress, Malatesta went secretly into Italy, where he spent some time organizing groups in the Carrara region; there was a strong anarchist tradition among the marble workers which continues to this day. Returning to Switzerland, he was arrested at Lugano; the Italians demanded his extradition, but the Swiss refused, and in September 1891 Malatesta returned to London. The following year he was in Spain, and in 1894 he was back in Italy. In 1896 he took part in the stormy sessions of the London Congress of the Second International, where the anarchists were finally expelled from the ranks of world socialism, and the next year he returned again to Italy and settled in Ancona. There he began to publish another newspaper, and gained such a wide influence among the factory and habour workers that the authorities soon became anxious about his presence; an excuse was found for arresting him and sentencing him to six months in prison for agitational activities. Perhaps it was as well for his own safety that he happened to be still in confinement during the May days of 1898, when severe rioting broke out in the Mezzogiorno and spread to Florence and Milan; in the cities there was fighting in the streets, and demonstrators were shot down by the government forces. It was in revenge for the severe repressions of this year that Bresci later killed King Umberto.

As a result of the tense atmosphere which followed the 1898 rising, Malatesta was not released at the end of his prison term, but instead, with a number of other leaders of the movement, was sent to exile for five years on the island of Lampedusa. He did not stay there long. One stormy day he and three of his comrades seized a boat and put out to sea in defiance of the high waves. They were lucky enough to be picked up by a ship on its way to Malta, whence Malatesta sailed to the United States. There his life once again took a sensational turn, which this time almost brought it to an end. He became involved in a dispute with the individualist anarchists of Paterson, who insisted that anarchism implied no organization at all, and that every man must act solely on his impulses. At last, in one noisy debate, the individual impulse of a certain comrade directed him to shoot Malatesta, who was badly wounded but obstinately refused to name his assailant. The would-be assassin fled to California, and Malatesta eventually recovered; in 1900 he set sail for London, which by now had become his favourite place of exile.

He did not return to Italy until 1913, and spent most of the intervening time running a small electrician's workshop and trying to influence affairs at home by writing for periodicals and publishing pamphlets which had a wide circulation in Italy, where his influence, even from exile, remained strong, particularly in the south and in Tuscany and Romagna.

Even in London, where he played a very slight part in the anarchist movement centred around Kropotkin and *Freedom*, Malatesta could not keep clear of trouble. He narrowly escaped being implicated in the famous Sidney Street affair, since one of the gang of Latvian terrorists involved in that strange battle had been a mechanic in his workshop. Two years later, in 1912, he was imprisoned for libel, because he had quite accurately described a certain Belleli as a police spy; he was also sentenced to deportation, and only the energetic representations which Kropotkin made to John Burns, then a minister in Campbell-Bannerman's government, prevented the order from being enforced.

During Malatesta's absence the Italian anarchist movement remained a minority, and not always an active one, in comparison with the parliamentary socialists. Nevertheless, its influence was maintained partly by recurrent economic distress and partly by the violent methods habitually used by the government in suppressing strikes and demonstrations, which led many of the workers in times of strike to be guided by anarchist counsels of direct action. For this reason the movement fluctuated greatly in the number of its adherents. Certain places, like Carrara, Forli, Lugo, Ancona, and Leghorn, consistently remained anarchist strongholds, and the movement was generally influential in Tuscany, the Romagna, and the Naples region, but everywhere groups tended to be impermanent because of police persecution, and attempts to create a national organization failed because of a stress on local autonomy which the Italians shared with the French. The Anarchist-Socialist-Revolutionary Party founded in the 1890s came to nothing, and a general anarchist congress held in Rome in 1907, under the influence of the Amsterdam International Congress of the same year, led to no effective national organization. Some of the anarchist intellectuals, led by Luigi Fabbri, attempted to create a progressive education movement centred around Fabbri's journal, *Università Populare*, and in this field they had a limited influence.

As in France, it was syndicalism that brought about a real revival of the libertarian trend in early twentieth-century Italy, and this explains the stress which Malatesta placed on the relationship between anarchist communism and syndicalism at the Amsterdam Congress. In the early years of the century two groups emerged in the Italian trade unions—the federalists, who advocated strong national unions, and the cameralists, who stressed local solidarity through Chambers of Labour similar to the French Bourses de Travail. At first the two trends worked side by side, but disputes quickly arose over the question of the general strike, which the cameralists (later to become the syndicalists) supported. A National Secretariat of Resistance was formed in 1904, and the syndicalists gained control of this, but in 1906, when a national congress of trade unions was called together to consider setting up a General Confederation of Labour (CGL), in imitation of the French CGT, they were in a minority. The Confederation was controlled from the start by the socialist moderates, against whom in 1907 the syndicalists set up a Committee of Resistance Societies based on Chambers of Labour and local unions. Many anarchist communists joined this organization, which gained strength and prestige through the adherence of the railway workers. Shortly after its formation the syndicalists led a general strike in Milan and a strike of agricultural workers in Tuscany which led to serious fighting between the police and the strikers. The failure of these strikes temporarily weakened the syndicalists, and in 1909 they held a Congress of Syndicalist Resistance in Bologna, attended by delegates of local Chambers of Labour and of the railway workers, at which they decided to join the reformist CGL for the purpose of infiltrating it. The tactic was ineffective, and in 1911 the railway workers left the CGL, followed by many of the Chambers of Labour and local syndicates. Finally, in November 1912, the syndicalists held a congress at Modena to consider founding their own organization. The delegates represented 100,000 workers, of whom the railwaymen, agricultural labourers, building workers, and metal-workers formed the largest groups.

Their resolutions showed the strong influence of French anarcho-syndicalism; they supported methods of direct action and stated that 'a general strike of all workers in all branches of production is the only way to bring about the definite expropriation of the bourgeois classes'. Finally, the Congress established the Unione Sindicale Italiana as an open rival of the CGL. Its influence grew rapidly, and although a minority of the USI which supported the Allies broke away during the war, by 1919 it claimed a membership of 500,000 largely among the industrial workers of Turin and Milan. It even developed its own group of intellectuals, of whom Arturo Labriola was the most important; his ideas were largely derived from Pelloutier, with a tinge of Sorelian mysticism.

Meanwhile, in 1913, Malatesta returned to Italy in the hope of reviving the orthodox anarchist movement so as to counter the growing influence of the syndicalists. Once again, he started a weekly newspaper in Ancona, and carried on his propaganda in spite of constant police interference, until, in June 1914, popular discontent suddenly flared up in the Adriatic region owing to the police shooting down a number of unemployed demonstrators. Under the leadership of Malatesta a general strike was immediately called in Ancona, and it spread rapidly through the Romagna and the Marches, involving both rural and urban workers, and then into other parts of Italy. During the 'Red Week' that followed, the railway services were largely at a standstill, and serious fighting broke out in many of the towns and also in the country districts. To the anarchists it seemed the beginning of what Malatesta called afterwards 'a period of civil strife, at the end of which we would have seen our ideal shining victoriously'. For a few days the nation-wide movement, under leadership of the anarchists and the Unione Sindicale Italiana, seemed on the verge of overthrowing the monarchy. Indeed, it was not the power of the government so much as the defection of the moderate trade-unionists that brought the movement to an end; after a brief period of hesitation, the CGL ordered its members back to work, and the strike collapsed.

The end of the First World War saw a new resurgence of revolutionary hopes in Italy, encouraged by the example of the Russian Revolution. When Malatesta returned at the end of 1919 from London, where he had spent the war years in renewed exile, he was welcomed as a popular hero, and in 1920 he founded in Milan the first Italian anarchist daily, *Umanità Nova*. In that year a wave of strikes ran through Italy, and in August, largely under the influence of the Unione Sindicale Italiana, led by Armando Borghi, the metal-workers of Milan and Turin occupied the factories. Once again it seemed the beginning of a revolutionary era, the chance of a generation. 'If we let this favourable moment pass,' said Malatesta, 'we shall later pay with tears of blood for the fear we have instilled in the bourgeoisie.' But the pattern established in the Red Week of 1914 was repeated. The CGL counselled moderation, the workers gave up the factories in exchange for vague promises of reform, and within a few weeks there were mass arrests of strike leaders and of anarchist and syndicalist militants, including Malatesta and Borghi, who were held for ten months without trial before they were eventually acquitted in 1922.

At this point, encouraged by the disillusionment that followed the breakdown of the general strike, the terrorist individualists who had always—despite Malatesta's influence—survived as a small minority among Italian anarchists, intervened frightfully and tragically. On the night of 23 March 1921, a group of them went to work in Milan, placing bombs in a theatre, a power station, and a hotel. In the theatre twenty-one people were killed and many more were injured. The deed did immense harm to the reputation of the anarchists, among the workers as well as with other classes, and, besides leading to further arrests, it provided the fascists with a justification for their campaign against the Left and with an excuse for counter-violence. They raided and destroyed the offices of *Umanità Nova*, and by threats and persecutions prevented its reappearance in Milan.

Italy was already on the downward slope toward dictatorship, and the anarchists were as paralysed by their own lack of decision as the socialists and the communists. Malatesta restarted *Umanità Nova* in Rome, but it survived only for a few months, until Mussolini took power. Then, as the fascist terror spread, all anarchist organizations, as well as the Unione Sindicale Italiana, were suppressed ruthlessly. The militants either fled abroad or disappeared into prisons and penal settlements. Only Malatesta was left, watched by the police but unharmed until his death, at eighty-two, in 1932. Perhaps there was after all some sincerity in the expressions of respect which the renegade revolutionary Mussolini had often made toward him; perhaps it was merely that his exploits had made him, like Tolstoy in Russia, too much a name in the world's ear to be easily shuffled into oblivion. He remained the symbol in Italy of a movement that otherwise lived out the fascist terror in exile. The expatriate groups, particularly in the Americas, kept Italian anarchism alive until after 1944, when it could revive again in its own country where, though its influence is far slighter than in the past, it has become the strongest of the minute libertarian movements that survive into the world of the 1980s.

During the fascist régime, Italian anarchism went either underground or abroad. It survived mainly in expatriate groups, of Italian immigrants in the United States and Argentina, of refugees in Paris and Geneva and

Lugano. Italian anarchists fought as volunteers against Italian fascists in the Spanish Civil War and here and there in their places of exile they maintained newspapers and small publishing houses that kept the tradition alive.

After World War II, the surviving refugees, as distinct from the immigrants, returned to Italy and, with those who had survived at home, they set about re-creating the movement. In 1945 the Italian Anarchist Federation (FAI) was refounded in the historic stronghold of Carrara, and shortly afterwards Malatesta's paper *Umanità Nova* resumed publication; it continues today. Anarchist traditions revived in many of the other former centres of activity in northern Italy, including Ancona, Genoa, Forli, Imola, Reggio Emilia, and Leghorn. In the south, where Italian anarchism had begun through Bakunin's efforts, Naples became a centre of activity once again, and there in 1946 Giovanna Berneri (Camillo's companion) and Cesare Zaccaria founded an anarchist review, *Volontà*, now published in Milan, which long remained the leading theoretical journal of the Italian libertarians. Recently a rival journal oriented to the younger generation of intellectuals, *Rivista A*, has begun to appear, also in Milan.

Post-fascism Italian anarchism differs in many respects from its earlier manifestations. Anarchists in the northern cities with old libertarian traditions have continued to instil their militancy into the local trade-union movements, but there has been no revival of a strong revolutionary syndicalist organization like the Unione Sindicale Italiana under Armando Borghi's leadership. Similarly, though in 1985 the anarchist-dominated town council of Carrara decided to put up a monument to Gaetano Bresci, the assassin of Umberto I, it has not been libertarians but the authoritarians of the Red Brigades and of the neo-fascist groups who have carried out the recent terrorist actions in Italy. The anarchists have been content with organizing cooperatives. They have also been especially active in fostering an international view of anarchism, so that the two most important post-war world gatherings, at Carrara in 1968 and Venice in 1985, have been hosted by the Italian movement. This is appropriate, since Bakunin founded the International Brotherhood in Naples in 1866 and in that act established the tradition of anarchist collaboration beyond national boundaries.

12. Anarchism in Spain

In relation to the rest of Europe, Spain has always been an isolated land, geographically, economically, historically; a land at once conservative and revolutionary, living by tradition and given to temperamental extremities; a land whose people are violent and generous, independent and morally rigorous; a land where most men live—as well as they can live—by the soil, and where to be poor is not to lose dignity. In the harsh face of this land and in the proud spirits of its inhabitants anarchism found the most congenial of all its homes, and for fifty years, until long after it had ceased to be an important movement anywhere else in the world, it gave to Spain an idea that stirred the imagination of the poor and a cause that counted its adherents in hundreds of thousands among the factory workers of Barcelona and the labourers of Madrid, and above all among the peasants of Andalusia and Aragón, of Levante and Galicia. In these favourable circumstances anarchism developed a moral intensity which made it overleap the merely social and political until, in many parts of Spain, it assumed the spiritually liberating form of a new religion. Spanish anarchists differed not merely in numbers, but also in nature from anarchists in the rest of Europe.

Yet their doctrine came from the same spring, and shared the same prophets—Proudhon first, and then Bakunin, with Kropotkin as a less important third. Proudhon's appeal came early, for in 1845 his disciple Ramón de la Sagra, whom Max Nettlau has described as the first Spanish anarchist, founded in Coruña a journal called *El Porvenir*, quickly suppressed by the authorities, which has a fair title to be regarded as the first of all anarchist journals, antedating Proudhon's more durable *Le Représentant du peuple* by three years. Ramón de la Sagra was in Paris during the 1848 Revolution, when he took part in Proudhon's activities, particularly the People's Bank, but his influence in Spain was relatively small, and he died in exile.

Nevertheless, the movement which we now think of as Spanish anarchism, with its extremism and its millenarian passion, was preceded by what Max Nettlau has called 'a federalist apprenticeship', a time when

Proudhon's influence in its moderate form played an important part in Spanish political history. The principal inspirer of Spanish federalism, and the most devoted of Proudhonian apostles, was a Madrid bank official named Pi y Margall; significantly, he was a Catalan by birth, and therefore predisposed to reject political centralization. Pi came into prominence at the time of the abortive Spanish Revolution of 1854, when he published his first book, *La Reacción y la revolución*. He did not advocate pure anarchism; indeed, politically he stood perhaps nearer to Jefferson than to Proudhon, since he envisaged the creation of a government that would proceed in a revolutionary direction by gradual reforms: 'I shall divide and subdivide power; I shall make it changeable and go on destroying it.' At the end of the perspective lay eventual anarchy, but Pi, unlike the true anarchists, was willing to contemplate the assumption of power in order to dismantle the structure of power.

Later Pi became the principal translator of Proudhon's works in Spanish, beginning with *Du principe fédératif*, and following later with *Solution du problème social*, *De la capacité politique des classes ouvrières*, and *Système des contradictions économiques*. By the time the last of these appeared, in 1870, enough of Proudhon's works were available in Spanish to provide an effective introduction to the most significant aspects of his thought. These translations were to have a profound and lasting effect on the development of Spanish anarchism after 1870, but before that time Proudhonian ideas, as interpreted by Pi, already provided much of the inspiration for the federalist movement which sprang up in the early 1860s. Federalism, of course, was by no means entirely the creation of external ideological influences; it arose from the traditional Spanish emphasis on regionalism, from the cult of the *patria chica*, and from the resentment of Castilian domination by Catalonia, Galicia, and Aragón. During the revolution of 1873, the federalists, led by Pi y Margall, were to have their brief hour of glory, but by that time a later and tougher strain of anarchism, derived from Bakunin had already entered Spain.

Pi y Margall's adaptation of Proudhon's federalism appealed mostly to the lower middle class, particularly outside Castile, who in the nineteenth century provided the main strength of Spanish revolutionary movements. Bakuninist anarchism made its immediate appeal to the artisans, particularly in Barcelona and Madrid, and here again a favourable climate already existed. Ever since the collapse of the revolutionary movement in 1854 there had been demonstrative discontent among both urban and rural workers. Eighteen fifty-five saw a general strike in Barcelona and other Catalan towns, 1861 a series of risings among the Andalusian landworkers,

1866 a serious riot in Madrid, and 1867, the year before the Bakuninists appeared, a widespread movement of rural insurrection which spread through Catalonia, Aragón, and Valencia.

Parallel with these outbursts of unorganized anger, working-class organizations of various kinds had been springing up ever since trade unions were legalized in 1839. The weavers of Barcelona began to associate in 1840, and tried unsuccessfully to establish a federation of trade unions in the city. There were even attempts to form socialist groups. In 1846 Fernando Garrido, a disciple of Fourier, founded in Madrid a socialist journal, *La Atracción*, and during the 1860s he became a fervent advocate of cooperation. Considerably to the left of Garrido was Antonio Gusart, who began to publish *El Obrero* in Barcelona during 1864, and in 1865 called together a congress of forty workers' associations to create a federation of cooperatives. In 1862 Spanish delegates to the London Exhibition appear to have taken part in the earliest discussions that preceded the founding of the First International, while in 1865 the Paris bureau of the Association announced that it was in correspondence with 'Spanish democrats'. Finally, at the Brussels Congress of the International in 1868, the first Spanish delegate, a Catalan metal-worker, appeared under the name Sarro Magallan; his real name was A. Marsal y Anglosa, and he represented the Workers' Association of Catalonia and the Legión Ibérica del Trabajo. Marsal provided a link between two stages of the working-class movement in Spain, since in 1870 he was to appear at the founding Congress of the Spanish Federation of the International.

But the real beginning of the anarchist movement in Spain was touched off by the revolution of September 1868, which drove Queen Isabella into exile. This seemed to Bakunin a golden opportunity for establishing the International—under his own rather than Marx's aegis—across the Pyrenees. Accordingly, he organized a missionary campaign of considerable dimensions. Élie Reclus, Élisée's anthropologist brother, and at least two of Bakunin's Marseilles disciples, Bastelica and Charles Alerini, went to Spain on Bakunin's behalf during the last months of 1868, but Spanish anarchist traditions have correctly given most of the credit for establishing their movement to Giuseppe Fanelli, who arrived in Barcelona, almost penniless, in October 1868. Curiously enough, considering Barcelona's later reputation as the centre of Spanish anarchism, Fanelli was unable to make any contacts there, and he went on to Madrid where Fernando Garrido passed him on to some young federalist printers who had already encountered libertarian ideas through Pi's translations of Proudhon, but had not even heard of the International. Gonzales Morago, the sole member of the group who knew a little French and could therefore communicate with Fanelli, arranged a meeting which can only be described as pentecostal. Several of the young men present that evening were to become lifelong leaders of anarchism in Spain, and one of them, Anselmo Lorenzo, has left an eloquent description of the occasion.

> Fanelli was a tall man with a kind and grave expression, a thick black beard, and large black expressive eyes which flashed like lightning or took on the appearance of kindly compassion according to the sentiments that dominated him. His voice had a metallic tone and was susceptible to all the inflexions appropriate to what he was saying, passing rapidly from accents of anger and menace against tyrants and exploiters to take on those of suffering, regret, and consolation, when he spoke of the pains of the exploited, either as one who without suffering them himself understands them, or as one who through his altruistic feelings delights in presenting an ultra-revolutionary ideal of peace and fraternity. He spoke in French and Italian, but we could understand his expressive mimicry and follow his speech.

In that extraordinary hour of communication over the barriers of language, Spanish anarchism began. Most of Fanelli's audience were converted immediately to the Bakuninist doctrine, and a few days later on his return to Barcelona Fanelli repeated his missionary feat. In the few weeks he stayed in Spain he learned hardly a word of Spanish, but he succeeded at meeting after meeting in converting those who had no other language. Neither before nor since did Fanelli show such extraordinary missionary powers, and the only explanation for his success can be found in the supposition that at this time of social disturbance, when the workers and the younger intellectuals found Pi y Margall's federalism too mild and gradual for their impatient wishes, Bakunin's anarchism—which contained but went beyond the basic doctrines of federalism—was the very creed for which they had been waiting.

A considerable movement grew rapidly from these small beginnings. Internationalist newspapers began to appear—*La Federación* in Barcelona and *Solidaridad* in Madrid. Sections of the International were formed in Andalusia, in Valencia, in the north of Spain, and by the beginning of 1870 the Spanish membership of the association had already reached 15,000. Two Spanish delegates, Dr Gaspar Sentiñon and the printer Rafael Farga-Pellicer, attended the Basel Congress of the International in 1869, and formed part of Bakunin's majority in that successful first round of his struggle with Marx. While they were there, Bakunin enrolled them in his skeleton International Brotherhood, and at his suggestion they founded on their return a Spanish Alliance of Social Democracy. This seems to have been a separate organization from the old Alliance, and it formed a secret core of initiate militants within the Spanish Federation of the International.

The Federation itself was founded at a general Congress held in Barcelona during June 1870. Ninety delegates represented 150 workers' societies with 40,000 members, but some of these were trade unions which had not yet affiliated themselves officially with the International, and the actual number of Internationalists was probably round about 20,000. The statutes of the Jura Federation were adopted for Spain, and the Congress left no doubt at all of its Bakuninist leanings. It is true that shortly afterward a split occurred owing to the activities of Paul Lafargue, whom Marx had sent to Madrid in the hope of weaning the Spaniards from their Bakuninist loyalties, but only a tiny minority joined the authoritarian sections, and the Spanish working-class movement as a whole remained oriented toward anarchism.

Meanwhile Amadeus of the House of Savoy had accepted the crown of Spain, and in the early months of his reign the International not only increased its membership but also led a number of successful strikes in Barcelona. Success brought repression; the police began to arrest internationalist leaders, and the Regional Council migrated to Lisbon, where they set up a section that became the first nucleus of anarchist activity in Portugal. They remained there for three months, living communally and awaiting a suitable time to return to Spain. The persecution of the International was soon relaxed, and in September the leaders were back for a Congress in Valencia, which created an elaborate structure of local federations and decided to establish unions for particular industries within the larger framework of the International. In the following January, disturbed by these signs of renewed activity, the government officially dissolved the International, on the grounds that it was an organization with affiliations outside Spain. The Association ignored the edict, and, during the spring of 1872, Anselmo Lorenzo went on an apostolic journey through the Andulusian countryside, where he began to convert the small peasants and landless labourers who were later to form such an important element in the Spanish anarchist movement.

Meanwhile the Spanish Federation had taken up its position in the dispute within the International. Anselmo Lorenzo had gone as a delegate to the London Congress of 1871, and shortly afterward the Spanish Internationalists gave their approval to the Sonvillier Circular. At the Hague Congress their delegates were among the Bakuninist minority, and later took an active part at Saint-Imier in founding the anti-authoritarian International. Finally, in December 1872, a general Congress in Cordoba unanimously approved the actions of the Saint-Imier Congress, and accepted within Spain the same kind of decentralized organization as had been established for the International, the local sections being regarded as autonomous and the Regional Council devolving into a bureau of correspondence and statistics. However, there remained a kind of shadow organization of leading militants which, though it had no official existence, virtually controlled the policy of the International.

By June 1873, when King Amadeus decided to abandon the uneasy Spanish throne and a new republic was proclaimed, the strength of the International had again grown considerably, and for the first time the majority of its members, now 50,000 strong, came from the rural districts of the south. In the new republic the federalist line of Proudhon's descendants played an important part. It was Pi y Margall who moved in the Cortes that Spain should become a federal republic and who became its President, pledged to lead the country toward a decentralized administration in which the regions would become largely autonomous cantons, in which the power of the Church would be sharply curbed, and in which peasant communities would take over the uncultivated lands of the great *latifundia* of the south. But Pi's presidency was short and unhappy, for the republic quickly broke down, partly because of the uprising of Carlist reactionaries in the north, and partly because the federalist enthusiasts in the south decided to take their independence for granted even before it had been legalized. Most of the large cities of Andalusia and Levante— Seville, Granada, Valencia, Cadiz, Malaga, and Cartagena—declared themselves free cantons. Committees of Public Safety were set up; the churches were closed and the rich taxed. Pi y Margall resigned in unhappy protest when the provisional government in Madrid decided to send its troops into the south. The risings collapsed quickly everywhere but in Cartagena, where the federalist extremists from the whole region gathered, and withstood a siege that lasted for almost five months.

The anarchists played only a minor part in this death struggle of their federalist cousins. The International as an organization abstained from any action, having passed a resolution condemning all political activity, but individual members were free to follow their own inclinations, and some of them joined the cantonalist risings and even served on the Committees of Public Safety. However, the anarchists did become involved in certain independent activities, slight but prophetic, during the events of 1873. They provoked a number of small Andalusian village risings, but the principal internationalist exploit of the period was the miniature revolution in the paper-making town of Alcoy, near Valencia. Alcoy was an early international stronghold, largely owing to the activities of an anarchist schoolteacher, Albarracín. As soon as the republic was declared, the paper-workers came out on strike in favour of the eight-hour day, which was part of the industrial programme of the federalist government. While the workers were demonstrating outside the town hall the police opened fire on them, and a general battle followed, which lasted all night and into the following day. Led, according to legend, by Albarracín on a white horse, the workers gained control of the town after killing a dozen policemen. They shot the mayor, whom they held responsible for starting the fighting, set fire to some factories and wealthy houses, and, in a last grotesque outburst, paraded the heads of their dead enemies through the streets in triumph.

Violence of the kind that happened at Alcoy was not new in Spain. It had happened often in connection with popular uprisings, and was mild in comparison with the cruelties committed by the Carlists of Navarre against liberals who fell into their clutches. Moreover, the very isolation of the Alcoy incident shows how far the International as a whole was at this time from a general policy of violence. But it aroused an outcry that was due not so much to the familiar presence of violence, as to the idea that popular unrest, which hitherto had been sporadic and undirected, was now being canalized by a powerful revolutionary organization. And there is no doubt that, despite its general inaction in 1873, and despite the fury unleashed against it after the Alcoy episode, the International gained in influence and membership alike as a result of the general tension of the early months of the republic. The Spanish delegates to the Geneva Congress of the Saint-Imier International in 1873 actually asserted that they represented 300,000 members; this was undoubtedly a gross exaggeration, and more reliable estimates place the real membership in 1873 at between 50,000 and 60,000.

This steady growth of the International attracted toward it the hostility of all the reactionary forces in Spain, and when the army seized control of the country in January 1874, and dissolved the Cortes in preparation for the restoration of the Bourbon monarchy, one of its first actions was to suppress the Spanish Federation. This time the intentions of the authorities were supported by rigorous action; local sections, trade-union branches, workers' discussion groups, all were dispersed, and 500 active militants were imprisoned, while many more went into exile. The ban on working-class organizations lasted for seven years, but the anarchists surreptitiously continued their activities with a fair amount of success. Only a few months after the official suppression of the International, in June 1874, a secret congress was attended by delegates from more than 400 sections in all parts of Spain. Other congresses followed, and underground newspapers were distributed widely, particularly in Andalusia, where anarchism survived as a mass movement during the years of clandestinity. In the towns the trade unions were unable to function, and only the skeleton élites remained, meeting furtively and achieving very little. But in the country districts of the south this was the time when peasant anarchism, with its peculiar semi-religious enthusiasm, first began to evolve into a movement which was to remain powerful in Andalusia for more than half a century. Its character has been well described by Gerald Brenan, who, at the end of this period, lived in southern Spain and closely observed the village anarchists in action:

> The character of the rural anarchism that grew up in the south of Spain differed ... from that developed in the large cities of the north. 'The idea,' as it was called, was carried from village to village by anarchist 'apostles'. In the farm-labourers' *gañaís* or barracks, in isolated cottages by the light of oil *candiles*, the apostles spoke on liberty and equality and justice to rapt listeners. Small circles were formed in towns and villages which started night-schools where many learned to read, carried on anti-religious propaganda and often practised vegetarianism and teetotalism. Even tobacco and coffee were banned by some, and one of these old apostles whom I knew maintained that, when the age of liberty came in, men would live on unfired foods grown by their own hands. But the chief characteristic of Andalusian anarchism was its naïve millenarianism. Every new movement or strike was thought to herald the immediate coming of a new age of plenty, when all—even the Civil Guard and the landowners—would be free and happy. How this would happen no one could say. Beyond the seizure of the land (not even that in some places) and the burning of the parish church, there were no positive proposals.

Naïvely millenarian though it may have been, this Andalusian peasant revolutionism was no perversion of the anarchist doctrine. Indeed, in its own pure and primitive way it exposed certain elements in anarchism which more sophisticated advocates have tended to gloss over; the moralistic element in particular, and that mental shift into a timeless world, out of progress and freed from material temptations, which seems the necessary leap of faith for the true black anarchist.

In 1878 a new and more violent era in Spanish anarchism began when a young Tarragonese cooper, Juan Oliva Moncasi, attempted to kill King Alfonso XII. Mass arrests of anarchists and trade-union militants followed, and during the next two years there were retaliatory strikes in Catalonia and farm burning in Andalusia, to which the government replied with further repressions. The vicious circle continued until 1881, when a liberal ministry decided to break it by legalizing working-class organizations once again. The International came into the open and immediately dissolved itself, to arise a few months afterward out of its own ashes under the new name of Federation of Workers of the Spanish Region. It quickly regained a membership close to that at the time of its dissolution in 1874, but from the beginning the Federation was ridden by regional differences between the Catalans, who wished to concentrate on trade-union activities, and the more fanatical Andalusian peasants, particularly the vineyard workers from Jerez, who favoured an emphasis on violent action. These differences came to a head at the Seville Congress in 1882, where a group who called themselves 'Los Desheredados' ('The Disinherited') broke away to form their own terrorist organization. The teachings of the Desheredados were denounced by the rest of the anarchists at the Federation's Valencia Congress in 1883, but this merely resulted in threats—never carried out—against the lives of Farga-Pellicer and other leaders of the Federation of Workers.

It is hard to determine how far the Desheredados really put their teachings of violence into practice, but it is certain that their indiscriminate advocacy of assassination was extremely useful to the Civil Guard in the mysterious affair of La Mano Negra (The Black Hand), which in 1883 served as an excuse for the temporary destruction of the anarchist movement in Andalusia. A tavern keeper from a village near Jerez, suspected of being a police informer, was murdered by some of the local peasants. The Civil Guard commander investigating the killing claimed to have discovered evidence that it was the work of a great secret society called La Mano Negra which was plotting the slaughter of all landowners and bailiffs in Andalusia. The police immediately set about arresting all the active anarchists they could find; informers and *agents provocateurs* flourished, and torture was used freely to extract confessions. In the end the majority of the prisoners were released, but a hundred were brought to trial, and fourteen were condemned to death, seven of them eventually being garrotted in the square of Jerez. The truth about La Mano Negra has never been satisfactorily established, but most of the impartial investigators who have studied the case have doubted the existence of any large-scale organization. It is likely that there were small terrorist groups in the Jerez area, of the same

primitive kind as the Black Band of Monceau-les-Mines, and that some of
the Desheredados were connected with them, but only three murders—of
informers—were proved, and it seems improbable that all the men executed or sent to prison were involved in these killings.

Whether it existed or not, the police used La Mano Negra as the excuse
for a widespread attempt to root out anarchism from Andalusia. For the
time being at least, they were largely successful. The remnants of the
Federation were forced underground in most of the south, and the membership of clandestine sections was pared down to the dedicated core of
convinced militants. Of the 30,000 Andalusian members which the
Federation could count in 1882, barely 3,000 were left after the Mano
Negra affair had run its course.

At the same time but for other reasons, the Federation was breaking up
in Catalonia. While the anarchists in Italy, Switzerland, and France had
moved on from Bakuninist collectivism to anarchist communism in the
late 1870s, the Spaniards did not become acutely aware of the conflict
between the two doctrines until the mid 1880s, when Kropotkin's writings
were first translated into Spanish. But it was not merely a struggle between
two views of the way of distributing the products of labour; the issue was
complicated by differing attitudes toward group organization. The anarchist communists who now began to appear in Barcelona adopted the view
now current in France and Italy, that it was necessary to organize in
groups consisting exclusively of dedicated anarchist propagandists of word
and deed. The collectivists, retaining the attitude of the old International,
thought in terms of large workers' organizations which would have a leav-
ening élite of convinced anarchists but would not demand complete conversion from the mass of the membership.

By 1888 the two factions in Catalonia had recognized their differences to
the extent of setting up separate organizations. The trade unions formed
the Pact of Solidarity and Resistance, and the purist militants created an
Anarchist Organization of the Spanish Region, some of whose members
belonged to the Pact of Solidarity, so that the division was never clearly
defined. This dual organization of libertarian unionists and anarchist militants continued in Spain down to the end of the 1930s; despite their
differences, the two tendencies constantly interacted upon each other, and,
indeed, would probably not have survived apart.

As in France, the early 1890s in Spain were characterized by a sudden
upsurge of insurrection, bomb throwings, and assassinations. Early in 1892
the country districts sprang to life again in one of those periodical surges
of enthusiasm characteristic of Andalusian anarchism. Four thousand
peasants, armed with scythes and shouting 'Long Live Anarchy!' marched

into Jerez and killed a few unpopular shopkeepers. After a night of sporadic fighting between the insurgents and the Civil Guard, a force of cavalry arrived and the rebellion was quickly crushed. Four of the peasant leaders were executed and many others were sentenced to long terms of imprisonment; the nature of Spanish justice at that period is shown by the fact that among the latter was a man actually in jail at Cadiz for another political offence when the rising took place.

At about the same time as the Jerez rising, the unions in Barcelona called a general strike for an eight-hour day, and a series of bombings, which had begun with an attempt to blow up the Fomento building in 1891, grew to epidemic proportions, without at first causing any great damage to either property or persons. Some of the bombs were undoubtedly thrown or planted by anarchists, among whom a small group of Italians was particularly active, but others were the work of agents employed by the police or by the employers' association, whose hired gunmen at this time began an intermittent guerrilla war of the streets with militant anarchists. By 1893 the violence assumed a more deadly form. A young anarchist named Pallas, who had been with Malatesta on his prospecting expedition in Patagonia, threw a bomb at Martínez Campos, Captain-General of Barcelona. He missed, but this did not prevent his being court-martialled and executed. In revenge, his friend Santiago Salvador threw a bomb into the Liceo Theatre and killed twenty people. The horror aroused by this frightful act was used by the government to justify the creation of a special anti-anarchist police force, called the Brigada Social, and also to round up indiscriminately as many anarchist leaders as could be found. A number of them, manifestly innocent, were executed at the same time as the real culprit, Salvador.

Such actions on the part of the authorities led to an intensification of the wave of violence in Barcelona. Bombings and shootings increased in number, and the police replied with further arrests and a liberal use of torture to extract confessions. Then, in June 1896, a bomb was thrown from an upper window on to the Corpus Christi procession as it passed through the streets of Barcelona. The perpetrator of this act was never found, but one fact that attracted notice was that the bomb was not thrown at the head of the procession, where all the officials hated by the anarchists marched, but at the tail of the procession, where it merely killed working men and women. The republicans as well as the anarchists accused the Clericals of perpetrating the outrage, but General Weyler, the new Captain-General of Barcelona (later to become notorious for his cruelties in Cuba), used it as an excuse for a general round-up of opponents of the régime and the Church—anarchists, republicans, socialists, freethinkers,

and Catalan separatists—until some 400 prisoners were herded into the
cells and dungeons of Montjuich prison, outside Barcelona, where the
thugs of the Brigada Social subjected them to such appalling tortures that
several prisoners died before they even reached trial. Some eighty-seven
were finally indicted, but by this time the news of the Montjuich tortures
had passed over the Pyrenees and aroused a storm of international protest,
so that the court sentenced only twenty-six of them, eight to death and
the rest to long terms of imprisonment. In the end five were executed, but
none of them was proved in any convincing way to have been connected
with the bombing in June 1896. Even the sixty-one acquitted men were
pursued vindictively by the government of Canovas, who decided to transport them to the deadly climate of the African colony of Rio d'Oro. Like
Sadi Carnot, Canovas reaped the consequences of his inhumanity; in the
Pyrenean watering place of Santa Aguada he was shot by Michele
Angiolillo, an Italian anarchist who had travelled from London with the
specific intention of avenging the horrors of Montjuich.

During the 1890s Spanish anarchism shared within the movement in
France not only its terrorism, but also its attractiveness for intellectuals
and artists. It was in 1896 that the most important anarchist theoretical
journal in Spain, *La Revista Blanca*, was founded, and to its pages university
teachers, engineers, professional men of letters, and even some former
army officers contributed. While Spanish anarchism never drew to itself so
many distinguished writers and painters as the movement in France, it
could include among its sympathizers not only—for a time at least—the
young Pablo Picasso, but also the great novelist Pío Baroja, who wrote at
least one book, *Aurora Roja*, derived from his direct association with the
anarchists. Another manifestation of anarchist intellectualism was the
growth of the movement to create libertarian schools. Owing to the acci-
dent of his manifestly unjust execution in 1909, which I shall discuss later
in more detail, Francisco Ferrer was to become by right of martyrdom the
most celebrated advocate of this movement. However, Ferrer's Escuela
Moderna was only one of many experiments in Catalonia and the villages
of Andalusia aimed particularly at bringing literacy to adult peasants and
industrial workers. For purposes of propaganda, Ferrer's personal reputation as an educationalist was inflated out of all proportion by the anarchists after his death; he was in fact a rather dully orthodox rationalist,
with a narrow unimaginative mind, and the few writings he left show little
in the way of an original conception of education. Yet to rebel at all
against the Church domination of education in Spain of the late nineteenth century was perhaps enough to expect of any man, as Ferrer's fate
was to show.

Even more important than the educational movement was the trade-union revival of the turn of the century, when the example of French revolutionary syndicalism gave a new life to the collectivist wing of Spanish anarchism. The conception of the general strike, refurbished by French theoreticians into the supreme revolutionary strategy, appealed immediately to Spanish millenarianism. A strike of the metal-workers in Barcelona in 1902 actually developed into a city-wide general strike; its failure brought about the collapse of the most recent attempt to re-create the old International—the new Federation of Workers of the Spanish Region which had been founded in 1900. Shortly afterward the movement spread to the rural districts, particularly in the provinces of Cadiz and Seville, where the strikes were accompanied by demands for a division of the great estates. All of them failed, because the labourers lived on the edge of starvation even when they were working, and had no resources for a sustained struggle; moreover, with their narrow view of the *patria chica*, the village community, they rarely looked beyond their own horizons, and so, instead of a coordinated movement that might at least have had some effect in improving their conditions, they indulged in a series of sporadic and isolated outbreaks which the Civil Guard suppressed individually without difficulty.

Meanwhile the success of the CGT in France, largely under the inspiration of anarchists who had gained influential positions in its hierarchy, continued to impress the workers of Barcelona, and in 1907 the libertarian unions of Catalonia came together in a specifically syndicalist federation known as Solidaridad Obrera, which quickly spread through the rest of Catalonia and held its first congress early in 1908.

The new movement took action on a dramatic scale in July 1909, when the Spanish army suffered a heavy reverse in one of its perennial wars with the Riffs in Morocco, and the government decided to call up the reservists of Catalonia. It is hard not to see a provocative intent in the fact that only men from this violently separatist province were included in the order. The anarchists, socialists, and syndicalists agreed on joint action, and Solidaridad Obrera called a general strike. During the 'Tragic Week' that followed there was heavy street fighting in Barcelona; it took the police and troops five days to establish control. Nearly 200 workers were killed in the streets alone, and—in an outburst of the anti-clerical passion that habitually attends popular uprisings in Spain—more than fifty churches and convents were burned and a number of monks were killed. The conservative government reacted in the customary manner with mass arrests, tortures in Montjuich, and summary executions, including that of Francisco Ferrer. Ferrer was actually in England during the Tragic Week, but he was nevertheless court-martialled and shot on a faked charge of having fomented the rising. As after the Montjuich atrocities of 1896, there were great protests abroad; Ferrer became an international martyr, and even in Spain the cry of disgust at the methods used by the authorities forced the conservative premier Maura to resign and brought into power the liberal government of Canalejas.

The Tragic Week and its aftermath impressed on Spanish libertarians the need for a stronger fighting organization, and in October 1910 representatives of trade unions from all over Spain gathered in Seville for a historic congress. Only the socialist unions already federated in the UGT remained aloof; the great majority of the remaining unions sent their representatives, and it was decided to form a new organization, the famous Confederación Nacional del Trabajo, better known as CNT.

The CNT was formed under the inspiration of the French CGT, but in the process of development it came to differ from it in a number of important ways. First, it fell immediately and remained always under the full control of anarchist leaders. It is true that many non-anarchist workers joined it, and even some socialists, but there was never a time when they gained any effective share of the leadership. Moreover, the dual organization of the CGT—the local Bourses de Travail and the national craft unions welded together into an elaborate confederational structure—was not at first imitated. The CNT tended rather to base itself on the local Sindicatos Únicos, which would bring together the workers of all crafts in one factory or even in one town. Thus the union and the locality tended to be identified, in accordance with the traditional anarchist stress on the commune as the basic social unit, and the Sindicatos Únicos were linked loosely in the regional and finally in the national federation. Anything in the form of a permanent bureaucracy was so carefully avoided that the CNT had only one paid official; the rest of this enormous organization was maintained by workers delegated by their comrades. This was possible because the CNT never adopted the benefit-society function of the ordinary trade union, and did not even maintain strike funds; the instinctive solidarity among workers was looked on as sufficient protection in a struggle which never saw the millennium as far distant. From the beginning the anarchists regarded the CNT as a revolutionary weapon, but it is in the nature of mass organizations to develop their own inertia, and the CNT in its turn was to reveal the reformist trends and the tendency to see the syndical organization of the revolution embodied (means *and* end) which led the French CGT far away from pure anarcho-syndicalism.

The enthusiasm generated by the founding of the CNT led to an immediate revival of anarchism in the rural areas of Andalusia and to a wave of strikes elsewhere. A spectacular general strike in Saragossa developed into an armed uprising. Other strikes broke out in Seville and Bilbao, where the socialist workers of the UGT made common cause with the anarcho-syndicalists. At Cullera, near Valencia, the striking workers declared the town a commune independent of Spain, a procedure which in later years was to be imitated by village insurrectionaries in many parts of the southern provinces. Canalejas replied to these manifestations of renascent anarchism by banning the CNT, and in 1912, when the railway unions went on strike, he forced the workers back by mobilizing them under military law. But the CNT continued to flourish as an underground organization, and Canalejas paid for his actions in the same way as Canovas; he was shot and killed by an anarchist gunman in a Madrid bookshop.

In 1914 the CNT emerged into the open again, greatly strengthened through the spread of rural anarchism during the intervening years from Andalusia into Levante, and during the First World War a number of circumstances led to further successes. In 1917 the UGT leaders declared a national general strike for a democratic and socialist republic. The CNT took part, but when the strike failed it reaped the benefit through the temporary discrediting of the socialist leaders. The success of the Russian Revolution also strengthened the appeal of the CNT as an avowedly revolutionary organization, and in 1918 the more dedicated militants held a National Anarchist Congress in Madrid to consider their attitude to syndicalism in the great struggle that seemed now to be dawning. Unlike anarchists in France and Italy, they were almost unanimous in deciding that, even though the CNT could not itself be regarded as a wholly anarchist organization, they must permeate and lead it, so that even its uncommitted members would be imbued with the libertarian spirit. By 1919, when the CNT held its Congress in Madrid, its membership had grown to 700,000, most of them in Catalonia, Andalusia, Levante, and Galicia, where the movement had recently established a new centre of activity.*

As the most influential revolutionary organization in Spain, the CNT was assiduously courted by the newly founded Communist (Third) International. At first its members were attracted by the glamour of the

*Here one should observe the necessary caution in accepting figures presented by Spanish anarchists, particularly since the CNT was notoriously slack in keeping records of membership. However, it is worth remarking that even so objective a writer as Gerald Brenan has suggested that 'there were moments when the anarcho-syndicalist movement was leading from a million to a million and a half workers', though he qualifies this statement with the remark that the CNT's 'core of persistently faithful adherents did not exceed 200,000'.

successful revolution in Russia, and a group of delegates to Moscow, headed by Andres Nin and Joaquin Maurin (later the leaders of the dissident
Marxist Partido Obrero de Unificación Marxista), pledged the Confederation's support to the communist organization. In 1921, however, another
syndicalist leader, Ángel Pestaña, returned from Russia with the news of
the persecution of anarchists there and of the brutal suppression of the
Kronstadt sailors' insurrection. His reports caused a general revulsion
among Spanish anarchists and syndicalists, and at its Saragossa Congress
in 1922 the CNT reasserted its faith in libertarian communism, and decided to withdraw from the Third International and give its allegiance to the
new syndicalist organization, the International Workingmen's Association,
which was being founded in Berlin. There was subsequently nothing
resembling the mass exodus of French anarcho-syndicalist militants into
the newly founded Communist Party during the early 1920s. The Spanish
anarchist ranks remained solid.

The years from 1919 to the establishment of Primo de Rivera's dictatorship in 1923 were clouded by a bitter warfare between the CNT and the
employers' organizations in Barcelona. The violence generated during this
period and during the remaining history of the CNT until the end of the
Spanish Civil War in 1939 must, as I have already suggested, be seen in the
context of the general tradition of political violence which has existed in
Spain since the Napoleonic wars. Repellent and futile as one may find the
Spanish anarchist tendency to resort easily to assassination, it is only fair to
remember that the police, the army, and the *pistoleros* in the pay of the
employers were even more inclined to violence and much more sadistic in
their methods. However mistakenly, the anarchists killed usually in revenge
for wrongs done to their comrades. It was, for instance, as a result of the use
of the *ley de fugas* (the euphemism describing the police practice of shooting
arrested men on the way to prison and claiming that they had been killed
while trying to escape) that the conservative prime minister Eduardo Dato
was killed in 1921. It was in revenge for the murder of the CNT leader
Salvador Segui by police gunmen in the street that the Archbishop of
Saragossa was shot by the celebrated guerrilla leader, Buenaventura
Durutti. Since the basic doctrines of anarchism deny retribution and punishment, such deeds were in fact unanarchistic, but they were typical of
Spain in their time, and they underline the need to consider Spanish anar-
chism as in many respects belonging in a category of its own.

Moreover, it must be remembered that even in the explosive situation
that existed between 1919 and 1923 by no means all the anarcho-syndicalists
favoured violent means. Salvador Segui himself and Ángel Pestaña led a
moderate trend within the CNT which was willing to seek compromises

with the employers and even with the state. On the other hand, the extremists, led by fanatics like Durutti and his inseparable companion Ascaso, were willing to use every means to speed the revolutionary millennium. Since they neither feared the authorities nor respected the moderates within their own ranks, these men continually forced the pace and committed the movement to the vicious repetition of murder and counter-murder. Moreover, men like Durutti, themselves idealists, gathered around them less pure elements, and in Barcelona at this time there arose a whole class of professional *pistoleros*, who shifted from side to side, sometimes fighting for the anarchists, sometimes for the employers or even the police, and in later years allying themselves to the nascent Falange. There is no doubt that the anarchist tendency to sentimentalize the criminal as a rebel against an authoritarian society was largely responsible for the barbarity that characterized industrial struggle in Barcelona during the years before Primo de Rivera forced an uneasy peace upon the city.

The period I have been describing began early in 1919 with a strike led by CNT moderates at the great Barcelona electric power plant known as the Canadiense. The strikers' demands were so reasonable that at first the management was inclined to reach agreement with them, but the Captain-General of Barcelona, Milans del Bosch, intervened and stopped negotiations. The strike spread, Barcelona was deprived of light, and Milans del Bosch, after arresting the union leaders, proclaimed martial law. Immediately the CNT declared a general strike, and there was a total stoppage of work in the Barcelona factories. It was a completely peaceful strike which demonstrated how effectively the workers could act without using violence. The army replied with the usual mass arrests, followed by courts-martial which imposed heavy sentences, and the succession of protest strikes and employers' lockouts continued for the rest of the year, with violence reasserting itself on both sides. The result was that by the end of 1919, having gained no clear victory, and having rejected a working arrangement with the socialist UGT which Segui had proposed, the CNT again began to lose ground among the Catalonian workers.

Meanwhile, stirred by rumours of the Russian Revolution and the news of the great general strike in Barcelona, the country districts of Andalusia once again sprang to life. As on other occasions, anarchist millenarianism swept over the countryside like a great religious revival. Díaz del Moral, in his *History of Agrarian Agitations in the Province of Cordoba*,* has left a fascinating description of the process at work:

*Quoted by E.J. Hobsbawm in *Primitive Rebels: Studies in Archaic Forms of Social Movement in the 19th and 20th Centuries*, Manchester, 1959.

We who lived through that time in 1918-19 will never forget that amazing sight. In the fields, in the shelters and courts, wherever peasants met to talk, for whatever purpose, there was only one topic of conversation, always discussed seriously and fervently: the social question. When men rested from work, during the smoking-breaks in the day and after the evening meal at night, whoever was the most educated would read leaflets and journals out aloud while the others listened with great attention. Then came the perorations, corroborating what had just been read, and an unending succession of speeches praising it. They did not understand everything. Some words they did not know. Some interpretations were childish, others malicious, depending on the personality of the man; but at bottom all agreed. How else? Was not all they had heard the *pure truth* which they had felt all their lives, even though they had never been able to express it? ...

In a few weeks the original nucleus of 10 or 20 adepts would be converted into one of 200; in a few months practically the entire working population, seized by ardent proselytism, propagated the flaming ideal frenziedly. The few who held out, whether because they were peaceable or timid, or afraid of losing public respect, would be set on by groups of the convinced on the mountainside, as they ploughed the furrow, in the cottage, the tavern, in the streets and squares. They would be bombarded with reasons, with imprecations, with contempt, with irony, until they agreed. Resistance was impossible. Once the village was converted, the agitation spread ... Everyone was an agitator. Thus the fire spread rapidly to all the combustible villages.

And with the sparks of conversion, strikes spread over the countryside until the whole of the south was aflame, and the landlords either granted the demands of their workers or fled in terror. Finally, in May 1919, a regular military expedition was sent into Andalusia, the CNT was proscribed in the province, and the strike movement fell away, as much because of the hunger of the landworkers as because of the presence of the soldiers.

Meanwhile there were new disturbances in Catalonia, where the employers had begun to form unions under their own control—the Sindicatos Libres—in rivalry to the CNT and the UGT. At the beginning of 1920 the CNT called a general strike in Barcelona. All the unions except those supported by the employers were immediately suppressed in Barcelona, and the National Committee of the CNT was imprisoned, but this did not prevent strikes continuing throughout the year, with considerable gains in terms of increased wages, which gave the CNT new prestige and enabled it to establish strong footholds in socialist strongholds such as Madrid and Asturias.

There was a temporary lull in violence during the latter part of 1920, but the bitter strife that was making Barcelona notorious throughout Europe returned when King Alfonso XIII forced the government to appoint as Civil Governor the brutal martinet, General Martínez Anido, who was to end his life as Franco's Minister for Home Affairs. Martínez Anido combined the brutality of the Spanish military caste at its worst with a wholehearted support of the most reactionary employers in the city, and it was he who organized, through his police department, a ruthless campaign of assassination against the CNT militants. During his period of office an average of fifteen political murders a week took place in the streets of Barcelona; approximately half of these were perpetrated by police-directed terrorists and half by anarchist *pistoleros*, who carried out their reprisals with mathematical exactitude. In the end Spanish public opinion became so deeply stirred by press exposures of his methods that Martínez Anido was dismissed, but the strife he had fostered did not die down until after the establishment of Primo de Rivera's dictatorship in September 1923, when an attempt was made by the government to promote reasonable compromises between workers and employers and to maintain control by less brutal means than those of Martínez Anido and his police officers.

The coming of Primo de Rivera meant a long period of clandestinity for anarchism in Spain. In comparison with General Franco, Primo de Rivera seems in retrospect a model of progressivism. He had a real sense of the economic problems of Spain, and no prejudices against the working class as such. His own desire for a balanced and ordered society—so different from his chaotic personal life—made him sympathetic to the socialists, and during his régime a curious alliance sprang up between this bibulous and likeable Andalusian aristocrat and the bombastic Madrid plasterer, Largo Caballero, who was later to fancy himself the Spanish Lenin. But between the anarchists and the dictator there was no common ground whatever, and the CNT heralded his appearance by declaring a general strike. It failed, because the socialist UGT refused to participate.

In May 1924 the CNT was dissolved on Primo de Rivera's orders, its newspapers were suppressed, and all its Sindicatos Únicos were closed down, while several hundred of its most active members were arrested. Primo de Rivera was less brutal but more efficient in repression than his predecessors, and as a mass organization the CNT virtually ceased to exist until his fall. Its members joined and did their best to disrupt the Sindicatos Libres patronized by the dictator; those of its leaders who remained at liberty either maintained the underground skeleton organization, which—as always happened in periods of clandestinity—fell under the influence of the anarchist extremists, or fled into exile in France. From there they organized a rather futile armed march into Navarre in the winter of 1924, and afterward settled down to the serious business of reorganizing the movement. Toward the end of 1926 they met in congress at Lyons, and decided to set up an Iberian Anarchist Federation in exile. The idea spread to Spain, and in July 1927, meeting secretly in Valencia, the representatives of the scattered anarchist groups accepted the idea of establishing the Iberian Anarchist Federation (better known as FAI) as an underground organization dedicated to the pursuit of revolution. The FAI, which only emerged into the open at the beginning of the Civil War in 1936, was the first closely knit national organization of anarchists to exist for any appreciable period in Spain, and its durability—for it lived on in exile after the destruction of the Republic in 1939—can be attributed largely to the fact that the whole of its life was a time of social unrest and excitement, beginning in the last phase of Primo de Rivera's dictatorship and continuing during the stormy years of the republic and the tragic years of the Civil War. It was founded largely with the intention of countering the reformist trend among the syndicalists, led by Ángel Pestaña, and it quickly established an ascendancy over the CNT so that the very small organized anarchist minority held almost all its important posts within the large trade-union body and dominated its bureaux and committees. In this way, probably for the only time in the history of anarchism, Bakunin's plan of a secret élite of devoted militants controlling a public mass organization of partially converted workers came into being. But the FAI not only included hard-working trade-union leaders and the theoreticians of Spanish anarchism; it also included a dubious contingent from the Barcelona underworld. As Franz Borkenau commented in *The Spanish Cockpit*:

> The FAI itself reflects exactly the queer phenomenon that Spanish anarcho-syndicalism is as a whole. Intended to group all those elements who are not simple CNT trade-unionists but convinced and able anarchists, it unites in its ranks on one hand the élite of the anarchist movement, the active guard which has passed through unnumerable fights, imprisonments, emigration, death sentences,

and which is undoubtedly one of the most idealistic elements existing in the world, together with doubtful elements which other groups might hesitate, not merely to trust with positions of responsibility, but simply to accept as members.

Here again, one might remark, the inheritance from Bakunin seems evident, for it was he who laid most stress on the alliance between idealists and the marginal social elements necessary to overthrow the state and prepare the ground for the free society. Yet the peculiar combination of tendencies within the FAI also has its parallels in Spanish history, particularly among the military religious orders, and even among the Jesuits in that period when they mingled idealistic devotion to a cause with a taste for conspiracy, a justification of illegality and tyrannicide, and—particularly in Paraguay—a leaning toward social experiments of a primitive communist nature.

This comparison begs an obvious question. The FAI claimed to be an anti-religious organization, and its members, during the republic and the early days of the Civil War, were among the most active of church burners. But Spanish anarchist opposition to the Church is a peculiarly passionate phenomenon, quite different from the calm rationality of free thinkers on the other side of the Pyrenees. Its advocates share the iconoclastic fervour of the radical sects of the Reformation, and this parallel brings us to the interesting suggestion made by Gerald Brenan, that in Spain, where the Inquisition effectively stifled any tendency toward religious dissent during the sixteenth century, anarchism has in fact taken on the character of a delayed Reformation movement.

All anarchism has, of course, a moral-religious element which distinguishes it from ordinary political movements, but this element is far more strongly developed in Spain than elsewhere. Almost every perceptive observer of anarchism in that country has remarked on the fact that here is what Borkenau has called 'a half-religious Utopian movement', and again it is Brenan who has shown most convincingly why its religious passion should have turned so fiercely against the Church. I can do no better than quote part of his excellent discussion of the subject in *The Spanish Labyrinth*, which is supported by a first-hand acquaintance with Spanish anarchists extending over many years.

The fanatical hatred of the anarchists for the Church and the extraordinary violence of their attack upon it during the Civil War are things which are known to everyone ... It can only, I think, be explained as the hatred of heretics for the Church from which they have sprung. For in the eyes of Spanish libertarians the Catholic Church occupies the position of anti-Christ in the Christian world. It is far more to them than a mere obstacle to revolution. They see in it the fountain of all evil, the corrupter of youth with its vile doctrine of original sin, the blasphemer against Nature and the Law of Nature, which they call *Salud* or Health. It is also the religion which *mocks* with its pretence of brotherly love and mutual forgiveness the great ideal of human solidarity ...

I would suggest then that the anger of the Spanish anarchists against the Church is the anger of an intensely religious people who feel they have been deserted and deceived. The priests and the monks left them at a critical moment in their history and went over to the rich. The humane and enlightened principles of the great theologians of the seventeenth century were set on one side. The people then began to suspect (and the new ideas brought in by liberalism of course assisted them) that all the words of the Church were hypocrisy. When they took up the struggle for the Christian Utopia it was therefore against the Church and not with it. Even their violence might be called religious. The Spanish Church, after all, has always been a militant Church, and down to the twentieth century it believed in destroying its enemies. No doubt the anarchists felt that if only, by using the same methods, they could get rid of all who were not of their way of thinking, they would make a better job than the Church had done of introducing the earthly paradise. In Spain every creed aspires to be totalitarian.

In that struggle of fundamentally religious men to win Spain from a perverted Christianity, the FAI has played a part not unlike that of the military orders in the more ancient struggle to win Spain from the infidelity of Islam. But, since anarchism is a social as well as a quasi-religious movement, the FAI has had other functions than the incitement of anti-clerical passions, and, most of all, it has sought from the beginning of its existence to give a consistently rather than intermittently revolutionary direction to the larger libertarian movement embodied in the CNT. In the year after the foundation of the FAI, the CNT began to form committees of action for struggle against the dictatorship, and to collaborate with other groups and movements attempting to change the régime. At this time the Spanish anarchists were willing to accept the temporary solution of a democratic republic, though they had no intention of using it as anything but a springboard from which to launch as quickly as possible their own revolution. In this they were not exceptional. When the dictatorship of Primo de Rivera fell in 1930 it was clear that the life of the monarchy was almost over, and every political faction in Spain began its preparations to make the most of the situation that would follow its collapse. The socialists, the communists, the Catalan separatists, and the army, as well as the anarchists, supported the republican cause, in so far as they did support it, for ends of their own.

The CNT emerged into the open in 1930, numerically stronger than ever, and inspired by the militancy of the FAI activities. The King departed in April 1931, as a result of anti-monarchist victories in the municipal elections, and the anarchists prepared for a revolutionary struggle which many of their leaders felt could only be a matter of months away. In June the CNT reorganized itself by creating national federations of each industry in addition to the Sindicatos Únicos, rather belatedly imitating the CGT's dual structure, under the conviction that the time was near when a coordinated structure of unions would be needed to run the affairs of a revolutionary Spain. In the late summer and autumn of 1931 they began to demonstrate, by a series of local strikes in Seville, Madrid, and Barcelona, that they had no thought of making distinctions between governments and intended to carry on their independent action as vigorously under a republic as under a monarchy. In this situation the FAI played a provocative part, embarrassing the CNT leaders almost as much as the republican government by organizing minor uprisings intended to create an atmosphere of tension throughout the country. They attempted to take the Central Telephone building in Madrid by assault, and early in 1932 led an uprising in the Llobregat valley of Catalonia which was designed as a rehearsal in miniature of the general revolution; one of its principal actions was the division of a number of large estates among the local peasants. The republican government played into the hands of the FAI by adopting a policy of firm repression unaccompanied by any serious attempt to solve the major problem that had plagued Spain for generations, the problem of land reform. In dealing with the Llobregat insurrection in particular they reverted to the bad old methods of past governments by deporting more than a hundred leading anarchists to Spanish Guinea without even the formality of a trial. In January 1933, as a protest against the continued illegal detension of these men, the anarchists organized a further insurrection in Barcelona and Valencia, the news of which sparked off a small uprising in the Andalusian village of Casas Viejas, where a group of labourers, led by a rural anarchist apostle nicknamed Six

Fingers, proclaimed the end of property and government, and laid siege to the barracks of the Civil Guard. On the orders of the central government to put down the rising at all costs, the army moved in on Casas Viejas, besieged Six Fingers and his men in their turn and killed most of them, either in the battle itself or afterwards according to the *ley de fugas.*

The tragedy of Casas Viejas aroused indignation against the government throughout Spain; especially it turned both the peasants and the industrial workers against the republicans and even against the socialists who supported them in the Cortes. Strikes spread through the country, and the CNT grew in prestige and power to such an extent that, though it was officially banned twice during the year, it continued to operate openly, and in December 1933 staged a considerable rising in Aragón, which lasted four days; factories in Saragossa and Huesca were taken over by the workers and collectivization of the land was attempted.

Meanwhile, the CNT was having its own internal troubles, largely through the differences of opinion between the leaders of the generation before Primo de Rivera's dictatorship, who had shifted toward reformism and were largely concerned with gaining better conditions for the workers within existing society, and the FAI élite, who saw every act only in terms of its usefulness in bringing about a social revolution at the earliest possible moment. Partly because of the unity of purpose of the FAI and the almost religious dedication of its members, and partly because of the charismatic appeal of the more flamboyant insurrectionary leaders like Durutti and García Oliver, the extremists were able to retain control of the CNT to such an extent that they ousted the veteran secretary of the organization, Ángel Pestaña, and Juan Peiro, the editor of the Confederation's newspaper, *Solidaridad Obrera.* Pestaña, Peiro, and a number of other leaders who distrusted the rule of the FAI in union affairs issued a public protest; since it bore thirty signatures, those who supported it became known as the Treintistas. With an almost totalitarian intolerance, their opponents engineered the expulsion of these dissidents from the CNT; but the reformists were not entirely without support, and a number of local unions in Valencia and the smaller Catalan towns followed them into a minority movement known as the Sindicatos de Oposición. The breach was eventually healed in 1936, but it left hard feelings within the movement which survived through the Civil War and even into the period of exile, when the Spanish anarchists in France, Britain, and Mexico once again split into rival factions over questions of revolution and reform.

Meanwhile the republican government resigned, largely because of the odium it had incurred over its handling of the Casas Viejas affair, and was heavily defeated by the right-wing parties in the elections of November 1933. More than anything else, the hostility of the anarchists was responsible for this setback. In the municipal elections which had precipitated the departure of the King, many anarchists had gone to the polls—against all their publicly proclaimed principles—for the tactical reason that a republic seemed more favourable to their aims than a monarchy. In 1933 the CNT carried on a vigorous abstentionist campaign; the lack of the million votes which it controlled meant defeat for the Left and two years of reactionary right-wing government.

The anarchists set about dealing with the new government in their own way, with strikes in Saragossa, Valencia, and Andalusia, but Catalonia remained relatively quiet, and toward the end of 1934 one of its periodic moods of lassitude came over the movement as a whole, so that in the rebellions set on foot in October of that year by the socialists and the Catalan separatists, the anarchists played no part, except in Asturias, where the CNT syndicates of Gijon and La Felguera (who ironically were supporters of the reformist Treintistas) fought loyally beside the socialists and suffered with them the atrocities perpetrated by the Foreign Legion and the Moors, used for the first time by Spaniards against Spaniards.

In spite of a temporary loss of ground among the workers because of the prestige gained by the UGT in Asturias, the CNT maintained its strength throughout the period of right-wing government. At the end of 1934 a police report estimated its following at a million and a half, and this was probably not far wrong, since during the republican period all the working-class organizations in Spain increased steadily in membership.

When the parties of the Left came together in a Popular Front coalition, Ángel Pestaña and a small group of his immediate followers were the only anarchists who joined them. The rest held aloof, but nevertheless decided to vote again in December 1935, justifying themselves by the argument that large numbers of their own militants were in prison and the Popular Front leaders had promised an amnesty. Once again they played the part of king-makers, and their votes brought success to the parties whom their abstention had defeated in 1933.

But, like most king-makers, the anarchists had no intention of obeying the government they had placed in power. With their ranks filled by the release of their most active leaders from prison and exile and by the return to the fold of the 60,000 members of the Sindicatos de Oposición at the Saragossa Congress of the CNT in May 1936, they kept aloof from the socialists, who talked of a revolutionary alliance between the UGT and the CNT (which did not materialize until 1938, when it was far too late), and followed their own policy of keeping the country in a state of expectancy and unrest by a succession of lightning strikes. The idea of revolution in the near future was certainly in their minds, but whether they would have attempted anything on a larger scale than the limited risings of the early days of the republic is an academic speculation in view of the fact that it was the Right and the army that set the pace and unleashed the Civil War by the rising of the generals in July 1936.

The story of the Civil War has been told in detail elsewhere. Here I will limit myself to discussing those aspects of the war which illuminate the nature and the development of Spanish anarchism. For this purpose the war can be divided into two phases: an earlier, dynamic period, lasting from July 1936 to the early days of 1937, in which the CNT and the FAI were among the dominant groups in republican Spain; and a later period, dating from May 1937, during which these movements declined in both influence and drive as centralization in military and administrative affairs successfully brought the loyalist regions of Spain under the control of the republican government, with a consequent strengthening of communist influence.

The events of the summer and autumn of 1936 revealed both the virtues and the shortcomings of the Spanish libertarian organizations. For years the FAI had been training for the kind of situation in which a general strike and a short, sharp period of insurrection would topple the state and bring in the millennium of *comunismo libertario*. They were expert street fighters and guerrilla warriors, and in the critical situation created by the military *coup* of 19 July they were at their best. In Barcelona and Valencia, in the rural districts of Catalonia and parts of Aragón, and even to an extent in Madrid and Asturias, it was the prompt action of the FAI élite and the workers of the CNT unions that defeated the generals locally and saved these cities and regions for the republic.

The triumph of the working-class organizations created a revolutionary atmosphere and even a temporary revolutionary situation in Catalonia, Levante, and parts of Aragón. For several months the armed forces in these regions were mostly anarchist-controlled militia units. The factories were largely taken over by the workers and run by CNT committees, while hundreds of villages either shared out or collectivized the land, and many of them attempted to set up libertarian communes of the kind advocated by Kropotkin. In a thousand minute details life changed its outward form, as George Orwell recorded vividly in *Homage to Catalonia* when he described Barcelona during the days of the anarchist ascendancy:

Every shop and café had an inscription saying that it had been collectivized; even the bootblacks had been collectivized and their
boxes were painted red and black.* Waiters and shop-walkers looked
you in the face and treated you as an equal. Servile and even cere-
monial forms of speech had temporarily disappeared. Nobody said
'Señor' or 'Don' or even 'Usted'; everyone called everyone else
'Comrade' and 'Thou' and said 'Salud!' instead of 'Buenos días' ...
There were no private cars, they had all been commandeered, and all
the trams and taxis and much of the other transport were painted red
and black. The revolutionary posters were everywhere, flaming from
the walls in clear reds and blues that made the few remaining adver-
tisements look like daubs of mud. Down the Ramblas, the wide central artery of the town where crowds of people streamed constantly
to and fro, the loudspeakers were bellowing revolutionary songs all
day and far into the night. And it was the aspect of the crowds that
was the queerest thing of all. In outward appearance it was a town in
which the wealthy classes had practically ceased to exist. Except for
a small number of women and foreigners there were no 'well-
dressed' people at all. Practically everyone wore rough working-class
clothes, or blue overalls, or some variant of the militia uniform. All
this was queer and moving.

Perhaps the most important element in the situation was the absence of
effective authority. The central government was weak and distant, and
locally in Catalonia the FAI and CNT were, at least for the time being,
more powerful than whatever shadowy authorities maintained a semblance of existence. But even the CNT and the FAI could not maintain a
uniformity of what they rather euphemistically called 'organized indisci-
pline'. Much that happened in Spain during those early days of the Civil
War was the work of small groups acting on their own anarchic responsibility. Sometimes their initiatives were good; often they were bad. It was
such groups of anarchists, for instance, who carried out most of the church
burnings that became a veritable epidemic in the summer of 1936, and in
the process destroyed many remarkable works of religious art; ironically,
their respect for culture made them preserve the celebrated paintings pro-

*The anarcho-syndicalist flag in Spain was black and red, divided diagonally. In the
days of the International the anarchists, like other socialist sects, carried the red flag,
but later they tended to substitute for it the black flag. The black-and-red flag symbol-
ized an attempt to unite the spirit of later anarchism with the mass appeal of the
International.

duced by an aristocratic culture, while it was mostly genuine works of folk art, examples of the popular achievement they valued so much, which they burned and hacked to pieces. It was such groups too who carried out many of the summary executions of suspected fascists which took place during the same initial period; these acts were usually committed, not by the ordinary working men of the CNT, or even by the more responsible FAI militants, but by relatively small groups, sometimes of professional *pistoleros*, but more often of hot-headed young fanatics belonging to the Libertarian Youth organization. Their favourite victims included priests and monks on the one hand, and pimps and male prostitutes on the other; both classes they shot from a moral bigotry that was characteristically Spanish—the priests having, in their eyes, mocked the ideal of human brotherhood and the pimps and male prostitutes having offended against the Law of Nature. Anarchism as a philosophy had little to do with such excesses, which took place in no other country than Spain. They sprang rather from a fatal conjunction of Bakunin's personal fantasies of destruction with the strange cult of death that has given violence to political and religious issues in Spain ever since the days of the Reconquest. On this level there is not really a great deal to choose between the anarchist minority who killed priests and pimps in Catalonia and the Falangist minority who killed trade-unionists in Granada; both were the products of Spanish history rather than of the political philosophies they claimed to represent.

Whether for good or ill, the Spanish anarchists were full of energy and practical capability during the early, fluid period of the Civil War. But theirs were dynamic virtues, which had always flourished in times of tension and flagged at other times. Strong in spontaneous impulse, they were incapable of the kind of tenacity necessary to hold whatever they gained. Their courage and enterprise in the first days of the military revolt fell away into boredom and inefficiency as the conflict lengthened, and their very resistance to discipline and authority unfitted them for the tasks of a real and prolonged war, which by its very nature is a totalitarian process. After the first spectacular push of Durutti's volunteer column into Aragón, that favourite anarchist front became one of the most static in the whole war, and the old anarchist stronghold of Saragossa, the objective of the campaign, was never taken. Partly this was because the anarchist units were starved of arms owing to the policy of the republican government, which tried to force the independent militias into a disciplined army under centralized control; partly it was because of local loyalties, which made affairs in Catalonia, in the factories and the collective farms, seem often more important than what was happening on the distant front; partly it was because of a half-conscious recognition that inevitably, as the war continued, an authoritarian pattern was being imposed upon the country in which the libertarian experiments undertaken so enthusiastically in 1936 could not survive.

Here one must remember that circumstances had placed the anarchists in a painful dilemma. Their organization, their tactics, their very mental attitude, had been shaped over a generation for the purpose of resistance to established authority, at the end of which the anarchic Armageddon would be fought and the libertarian saints would march into the Zion of *comunismo libertario* that would arise from the ruins of a dead world. But by the late autumn of 1936 it became clear that the real revolution had not taken place, that *comunismo libertario* had at best been achieved on a piece-meal scale, that in order to carry on the struggle against the external aggressor the anarchists must collaborate against the grain with the republican government and the authoritarian parties they had formerly resisted.

In this situation the anarchist leaders chose the way of compromise and, having chosen it, they followed it to the extent of denying all anarchist tradition and entering first the government of Catalonia in September 1936 and then the Madrid government of Largo Caballero in December 1936. It was not merely members of the reformist trend in the CNT who took ministerial portfolios; they were joined by the FAI insurrectionist leader, García Oliver, who became Minister of Justice and seems to have enjoyed his position. The FAI Peninsular Committee went on record in October 1936 to justify participation in governmental institutions because the situation demanded it. But participation meant a virtual abdication of anarchist revolutionary hopes; it meant that the anarchist leaders were strengthening the governmental institutions which were their natural enemies, and which must seek to destroy their influence as libertarians.

The presence of anarchist ministers did not prevent, and perhaps even encouraged, the government *coup* of May 1937, when fighting broke out in Barcelona because of an assault by the communist-dominated PSUC party in the Telephone Building, which had been in the hands of the anarchists since the beginning of the Civil War. After several days of fighting in the streets, when many of the anarchist rank-and-file resisted the PSUC and the government forces in defiance of their own leaders' calls for a cease-fire, the preponderant anarchist influence in Catalonia was destroyed. From that time the CNT ceased to count in the Spanish scene. Its membership remained high, reaching approximately two million, and the FAI, having decided to loosen its organization, grew from 30,000 in

1936 to 150,000 in 1938. But both organizations had lost spirit as a result of living by compromise rather than by resistance, and from mid 1937 they retreated slowly in every field of action. The conduct of the war itself fell more and more under the control of communists and the Russian military experts. The collectivized factories were taken over by the government, and many of the agricultural collectives were destroyed when Lister's communist troops marched into Aragón. All this happened without any appreciable anarchist resistance, and the demoralization of the movement was finally revealed in January 1939, when Franco's troops entered Barcelona, the stronghold of Spanish anarchism, without the least opposition.

Even after the fall of Barcelona the anarchists did achieve a bitter kind of triumph, not over the Nationalists but over their communist enemies behind the republican lines, for a number of their leaders, including José Garcia Pradas, Gonzalez Marin, and Eduardo Val, carried compromise to a final stage by taking part in the plot by which Colonel Casado and other republican officers seized power in Madrid after the flight of Negrin's government in March 1939; Casado's *coup* was made possible only by the use of the army corps commanded by the anarchist Cipriano Mera. But though this meant that at last the communists were thrust out of power in what remained of republican Spain, and the anarchists in this sense had their revenge, it did nothing to change the course of the war. Franco's military superiority was by now overwhelming and unconditional surrender was inevitable.

It is true that not all the anarchists in Spain agreed with the policy of compromise. Some of the more intransigent members of the FAI stood out for a thoroughly anarchist approach to the situation; they centred around a select group who called themselves Friends of Durutti (in memory of the guerrilla leader who was shot in the back in the winter of 1936 by political enemies on the Madrid front) and who led the anarchist resistance during the May fighting in Barcelona. They were supported by some of the Italian, French, and German anarchists who had gone to Spain at the outbreak of the Civil War, and particularly by the Italian intellectual Camillo Berneri, whom the communists regarded as so dangerous to their plans for immobilizing the anarchists that their agents murdered him in a Barcelona street. But to point out that there were anarchists in Spain who kept vigorously to their ideals is not to suggest that even they would have found a way to create and conserve an anarchist society in the middle of an event so antithetical to libertarian principles and practice as a modern war. Given the situation, the problem seems to have been insoluble in anarchist terms.

The anarchists in Spain in fact failed both militarily and politically because they could not remain anarchists and take part in governments and total war. By compromising they did not make their failure less certain; they merely made it more humiliating. But in making a final accounting one must consider what the survivors of those tragic days regard as their constructive achievements. In their running of the factories, in their effective collectivization of agriculture, it has often been suggested by libertarian apologists, the Spanish anarchists demonstrated triumphantly that workers can effectively control their own industries and that Kropotkin's ideal of libertarian communism is indeed practicable in the modern world.

The full history of anarchist industrial and agricultural collectivization in Spain has never been written, and it is possible that the records no longer exist on which it might be based. But what evidence has been preserved suggests that these experiments were to a great extent successful. Spain, with its traditions of village democracy and communal enterprise, was a country naturally adapted for such undertakings. In the rural districts of Navarre, Asturias, and the Pyrenees there still existed villages where land was farmed and herds were owned collectively on a system that in the past must have been far more widely spread. Even in the rural districts of the south, divided into great estates, traditions of a golden age of village communism still survived, and it was from these districts that the factories of Barcelona recruited their workers. In their propaganda for collectivization the Spanish anarchists in fact appealed—as anarchists so often do—to a nostalgic dream of a lost past as well as to an aspiration toward a better future.

The beginnings of collectivization seem to have been similar in villages and factories. The landlords in the villages had fled, the Civil Guards had been killed or chased away, and the village syndicate would transform itself into a popular assembly in which every villager could participate directly in the affairs of the community. An administrative committee would be elected, but this would operate under the constant supervision of the population, meeting at least once a week in full assembly to hasten the achievement of free communism. In the factories the process was similar, with a workers' committee becoming responsible to the general assembly of the syndicate, and technicians (in a few cases the former owners or managers) planning production in accordance with the workers' views.

The period of almost complete workers' control in Barcelona lasted from July until 24 October 1936, when the Generalitat, the provincial government of Catalonia, passed a Collectivization Decree which recognized the accomplished fact of the workers having assumed responsibility for the factories, but at the same time set up a machinery of coordination which was the first stage in governmental supervision and—eventually—government control. But for more than four months, from 19 July until the decree began to take effect, the factories of Barcelona were operated by the workers without state aid or interference, and for the most part without experienced managers.

Public services were conducted in the same way, and Barcelona, a large modern city with complex needs, was kept functioning by the CNT with a surprising degree of efficiency. As the English libertarian writer Vernon Richards has pointed out:

> It speaks highly of their organizing capacities and intelligence that the Catalan workers were able to take over the railways and resume services with a minimum of delay; that all transport services in Barcelona and its suburbs were reorganized under workers' control and functioned more efficiently than before; that public services under workers' control, such as telephones, gas and light, were functioning normally within 48 hours of the defeat of General Goded's attempted rising; that the bakers' collective of Barcelona saw to it that so long as they had the flour (and Barcelona's needs were an average of 3,000 sacks a day), the population would have the bread.[*]

A less partial commentator, Franz Borkenau, who arrived three weeks after the July rising, gives in *The Spanish Cockpit* (1937) a very similar impression from direct observation:

> The amount of expropriation in the few days since 19 July is almost incredible [he noted in his diary for 5 August]. In many respects, however, life was much less disturbed than I expected it to be after newspaper reports abroad. Tramways and buses were running, water and light functioning.

The comments on the efficiency of the collectivized factories have varied considerably, and there is no doubt that some of them were unable to operate satisfactorily for lack of raw material. However, Gerald Brenan remarks that the evidence shows collectivization to have been successful on many occasions 'to a surprising degree', and here again Borkenau gives a guarded but favourable report of what he saw on 8 August 1936, when he visited the collectivized workshops of the general bus company in Barcelona:

[*]*Lessons of the Spanish Revolution*, London, 1953.

Undeniably, the factory which I saw is a big success for the CNT. Only three weeks after the beginning of the Civil War, two weeks after the end of the general strike, it seems to run as smoothly as if nothing had happened. I visited the men at their machines. The rooms looked tidy, the work was done in a regular manner. Since socialization this factory has repaired two buses, finished one which had been under construction and constructed a completely new one. The latter wore the inscription 'constructed under workers' control'. It had been completed, the management claimed, in five days, as against an average of seven days under the previous management. Complete success, then.

It is a large factory, and things could not have been made to look nice for the benefit of a visitor, had they really been in a bad muddle. Nor do I think that any preparations were made for my visit ...

But if it would be hasty to generalize from the very favourable impression made by this particular factory, one fact remains; it is an extraordinary achievement for a group of workers to take over one factory, under however favourable conditions, and within a few days to make it run with complete regularity. It bears brilliant witness to the general standard of efficiency of the Catalan worker and to the organizing capacities of the Barcelona trade unions.

On the basis of what we do know of anarchist urban collectivization I think we can safely say that the public services in the cities and towns were as adequately operated as they had been before the Civil War, and that some at least of the factories were run remarkably well. Spanish communal traditions and the long absorption of anarchist teachings of voluntary cooperation seem here to have borne good fruit. In his extensive study *Collectives in the Spanish Revolution*, Gaston Leval points out that all industry and all public services were collectivized in Catalonia, the anarchist heartland, and about 70 per cent in Levante, though in Castile, where libertarian traditions were weaker, the proportion was not so high. In the three provinces of Levante, Aragón, and Castile alone he estimates that there were 1,600 agrarian collectives, each usually consisting of an entire village; this does not count Catalonia or Andalusia, where every village that escaped the first onslaught of the Nationalists automatically collectivized its land. Like many statistics connected with anarchism in Spain, his estimate that between five and seven million people were directly or indirectly involved in industrial and agrarian collectives is doubtless excessively high; other estimates run as low as two million, and the reality lies somewhere in between. But even if one assumes that only

three million people were involved, that is an impressively high proportion of the population behind the republican lines.

Certainly in the areas of anarchist influence most of the villages were
collectivized and the great majority of the peasants participated. How
completely the participation was voluntary it is hard to tell. Leval insists
that 'it is untrue to say that those who took part in the collectives were
forced to do so', but there is evidence that in many villages reluctant peasants were brought in by fear for their lives, or, perhaps more often, by fear
of that great anarchist substitute for overt authority, the power of public
opinion; besides, those who disagreed deeply with the new order would
have fled before collectivization began.

The village collectives usually regarded themselves as independent
communes, each in its own *partria chica*, entering into equal relations with
surrounding villages. In general, the land was worked communally instead
of being divided into equal plots, though there were wide variations in
methods of organizing work and distributing produce. Almost all the villages set out to abolish the use of money, on which subject they were in
full agreement with St Paul; some resorted to labour cheques in the
Proudhonian manner, but others went all the way to *comunismo libertario*
and established a system by which the peasants were supplied with goods
from the village store without any kind of payment. Standards of living
and work varied from region to region. In Andalusia the ascetic strain was
strong, and a simplification of living that would produce a dignified, free,
and equal poverty was the goal. In Aragón and Catalonia the progressive
temper of the people produced a desire for improving methods of cultivation, so that here the tendency was toward scientific agriculture and as
much mechanization as possible. Almost all the collectivized villages seem
to have been highly conscious of the need for education, so that they set
up ambitious plans for ending adult illiteracy, as well as attempting to create medical services and to provide for the care of people unable to work.

It is hard to generalize about the success of agrarian collectivization,
since nowhere did it survive more than two and a half farm seasons, and in
some places where the nationalist advance was rapid it did not last far
beyond the first harvest. The one great achievement was that, for the first
time within living memory in many parts of rural Spain, there was work
and food, if not luxury, for all. Land that had gone untilled for generations
was cultivated again, and no man starved. But, as happens often in Spain, it
was beyond the boundaries of the villages or the districts that trouble
began. The distribution systems, in which the government soon began to
interfere, were often inefficient, and peasants who grew specialized crops,

such as oranges or olives, which had lost their normal foreign markets, probably suffered a great deal more than those who carried on mixed or grain farming and lived largely from their own produce.

Yet here again the final verdict must be favourable. The peasants of the anarchist regions of Spain were successful enough to convince many observers that collectivization of some kind is still the only real solution to the perennial problem of the land in Spain.

Collectivization during the early months of the Civil War is therefore a field of achievement that must be placed to the credit of the last and largest of the world's major anarchist movements. In the arts of war the Spanish anarchists failed for the most part, and their organization was destroyed, at least in Spain itself, and their following dispersed.

But in the arts of peace they showed that their faith in the organizing powers of workers and peasants, in the natural social virtues of ordinary people and their power to extemporize in circumstances of crisis, had not been misplaced. Even if one takes into account the special circumstances of the country and the times, the collectivization of Spanish factories and farms under anarchist inspiration remains a practical experiment on a large scale that cannot be ignored in a final assessment of the anarchist claims to have discovered a way to live in a free and peaceful community.

During the long period of Franco's rule, which lasted from 1939 to his death in 1975, Spanish anarchism reverted to clandestinity. A small underground movement survived in the country under circumstances of great difficulty and peril and it is almost impossible to reconstruct its history, though it appears that no less than eighteen national committees were formed during this period and broken up by the authorities, their members either being imprisoned or fleeing over the Pyrenees. All one can say is that this dangerous and dedicated activity had little effect on the trend of events in Spain.

After the fall of Barcelona in 1939, many members of the CNT, FAI, and anarchist militia units fled over the border into France, and others found their way to Britain and to certain Latin American countries. Difficult years followed, particularly in France during the Vichy régime, but the CNT-FAI revived as an expatriate organization, particularly after 1945 in France, where it was led by Federica Montseny, and in Mexico, where García Oliver had fled.

Gradually, however, over the thirty-six years of Franco's rule, the movement in exile shrank in numbers as its members died off or became discouraged, and when the time came with the end of the dictatorship for it to re-emerge into the open, and those who had survived in exile were reunited uneasily with those who had stayed to work clandestinely, they faced a Spain that had changed dramatically from the country of 1939. A middle class had emerged, largely filling the traditional Iberian chasm between the rich and the poor, and even the poor had for the most part escaped from the classic Spanish destitution under which a labourer on one of the *latifundias* would have to be content with a meal of bread smeared with garlic.

The CNT re-emerged as an open organization in January 1976, and in March 1977 a public rally in the bull ring at San Sebastian de los Reyes attracted more than 20,000 people. By the summer of 1977 the movement claimed 24,000 members, and while such figures are large compared with contemporary anarchist movements in other countries, they represent a striking reduction from the membership of the CNT in the 1930s and especially during the Civil War. Since 1976 the CNT has grown slowly as a combination of doctrinaire veterans and young people with less tradition-al views of the role of anarchism. Even in its old centre of Barcelona, anar-chism is no longer a mass movement, the acknowledged rival of the social-ists and the communists, and this is largely because education and growing prosperity have eroded its traditional constituencies of downtrodden Andalusian peasants and Catalan workers locked in violent conflict with ruthless employers.

13. Anarchism in Russia

AT first the history of Russian anarchism seems puzzlingly slight. In the writings and lives of Bakunin, Kropotkin, and Tolstoy, Russia probably contributed more than any other country to anarchist theory and even to the creation of an international anarchist movement. Yet in Russia itself a specifically anarchist movement did not appear until the middle of the 1890s, and throughout the quarter of a century of its existence it remained the smallest of the revolutionary groupings, dwarfed in the rural districts by the Social Revolutionary Party, in the cities by the Menshevik and Bolshevik halves of the Social Democratic Party, in Poland by the Bund. Only at the very end of its life, between 1918 and 1921, did Russian anarchists gain a brief and sudden glory when the peasants of the southern Ukraine flocked in their tens of thousands to the black banners of the anarchist guerrilla leader Nestor Makhno. With the final destruction of Makhno's Revolutionary Insurrectionary Army in 1921, Russian anarchism declined rapidly to extinction under the relentless persecution of the Cheka.

Yet parallel to this meagre history of a definable anarchist movement there runs a much deeper history of the anarchist idea. It was not until the foundation of the earliest Marxist group in 1883 by Plekhanov, Axelrod, and Vera Zasulich that revolutionaries within Russia began to divide along the rigid party lines which had parted anarchists from authoritarian socialists in western Europe since the schism within the International. The sectarian forms of anarchist organization which Bakunin had already created in Europe did not attract the Russian activists of the 1870s, yet the whole of the populist movement down to 1881 was permeated with libertarian attitudes and ideals. As Isaiah Berlin remarks in his introduction to Franco Venturi's monumental work on the populists, 'violent disputes took place about means and methods, about timing, but not about ultimate purposes. Anarchism, equality, a full life for all, these were universally accepted.'

In so far as the anarchistic elements in Russian revolutionary thought of the 1860s and 1870s came from western Europe, they were transmitted through the writings of individual theoreticians rather than through the organized anarchist movement, which until the end of the century had few and tenuous contacts with revolutionaries inside Russia. Professor Venturi has justly remarked of Bakunin that 'he was able to inspire a revolutionary spirit within Russia but not an organization'. Indeed, even when an avowedly anarchist movement did appear in Russia toward the end of the 1890s, it grew in its own independent way, largely ignoring the exhortations of respected expatriate leaders like Kropotkin, and it ended by producing in the Makhnovist movement of 1918-21 a fruit of prodigious Russianness.

Indeed, students of Russian revolutionary movements have at times been inclined to minimize the influence of teachings from abroad, and to attribute the wide appeal of libertarian ideas during the greater part of the nineteenth century to an anarchistic tradition native to Russian society. Like Bakunin, they have pointed particularly to the great peasant revolts led by Stenka Razin and Pugachev, and to the resistance to centralized authority shown in the struggles for independence of the early Cossacks, and in the tendency of Russian dissenting sects to reject all mundane authority and live by the Inner Light.

What most significantly united all the native Russian movements of rebellion was not so much their thirst for liberty as their hatred of distant power; they were the rebellions—either through insurrection or withdrawal—of peasants who wished to live according to their own customs and in their own communities. They fought against serfdom and against domination by alien rulers. But they did not fight as anarchists. The peasant revolts produced their own autocratic leaders and pretended Tsars, and even such religious sects as the Doukhobors merely rejected a Romanov autocrat so as to accept the domination of a prophet or 'living Christ' of their own breed, who wielded both temporal and spiritual authority within the community.

All these movements stressed the autonomy of the *mir* or *obshchina*, the natural peasant community, and the idealized image of this institution became a kind of Platonic myth that united a wide variety of Russian thinkers during the nineteenth century. Men who in other ways seemed each other's natural opposites—Aksakov and Bakunin, Dostoyevsky and Tolstoy—made it the cornerstone of their visionary Russia. For both anarchists and Slavophils it seemed the magic link between a lost age of gold and a future of idyllic promise.

Indeed, their tendency to oppose to the centralized Western state an organic society based on natural peasant institutions brought the Slavophils at certain points so near to the libertarian position that some of their early leaders—particularly Konstantin Aksakov—have been counted among the ancestors of Russian anarchism. Even Bakunin remarked, at the height of his anarchist period in 1867, that as early as the 1830s 'Konstantin Sergeevich and his friends were enemies of the Petersburg State and of statism in general, and in this attitude he even anticipated us'. Here again, however, it is necessary to approach the claims of a putative ancestor with scepticism.

It is true that Aksakov, like Dostoyevsky, posed the contrast between the way of conscience and the way of law and compulsion. This led him to a discussion of the political state as developed in western Europe and imported into Russia by Peter the Great:

> However widely and liberally the state may develop, were it even to reach the extreme form of democracy, it will none the less remain a principle of constraint, of external pressure—a given binding form, an institution. The more the state evolves the more forcefully it turns into a substitute for the inward world of man, and the deeper, the more closely man is confined by society, even if society should seem to satisfy all his needs. If the liberal state were to reach the extreme form of democracy, and every man to become an officer of the state, a policeman over himself, the state would have finally destroyed the living soul in man ... The falsehood resides not in this or that form of the state, but in the state itself, as an idea, as a principle; we must concern ourselves, not with the good or evil of a particular form of state, but with the state as false in itself.

Thus Aksakov, like the rest of the great Slavophils down to Dostoyevsky, rejected the modern state—autocratic or democratic—in terms that are deceptively similar to those used by the anarchists. As Herzen, his ideological enemy, said of him:

> His whole life was an uncompromising protest against the Russia of officialdom, against the Petersburg period, in the name of the unrecognized, oppressed Russian people ... He was ready to go into the market place for his faith: he would have gone to the stake, and when that is felt behind a man's words, they become terribly convincing.

Yet, if Aksakov rejected the state in its modern form, he did not reject the idea of government. On the contrary, he dreamed of an ideal autocracy, an autocracy returning to a primitive form that had never really existed in the Slavophil imagination as part of the myth of Holy Russia. In such an autocracy the Tsar would become a kind of sacrificial king on whom the people would place the burden of authority so that they might be liberated from its moral evil and set free to concentrate on the real, non-political business of living good lives. Aksakov hated authority, but he could not convince himself that it was unnecessary, so he chose to imagine its transference rather than its abolition. His real contribution to the Russian libertarian tradition sprang from his insistence on the value of the basic units of social cooperation: the peasant community and the traditional cooperative association of artisans.

A truer bond links anarchism with Alexander Herzen, who stands at the beginning of the whole Russian tradition of rebellion that began to emerge in the decades after the defeat of the Decembrists. Herzen was the first Russian to realize the importance of Proudhon's objections to authoritarian communism, and in the 1840s he began to spread the French anarchist's ideas among the radical discussion groups of Moscow. Later, exiled in Europe, disillusioned by the Revolutions of 1848 and 1849, he found in Proudhon the man who most eloquently expressed his own misgivings about the failures of Jacobin politics and socialist Utopianism. It was for this reason that he financed Proudhon in publishing *La Voix du peuple*. He recognized at that early time what one now sees in the perspective of history: that the strength of thinkers like Proudhon lies in their denials rather than in their affirmations.

> It is in the denial, the destruction of the old social tradition, that the great power of Proudhon lies; he is as much the poet of dialectics as Hegel is, with the difference that the one rests on the calm heights of the philosophic movement, while the other is thrust into the turmoil of popular passions and the hand-to-hand struggle of parties.

Herzen himself was a gentle sceptic, tenacious in his purposes, as was shown by his years of almost single-handed effort to stimulate Russian radical thought through his expatriate journal, *The Bell*, yet perpetually doubtful of them. He longed for peaceful and constructive change, but he felt that the world in which he lived would make any change stormy and destructive. There is a true ring of negative anarchism in the message to his son which in 1855 he prefaced to his book, *From the Other Shore*:

> We do not build, we destroy; we do not proclaim a new revelation, we eliminate the old lie. Modern man, that melancholy *Pontifex Maximus*, only builds a bridge—it will be for the unknown man of the future to pass over it. You may be there to see him ... But do not,

I beg, remain *on this shore* ... Better to perish with the revolution than
to seek refuge in the alms-house of reaction.

Like Proudhon, Herzen did not create systems and he was reluctant to
assume labels. Yet he did at times speak of anarchy in the Proudhonian
sense as an ideal for society, and placed his hopes of Russia in the 'anarchism' of the nobles and the 'communism' of the peasants. By 'communism' he meant voluntary economic arrangement quite unlike anything
Marx contemplated; communism as conceived by the political thinkers of
western Europe he dismissed with the remark that it was 'Russian autocracy turned upside down'.

In his disillusionment with the West after 1848, he turned toward Russia
once again, yet the point of view from which he now saw it was inevitably
shaped by the very events and tendencies he rejected, and so the attitude
he bequeathed to the populist tradition was a mixture of Russian and
Western elements in which Proudhonism was curiously reconciled with
Slavophilism.

Herzen remained a socialist in the Proudhonian sense, rejecting governmental socialism as an ideal in favour of a society based on
modifications of the peasant *mir* and the workmen's *artel*. He was always
anti-bourgeois and looked with distrust on conventional democracy
which, like Tocqueville, he feared might end in the reign of universal
mediocrity. He disliked industrialism as he saw it developing in England
and France, but he did not dismiss the idea of applying science to production, provided it was based on 'the relation of man to the soil', which he
considered 'a primordial fact, a *natural fact*'. Above all, he regarded the
monolithic state as inimical to freedom and also as un-Russian.

Centralization is alien to the Slav spirit—freedom is far more natural to it. Only when grouped in a league of free and independent peoples will the Slav world at last enter upon its genuine historical existence.

The primitive communal forms of rural Russia, it seemed to him, provided the settings in which the people learned to be responsible and socially
active.

The life of the Russian peasantry has hitherto been confined to the
commune. It is only in relation to the commune and its members
that the peasant recognizes that he has rights and duties.

And in the extraordinary durability of the communal system he saw, like
others of his fellow countrymen, a means by which Russia could achieve a
free society without going through the stages of capitalism and socialist
revolution to which western Europe seemed committed.

> The communal system, though it has suffered violent shocks, has
> stood firm against the interference of the authorities; it had success-
> fully survived up to the development of socialism in Europe. This
> circumstance is of infinite consequence for Russia.

The thought that the world's future lay in the untried countries haunted Herzen's imagination, and behind all the writings of his later years
there stood the vision—how prophetic one is now uneasily aware—of
Russia and America facing each other over a dispirited Europe. In all this
he saw the complete elimination of the state as a desirable but almost
infinitely receding possibility. Like Thomas Paine, he was never enough of
an optimist to let his natural anarchism run its full course. Almost alone,
except for his friend, the poet Ogarev, he awoke the youth of his country
to a sense of responsibility for the liberation of the Russian people, but
like Moses he had no more than a glimpse of the promised land, and by
the end of his career he had retreated into a caution that made constitutional liberalism the effective goal of his efforts.

Yet even if Herzen's anarchism was never fully developed and even if
he deliberately used his influence in the direction of moderation, his evident distrust of the state and his faith in the social potentialities of the
people prepared the way not only for the great populist movement that
began to emerge in the early 1860s, but also for its essentially anarchistic
attitude toward the political organization of society.

That anarchistic attitude was sharpened and given form by Bakunin.
Bakunin's influence in Russia was necessarily indirect and intermittent. He
himself did not become a completely convinced anarchist until at least
three years after his escape from Russian soil in 1861. He influenced a number of young populists while he was in Siberia, but there is little evidence
that they played any part in spreading his ideas, with the possible exception of Ivan Yakovlevich Orlov, who became the first Russian revolutionary to 'go to the people' by preaching the populist doctrine on an 'apostolic journey' through the Russian countryside and who later became
involved in the Kazan conspiracy of students and officers to incite a peasant rebellion in conjunction with the Polish uprising of 1863. Orlov's
actions suggest that he may have been influenced at least by the emphasis

on peasant insurrections which was a feature of Bakunin's teaching in all his revolutionary phases.

In his last, anarchist period Bakunin spread his doctrine in Russia both orally, through returning *émigrés*, and by means of his writings, which were smuggled into the country and distributed by the network of revolutionary groups. His direct contacts with activists within Russia were few and brief, owing to an inevitable difficulty of carrying on secret correspondence, complicated by lack of discretion on his own part which led more than one of his associates to a Tsarist dungeon. Like all the Russian leaders in exile, he knew little of the quickly changing situation within the country whose political fate he was trying to influence, and this led to differences of opinion and interpretation between him and the militants actually involved in the struggle against Tsarism. By the very nature of the situation he had no influence at all on the specific actions of the revolutionaries, but his influence on their attitudes was strong enough for a recognized Bakuninist trend to flourish throughout the 1870s, particularly in the Ukraine.

Bakunin's anarchism gained its first substantial influence within Russia in 1869. It is true that shortly after his escape from Siberia he established tenuous contacts with the leaders of the first Zemlya i Volya (Land and Liberty) movement, and that in September 1862, after a strongly political manifesto had been issued by a group calling itself Young Russia, he published with Herzen's Free Russian Press a pamphlet entitled *The People's Cause: Romanov, Pugachev or Pestel?* But this was little more than a call for unity among the various forces that were working toward a full emancipation of the people. After 1863 and the fiasco of his Polish adventure, Bakunin's attention turned away from Russian affairs to those of the socialist movement in western Europe. While he was building up his succession of Brotherhoods in Italy he seems to have made little effort to establish contact with his own countrymen. Russians passing through Italy would often visit him, but the young scientist L. Mechnikov was the only one of them who became closely associated with him. And Mechnikov, who was probably a member of the Florentine Brotherhood, had fought under Garibaldi and, like Bakunin himself, was something of an international revolutionary.

It was Bakunin's return to Geneva in 1867 that brought him back to the world of Russian exiles. Many had settled in Geneva itself and along the shore of Lake Leman at Vevey. Among them was Nicholas Zhukovsky, whom Bakunin had met in 1862, and who now served with him on the Committee of the League for Peace and Freedom, later becoming a founding member of the Alliance. At Vevey Bakunin formed a small Russian section of the International Brotherhood; this was the first Russian anarchist organization; but it was neither active nor large, since most of the exiles, led by Nicholas Utin and Alexander Serno-Soloveich, joined the Marxist-oriented Russian section of the International which was founded at Geneva in 1869.

Bakunin's sole real achievement in the field of Russian affairs at this time was the foundation, in collaboration with Zhukovsky, of *Narodnoe Delo* (*The People's Cause*). The first number of this journal, written entirely by Bakunin and Zhukovsky, was successfully smuggled into Russia by Ivan Bochkarev, later a close associate of Tolstoy, and distributed in St Petersburg by Stepniak. To the students who read it, *Narodnoe Delo* seemed to give the guidance for which they had been waiting anxiously in a stage of transitional indecision, and its stimulative influence within Russia was very great.

In *Narodnoe Delo* Bakunin declared that the time had now come for the intellectuals to abandon their detachment from the people and to arouse in them the revolutionary spirit. The revolution, the 'socio-economic' liberation of the peasants, should have first place; after that, their mental chains would fall away. They must be weaned of their ancient faith in the Tsar, and in their minds must be awakened 'an awareness of their own strength, which has slept ever since Pugachev'. The aims of the revolution must be collectivist and anarchist; the return of the land to those who worked it and the complete destruction of the state, to be replaced by 'a future political organization made up exclusively of a free federation of free workmen's *artels*, agricultural and industrial'. In *Narodnoe Delo* Bakunin sought to adapt to Russian circumstances the programme he was about to defend among the western European revolutionaries of the International, and he declared that any view of Russia's messianic destiny must be abandoned, for 'the cause of the revolution is the same everywhere'.

From this comprehensive exposition of the anarchist viewpoint as it had been developed in the International Brotherhood, the Bakuninist trend in the Russian revolutionary movement really began. So far as Bakunin himself was concerned it remained for some years an isolated effort, since the anti-Bakuninist refugees, led by Utin, managed to win over to their side the rich Olga Levashov, who was financing *Narodnoe Delo*, and the journal passed from Bakunin and Zhukovsky to the Russian section of the International.

Apart from his disastrous association with Nechayev, his involvement in the International and the Lyons Commune drew Bakunin away from

Russian affairs in the years immediately following the loss of *Narodnoe Delo*. In 1872, however, he was attracted by the great concentration of Russian students and radicals of all kinds who had settled in Zürich. Here at last he gathered around him a circle of young men who absorbed his ideas with enthusiasm and created an organization to disseminate them. They came to him by various paths. Some had been associates of Nechayev; these included the two men who were possibly most influential in transmitting Bakunin's ideas to the clandestine groups of Russia—Z. K. Ralli and Michael Sazhin, better known by the name Armand Ross, which he had adopted during a brief visit to the United States. Others, like Varfomeley Zaystev and Nicholas Sokolov, had been members of the loose nihilist group which gathered around Pisarev and his magazine *Russkoe Slovo* in the early 1860s. An even younger group of medical students had come straight from agitation and expulsion at the University of St Petersburg; of these the most active were V. Holstein and A. Oelsnitz.

Already, in the spring of 1872, Bakunin had re-formed his Russian Brotherhood as a branch of the Alliance, with Ralli, Holstein, and Oelsnitz as founding members. In Zürich the Brotherhood increased its numbers and came into sharp conflict with the followers of Peter Lavrov, who represented the gradualist trend in the populist movement. The Brotherhood set up its own press in Zürich and began early in 1873 to print a series of pamphlets, including Bakunin's *The State and Anarchism*. But internal disputes quickly destroyed this effort. Michael Sazhin was a man of proud and explosive character, and he soon quarrelled with Ralli and other members of the group. Bakunin tactlessly took sides with Sazhin; as a result he lost the majority of his Russian followers. Ralli, Holstein, and Oelsnitz departed from Geneva, where, in collaboration with Nicholas Zhukovsky, they set up their own Revolutionary Community of Russian Anarchists and established a new press, which went into operation in September 1873 with the publication of a pamphlet entitled *To The Russian Revolutionaries*.

The personal conflict did not become a conflict of principles, for the Revolutionary Community continued to propagate Bakunin's ideas and fit them to Russian problems. Bakunin withdrew into semi-retirement, concerning himself almost exclusively with Italian affairs until his death in 1876; he seems to have found the Italians temperamentally more sympathetic than his own fellow countrymen. But the 'young Bakuninists' continued, and for some years the press they operated was one of the most important centres in western Europe for the production of literature distributed clandestinely in Russia.

In 1875, in collaboration with the Pan-Russian Social Revolutionary

Organization, a group in Moscow led by Vera Figner, they began to publish a monthly journal called *Rabotnik* (*The Worker*). This was the first Russian periodical deliberately aimed at the workers in both towns and rural areas; thanks to the close contacts its writers maintained with the group in Moscow, they were able to devote considerable attention to actual working conditions in Russia itself, though they never lost sight of the Bakuninist emphasis on the unity of the international revolutionary struggle. *Rabotnik* continued into the early months of 1876; it was followed in 1878 by *Obshchina* (*Community*), in which the members of the Revolutionary Community collaborated with Stepniak, Axelrod, and other Bakuninists recently fled from Russia. The tone of *Obshchina* was cautious and conciliatory, but it remained Bakuninist in its rejection of the liberal idea of constitutional government and in its insistence that the peasants and workers must win their freedom for themselves.

The Revolutionary Community and the press it operated were openly and frankly anarchist, responding to the situation in western Europe, where Ralli and Zhukovsky maintained close links with the Saint-Imier International and particularly with Élisée Reclus and the group connected with the Geneva anarchist paper, *Le Travailleur*. Curiously enough, they had little to do with Kropotkin, who adhered at this time to Brousse's rival paper, *L'Avant-garde*, whose contacts with the Russian movement after his escape in 1876 were to remain scanty for almost twenty years during which he gave himself to the cause of international anarchism.

Though the publications of the Revolutionary Community circulated widely and influentially in Moscow, St Petersburg, and the cities of the Ukraine, no corresponding anarchist group arose during the 1870s on Russian soil. Rather there appeared a Bakuninist tendency within the larger Zemlya i Volya movement; its adherents were usually called Buntars, from their emphasis on *bunt*, or insurrection. The situation in Russia rapidly became the reverse of that among the refugees in Switzerland, where the Lavrovists were in the majority. During 1875 and 1876 strong Buntar movements grew up in Kiev and Odessa, living in communities, surreptitiously gathering arms, and endlessly plotting rural insurrection.

In one area, the district of Chigirin near Kiev, three Bakuninist agitators succeeded in organizing a considerable conspiracy, and their oddly Machiavellian methods—if somewhat inconsistent with anarchist orthodoxy—at least showed a certain realism in their grasp of peasant psychology. Relying on the widespread rural belief that the Tsar loved his people and was unaware of the atrocities committed in his name, the conspirators prepared two documents for circulation among the peasants of Chigirin.

One was a Secret Imperial Charter, in which 'the Tsar' recognized the right of the peasants to the land, complained that he was not strong enough to force the noblemen to give up their estates, and instructed the landworkers to create their own secret militia organizations so as to be ready to revolt at the appropriate moment. The other document—the Statutes of the Secret Militia—laid down the plan for organizing the rebels; it included complicated oaths and gave the revolutionary organization an elaborate hierarchical structure that would have delighted Bakunin in his conspiratorial days. This bizarre plot appealed to the peasants. They believed implicitly all the fictions that were presented to them, and more than a thousand of them joined the militia. They kept the secret so well that it was almost a year before a chance indiscretion put the police on the track of the plot. Hundreds of peasants were arrested and sent to Siberia. The three Bakuninists responsible for it all were also imprisoned, but they escaped through a device almost as strange as their original plot; one of their comrades became a warder in the prison where they were held and worked faithfully for months until the opportunity came for him to free his friends and escape in their company.

Other Bakuninists devoted themselves to attempts to organize the urban workers. They were particularly active in the various ephemeral Unions of Southern Workers which were organized in Odessa (1875) and Kiev (1879 and 1880). Even the Northern Union of Russian Workers, founded in 1878, adopted a basically anarchistic programme calling for the abolition of the state and its replacement by a federation of peasant communes and industrial *artels*.

By the end of the decade a new trend toward organized terrorism entered the Russian revolutionary movement. The Bakuninists were not opposed to terrorism in itself, but they were opposed to the concept of a disciplined organization that now accompanied it in the minds of the group who called themselves the Executive Committee, led by Zhelyabov and Sofya Perovskaya. These organized terrorists, who sought by selective assassination to bring about a political and constitutional solution to Russia's difficulties, formed themselves into the party of Narodnaya Volya (the People's Will). The Bakuninists, who wished to continue their work among the peasants and factory workers and to aim at a general revolt leading to a social-economic solution through a federation of communes, split away from them and formed the organization known as Cherny Peredel (Black Partition).

But the period of Bakuninist ascendancy, when a strong libertarian trend existed within the Russian revolutionary movement without accepting the name of anarchism, was now drawing to a close. The assassination of Alexander II in 1881 by Narodnaya Volya led to a relentless persecution of all revolutionaries operating on Russian soil, until almost every militant of any shade of opinion was in prison, in exile, or dead. For almost a decade the revolutionary movement existed in the most tenuous form, except among the many expatriates of western Europe. And even there the anarchist tendency was reversed when the leaders of Cherny Peredel, Plekhanov, Axelrod, and Vera Zasulich, became converted to Marxism and formed the earliest organization of Russian Social Democrats.

Only in the later 1890s was the initiative of Ralli, Zhukovsky, and the Revolutionary Commune of Russian Anarchists resumed in western Europe; from the same period date the first avowedly anarchist groups in Russia itself. Their very presence was an indication of the changed character of the revolutionary movement that re-formed itself in Russia during the last years of the nineteenth century. The persecutions after 1881 had virtually destroyed both Narodnaya Volya and Cherny Peredel. The heirs of Narodnaya Volya transformed themselves into the Russian Social Revolutionary Party, which inherited the terrorism of its predecessors, became even more constitutionalist in its aims, and developed a considerable following among the peasants. The leaders of Cherny Peredel formed themselves in 1883 into a Marxist group called Liberation of Labour, and were henceforth lost to Bakuninism; in 1898 their organization developed into the Russian Social Democratic Party, out of which, by schism, eventually emerged the Mensheviks and the Bolsheviks.

In this changed situation the influence of libertarian ideas was much slighter than it had been in the 1870s. In aims and in organization the major groups tended to become more rather than less authoritarian. The urge to create an anarchist movement on Russian soil now came from outside and mainly from Kropotkin's disciples in western Europe. In 1893 an Armenian doctor, Alexander Atabekian, visited Kropotkin in England with plans for the clandestine distribution of anarchist literature in Russia, and shortly afterwards he founded the Anarchist Library in Geneva. His group did not have enough funds to print a periodical, but they did produce pamphlets by Bakunin and Kropotkin which were used by the first anarchist groups to spring up in southern Russia during the 1890s. By a natural process, the appearance of a movement in Russia gradually increased the number of anarchist exiles in Switzerland, France, and England, and from 1903 onward a succession of expatriate groups appeared in Paris, Geneva, London, and Zürich, dedicated to producing material for propaganda. At least ten expatriate papers were published from these centres between 1903 and 1914; some lasted only for a few issues, but three of them were journals which deeply stimulated the development of anarchism within Russia. These were *Hleb i Volya* (Geneva, 1903-5), *Burevestnik* (Paris, 1906-10), and *Rabotchi Mir* (Paris, 1911-14).*

Hleb i Volya was the first Russian-language anarchist periodical to appear since *Obshchina* in 1878. It was under the direct inspiration of Kropotkin, who contributed regular articles to its pages. The editor, and virtual leader of the group in Geneva, was a Georgian who went under the *noms de guerre* of K. Orgheiana and K. Illiashvili; his real name was G. Goghelia.

The time was indeed opportune for starting a paper under the prestigious shadow of Kropotkin's name, for the situation in Russia during 1903 was one of growing unrest; industrial strikes, peasant riots, and student demonstrations succeeded each other with mounting impetus, and there was disaffection in the army and even among the Cossacks. *Hleb i Volya* aimed deliberately to influence this situation in a libertarian direction, and from the time of its appearance the number of anarchist groups in Russia increased steadily.

It is hard to estimate how far these groups helped to bring about the 1905 Revolution, which was largely an outburst of popular indignation and took many of the professional revolutionaries by surprise. 'It is not Social Democrats, or Revolutionary Socialists, or anarchists, who take the lead in the present revolution,' said Kropotkin. 'It is labour—the working man.' The anarchist theories about spontaneous revolution seemed to be confirmed, and the events of October 1905 appeared also to vindicate the anarchist advocacy of the general strike. Moreover, when the Revolution had failed, there was a revulsion of feeling against the Social Democrats, who had attempted to assume its leadership, and the anarchists gained from this. By 1906 they had formed groups in all the larger towns, and the movement was particularly strong in the Urals, among the Jewish population of Poland, and above all in the Ukraine, the old stronghold of the Buntars and Cherny Peredel, where anarchism appeared as a rural movement in the market towns and even in the villages.

By 1907, when governmental reaction grew strong again, the impetus of anarchism began to weaken, and the libertarian movement never grew out of its numerical inferiority to the Social Democrats and the Social

---

*In addition to the Russian-speaking expatriate groups of this period there was the Yiddish-speaking movement of Russian and Polish Jews in the East End of London, who formed a whole federation of their own. This was the largest group of Russian anarchist exiles in western Europe. For many years they published their own paper, *Der Arbeter Fraint.* However, it was written primarily for distribution in England, whereas the Russian-language papers I have mentioned were all prepared for use in Russia, and therefore formed an integral part of the Russian movement.

Revolutionaries. This was probably due largely to the fact that it was a movement of isolated groups which were often very loosely linked and differed considerably in philosophy and tactics. Only the refugees in the West seriously attempted to create federal organizations, holding conferences for this purpose in Geneva in 1906 and in Paris in 1913, but even their efforts came to nothing. The anarchist groups within Russia could be divided roughly into three trends: the anarchist communists, the individualists (who were given to 'terror without motive' and much feared by the police), and the anarcho-syndicalists. Anarcho-syndicalism did not appear until the time of the 1905 Revolution, but it quickly gathered a strong following; among the exiles in the United States alone the anarcho-syndicalist Union of Russian Workers recruited 10,000 members, and the clandestine movement in Russia was correspondingly strong. From the Tolstoyans, who might be regarded as a fourth anarchist trend of the time, all these tendencies were distinguished by their emphasis on the use of violence, which by now had become a standard practice of every Russian revolutionary party, including the Social Democrats. Leaders outside Russia were often distressed by this situation, and at a secret conclave held in London during December 1904, and attended by delegates of groups within Russia, Kropotkin pleaded with them to give up at least the practice of 'expropriation' which they and members of other movements used to obtain funds. (It will be remembered that Joseph Stalin was an adept bank robber for the Bolsheviks.) 'Bourgeois money is not necessary for us,' Kropotkin argued, 'either as donations or as thefts.' But the revolutionaries within Russia insisted on going their own way in spite of his appeals. However, as anarcho-syndicalism grew stronger, there was a perceptible shift from assassinations and banditry to the incitement of strikes as a means of undermining the Tsarist state.

Activity both in Russia and among the expatriates fell away during the years of the First World War, and the anarchists played a surprisingly small part in the February Revolution of 1917. Indeed, it was not until the expatriates began to return from abroad during the summer that the libertarian movement in Russia took on more than the semblance of renewed life. The poet Voline, the most important Russian anarchist intellectual of this period,* recollected that, when he reached St Petersburg from America in July 1917, he did not see a single anarchist newspaper or poster, nor did he encounter any evidence of oral propaganda by 'the few very primitive libertarian groups there.' In Moscow the situation was somewhat better, since there a local federation had been established and a daily

---

*His real name was Vsevolod Mikhailovich Eichenbaum.

newspaper, *Anarchy*, was being published. A few army units in Moscow and many of the sailors at Kronstadt had anarchist sympathies, while there was a strong anarcho-syndicalist influence in the factory committees which opposed the centralizing efforts of the Menshevik-dominated trade unions. Finally, far in the south, in the sprawling Ukrainian 'village' of Gulyai-Polye (it actually had 30,000 inhabitants), a young labourer named Nestor Makhno, recently released from the Butirky prison in Moscow, had been elected president of the local Soviet. Already, in August 1917, he and the handful of local anarchists who supported him had gained the confidence of the poor peasants and had begun to divide the local estates among the landless and to hand over the small industries of the district to the workers.

The October Revolution, in which many of the anarchists took part under the illusion that it would really lead to their kind of millennium, gave a temporary impetus to libertarian activities. An anarcho-syndicalist Propaganda Union was created in St Petersburg and began to publish a daily paper, *Golos Truda* (the *Voice of Labour*), which was later transferred to Moscow. The Federation of Anarchist Groups in Moscow began to spread its propaganda into the rural districts of central Russia, and Kropotkin's old lieutenant, Atabekian, started a theoretical review. Finally, toward the end of 1918, the anarchists of the south came together in the Nabat (Tocsin) Confederation of Anarchist Organizations of the Ukraine. The Nabat movement, whose activities centred on the cities of Kharkov and Kursk, attracted the most energetic of Russian anarchists during the period of the Revolution and the Civil War, including Voline, Yarchuk, Peter Arshinov, Olga Taratuta, Senya Fleshin, and Aaron and Fanya Baron. Its members sought to unite the various Kropotkinist, individualist, and syndicalist trends into one vigorous movement, and it maintained a close relationship with Makhno when his movement in the far south entered its militant phase.

The anarchists in Russia were at first divided in their attitudes toward the Bolshevik government and also toward the Soviets. Some of them became communists. Others, like the idealistic Alexander Schapiro, hoped to bring about an amelioration of conditions through working with the new régime, and briefly and unhappily collaborated. But the majority accurately assessed the Bolshevik government as a party dictatorship alien to all their libertarian values and set out to oppose it. Toward the Soviets their attitude changed more slowly. At first they regarded these councils as genuine expressions of the will of the workers and peasants who composed them, but later they decided that the Bolsheviks were turning them into instruments of their own policy. The general anarchist attitude was expressed in a resolution of the Nabat Congress of April 1919; it opposed 'all participation in the Soviets, which have become purely political organs, organized on an authoritarian, centralist, statist basis'.

Such an attitude inevitably provoked the hostility of the Bolsheviks, and it is one of the more curious historical ironies of the time that Leon Trotsky, a later martyr of communist intolerance, should have been the most violent in his justification not merely of the political suppression but also of the physical liquidation of his anarchist opponents, whom he habitually described as 'bandits'. Little more than six months after the October Revolution the persecutions began with a Cheka raid on the offices of *Anarchy* in Moscow. At the same time, anarchist activities in Petrograd were suppressed. The Nabat Federation was left alone for a while, and even in the northern cities the repression was not immediately complete. A restricted activity was still allowed, particularly to the anarcho-syndicalists, until the beginning of 1921, though unduly active militants were always liable to be imprisoned by the Cheka. Then, in February, came the funeral of Kropotkin, with its great public expression of support for the libertarian criticisms of the régime, and, in March, the rising of the Kronstadt sailors against what they regarded as the communist betrayals of the Revolution. The men of Kronstadt had certainly been influenced by anarchist arguments, and the Bolsheviks decided that the time had come for a final reckoning. The remnants of the anarchist movement were quickly eliminated in Petrograd, Moscow, Kharkov, and Odessa. Hundreds of anarchists were arrested. Fanya Baron and eight of her comrades were shot in the cellars of the Cheka prison in Moscow during September 1921. Other executions followed, and soon the Tolstoyans also were being killed in the dungeons; since they could hardly be accused of banditry, they were shot for refusing to serve in the Red Army. The clock of history had turned more than full circle in a brief four years, for never were the Tsarist authorities so ruthless in their persecution of opponents as the Bolsheviks in those days when the great purges of Stalin were still a mere shadow on the horizon. By the end of 1922 the anarchists in Russia were either dead, imprisoned, banished, or silent. For those in exile there remained the bitterness of having seen the Revolution turn into the very opposite of all their hopes; at most there could be the melancholy consolation that their ancestor Bakunin, looking at Marxist socialism half a century before, had prophesied it all.

Yet it was during those last disillusioning years that Russian anarchism made its one dramatic appearance on the stage of history, with the movement centred around the dynamic and Dostoyevskian personality of Nestor Makhno. We left Makhno in August 1917, as a rural anarchist leader organizing his countryside on the principles of free communism. It was the Treaty of Brest Litovsk that brought about his metamorphosis from the political boss of an overgrown village to the most formidable of all anarchist guerrilla warriors.

As a result of the treaty, the German and Austrian armies marched into the Ukraine and set up the puppet régime of Hetman Skoropadsky. Makhno fled eastward to the relative safety of Taganrog and then went on to Moscow to seek for help and advice from the anarchist leaders there. The persecution of the movement had already begun when he arrived, and he decided to return to his own territory and rely on the loyalty and the natural anarchy of his peasant neighbours.

He was not mistaken in his decision. The Hetman's régime and the invading armies had aroused bitter resentment by returning the land to its former owners, and Makhno quickly recruited a band of peasant partisans. He began to attack large estates in the region between the Dnieper and the Sea of Azov; the tales of his exploits at this period present him as an anarchist Robin Hood, for he and his men would often disguise themselves as officers in the Hetman's army, call on landlords, enjoy their hospitality, and then at a dramatic moment unmask themselves and wreak the justice of the vendetta on the enemies of the people. Every raid brought arms, supplies, and horses, and the recruits came in by the hundred to Makhno's headquarters, which seems to have been unknown only to the authorities. In September 1918 he was strong enough to capture Gulyai-Polye; he was driven out again, but shortly afterward defeated a whole German division that had been sent in pursuit of him. By the time the Central Powers began to withdraw from Russian territory after the armistice of November 1918, Makhno was already a legend throughout the southern Ukraine; the peasants thought of him as another Pugachev sent to realize their ancient dream of land and liberty, and his band had grown into an insurgent army so large that by January 1919, when he encountered the Red Army at Alexandrovsk, the Bolshevik authorities were glad to reach an agreement with him for common action against the White Army advancing north-ward under General Denikin.

For seven months, from November 1918 to June 1919, Makhno's region east of the Dnieper was untouched by either the White or the Red Armies. During the brief period of peace an attempt was made to create a free communist society, and, if one can accept the rather naïve description of the peasant communities which Makhno gave in his own account of the rebellion in the south, their efforts rather resembled those of the anarchist peasants in Andalusia:

In every one of these communes there were a few anarchist peasants, but the majority of their members were not anarchist. Nevertheless, in their communal life they behaved with that anarchist solidarity of which, in ordinary life, only toilers are capable whose natural simplicity has not yet been affected by the political poison of the cities. For the cities always give out a smell of lying and betrayal from which many, even among the comrades who call themselves anarchists, are not exempt.

Every commune comprised ten families of peasants and workers, i.e., a total of 100, 200, or 300 members. By decision of the regional Congress of agrarian communes every commune received a normal amount of land, i.e., as much as its members could cultivate, situated in the immediate vicinity of the commune and composed of land formerly belonging to the *pomeschiki*. They also received cattle and farm equipment from these former estates ...

The absolute majority of the labourers ... saw in the agrarian communes the happy germ of a new social life, which would continue as the revolution approached the climax of its triumphal and creative march, to develop and grow, and to stimulate the organization of an analogous society in the country as a whole, or at least in the villages and hamlets of our region.*

The last phrase reveals the whole secret of Makhno and his movement, their strength and their weakness. At heart he was both a countryman and a regionalist; he hated the cities and urban civilization, and he longed for 'natural simplicity', for the return to an age when, as in the past of peasant legends, 'the free toilers' would 'set to work to the tune of free and joyous songs'. This explains why, in a later phase, when the Makhnovists captured a number of fairly large towns in the Dnieper valley, they never really faced the problem of organizing industry and never gained the loyalties of more than a few urban workers.

But there was another factor in the situation—the Revolutionary Insurrectionary Army. Theoretically, this was under the control of the Congress of Peasants, Workers, and Insurgents, but in practice it was ruled by Makhno and his commanders, and, like all armies, was libertarian only in name. It used its own form of conscription, and a rough-and-ready discipline was observed which left no doubt that Makhno was master and often involved swift and violent punishments. The character of the army

*La Révolution russe en Ukraine, Paris, 1927.

was in fact largely a projection of Makhno's own character. He was very courageous, and extremely resourceful in the arts of guerrilla warfare. His army at times contained as many as 50,000 men, but it never ceased to be swift in its operations; even the infantry never marched, but rode in light peasant carts, and it was Makhno's extraordinary mobility that brought him most of his victories and preserved him so long from final annihilation. But he had the faults that often accompany reckless skills. His debaucheries were on a Karamazovian scale; even his admirer Voline admitted them and added grave accusations:

> Under the influence of alcohol, Makhno became irresponsible in his actions; he lost control of himself. Then it was personal caprice, often supported by violence, that suddenly replaced his sense of revolutionary duty; it was the despotism, the absurd pranks, the dictatorial antics, of a warrior chief that were strangely substituted for the calm reflection, perspicacity, personal dignity, and self-control in his attitude to others and to the cause which a man like Makhno should never have abandoned.
>
> The inevitable result of these disorders and aberrations was an excess of 'warrior sentiment' which led to the formation of a kind of military clique or camarilla about Makhno. The clique sometimes made decisions and committed acts without taking account of the opinion of the Council or of other institutions. It lost its sense of proportion, showed contempt toward all those who were outside it, and detached itself more and more from the mass of the combatants and the working population.

The parallel between the Makhnovists and the anarchists in the Spanish Civil War is striking. Both appear to have had some success when they set about creating rural economic institutions which responded both to anarchist ideals and to peasant longings. Both lost the purity of their ideals when they became involved in military activities. But there is the notable difference that, while the Spanish anarchists, with rare exceptions like Cipriano Mera, were military failures even when they had made their compromises with modern war, Makhno was one of the most brilliant tacticians of military history. I will end with a brief account of his achievements.

From January to June 1919, the Revolutionary Insurrectionary Army acted as a semi-autonomous unit within the Red Army in its rather inefficient resistance to Denikin. Then, in the middle of June, when the anarchists had called a Congress at Gulyai-Polye and invited the Red Army soldiers to send their delegates, Trotsky high-handedly forbade the Congress and ordered Makhno to surrender his command. Makhno bluffed. He left his units, with instructions to meet him whenever he summoned them, and set off with a cavalry bodyguard to new territory west of the Dnieper. There he carried on guerrilla war against the Whites and in the meantime started ridding the villages of their Bolshevik Commissars and setting up libertarian communes. In August 1919 he called back the men he had left in the Red Army, and started a general campaign against Denikin, whom the Red Army was obviously unable to defeat. At first the campaign seemed to be going badly, and Makhno was driven north-west to Uman, far away from his own country. Then he counter-attacked, inflicted a decisive defeat on the Whites, and drove across their rear to the Sea of Azov and then north to Ekaterinoslav in a ruthless sweeping movement that covered hundreds of miles of territory in barely three weeks. Denikin's supply lines were cut, and he was forced to retreat. An area of many thousands of square miles was now under anarchist control, and in the region where the Revolutionary Insurrectionary Army marched and counter-marched no civil authority existed; the peasants conducted their own affairs in a relative freedom, marred only by the constant demands of the army for food and men.

In December 1919 the Red Army reached the south again, and at the end of the year—after acknowledgements for services rendered—ordered Makhno to take his army to the Polish front, a move clearly intended to leave the Ukraine open to the intensive establishment of communist control. Makhno refused and was outlawed; immediately a bitter guerrilla war began in which Makhno fought back for nine months against numerically superior forces and, while he lost and won territory in bewildering succession, managed to keep intact the organization of the Revolutionary Insurrectionary Army.

This phase of the struggle ended when a new White Army, led by Wrangel, began to advance successfully northward from the Crimea. Again the Red Army decided it could not do without Makhno, and a truce, followed by a treaty, was arranged. Among other promises, the Bolsheviks undertook to free all the anarchist prisoners and to allow them complete freedom to propagate their ideas. The undertaking was never carried out. Indeed, only a few weeks later, when Makhno's forces had played an indispensable part in the forcing of the Perekop isthmus and the destruction of Wrangel's army in the Crimea, the Red Army leaders and the Cheka between them carried out one of the most perfidious *coups* in communist history. On 26 November 1920, in a concerted series of moves, the Cheka arrested all the known anarchists in the parts of the Ukraine under their control, invited the Makhnovist commanders in the Crimea to a conference at which they were seized and immediately shot, and disarmed all their men except a single cavalry unit which fought its way out and set off to Gulyai-Polye.

There, in the meantime, Makhno was attacked by large Red Army forces. In the first weeks he rallied what remained of his army, and inflicted heavy defeats on the enemy units, many of whose men were themselves Ukrainian peasants and fought reluctantly against him. But he could not fight indefinitely against the whole Red Army, though he did carry on the war nine months longer, until his supplies were exhausted and almost all his followers were killed. He never surrendered. On 28 August 1921 he escaped into Romania, and began a miserable pilgrimage through the prisons of Romania, Poland, and Danzig until he reached the freedom of exile in Paris, where he lived on, tuberculous, alcoholic, a bitter and lonely peasant who hated the city, until 1935. Only the Spanish anarchists remembered his epic years and kept him from starvation.

On the day when Makhno fought his way across the Dniester into exile, anarchism as a vital force ceased to exist in Russia. That the Bolsheviks should have fought it so fiercely and so treacherously suggests that, in the south at least, they regarded it as a real danger to their own ascendancy. From their own viewpoint they were doubtless correct. Only when the anarchists had been expelled from the Ukraine could the procrustean task of fitting the peasant world into the Marxist state be seriously undertaken.

Some of the leading anarchists who had been able to leave Russia at the beginning of the 1920s were among the first to expose from the Left the repression instituted by the Bolsheviks almost from the beginning of their régime. These included Emma Goldman with *My Disillusionment with Russia* (1923), Alexander Berkman with *The Bolshevik Myth* (1925), and G.P. Maximoff with *The Guillotine at Work: Twenty Years of Terror in Russia* (1940). Largely excluded from the United States because of the immigration laws, and often unwelcome in the countries of Western Europe, the Russian anarchists in exile lived unstable and difficult lives, and there was no revival of the kind of expatriate Russian anarchist groups that had existed in many places, from Switzerland to the United States, before the Great War.

Some anarchists survived inactively in Russia, mainly in prisons and labour camps until the early 1930s, but all trace of them vanished during the Stalinist repression later in the decade, and it is safe to assume that the last of them were eliminated in the purges of that era. In 1938 the Kropotkin Museum was closed down, and this was the final break with the libertarian current in Russia's revolutionary tradition. In 1949 when Ivan Avakumović and I were preparing our biography of Kropotkin, *The Anarchist Prince*, we tried through various channels to obtain information from Russia. We encountered an unbroken silence. The great Russian anarchists had become unpersons in history as rewritten by the Russian communists.

14. Various Traditions:
Anarchism in Latin America, Northern Europe, Britain, and the United States

ANARCHISM has thrived best in lands of the sun, where it is easy to dream of golden ages of ease and simplicity, yet where the clear light also heightens the shadows of existing misery. It is the men of the South who have flocked in their thousands to the black banners of anarchic revolt, the Italians and Andalusians and Ukrainians, the men of Lyons and Marseilles, of Naples and Barcelona. But though the Mediterranean countries and southern Russia have been its great strongholds, anarchism has a place that cannot be ignored in the political and intellectual life of many other countries. In a general history one cannot describe every libertarian movement as thoroughly as it might intrinsically deserve, but in this penultimate chapter I intend at least to sketch out the record of anarchism in Latin America, in Northern Europe, and particularly in Great Britain and the United States.

During the nineteenth century the countries of Latin America were related to Spain and Portugal not only by cultural and linguistic ties, but also by similar social conditions. This was a relationship that favoured the transmission of revolutionary ideas, and it was mostly the Spanish immigrants who spread anarchist ideals in Latin America, though in Argentina, as we have seen, the Italians also played an important missionary role. The earliest anarchist groups appeared in Mexico, Cuba, and Argentina at the beginning of the 1870s; these countries and Uruguay were represented at the last Congress of the Saint-Imier International in 1877, while in 1878 a Bakuninist League was founded in Mexico City.

The anarchists quickly became active in organizing craft and industrial workers throughout South and Central America, and until the early 1920s most of the trade unions in Mexico, Brazil, Peru, Chile, and Argentina

were anarcho-syndicalist in general outlook; the prestige of the Spanish
CNT as a revolutionary organization was undoubtedly to a great extent
responsible for this situation. The largest and most militant of these organizations was the Federación Obrera Regional Argentina, which was
founded in 1901, largely under the inspiration of the Italian Pietro Gori; it
grew quickly to a membership of nearly a quarter of a million, which
dwarfed the rival social-democratic unions. From 1902 until 1909 the
FORA waged a long campaign of general strikes against the employers
and against anti-labour legislation. Toward the end of this period there
arose in Buenos Aires a situation in which the brutality of the authorities
and the militancy of the workers incited each other to greater heights,
until, on May Day 1909, a gigantic demonstration marched through the
streets of Buenos Aires and was broken up by the police, who inflicted
many casualties on the trade-unionists. In retaliation, a Polish anarchist
killed Colonel Falcon, the Buenos Aires police chief who had been
responsible for the deaths of many syndicalists. After this event a rigorous
suppression of anarchist groups and papers took place, but the movement
revived, and FORA and its paper, *La Protesta*, continued vigorously into
the 1930s, though it lost some ground after the socialist-dominated and
reformist union, the CGT, was founded in 1929. Meanwhile, after a long
period of disunity, the anarchists came together in 1935 to form the
Argentine Anarcho-Communist Federation, which eventually, in 1955,
became the Argentine Libertarian Federation. Under the Peron régime,
the anarchists and syndicalists were forced underground, as only the
unions which supported the dictator were allowed to function. After the
dictatorship, the anarchist groups and FORA re-emerged, but much
diminished in numbers and influence, and since that time, whether operating legally or clandestinely as Argentina has swung repeatedly from
democracy to dictatorship and back again, the anarchist movement has
shrunk to a small, nostalgic and relatively inactive movement.

In Mexico the anarchists played a considerable part in the revolutionary era that followed the downfall of the dictator Porfirio Díaz in 1910. One
anarchist in particular, Ricardo Flores Magon, is still remembered among
the fathers of the Mexican Revolution. With his brothers Jesús and
Enrique he founded in 1900 an anarcho-syndicalist journal, *Regeneración*,
which played a very important part during the next ten years in arousing
the urban working class against the Díaz dictatorship. The Flores Magon
brothers spent much of their lives in exile, carrying on propaganda from
across the border in the United States, where they were several times
imprisoned for their activities and where Ricardo died in jail in 1922.

Although Ricardo Flores Magon was concerned primarily with converting the urban workers to his anarcho-syndicalist ideas, he established links with the great agrarian leader Emiliano Zapata, whose activities in southern Mexico during the revolutionary era resemble strikingly those of Makhno in the Ukraine, for like Makhno he was a poor peasant who showed a remarkable power to inspire the oppressed farmers of southern Mexico and to lead them brilliantly in guerrilla warfare. The historian Henry Bamford Parkes remarked that the Zapatista army of the south was never an army in the ordinary sense, for its soldiers' 'spent their time ploughing and reaping their newly won lands and took up arms only to repel invasion; they were an insurgent people'. The philosophy of the Zapatista movement, with its egalitarianism and its desire to re-create a natural peasant order, with its insistence that the people must take the land themselves and govern themselves in village communities, with its distrust of politics and its contempt for personal gain, resembled very closely the rural anarchism which had arisen under similar circumstances in Andalusia. Undoubtedly some of the libertarian ideas that inspired the trade unions in the cities and turned great Mexican painters, like Rivera and Dr Atl, into temporary anarchists, found their way to Zapata in the south, but his movement seems to have gained its anarchic quality most of all from a dynamic combination of the levelling desires of the peasants and his own ruthless idealism. For Zapata was the one leader of the Mexican Revolution who never compromised, who never allowed himself to be corrupted by money or power, and who died as he lived, a poor and almost illiterate man fighting for justice to be done to men like himself.

Since the Revolution, anarchism has lived a curious double life in Mexico. On the one hand the permanently ruling Party of Revolutionary Institutions has virtually canonized some of the past libertarian leaders, like Zapata and Ricardo Flores Magon, who, safely dead, have entered the national revolutionary myth, without the policies of the government approximating in any way to the teachings of anarchism. This incorporation of the anarchist past into the national tradition meant that at the end of the Spanish Civil War the government of President Cardenas welcomed many Spanish anarchists who fled from Franco's victory, and also a number of European militants who had worked in Spain and could not return to their own countries; in 1953, in Mexico City, I encountered the Russians Mollie Steimer and Senya Fleshin, and also the German Augustin Souchy. It also meant that the anarchist groups in Mexico did not undergo the persecutions they endured from dictatorships in other Latin American countries, whether of the Right or the Left, for since the early 1960s anarchists have not been allowed to operate in Castro's Cuba. But this somewhat indifferent benevolence has not encouraged the survival of a vigorous movement, though groups do continue and occasionally I receive an issue of the anarchist paper which bears as its title the slogan of Flores Magon's movement, *Tierra y Libertad.*

In Mexico anarchy strikes one as the appropriate product of a chaotic history, a dramatic, divided land, and a localism as inveterate as that of Spain. In the Teutonic lands that face the North Sea and the Baltic its presence is less expected, yet at least three of these countries, Germany, Holland, and Sweden, have produced libertarian movements of considerable historical interest.

German anarchism followed a course that curiously parallels the country's national development. In the 1840s, when Germany was a patchwork of kingdoms and principalities, the tendency was toward individualism, represented most extremely by Max Stirner. From the 1870s onward, it turned toward collectivism, until, in the twentieth century, the prevalent trend became a moderate anarcho-syndicalism, relatively non-violent in practice and inspired by a respect for efficiency and intellect.

Anarchism first appeared in Germany under the influence of Hegel and Proudhon; it began in the 1840s with the very difference personalities of Max Stirner and Wilhelm Weitling. Stirner, as we have seen, represented unqualified egoism; Weitling became a communist much influenced by Fourier and Saint-Simon. Like the anarchist communists he rejected both property and the wage system, and in his earlier writings, such as *Garantien der Harmonie und Freiheit* (1842), he put forward a basically Phalansterian plan of a society in which liberated human desires would be harmonized for the general good. Though Weitling wished to destroy the state as it existed, there were elements of Utopian regimentation in his vision of a 'harmonious' communist society, but in time these were tempered by the influence of Proudhon.

After Weitling's final departure to the United States in 1849, he abandoned his communism and moved even closer to Proudhonian mutualism. In the monthly journal *Republik der Arbeiter*, which he published in New York from 1850 to 1854, he criticized the experimental Utopian colonies that were still numerous in the United States as diversions of the workers' energy, which in his view should attack the vital problem of credit by the foundation of a Bank of Exchange. The Bank of Exchange, he tells us in truly Proudhonian tones, 'is the soul of all reforms, the foundation for all cooperative efforts'. It will set up stores for raw materials and finished products, and issue paper money based on labour value to facilitate their

exchange. Associated with the Bank will be trade associations of journey-
men for cooperative production, and the profits from exchange transactions will enable the Bank to provide for education, hospitals, and the care
of the aged and the disabled. By these means, and without state intervention or the elimination of the individual producer, the Bank will destroy
the monopoly of the capitalist and provide an economic structure which
will render political institutions unnecessary. These later ideas of Weitling
were undoubtedly much more influential in the neo-Proudhonian movement of the nineteenth-century United States than in Germany.

Several other German social theoreticians fell under the influence of
Proudhonian anarchism during the 1840s. Karl Grün, possibly the most
ardent convert, met Proudhon in Paris during 1844, and his *Die Soziale
Bewegung in Frankreich und Belgien* was the first work to introduce
Proudhon's ideas to the German public. Grün was a versatile man of letters who, like Proudhon, served a short, disillusioned period as a parlia-
mentarian—in the Prussian National Assembly during 1849—and spent
much of his life in exile, dying in Vienna in 1887. It was during his earlier
period that Grün was most attracted to the mutualist philosophy; in fact,
he ventured beyond it, for he criticized Proudhon for not attacking the
wages system, and pointed out that the growing complexity of industry
made it impossible to decide on each man's product with any accuracy or
justice. Therefore consumption and production must alike depend on
choice. 'Let us have no right at all against the right of the individual.'

Moses Hess, another German socialist, who knew Proudhon and
Bakunin in Paris during the 1840s, actually adopted the title 'anarchy' for
his own social philosophy, expounded in 1843 in *Die Philosophie der Tat.*
Hess was a rather solitary and truculent figure who stood out among the
Rhineland socialists as Marx's most important rival. He was never so close
to Proudhon as Grun became, and he later quarrelled bitterly with
Bakunin, but he agreed with both in rejecting the state and dismissing
organized religion as a form of mental bondage. Yet his doctrine was curiously muddled. In declaring that all free actions must proceed from individual impulses, unmarred by external influence, he came near to Stirner.
In envisaging a social system under which men would work according to
inclination and society would provide automatically for every man's reasonable needs, he anticipated Kropotkin. But he grafted on to his libertarian dream a number of features, such as universal suffrage and national
workshops, which no true anarchist would entertain.

Neither Stirnerite nor Proudhonian anarchism had a lasting influence
in Germany. Stirner gained no German following at all until after
Nietzsche had become popular, and the interest in Proudhon's ideas dis-

appeared in the general reaction that followed the failure of the revolutionary movements of 1848 and 1849. A whole generation now passed before the reappearance of any perceptible anarchist tendency. In the early years of the First International neither Bakunin nor Proudhon had any German supporters, and the Lassallean delegates who attended one Congress of the Saint-Imier International agreed with the anarchists only in their desire to stimulate cooperative experiments.

During the latter part of the century, however, anarchistic factions began to appear within the German Social Democratic Party. In 1878, for example, the bookbinder Johann Most, who had formerly been a fiery member of the Reichstag, was converted to anarchism while in exile in England. With Wilhelm Hasselmann, another anarchist convert, he was expelled by the Social Democrats in 1880, but his journal, *Die Freiheit*, published first in London in 1879 and then in New York, continued to wield an influence until the end of the century on the more revolutionary socialists both in Germany and in exile. A few small anarchist groups were formed under his influence in Berlin and Hamburg, but it is doubtful if their total membership in the 1880s much exceeded 200; the particular kind of violence preached by Most encouraged the conspiratorial group rather than the mass movement. One such group, led by a printer named Reinsdorf, plotted to throw a bomb at the Kaiser in 1883. They were unsuccessful, but all of them were executed.

Most's influence was also felt in Austria, where the powerful Radical faction of the Social Democratic Party was anarchist in all but name. Libertarian ideas also penetrated deeply into the trade unions in Austria, Bohemia, and Hungary, and for a brief period from 1880 to 1884 the Austro-Hungarian labour movement was probably more strongly impregnated with anarchist influences than any other in Europe outside Spain and Italy. More influential even than Most was the Bohemian Joseph Peukert, who published in Vienna a paper of anarchist communist leanings called *Zukunft*. When the Austrian authorities began to suppress meetings and demonstrations in 1882, the anarchists and radicals resisted violently, and a number of policemen were killed. Finally, in January 1884, the authorities became so disturbed by the spread of anarchist propaganda and the increase of violent clashes between police and revolutionaries that they declared a state of siege in Vienna and promulgated special decrees against anarchists and socialists. One of the anarchist leaders, Most's disciple Stellmacher, was executed, and the rest, including Peukert, fled from the country. From that time onward anarchism ceased to be a movement of any importance in the Austrian Empire, though small propaganda groups did emerge in later years, and one libertarian literary circle in Prague counted among its sympathizers and occasional visitors both Franz Kafka and Jaroslav Hašek, author of *The Good Soldier Schweik*.

In later years Germany produced at least three outstanding anarchist intellectuals, Erich Muehsam, Rudolf Rocker, and Gustav Landauer. Muehsam, one of the leading socially engaged poets of the Weimar Republic, played an important part in the Bavarian Soviet rising of 1919, and was eventually beaten to death in a Nazi concentration camp. Rudolf Rocker spent many years in England, about which I shall say more in the following pages; after internment during the First World War, he returned to Berlin, and became one of the leaders of the anarcho-syndicalist movement during the period up to the Nazi dictatorship. He was a prolific and able writer, and at least one of his works, *Nationalism and Culture*, is a classic statement of the anarchist case against the cult of the national state.

Gustav Landauer, who called himself an anarcho-socialist, was one of those free spirits who never find a happy place in any organized movement. As a young man during the 1890s he joined the Social Democratic Party, and became the leader of a group of young rebels eventually expelled because of their anarchistic leanings. For some years as a disciple of Kropotkin he edited *Der Sozialist* in Berlin, but by 1900 he had shifted toward a position much closer to Proudhon and Tolstoy, advocating passive resistance in the place of violence and looking toward the spread of cooperative enterprises as the really constructive way to social change. He differed from most other anarchists in appealing particularly to the intellectuals, whose role in social change he regarded as extremely important. This led to the failure of *Der Sozialist*, which never gained a mass readership, and to a growing sense of isolation on Landauer's part. Today Landauer's books—both his political commentaries and his essays in literary appreciation—seem excessively romantic. Yet he was one of those men of complete integrity and passionate love for the truth who represent anarchism at its best, perhaps all the more because they stand alone. Despite his distrust of political movements, Landauer was taken up in the wave of revolutionary excitement that swept Germany during the years immediately after the First World War, and, like Muehsam and Ernst Toller, he became one of the leaders of the Bavarian Soviet. In the repression that followed its downfall he was killed by the soldiers sent from Berlin. 'They dragged him into the prison courtyard,' said Ernst Toller. 'An officer struck him in the face. The men shouted, "Dirty Bolshie! Let's finish him off!" A rain of blows from rifle-butts descended on him. They trampled on him till he was dead.' The officer responsible for Landauer's murder was a Junker aristocrat, Major Baron von Gagern; he was never punished or even brought to trial.

Early in the present century the anarcho-syndicalist tendency quickly outgrew the small groups of anarchist communists and the circles of individualists upholding the ideas of Stirner and of John Henry Mackay.* Syndicalism originated in Germany with a dissident group calling themselves Localists, who in the early 1890s opposed the centralizing tendencies of the Social Democratic trade unions and in 1897 broke away to form a federation of their own, the Freie Vereinigung Deutscher Gewerkschaften. In its early days most of the members of this organization still adhered politically to the left wing of the Social Democratic Party, but in the years immediately preceding the First World War they fell under the influence of the French syndicalists and adopted an anti-parliamentarian attitude. At this time the FVDG was still a small organization, with about 20,000 members, mostly in Berlin and Hamburg. After the war, in 1919, a congress held in Düsseldorf reorganized the federation on anarcho-syndicalist lines and renamed it the Freie Arbeiter Union. The re-formed organization expanded rapidly in the revolutionary atmosphere of the early 1920s, and by the time of the Berlin International Syndicalist Congress of 1922 it had reached a membership of 120,000, which expanded further during the decade to a high point of 200,000. Like all other German organizations of the Left, the Freie Arbeiter Union was destroyed by the Nazis on their accession to power in 1933, and its militants either fled abroad or were imprisoned in the concentration camps, where many of them were killed or died of privation.

If the anarchist movement in Germany was destroyed by the Nazis, not all its members were, and I remember vividly the delighted astonishment with which at *Freedom* in London we received in 1945—clandestinely through a sympathetic GI in the American occupation forces—the first message from an anarchist who had survived the concentration camps and emerged with his ideals unbroken. But though the few remaining veterans from the past came together in attenuated groups, anarchism did not gain much attention in post-war Germany until the movement of youth revolt during the 1960s, and even then, in Marx's homeland, it had to compete with various forms of left communism, from the intellectualism of Adorno's and Marcuse's followers to the authoritarian terrorism of the

---

*Mackay was a wealthy Scot, born in Greenock, who became a naturalized German and, besides writing Stirner's biography, published a novel of his own, *The Anarchists: A Picture of Society at the Close of the Nineteenth Century*, which revealed him as a kind of inferior libertarian Gissing.

Baader-Meinhof gang and similar formations, who shared only their violence with the anarchist assassins of the past. The anarchists should have found their natural constituency in the vigorous peace and ecological movements that have flourished in Germany, but even here they had to compete with organizations like the Green Party which have diverted such interests into parliamentary channels. Yet the Freie Arbeiter Union has revived, and flourishes modestly in Cologne, Düsseldorf and other towns of the Ruhr, while autonomous groups devoted to propaganda and publication are to be found scattered all over West Germany, and from these emerge such papers as *Graswurzelrevolution* and the excellent cultural review, *Trafik*.

In Sweden there still exists an organization very similar to the German Freie Arbeiter Union. This is the Sveriges Arbetares Central; in the Baltic amber of Swedish neutrality it has been preserved from the disasters of oppression and war which destroyed almost every other anarcho-syndicalist organization, and it still functions as a working federation of trade-unionists.

There were anarchists in Sweden since the 1880s, when they infiltrated the newly formed Social Democratic Party, from which they were expelled in 1891 during the general purge of anarchists from parties belonging to the Second International. Thereafter, as anarcho-syndicalists, they worked within the trade unions until, after a disastrous general strike in 1909, they decided to break away and set up their own federation in imitation of the French CGT. In 1910 they founded the Sveriges Arbetares Central. It was a tiny organization at first, with a mere 500 members, but its militant call to direct action appealed particularly to the lumbermen, miners, and construction workers, whose work was heavy and whose wages were generally low. By 1924, at the peak of its influence, the SAC had 37,000 members; still, after World War II it retained more than 20,000 members, published its own daily paper, *Arbetaren*, in Stockholm, and loyally kept alive the syndicalist International Workingmen's Association.

There is a certain historical interest in considering how this rare survivor from the golden age of revolutionary syndicalism has adapted itself to the contemporary world, and a survey of world labour by American sociologists* includes a valuable description of the Sveriges Arbetares Central in the later twentieth century.

The structure of the federation has apparently remained that of an orthodox syndicalist organization, based on 'local syndicates, each

---

*Walter Galenson (ed.), *Comparative Labour Movements*, New York, 1952.

embracing all members within a geographical area without regard to trade
or industry'; 'the local syndicate remains the chief repository of union
power', being 'affiliated directly to the national centre'.

It seems clear, however, that union practices have been modified by
changing social conditions. Theoretically, as the authors of the survey
point out, collective bargaining is opposed by the Swedish syndicalists:

> As a means of exercising control over labour conditions each local
> syndicate has established a register committee, the function of which
> is to prepare wage schedules. After approval by the syndicate these
> schedules constitute the wages for which members may work. The
> failure of the register method to provide binding wages for definite
> periods of time enabled employers to cut rates during periods of
> unemployment, and some of the syndicates have been forced to
> enter into agreements. The syndicalists have advocated as means of
> enforcing their demands, the sympathetic strike, the slow-down
> through literal observance of working rules, shoddy work, and ca'-
> canny. But these methods have proved incongruous in a so highly
> organized society as the Swedish, and, in fact, the syndicalists have
> practised collective bargaining.

The survey goes on to remark that 'the Swedish syndicalists have
remained faithful to the political tenets of their doctrine', and that their
unions 'abstain strictly from political activity'. Officially, 'the eventual
overthrow of capitalism through the revolutionary general strike' is still
professed by the leaders of the SAC, but, the survey concludes, 'as far as
practical trade-unionism is concerned ... there is not a great deal of
difference between the socialist and the syndicalist unions'.

Theoretically, in other words, the Sveriges Arbetares Central has
remained faithful to the kind of revolutionary syndicalism preached by
Pierre Monatte at the Amsterdam Congress in 1907; practically it has
accepted standard modern procedures in industrial relationships; and in
theory and practice alike it has gone far away from pure anarchism.

In Holland, anarchism has shared with the movements in Germany and
Sweden their tendency toward syndicalism, but it has gained a character of
its own from the militant pacifism of many of its leaders, and particularly
of Ferdinand Domela Nieuwenhuis.

It was under the dynamic influence of Nieuwenhuis that Dutch anarchism really developed. In the First International the small Dutch
Federation worked closely with the Belgians led by Caesar de Paepe; it

supported Bakunin in his quarrel with Marx, opposed the centralism of the General Council, and joined the Saint-Imier International without ever becoming an organization of true anarchists. It was not, in fact, until the late 1880s that a clearly defined anarchist movement began to appear in Holland.

It arose out of the revival of the Dutch socialist movement under the inspiration of the Nieuwenhuis at the end of the 1870s. Nieuwenhuis began his active life as a famous Lutheran preacher in a fashionable church of The Hague. He was still in his early thirties when he underwent a crisis of conscience rather similar to William Godwin's, and decided to leave the Church and devote his life to the cause of the workers. In 1879 he resigned his pastorate and founded a journal, *Recht voor Allen*, in which he advocated an ethical socialism based on a strong emotional revulsion against oppression and war, and a deep sense of human brotherhood; it was a distillation of Christian principles into modern social terms. Nieuwenhuis ceased to be a pastor, but he never ceased in the real sense to be a religious man. His strength of personality and his idealistic fervour soon made him the most influential personality among the scattered groups of Dutch socialists, and when they came together in 1881 to found the Socialist League, he became its undisputed leader.

The early years of the League, when it directed its efforts to anti-war propaganda and trade-union organization, were very stormy, and most of its active members were imprisoned at one time or another, including Nieuwenhuis himself, but they gained enough ground for Nieuwenhuis to be elected to parliament in 1888 as a Socialist; he remained there for three years, but like Proudhon and Grün, he found it a saddening experience, and emerged a convinced anti-parliamentarian. It was during his period in parliament that he began to turn toward anarchism, and to advocate, before French revolutionary syndicalism had been developed, the idea of industrial direct action and the general strike as means for the workers to free themselves from political and economic oppression and to combat war.

Already, at the International Socialist Congress in 1889, Nieuwenhuis had attacked the participation of socialists in parliamentary activity, and at the Zürich Congress in 1891 he raised, in violent opposition to Wilhelm Liebknecht, the idea of turning a war between nations into an international revolutionary war between classes by means of the general strike. At these congresses, and again in 1893 and 1896, he stood out in defence of the idea that the International should include socialists of every shade, from the most moderate reformists to the most extreme anarchists, and in the end he led the Dutch delegation out of the London Congress of 1896 as a final protest against the Second International's expulsion of the anarchists.

Meanwhile dissension had arisen within the Dutch Socialist League itself, between the majority, who followed Nieuwenhuis in his drift toward anarchism, and a strong minority attracted by German Social Democracy. The differences came to a head at the Groningen Congress of 1893, when the majority carried the League into the anarchist camp and the parliamentarians departed to form their own Socialist Party.

While Nieuwenhuis and his followers were winning the Socialist League to anarchism, their efforts to organize trade unions had also been largely successful, and in 1893 a syndicalist federation, the National Arbeids Sekretariat, was created. It developed under the ideological influence of Christian Cornelissen, who eventually became one of the most important of anarcho-syndicalist theoreticians. He was particularly interested in the international organization of syndicalism, and the intellectualism of his attitude made him one of the few links between the working-class militants of the CGT such as Pouget and Yvetot, with whom he was in direct contact, and the theoretical syndicalists who gathered around Sorel and Lagardelle, and to whose journal, *Le Mouvement socialiste*, he contributed. Cornelissen's influence in the European anarchist movement was very considerable during the early years of the present century, but it dwindled away to nothing when he joined Kropotkin and Guillaume in supporting the Allies during the First World War.

For almost a decade the National Arbeids Sekretariat, whose membership at this time did not reach more than 20,000 remained the most active and influential organization among the Dutch trade unions. Its fall from this ascendant position came rather dramatically during the general strike of 1903, which started on the railways, spread to other industries, and then, at the moment of apparent success, collapsed suddenly when the government began to arrest the leaders and to use soldiers as blacklegs. The Social Democrats reaped the benefit of this defeat, and there was a mass exodus from the anarcho-syndicalist unions. For several years the National Arbeids Sekretariat maintained no more than a small bridgehead among the dock-workers of Amsterdam and Rotterdam, and by 1910 its membership had shrunk to little more than 3,000.

The anarchist movement outside the trade unions also diminished in numbers and influence, but the personal prestige of Nieuwenhuis did not suffer greatly. He was the kind of idealist who does not need a movement to establish a moral influence, and he continued through the First World War and until his death in 1919 to wage his passionate anti-militarist campaigns, which were afterward continued by younger Dutch anarchist pacifists like Albert de Jong and Bart de Ligt, author of that extraordinary

manual of passive resistance, *The Conquest of Violence*, which was read widely by British and American pacifists during the 1930s and led many of them
to adopt an anarchistic point of view.

The Dutch anarcho-syndicalists slowly recovered some of the ground
they had lost in 1903, and by 1922 the National Arbeids Sekretariat, though
now a minority in comparison with the other trade unions, had regained
its earlier membership: when it joined the International Workingmen's
Association in 1922 it had almost 23,000 members. But like the syndicalist
movement in France, it soon began to suffer from the spell which Russian
communism cast over its younger militants. Eventually the organization
itself was captured by the communists, and a large minority who remained
faithful to anti-parliamentarian traditions broke away in 1923 to form the
Nederlandisch Syndikalistisch Vakverbond. It never gained more than a
fraction of the dominant influence which the National Arbeids Sekretariat
had once wielded in the Dutch labour movement. After 1903, in fact, Dutch
anarchism reconciled itself to having become a permanent minority
movement whose widely respected leaders, like Nieuwenhuis and
Cornelissen, enjoyed the prestige that in northern lands is granted to those
voices crying in the wilderness which form the conveniently externalized
consciences of peoples largely devoted to the acquisition and enjoyment
of material prosperity. During the 1930s the shrinking movement settled
into a mood of nostalgic inactivity, and in World War II anarchists participated in the Resistance as individuals, not as groups. After the war ended
the movement stirred sluggishly into life, but the gatherings of old comrades were little more than discussion groups.

This inertia makes all the more striking the awakening of anarchism
during the 1960s and 1970s under various names as a movement of the
young. The first manifestation was the group known as Provos, whose
name derived from the word Provokant or provoker; they had no relationship with the Provisional wing of the IRA, who are also often called
Provos. The Provo movement began in 1965, as a coalition of mostly young
malcontents who were partly in revolt against the tyrannous police system
in existence at the time and partly dedicated to the idea of social revolution. In April the first issue of its magazine *Provo* appeared, and the style of
the movement—radical, disrespectful and improvisational—was evident
from its declaration of principles.

PROVO is a monthly sheet for anarchists, provos, beatniks, pleiners,
scissor-grinders, jailbirds, Simple Simon stylites, magicians, pacifists,
potato-chip chaps, charlatans, philosophers, germ-carriers, grand

masters of the Queen's horse, happeners, vegetarians, syndicalists, Santa Clauses, kindergarten teachers, agitators, pyromaniacs, assistant assistants, scratchers and syphilitics, secret police and other riffraff.

Provo has something against capitalism, communism, fascism, bureaucracy, militarism, professionalism, dogmatism, and authoritarianism.

Provo has to choose between desperate resistance and submissive extinction.

Provo calls for resistance wherever possible.

Provo realizes that it will lose in the end, but it cannot pass up the chance to make at least one more heartfelt attempt to provoke society.

Provo regards anarchism as the inspirational source of resistance.

Provo wants to revive anarchism and teach it to the young.

The Provos indulged in noisy demonstrations and even violent riots, largely intended to provoke the police to counter-violence and thus to expose their brutality. But they also conceived original kinds of mutual aid, such as a plan to place several thousand white-painted bicycles at various spots over Amsterdam for the people to use freely and thus lesson the flow of motorized traffic in the streets. The Provos were never a united, tightly knit group. One of their slogans was 'We agree to disagree', and in spite of their statement of anarchist principles, their following was a heterogeneous throng of youthful malcontents, with a high proportion of people who joined just for the excitement that Provo tactics generated. Nor were the Provos dogmatic in their adherence to anarchist principles, for they contested the municipal elections in 1966, gained 13,000 votes and won a seat in the Amsterdam city council. Then, at a happening on 13 May 1967, less than two years after the first Provo manifesto appeared, they declared the 'death of Provo'. They evidently considered that their manifestations had aroused the conscience of the Dutch people to such a degree that police powers were notably relaxed and felt that their special form of agitation was no longer appropriate or necessary.

Such flexibility of attitude has tended to be generally characteristic of the 'new' anarchism that appeared widely in the 1960s, distinguishing it from the organizational rigidity that had overtaken the 'old' movement and prevented it from responding freely to the turn of events. The ferment generated by the Provos did not in fact die down, and student revolts, alternative schools, occupation of empty houses by squatters, and feminist protests were among its manifestations during the following years of the quiet revolution that was turning Amsterdam into one of the freest cities—in terms of life style—in Western Europe. The ground was ready for a new movement to spring up, and in January 1970 a group calling themselves the Kabouters (gnomes) proclaimed the existence of a new political order which they called the Orange Free State. In their manifesto of 5 February they declared:

> Out of the subculture of the existing order an alternative society is growing. The underground society grows out of the ground now and it begins—independent of the still ruling authorities—to live its own life and to rule itself. This revolution takes place now. It is the end of the underground, of protest, of demonstrations; from this moment we spend our energy on the construction of an anti-authoritarian society.

Greatly influenced by Peter Kropotkin, the Kabouters sought to make people aware of the alternatives to existing authoritarian and capitalist solutions to social problems, and in the process they became involved in many kinds of constructive direction action—planting trees, helping the old, cleaning playgrounds, establishing shops selling unsprayed fruit and vegetables, running papers with original titles like *Ontbijt op Bed* (*Breakfast in Bed*). Eventually, like the Provos, they entered municipal politics, and in the elections of June 1970 they won more than 37,000 votes—11 per cent of the total for Amsterdam, and gained five seats in a city council of forty-five. They won another 17,000 votes and seven more seats in five other municipalities. Their relative effectiveness as councillors tended to sap their radical urges, and it was not long before the Kabouters began to look like yet another unorthodox political party, like the Greens in Germany, rather than a genuine anarchist movement.

English anarchism has never been anything else than a chorus of voices crying in the wilderness, though some of the voices have been remarkable. At no time did the anarchists have even a remote chance of controlling the British labour movement. They have always been a small movement, for many years hardly existent outside London and Glasgow, and in adapting themselves to their situation without admitting it, they have concentrated more than libertarians in many other countries on the graces of art and intellect. The only casualty of anarchist violence in England was a Frenchman named Marcel Bourdin, who in 1894 accidentally blew himself up in Greenwich Park with a home-made bomb intended for use abroad, and even that incident became material for literature, since it provided Joseph Conrad with a plot for *The Secret Agent*, just as the activities of Johann Most in England provided Henry James with a theme for *The Princess Casamassima*.

But though there has been a recurrent libertarian itch among English writers ever since Shelley, some of whose effects we shall shortly see, it would be wrong to give the impression that anarchism in England has been entirely or even principally an affair of men of letters. On the contrary, the modest record of the English movement shows an experimental spirit which has embraced every kind of anarchist thought and has produced every type of anarchist individual, with the sole exception of the practising terrorist.

Anarchism as a movement began in Britain during the 1880s, under the influence of foreign rather than native models. Neither the writings of Godwin and his disciples nor the primitive syndicalism of Robert Owen's Grand National Consolidated Trades Union or of William Benbow with his early version of the millennial strike, made any direct contribution to the anarchism of the later nineteenth century. If anything, their lingering influence impeded it, since the rejection of power which was their legacy to the general English labour movement produced an obstinate and long-maintained distrust of centralized authority that at times made anarchism seem a needless extremity. The real birth-places of modern British anarchism were the clubs for foreign workers which appeared in Soho as early as the 1840s, and somewhat later in the East End of London. The Rose Street Club in Soho, the Autonomie Club in Windmill Street, and later (after 1885) the International Club in Berners Street, Whitechapel, were the most favoured centres of the anarchist faction among the expatriates.

The Rose Street Club was a stronghold of the followers of Johann Most, who arrived in England in 1878, and in the next year founded *Die Freiheit*, the first anarchist paper published in England. The discreetly blind eye of Scotland Yard usually allowed expatriate political activities in London to go unmolested; by a tacit gentlemen's agreement most of the foreign revolutionists refrained from dabbling in English affairs or embarrassing the British government internationally. But Most went beyond discretion in 1881 when he devoted an editorial of gloating enthusiasm to the assassination of Tsar Alexander II; he was sent to prison for eighteen months. The comrades he left in charge of *Die Freiheit* had no desire to appear less courageous than their leader, and when the Irish rebels assassinated Lord Cavendish in Phoenix Park they loudly proclaimed their solidarity with the killers. This was interfering with a vengeance in British affairs, and *Die*

Freiheit was raided and suppressed. For a few issues it appeared in Switzerland, and on Most's release moved to New York for a further sensational career, which belongs to a later part of this chapter.

Die Freiheit was intended as propaganda for Austria and Germany, and it had little influence in England except among the expatriates. It was rather through the personal activity of a small number of Englishmen who attended the foreign clubs that continental anarchism spread into the slowly awakening socialist movement of the 1880s. Out of six English delegates who attended the International Anarchists' Congress of 1881, four carried the credentials of clubs in Soho.

It was shortly after the international congress that the earliest anarchist organization in Britain, the Labour Emancipation League, was formed by a revolutionary faction of the Stratford Radical Club. Its leader was Joseph Lane, an elderly carter who remembered the days of the Chartists and had long been an active open-air speaker. The Labour Emancipation League, which gained a modest following among East End working men, was dominated by the anarchism of Lane and Frank Kitz, one of the militants of the Rose Street Club, and it sharply opposed both state socialism and parliamentary activity.

In those halcyon early days of the English labour movement there was yet no thought of the strict boundaries between socialism and anarchism later enforced by the Second International, and in 1884 the Labour Emancipation League became affiliated to the Social Democratic Federation, which united almost all of the small socialist factions in England, with the notable exception of the aloofly intellectual Fabian Society. The union did not last long, thanks to the dictatorial nature of H.M. Hyndman, the Marxist leader of the Federation. By December 1884 the whole federation was in revolt, and most of its leading personalities, including William Morris, Belford Bax, and Eleanor Marx Aveling, resigned in protest. The Labour Emancipation League accompanied them into the new organization they created, the Socialist League, which shortly afterward began to publish *Commonweal* under the editorship of William Morris. Within the League the anarchist faction, under the leadership of Lane, Kitz, and C.W. Mowbray, rapidly made converts and moved towards dominance.

They found a temporary ally in William Morris, whose relationship to anarchism is not easy to define. In *News from Nowhere* he portrayed nothing less than that paradisaical anarchy dreamed of by libertarians for three centuries. Even in the non-Utopian present he shared to the full the anarchist contempt for shifts and compromises of politics, and his anti-parliamentarianism continued to the end, since the most he would concede was that the socialists might in the last resort be justified in entering parliament if they were sure of getting a majority large enough to vote it out of existence for good and all. For him, as for the anarchists, it was necessary to find a way by which people could 'themselves destroy their slavery'. It is true that he disagreed with the anarchists of the Socialist League over their extreme stress on violence and the destructive aspects of revolution. In his view a long process of education was necessary before the struggle to transform society would even begin. But, while this gave an element of gradualism to Morris's socialism, it did not fundamentally divide him from the libertarian tradition; Godwin and Proudhon thought the same, and Kropotkin came very near to doing so in his later years.

It is true that, when he was sore from his experiences in the Socialist League, Morris categorically denied that he was an anarchist. But this statement on the subject showed clearly that he was considering anarchism in the narrow sense of individualism.

> Anarchism means, as I understand it, the doing away with, and doing without, laws and rules of all kinds, and in each person being allowed to do just as he pleases. I don't want people to do just as they please; I want them to consider and act for the good of their fellows, of the commonweal, in fact. Now, what constitutes the commonweal, or common notion of what is for the common good, will and always must be expressed in the form of laws of some kind—either political laws, instituted by the citizens in public assembly, as of old by folk-moots, or if you will by real councils or parliaments of the people, or by social customs growing up from the experience of society.

No anarchist except an extreme Stirnerite would dispute Morris's ideal of men acting for the good of their fellows; indeed, it is a central anarchist dogma that freedom releases human sociability to follow its natural course, while the stress which anarchists have placed on the power of public opinion in disciplining the anti-social individual suggests that none of them would object to Morris's idea of the common good being protected by 'social customs growing up from the experience of society'. An anarchist, on the other hand, would object to Morris's acceptance of laws voted by assemblies or popular councils. And it is in this narrow borderline that the real difference between Morris and the anarchists is to be found. Morris admitted a measure of direct democracy which would leave sovereignty to the people; the anarchists deny democracy of any kind and reserve sovereignty for the individual. But Morris appears to have allowed only reluctantly for his shreds of poular authority. In *News from Nowhere*, which was intended as the picture of society as he would really have liked it to be, no fragment of true authority or government is left; it is a thoroughly anarchist world that Morris invites us to enter. One is forced to the conclusion that the important differences which later developed between Morris and the anarchists in the Socialist League were matters of personality rather than ideology, and that a closer association with Kropotkin might have given Morris a clearer conception of anarchism and of his own relationship to it.

But in the early days of the Socialist League Morris and the anarchists still worked in apparent harmony, and together they secured, in June 1887, a majority decision that pledged the League to anti-parliamentarianism. The Marxists and the moderate socialists thereupon resigned, and the anarchists soon gained control. In 1889 they won a majority on the executive council, and immediately turned on their old ally Morris, depriving him of the editorship of *Commonweal*. It became an exclusively anarchist journal, expressing a point of view very close to that which Most had expounded in *Die Freiheit*.

The conquest of the Socialist League was only one manifestation of a general upsurge of anarchist activity during the later 1880s. This was shown particularly by the appearance of two libertarian periodicals expressing greatly differing tendencies. *The Anarchist* was first published in 1885 under the editorship of Henry Seymour, a disciple of the American individualist Benjamin Tucker, and the founder of the English Anarchist Circle, a small group of neo-Proudhonians who regarded individual possessions as essential to freedom and a rational exchange system as the key to social liberation. However, Seymour's interests were wide—they even included an ardent partisanship of the Baconian theory of the authorship of Shakespeare's plays—and he not only published as a pamphlet the only translation of Bakunin to appear in England for many years (the fragmentary essay entitled *God and the State*) but also included among the contributors to *The Anarchist* writers of such diverse opinions as George Bernard Shaw and Élisée Reclus. For a short period in 1886 Seymour offered the hospitality of his column to Kropotkin and his disciples, but the divergence between individualism and anarchist communism was too wide for the collaboration to last more than one issue. *The Anarchist* ceased publication in 1888, but the individualist tendency continued strongly into the 1890s. In 1889 Seymour himself brought out a few issues of a new journal, *The Revolutionary Review*, and from 1890 to 1892 Albert Tarn maintained the individualist position in *The Herald of Anarchy*.

But the dominant trend within the growing anarchist movement was toward free communism, and this was expressed particularly in *Freedom*, founded in 1886 by the group centred around Peter Kropotkin, who in that year began his long residence in England. The Freedom Group was a small circle of propagandists in the classic anarchist tradition, devoted to publication and lecturing, and eschewing any ambition to turn itself into a mass movement, though it maintained loose associations with various anarchist groups that began to spring up in London and the north. Kropotkin was the intellectual mentor of the group, and around him clustered a number of distinguished expatriates, including Merlino and some old associates from the days of agitation in Moscow, particularly Stepniak and Nicholas Chaikovsky. The more active members, however, were English, and none was more militant than the sharp-tongued, black-haired Charlotte Wilson, a Girton girl who wore aesthetic gowns and had gone to live in a cottage on the edge of Hampstead Heath rather than accept the earnings of her stockbroker husband.

Charlotte Wilson had been an active member of the Fabian Society, and, since her conversion in 1883, she was its only voluble anarchist. She became and for a decade remained the editor and the real organizing force of *Freedom*, while Kropotkin provided its ideological inspiration, as he continued to do until his break with the Freedom Group over his support for the Allies in the First World War.

For eight years *Freedom* and *Commonweal* continued to advocate anarchism from slightly varying points of view. *Freedom* represented the intellectuals of the movement, and *Commonweal* the plebeian activists. But after Morris's departure *Commonweal* declined rapidly in tone until it became a shrill sheet without ideological or literary significance. The Socialist League itself shrank to a hard core of devoted militants, whose verbal terrorism led to the repeated prosecution of *Commonweal* until, in 1894, it collapsed under the weight of fines and the loss of circulation. Finally, in 1895, the surviving rump of the Socialist League joined the Freedom Group, and *Freedom* became the organ of a united anarchist movement of small dimensions but considerable enthusiasm.

The late 1880s and the 1890s were the first heyday of English anarchism, when its gospel spread in many directions and influenced a considerable fraction of the numerically small socialist movement. Recollecting those days, the Fabian historian Edward Pease, who certainly had no reason to exaggerate anarchist influence, remarked:

In the eighties the rebels were Communist Anarchists, and to us at any rate they seemed more portentous than the mixed crowd of suffragettes and gentlemen from Oxford who before the war seemed to be leading the syndicalist rebels. Anarchism Communism was at any rate a consistent and almost sublime doctrine. Its leaders, such as Prince Kropotkin and Nicholas Chaikovsky, were men of outstanding ability and unimpeachable character, and the rank and file, mostly refugees from European oppression, had direct relations with similar parties abroad, the exact extent and significance of which we could not calculate.

Two specific groups to which anarchism appealed particularly were the Jewish immigrants of East End of London and the literary and artistic rebels of the 1890s. The Jewish immigrants were mostly working people employed—often under appalling sweatshop conditions—in various branches of the clothing trade. They burned with an understandable resentment at the thought that they had exchanged political tyranny and pogroms under the Tsars for exploitation by members of their own race and religion in free England, and for thirty years, from the mid-1880s to 1914, they provided more recruits to anarchism than the rest of the population of Britain.

Jewish anarchism in London centred around *Der Arbeter Fraint*, a Yiddish journal which began to appear in 1885 to give a literary expression to the various socialist points of view that were so volubly discussed week after week in the Berners Street International Club in Whitechapel. In 1891, owing largely to the expulsion of the anarchists by the Second International, the Berners Street Club was riven by political dissension, out of which the anarchists emerged triumphant, in possession of both the club and *Der Arbeter Fraint*.

The most active period of Jewish anarchism in London began with Rudolph Rocker's arrival in England in January 1895. Rocker was a bookbinder by trade, of unmixed German blood, who spoke no Yiddish and had known no Jews until he was introduced to the anarchists from the Polish ghettos in Paris on his arrival there as a political refugee in 1893. When he reached London he made immediate contact with the Jewish group in Whitechapel, learned Yiddish, and in 1896 began to write for *Der Arbeter Fraint*. Two years later he went to Liverpool and collaborated in editing a small paper, also in Yiddish, called *Dos Freie Vort*.

At the end of 1898 the group that published *Der Arbeter Fraint* offered him the editorship; he accepted, and remained the German editor of a Yiddish paper until his internment by the British authorities in 1914.

Rocker quickly overcame any difficulties that might arise from differences of background, and soon won the confidence and loyalty of his

Jewish comrades. In time he became a great influence in the labour movement in the East End, where the anarchists were for long the most active
political element among the Jewish population, and during the great strike
of the sweatshop workers in 1912, when he turned *Der Arbeter Fraint* into a
daily paper for the benefit of the strikers and eventually led them to a
notable victory, he gained the respect and gratitude of thousands of people who did not share his views.

> One day as I was walking along a narrow Whitechapel street [he rec-
> ollected many years afterward], an old Jew with a long white beard
> stopped me outside his house, and said: 'May God bless you! You
> helped my children in their need. You are not a Jew, but you are a
> man!' This old man lived in a world completely different from mine.
> But the memory of the gratitude that shone in his eyes has remained
> with me all these years.

Between 1898 and 1914 the movement that centred around *Der Arbeter
Fraint* developed into a complex network of social and cultural activities.
In 1902 the Federation of Jewish Anarchist Groups in Great Britain and
Paris was formed; it maintained until 1914 a continuity of action and cooperation rare among anarchist organizations of comparable size. *Der Arbeter
Fraint* gradually became the centre of a considerable Yiddish publishing
enterprise, which brought out not only the journal itself, but also a cultural review, *Germinal*, and a notable series of translations of the great contemporary novelists and dramatists. In 1906, after the establishment of the
Jubilee Street Institute, an educational programme was started, with classes in English for immigrants from Poland and Russia and lectures in history, literature, and sociology on the lines of the People's Universities in
France. Finally a mutual-aid organization called The Workers' Circle was
founded, devoted both to progressive education and to the care of the sick
and needy. The success of these many-sided activities seemed to vindicate
anarchist ideas of voluntary organization, but it must be remembered that
they were carried out by people whose traditions had inclined them for
centuries to practise a high degree of cooperation as a protection against
external threats.

The literary rebels who skirmished on the verge of the anarchist movement during the 1890s were united only by a belief that anarchism and
similar doctrines provided a social counterpart to their own emotional
conviction that the freedom of the individual was necessary for the
flowering of art. They ranged from important writers like William Morris

and Edward Carpenter, who defended Libertarian dreams without fully accepting the label of anarchism, to minor decadent poets like Evelyn Douglas, who once gave the propaganda by deed a twist of English eccentricity by firing off a revolver at the stony face of the Houses of Parliament. The most delightful inhabitants of the literary-aesthetic fringe were undoubtedly the two teenage daughters of William Michael Rossetti, Olivia and Helen, who were inspired by their admiration for Kropotkin to publish from their Pre-Raphaelite home in 1895 a journal of the most fiery earnestness; it was called *The Torch: A Revolutionary Journal of Anarchist Communism*. In loyalty to their foreign ancestry, the Rossetti sisters specialized in introducing the writings of continental anarchists, and Louise Michel, Malato, Malatesta, Zhukovsky, and Faure all contributed to *The Torch*. So also, on the literary side, did Octave Mirbeau and even Émile Zola, while one of the younger contributors was the youth who became Ford Madox Ford. But *The Torch* burned out quickly, and in later years both the Rossetti girls wrote with amusing asperity on their anarchist childhood.

The most ambitious contribution to literary anarchism during the 1890s was undoubtedly Oscar Wilde's *The Soul of Man Under Socialism*. Wilde, as we have seen, declared himself an anarchist on at least one occasion during the 1890s, and he greatly admired Kropotkin, whom he had met. Later, in *De Profundis*, he declared Kropotkin's life as one 'of the most perfect lives I have come across in my own experience' and talked of him as 'a man with a soul of that beautiful white Christ that seems coming out of Russia'. But in *The Soul of Man Under Socialism*, which appeared in 1891, it is Godwin rather than Kropotkin whose influence seems dominant.

Wilde's aim in *The Soul of Man Under Socialism* is to seek the society most favourable to the artist. We immediately notice a difference between his approach and that of other libertarian writers, such as Proudhon and Tolstoy, who have also written on art. For Proudhon and Tolstoy, art is a means to the end of social and moral regeneration. But for Wilde art is the supreme end, containing within itself enlightenment and regeneration, to which all else in society must be subordinated. If Proudhon and Tolstoy represent the anarchist as moralist, Wilde represents the anarchist as aesthete.

Since art, in Wilde's view, depends on the full and free development of personal capacities, society must make individualism its goal, and Wilde seeks—with what at first seems a characteristic paradox—to attain individualism by way of socialism. Wilde is as passionate as Stirner in his advocacy of the individual will, and in his denunciation of the 'altruistic impulses of charity, benevolence, and the like', but he is not an orthodox individualist in the sense of regarding individual possession as a guarantee of freedom. On the contrary, he contends that the burden of property is intolerable and that society must lift it from the shoulders of individuals. This can only be done by 'Socialism, Communism, or whatever one chooses to call it', which by converting private property into public wealth, and substituting cooperation for competition, will restore society to its proper condition of a thoroughly healthy organism. So far, no Fabian could disagree. But Wilde adds that mere socialization of property is not enough. Individualism is needed as a corrective:

> If the Socialism is Authoritarian; if there are Governments armed with economic power as they are now with political power; if, in a word, we are to have Industrial Tyrannies, then the last state of man will be worse than the first.

Here Wilde turns aside into a discussion of present-day society, in which a few privileged people enjoy a limited individualism, and the rest are condemned to uncongenial work 'by the peremptory, unreasonable, degrading Tyranny of want'. When he looks at the poor, Wilde finds hope, not among the virtuous, but among those who are 'ungrateful, discontented, disobedient, and rebellious'.

> Disobedience, in the eyes of any one who has read history, is man's original virtue. It is through disobedience that progress has been made, through disobedience and through rebellion ... I can quite understand a man accepting laws that protect private property, and admit of its accumulation, as long as he himself is able under those conditions to realize some form of beautiful and intellectual life. But it is almost incredible to me how a man whose life is marred and made hideous by such laws can possibly acquiesce in their continuance.

Wilde's interest in rebellion was not a mere romantic pose. He saw his own life as a rebellion, and he genuinely respected sincere revolutionaries—'these Christs who die upon the barricades'—even if he loathed indiscriminate violence. In 1886 Shaw found him the only English man of letters willing to sign a petition for the lives of the Chicago anarchists, and in *The Soul of Man Under Socialism* he makes quite clear his sympathy for those who try to rouse the poor to rebellion:

What is said by great employers of labour against agitators is unquestionably true. Agitators are a set of interfering, meddling people, who come down to some perfectly contented class of the community and sow the seeds of discontent among them. That is the reason why agitators are so absolutely necessary. Without them, in our incomplete state, there would be no advance towards civilization.

This discussion of rebellion leads Wilde back to his opposition to an authoritarian socialism, which will only make universal the economic tyranny that now at least a few escape. A voluntary system is the only possible solution:

Each man must be quite free to choose his own work. No form of compulsion must be exercised over him. If there is, his work will not be good for him, will not be good in itself, and will not be good for others ... All association must be quite voluntary. It is only in voluntary associations that man is fine.

From this point Wilde expands, in almost Godwinian tones, on the tyranny which property exercises even over the wealthy, and there is yet another touch of *Political Justice* in the passage where it points out that the abolition of property will mean also the abolition of family and marriage. There must be no claims on personality that are not granted freely; in such freedom love itself will be 'more wonderful, more beautiful, and more ennobling'.

Wilde's rejection of restraint, his consciousness that 'to the claims of conformity no man may yield and remain free at all', leads him naturally to his criticism of government. Authority is degrading to ruler and ruled, and no form is exempt; even democracy 'means simply the bludgeoning of the people by the people for the people'. With authority and property, punishment also will cease, since crime—when men are no longer hungry—will mostly vanish, and where it does not 'will be treated by physicians as a very distressing form of dementia, to be cured by care and kindness'. So the machinery of the state that governs must be dismantled, and all that remains will be an administrative apparatus (which Wilde still rather misleadingly calls a state) to arrange the production and distribution of commodities. Here—since Wilde has no illusions about the dignity of manual labour—machinery will take the place of men freed to follow their artistic or scientific or speculative pursuits and to produce the thoughts and things that only individuals can devise.

If Wilde follows Godwin in so much, there is one important respect in which he differs from him. Nowhere in *The Soul of Man* does one find a hint of that tendency to fall back on public opinion as a means of restraint which Godwin and so many other anarchists have shown. Wilde detested moralists of every kind; he hated cant about duty and self-sacrifice; he maintained that 'individualism ... does not try to force people to be good'. What he would put in the place of public opinion is 'sympathy', and sympathy is the product of freedom; when men have no need to fear or envy their fellows, they will understand them and respect their individualities. It is a vision not unlike Stirner's, but it is tempered by Wilde's natural amiability.

Britain did not escape the trend toward syndicalism, though it came late and never produced an independent movement; moreover, the anarchist element was diluted almost to the point of disappearance. Tom Mann, who returned from Australia in 1910 with his head filled with IWW theories, was the real inspirer of the movement, which was most significant as a rebellion against the hierarchy that had formed in the trade unions and was in the process of formation in the Labour Party. The arguments of Mann and his associates in *The Industrial Syndicalist* (1911) spoke for a wide rank-and-file movement which aimed at the creation of industrial unions, on the lines of the IWW, and at substituting the concept of workers' control for that of nationalization in the socialist programme. These ideas were particularly strong in South Wales, where a celebrated anonymous pamphlet, *The Miner's Next Step* (1912), advocated the struggle against the capitalist state by a strong, centralized workers' organization, proceeding by strike after strike to the point where capitalism would collapse and the workers would take over the industries in which they worked. The emphasis on centralization in such propaganda was really anti-libertarian, and a closer approach to anarcho-syndicalism was adopted by a smaller group, led by Guy Bowman of *The Syndicalist* (1912), who was influenced by the Bourses de Travail and stressed the need for local unions as the basic industrial pattern. Both groups were impressed by the idea of the millennial general strike, and their theories continued to influence the British labour movement until the general strike in 1926.

The truer forms of anarchism lost their impetus in Britain before 1900. There were probably no fewer anarchists during the next decade, but their numbers did not keep proportional pace to the growth of the general socialist movement, and in spite of the fact that they branched out into educational and community-living experiments, of which Clousdon Hill and Whiteway were the most important, they gained little new ground.

The First World War, which led to the suppression of their journals and to the split between pro-war and anti-war elements, set going a positive decline, which affected both the Jewish movement and the English-speaking groups in London, Glasgow, and South Wales. When Emma Goldman reached England in 1924 she found the movement almost dead, and in 1927 *Freedom* came to an end from lack of support.

It was almost a decade afterward that the enthusiasm aroused by the Spanish Civil War gave anarchism in Britain a new lease of life. In 1936 *Spain and the World* began to appear; its most active founders, and the real inspirers of British anarchism during the 1930s and 1940s, were Vernon Richards, a young engineer whose father had been a friend of Malatesta, and his wife, Marie Louise Berneri, the talented and beautiful daughter of Camillo Berneri. The revivified movement was small but vigorous; *Spain and the World* and its successor, *Revolt* (1939), attracted not only many younger radicals but also a number of literary intellectuals; John Cowper Powys, Ethel Mannin, and Herbert Read were all contributors. Read, who had long been sympathetic to libertarian ideas, published in 1938 his *Poetry and Anarchism*, which he followed shortly afterward by *The Philosophy of Anarchism*, and these works marked the beginning of a period, when anarchism became for a time a recognizable feature of the British literary landscape.

The vitality of British anarchism continued through the years of World War II, when the movement with its publications became one of the centres of resistance to the war. In the autumn of 1939 *Revolt* was replaced by *War Commentary*, which continued to appear regularly until May 1945, when the title was changed to that of Kropotkin's old paper, *Freedom*; *Freedom* still appears.

At the beginning of the war the anarchist movement received an access of strength because the militant pacifists of the Forward Movement grew impatient with the Quakerish timidity of the Peace Pledge Union, and a number of them—including John Hewetson, Tony Gibson, Laurie Hislam, and Fredrick Lohr—seceded and began to work in varying degrees of closeness with the Freedom Group, which operated the Freedom Press and published *War Commmentary*.

Shortly afterwards, in 1941, George Woodcock, who was already editing *Now* as a pacifist literary journal, joined the Freedom Group, and *Now*, in a new series and an enlarged format, became an anarchist-oriented review of the arts. Continuing until 1947, it published writings by poets and fiction writers from a wide range of the non-communist Left, and Julian Symons, who was one of the contributors, remembered it thirty years later as 'much the best periodical of a radical kind in England during those years ... For anybody wanting to know what non-communist radicals thought and hoped during those years *Now* must be an indispensable document, as *Horizon,* for example, is not.' Among the writers who contributed to *Now* were not only avowed anarchists like Woodcock, Read, and Comfort, like Denise Levertov, Kenneth Rexroth, and Paul Goodman, but also left-wing writers who at most could be regarded as libertarians, like George Orwell, Henry Miller, George Barker, Roy Fuller, Lawrence Durrell, André Breton, e.e. cummings, Victor Serge, and William Everson.

In fact, rather unexpectedly, it was in the English-speaking countries that during World War II anarchism demonstrated the greatest variety in the sense of interpreting the tradition in new ways. The most creative insights often came from writers outside the organized movement like—in Britain—Read and Comfort, who never joined any specific group, and this was a foreshadowing of the later opening out of anarchism in many new directions.

In two particular directions anarchist perspectives widened notably during the 1940s. Ever since Kropotkin, libertarian theoreticians had attempted to relate their doctrines to the current sciences of man, and towards the middle of the twentieth century the place biology had held in the speculations of the author of *Mutual Aid* was assumed by psychology. Alex Comfort wrote on the psychology of power (*Authority and Delinquency in the Modern State,* 1950), and Herbert Read applied the insights of Freud, Jung and Adler to aesthetic and political criticism; the teachings of Erich Fromm (particularly *The Fear of Freedom*) and of Wilhelm Reich (especially as applied to libertarian problems in the essays of Marie Louise Berneri) were notably appealing to the anarchist intellectuals of the time. The other new departure was an intensified recognition of the need for a new type of education so that men could endure and accept freedom. This recognition was expressed partly in the practical involvement of anarchists in free schools, notably Burgess Hill in North London, and partly through their writings. Herbert Read's *Education through Art* and *The Education of Free Men* not only had a deep and wide effect on teaching methods in the schools of many countries, but also offered anarchists a new revolutionary technique; through the transformation of the schools by substituting the education of the senses for the education of the mind, Read taught, the kind of peaceful transformation of society of which anarchists had long dreamed might yet be attained. Other anarchists, who were themselves teachers, like Tony Gibson and Tom Earley, wrote important pamphlets contributing the insights acquired in practice.

Before the war ended, the anarchist movement in Britain underwent a series of crises. At the beginning of the war a clandestine Anarchist Federation of Great Britain had been founded; its principal branches were in London, Glasgow and Kingston. In 1944 a group of syndicalists gained control of the Federation and the Freedom Group withdrew, taking with them the movement's press and *War Commentary*. In 1954 the syndicalists eventually transformed the rump of the Anarchist Federation into the Syndicalist Workers' Federation, which published *Direct Action* until 1968, and then appears to have expired from lack of relevance in this period when the revolt of the young had changed the perspectives of anarchism.

Shortly after the split in the Anarchist Federation, four of the editors of *War Commentary* were arrested under a wartime regulation on charges of spreading disaffection in the army. The bringing of such charges in 1944, when the end of the war was already in sight, aroused indignation throughout the English Left, except for the communists. Three of the editors, Vernon Richards, John Hewetson, and Philip Sansom, were convicted and imprisoned for nine months. In compensation the anarchists gained unprecedented publicity, for articles that had reached *War Commentary's* four thousand subscribers were reprinted, once they had been quoted in court, by national newspapers with circulations of millions. Marie Louise Berneri was acquitted on a technicality, and she and George Woodcock carried on the editing of *War Commentary*, transformed it into *Freedom* at the war's end, and prevented the collapse of the Freedom Group, the nerve centre of British anarchism at the time, on which the Special Branch of Scotland Yard had counted as a result of the prosecution.

One result of the anarchist trial in 1945 was the continuation of the Freedom Press Defence Committee as a broader Freedom Defence Committee, devoted to defending all people who were arbitrarily imprisoned or otherwise persecuted under wartime regulations. Herbert Read was the Chairman, and the organizational work was mainly done by anarchists, but George Orwell was a closely involved Vice-Chairman, and leading members of the ILP and the Peace Pledge Union, as well as independent writers like Julian Symons, played active roles, while the work of the Committee, which also included monitoring freedom of the press, appealed to a wide spectrum of intellectuals, writers and artists, from Harold Laski to Henry Moore, from Cyril Connolly to Bertrand Russell, from Augustus John to Osbert Sitwell, who all contributed funds and gave their names as sponsors. At that time the National Council for Civil Liberties was under communist control and virtually inactive except in very limited directions, and the Freedom Defence Committee usefully filled a gap until the end of the 1940s, when the revival of the NCCL as an effective body made its existence unnecessary and it quietly folded up its operations. The Freedom Defence Committee was an early example of the kind of cooperation between anarchists and other libertarian-inclined groups and individuals that would later become a much more general pattern in Britain.

The British anarchists at this period showed a special interest in the housing of the poor. As early as 1944 George Woodcock published a pamphlet entitled *Homes and Hovels*, and when Colin Ward came actively into the Freedom Group in 1945, he brought with him an expertise in town planning and the urban environment that led the anarchists of this time to give support and encouragement to the squatters of that period, men and women lacking homes who took matters into their own hands, occupying disused army camps and moving into long-vacant houses. A few anarchists were active among the squatters and the movement as a whole hailed their actions as instances of the kind of direct action that anarchists had been advocating ever since Kropotkin.

The 1950s were a period of somnolence for anarchism in Britain. The movement lost two of its leading figures in 1949 when Marie Louise Berneri died and George Woodcock departed to start a new kind of life in Canada. *Freedom* survived, though its circulation fell to low levels, and the flow of pamphlets and books from Freedom Press that had been characteristic of the war years dried up. In the dreary welfare state that arose after 1945 issues were not as clearcut as in the earlier part of the decade, and the young were no longer attracted as they had been during the Spanish Civil War and World War II.

But in the 1960s everything changed. The first notable event of the renaissance that now began, and perhaps the most important in its long-term consequences, was the foundation of *Anarchy*, a monthly of anarchist thought and proposal that was started by Colin Ward in 1961. *Anarchy* ran under Colin Ward's editorship for ten years, until the end of 1970, and then was handed over to other editors who unfortunately killed it by turning it into a mere propaganda sheet.

Ward produced the 118 issues of *Anarchy* which he edited on the principle, as he put it, of 'moving with the times, but not in step', and in fact *Anarchy* did represent a new kind of anarchism that had escaped from out of doctrinaire loyalty to the historic movement and had become responsive to the urgent currents of the time, just as in the mid nineteenth century anarchists had responded more sensitively and more originally than the Marxists to the situation created by the industrial revolution and the rise of the nation-state.

Anarchy was not a literary magazine in the same way as *Now* had been, though it showed a lively interest in such aspects of contemporary culture as painting, the cinema, and the theatre, to all of which issues were devoted, and Colin Ward persuaded some of the more vital younger writers of the period to contribute, including Alan Sillitoe, Colin MacInnes, Simon Raven, Arnold Wesker, Adrian Mitchell, and Maurice Cranston.

As the new pacifism of the Campaign for Nuclear Disarmament developed during the 1960s, *Anarchy* followed it closely and showed how much the campaign could gain from the study of anarchist concepts of organization by affinity groups and how much the anarchists, on the other hand, could gain in both inspiration and support from taking part in such a movement.

Anarchy was naturally, given the bent of the British movement at this time, much interested in various aspects of education, to which it devoted a number of issues. It was one of the first leftist magazines to sense the coming wave of militant feminism and to discuss in depth the problems of women in a male world. When housing became a problem once more in the later 1960s and the squatters appeared again in the cities of Britain, *Anarchy* gave them support and used the occasion for studies in depth of urban problems. It devoted space—and more of it as the decade went on—to environmental and ecological questions and to the significance of new technologies in the context of anarchist aims. And it inevitably devoted an issue to Wilhelm Reich, the maverick psychiatrist who became such a hero among mid-twentieth-century anarchists.

Anarchy was naturally alive to the particular radical issues of the 1960s. It devoted two whole issues and many articles to student revolt and the causes that led to the rebellion of the young, but it identified with no particular group, which was wise, since the student rebels had a very shaky theoretical base and were as likely to be captured by authoritarian Marxist factions as to be consistent in the libertarian impulses by which so often their actions seemed to be governed. An awareness of the degree of charlatanry that often afflicted student groups was demonstrated by an issue on the subject entitled 'Playing at Revolution'. To false concepts of revolution *Anarchy* opposed what it sometimes called 'do-it-yourself anarchism', by which it—and Colin Ward—meant the constant search, within society as it is, for the opportunities to put anarchist principles into action without waiting for a revolution, the underlying thought being that governments and especially welfare states are so destructive of freedom and of individual and mutual initiatives that, if we wait for a revolution, it may be too late to create the free society of which the anarchists dream, because the natural social impulses will all have been atrophied. More than any other publication of the time, more than *Freedom*, which continued its parallel course, more than the lesser sheets with their limited constituencies like *Black Flag* and *Ludd* and the *University Libertarian, Anarchy* exemplified the extraordinary outgoing of anarchist interests in Britain during the 1960s, personified in the confident and mostly young contingents who would be there behind the black banners in every Aldermaston March and would figure prominently and often uproariously in the demonstrations in London and in the larger cities. It was an extraordinary shift of climate from the preceding radical decade, the 1930s. Where young British rebels in the decade before World War II joined the communists, in the 1960s they were more likely to become anarchists. Mark the change; becoming rather than joining, a change of heart rather than a party ticket. Doctrinaire earnestness tended to be replaced by rebellious gaiety as the current mood.

For large numbers of the young during the 1960s, anarchism was an insurgent phase, a *rite de passage*, and many did not remain, just as many abandoned their roles as beats or hippies. The 1970s, like the 1950s, was a period when the movement tended to shrink towards its core of dedicated converts. But each time the surviving core has been larger. Looking at the pages of *Freedom* in the 1980s, I find it the kind of paper, cautious and raucous by turn, that radical groups operate in periods when their popularity is not at its peak. But I also see signs of countrywide anarchist activity of a kind that did not exist forty years ago, when any kind of anarchist organization seemed to be confined to the London and Glasgow areas. Now, when I look at the back pages of *Freedom*, I find more than fifty groups in all parts of the country, listing their addresses and sometimes advertising their local propaganda sheets—an *Anarchist Times* in Derby, a *Clydeside Anarchist* in Glasgow. Even in times when it is in temporary retreat, anarchism is now taken seriously as a political theory represented by an identifiable minority movement—more seriously in fact than at any time since Kropotkin's heyday.

In fact there are signs of another upward undulation of British anarchism. Anarchists, who were very active in the original Committees of 100 in the 1960s, have retained their importance in the Campaign for Nuclear Disarmament, and indeed everywhere that an element of civil disobedience enters into the anti-war movement. During the 1960s there was indeed a tendency for a few groups like the Angry Brigade to move beyond ordinary civil disobedience into violent sabotage, though in characteristic British fashion nobody was killed in the Brigade's relatively few exploits. However, in recent years, though a certain amount of verbal violence still rumbles in the anarchist press, it is not translated into action, and methods that one associates with Gandhi rather than Bakunin tend to prevail in a movement that remains sensitive to the issues of its time, agitating against industrial pollution and urban spread, and providing something of a magnet to the unemployed youth of the country in their reaction against Big Sister policies and the neo-imperialist adventures of the Thatcher government.

American anarchism has a double tradition—native and immigrant. The native tradition, whose roots run back to the early years of the nineteenth century, was strongly individualist. The immigrant tradition, which begins among the German revolutionary socialists of the later 1870s, was first collectivist and afterwards anarchist communist.

The native tradition stems largely from the writings of Thomas Paine, from the experiences of the early nineteenth-century socialist communities, and from Godwin's *Political Justice*, of which an American edition appeared in Philadelphia in 1796. Godwin's influence on early American literature and political thought was profound; Charles Brockden Brown, his principal American disciple, transmitted the nightmare of Caleb Williams to the darker traditions of the American novel, while the brighter dream of liberty and justice that is enshrined in *Political Justice* found an echo in the writings of Emerson and Thoreau.

For Emerson the state and its laws were always the enemies of liberty and virtue. The very existence of political institutions implied a diminution of individual human dignity.

> Every actual State is corrupt. Good men must not obey the laws too well ... Wild liberty develops into conscience. Want of liberty, by strengthening law and decorum, stupefies conscience.

Yet one cannot regard Emerson as a complete anarchist. For him the state was a poor makeshift, but a makeshift that might be necessary until education and individual development had reached their goal in the production of the wise man. 'To educate the wise man the State exists, and with the appearance of the wise man the State expires.'

Thoreau's condemnation of the state was more thorough, and in many other ways he fits more closely into the anarchist pattern than Emerson could ever do. *Walden*, the record of a modest attempt to live simply and naturally, in a poverty of material goods that provides its own immaterial riches, is inspired by that desire to simplify society and to disentangle the needless complexities of contemporary living which underlies the anarchist demand for the decentralization of social life and the dismantling of authority. Behind both is the faith in natural as distinct from human law which makes all libertarians trust to impulses rising freely rather than to rules applied mechanically.

The essay *On the Duty of Civil Disobedience*, which Thoreau wrote in 1849, has remained one of the classic justifications of passive and principled resistance to authority; it shows Thoreau firmly placing the final judgement of any action within the conscience of the individual, and demonstrating clearly the incapacity of government:

> I heartily accept the motto—'That government is best which governs least'; and I should like to see it acted up to more rapidly and systematically. Carried out it finally amounts to this, which I also believe—'That government is best which governs not at all', and when men are prepared for it, that will be the kind of government which they will have. Government is at best but an expedient; but most governments are usually, and all governments are sometimes, inexpedient.

For Thoreau freedom was not merely a matter of politics, and he believed that the War of Independence had left his fellow countrymen both economically and morally enslaved. As a complement to the Republic—*res publica*—he asked that attention be paid to the *res privata*—the private state of man:

> Do we call this the land of the free? [he asked bitterly]. What is it to be free from King George and continue the slaves of King Prejudice? What is it to be born free and not to live free? What is the value of any political freedom but as a means to moral freedom? Is it a freedom to be slaves, or a freedom to be free, of which we boast?

Thoreau was most concerned with individual protest; his instinctive distrust of the mass mind made him eschew the collective deed. 'Action from principle' was in itself, for him, 'essentially revolutionary'; each man must act according to his conscience, not according to the laws of the state, and for men who so acted, like John Brown, Thoreau's admiration was boundless. Always he came back to the fresh, untrammelled, personal judgement, and it was for this reason that he hated 'the institutions of the dead unkind'.

Thoreau hesitated always between the rebel and the artist, and, while he wrote some of the most remarkable pleas for the individual against the state, he left it for other men to give an extensive practical expression to such sentiments.

It is here that we come to American individualist anarchism as a social doctrine. It begins in the heyday of the Utopian communities, the age when Owenites and Fourierites and Icarians and a host of minor religious and political sects sought to create in the broad lands of the young United States prototypes of their ideal worlds. Most of the socialist colonies were based on rigid Utopian theories of organization; leaders like Owen, Cabet, and Considérant, Fourier's principal heir, tried to create model villages that would reconstruct in every possible detail their predetermined plans of a just society. Inevitably, since the success of the community was held to depend on the proper working out of an inspired project, there had to be rules and an austere discipline. A sense of their own essential rightness of judgement turned men like Owen and Cabet into paternalistic autocrats, and the dialectic of autocracy and resentful rebellion brought an end to many of the communities.

One of the men who sadly watched this process working out in Robert Owen's colony of New Harmony was a talented musician and inventor named Josiah Warren. Warren left New Harmony in 1827 with the firm conviction that Owen's way was not the right way to solve the problems of cooperative living.

> It seemed [he said afterward when he analysed the causes of New Harmony's failure] that the difference of opinion, tastes, and purposes *increased* just in proportion to the demand for conformity ... It appeared that it was nature's own inherent law of diversity that had conquered us ... Our 'united interests' were directly at war with the individualities of persons and circumstances and the instinct of self-preservation ... and it was evident that just in proportion to the contact of persons and interests, so are concessions and compromises indispensable.

Warren did not abandon the general idea of the cooperative community. All his life he felt that the way to social change lay in teaching men and women by practical experiment how they could live together in fellowship. But he took to heart the lessons of New Harmony, and in doing so he developed the theory of the sovereignty of the individual which has led to his being regarded, rightly I think, as the first American anarchist. It was not, he contended, the individual that must be made to conform to society, but society that must be fitted to the individual:

> Society must be converted so as to preserve the SOVEREIGNTY OF EVERY INDIVIDUAL inviolate. That it must avoid all combinations and connexions of persons and interests, and all other arrangements which will not leave every individual at all times at liberty to dispose of his or her person, and time, and property in any manner in which his or her feelings or judgement may dictate, WITHOUT INVOLVING THE PERSONS OR INTERESTS OF OTHERS.

Seeking the causes of the wreck of New Harmony, Warren came to the conclusion that they had centred around the failure to deal adequately with the question of property. His conclusions were surprisingly like those which Proudhon reached, apparently quite independently, a few years later in France. All that a man had a right to individually was the material result of his own labour. But the complexity of civilization had made it impossible for each individual to live self-subsistently; division of labour was a reality that could not be ignored, and the economic relationships between men must be based upon it. He therefore made 'labour for labour' his formula, and sought to find a means of putting into effective practice Owen's original proposal for an exchange of labour time on an hour-for-hour basis, but with a flexibility that would allow individuals to agree on some kind of adjustment when one man's work, irrespective of time, had clearly been more arduous than another's.

Immediately on his return from New Harmony to Cincinnati, Warren started his first experiment, which he called a Time Store. He sold goods at cost, and asked the customers to recompense him for his own trouble by giving him labour notes, promising to donate to the storekeeper an equivalent time at their own occupations for that consumed in serving him. By this means he hoped to educate his customers in the idea of exchange based on labour and to recruit supporters willing to take part in his plans to found a chain of mutualist villages. The Time Store lasted for three years, and Warren came out of the experiment convinced that his plan was workable. He spent the next two years on what seems to have been the first design for a rotary press, and out of the earnings from his patents in stereotyping he accumulated enough money to start in 1833 a journal entitled *The Peaceful Revolutionist.* The final stage in his carefully planned scheme of action was to found a model village as soon as his ideas became known through his publications.

In 1834 Warren and a group of his disciples bought a stretch of land in Ohio and founded the Village of Equity with half a dozen families, who built their houses and operated a cooperative sawmill on a labour-for-labour exchange basis. The hierarchical structure of the Owenite and Fourierite communities was abandoned in favour of simple mutual agreements, and it was in fact the first anarchist community in any country since Winstanley's venture on St George's Hill almost two centuries before. Its failure was not due to any breakdown of the exchange system, which hardly had time to prove itself, but to sickness, for there was malaria in the low-lying land of the settlement, and a final epidemic of influenza brought the community to an end.

Warren was too persistent and too convinced of the essential practicality of his theories to abandon his attempts. In 1846 he founded a second colony called Utopia, largely populated by disillusioned Fourierites. Here brick kilns, stone quarries, and sawmills were worked on the Warrenite basis, and the community remained for some years virtually independent of outside society. As for the organization of the colony, it was as near pure individualist anarchism as seems humanly possible. In the spring of 1848 Warren wrote:

> Throughout our operations on the ground, everything has been conducted so nearly upon the Individualist basis that not one meeting for legislation has taken place. No Organization, no indefinite delegated power, no 'Constitution', no 'laws' or 'Bye-laws', 'rules' or 'Regulations' but such as each individual makes for himself and his own business. No officers, no priests nor prophets have been resorted to—nothing of either kind has been in demand. We have had a few meetings, but they were for friendly conversation, for music, dancing, or some other social and pleasant pastime. Not even a single lecture upon the principles on which we were acting has been given on the premises. It was not necessary; for (as a lady remarked yesterday) 'the subject once stated and understood, there is nothing left to talk about'—All is action after that.

Utopia lasted as a mutualist village for almost twenty years, into the 1860s, with about a hundred inhabitants and some small woodworking industries. It survived Warren's own departure, when he set off in 1850 to found yet another community, Modern Times, on Long Island, which also maintained its mutualist character for at least two decades, eventually turning, like Utopia, into a more or less conventional village with cooperative tendencies. Neither community can be counted an actual failure, but both of them owed their success in great measure to the fluidity of American society during the period in which they operated, and both tended to dissolve rather than collapse as society in the eastern United States became more stabilized after the Civil War.

Because he combined theory so extensively with practice, Warren was undoubtedly the most important of the American individualist anarchists, though both Stephen Pearl Andrews and Lysander Spooner eloquently elaborated on the ideas he had originally put forward. Later, largely through the influence of William B. Greene, Proudhon's mutualism was introduced into the United States, and its similarity to native individualism was quickly recognized. The Proudhonians remained a small sect, but they and the disciples of Warren both contributed much to American Populist thought, with its strong emphasis on currency reform.

In later years the leading American individualist anarchist was Benjamin R. Tucker, who founded the *Radical Review* in 1878, and three years later *Liberty*, which lasted until Tucker's printing shop burned down in 1907. Tucker's own ideas were a synthesis of Warren and Proudhon, with little original added to them, and he is perhaps most important for the fearlessness which made *Liberty* a forum for native American radicalism, and which earned the admiration of H.L. Mencken, George Bernard Shaw (a contributor to *Liberty*), and Walt Whitman, who declared, 'I love him; he is plucky to the bone.' Tucker called himself a scientific anarchist; he remained firmly individualist throughout his career, and opposed both the collectivist schools of anarchism—since he believed that freedom was incompatible with any kind of communism—and the advocates of the propaganda by deed, which struck him as essentially immoral. With the disappearance of *Liberty*, the tradition of native individualist anarchism virtually came to an end. Tucker himself lived on to die in Monaco at the age of eighty-five in 1939; during his last years he was plagued by doubts, and, while he still regarded anarchism as 'a goal that humanity moves towards', he doubted whether the path to that goal had yet been discovered.

As I have already suggested, there was little direct connection between the native individualist anarchists and the immigrant anarchists. This was not because of any insularity on the part of the individualists. Both Lysander Spooner and William B. Greene had been members of the First International; Tucker made the pioneer translations into English of Proudhon and Bakunin, and at first was enthusiastic about Kropotkin, to whose trial in Lyons as late as 1883 he devoted considerable space in

Liberty. What detached him and his associates from the immigrant anarchists was the cult of violence that marked and marred their movement from the beginning.

The rise of immigrant anarchism begins with the split between revolutionaries and reformists in the Socialist Labour Party in 1880. This party consisted mostly of German immigrants, and even the rebels were theoretical Marxists, so that their founding of the Socialist Revolutionary Clubs in New York, Chicago, and other large cities was only the prelude to the appearance of anarchism. The event that took the Socialist Revolutionaries into the anarchism camp was the International Anarchist Congress of 1881. No delegates from the German groups in the United States actually took part in the Congress, though they were represented by proxy; it was perhaps the combination of distance and imagination that made the Congress seem so important in America. The new International founded at the Congress, which in reality led a phantom existence, seemed from New York and Chicago a powerful and portentous organization. As a consequence, by the end of 1881 there were actually two Federations in the United States that pledged adherence to the International. A convention in Chicago of Socialist Revolutionaries from fourteen cities in the East and Mid-West formed the International Working People's Association, known also as the Black International and consisting mostly of immigrants from Germany and the Austro-Hungarian Empire. It declared, after long debate, against political activity, and its resolutions clearly premeditated the use of violence.

At the same time a group of native Americans in San Francisco, led by Burnette G. Haskell, had formed a secret society, organized on the old conspiratorial system of small closed groups of nine men each, which also affiliated to the London International and called itself the International Workingmen's Association, or Red International. Haskell was a wealthy lawyer who also supported the anti-Chinese movement in California, and his links with real anarchism were too slight to be taken seriously.

Any doubts the Revolutionary Socialists in the East may have had about the choice between Marxism and anarchism seem to have been dissipated by the arrival of Johann Most in 1882. Most immediately refounded *Die Freiheit* in New York, and started a speaking tour through all the cities where revolutionary groups existed. His trenchant journalism, his fiery oratory, and his enthusiastic advocacy of violence, in a manner that rivalled Nechayev's, had a most malign influence on coming events.

Most was in fact so obsessed by revolutionary violence that he secretly found employment in an explosives factory in Jersey City, and afterward wrote an extraordinary pamphlet entitled *Revolutionäre Kriegswissenschaft*, which is really a manual on the making and use of bombs, on burglary and arson for the good of the cause, and on certain aspects of toxicology already known to the Borgias. This was supplemented by articles in *Die Freiheit* in praise of dynamite and on easy ways to manufacture nitroglycerine. All these matters Most discussed with the sinister enthusiasm of a malevolent and utterly irresponsible child. He never used and probably never intended to use such methods himself; he recommended them to others instead, and his responsibility in the tragedy that followed in Chicago in 1886 was undoubtedly great.

Chicago was the centre in which immigrant anarchism took strongest root, doubtless owing to the city's bitter industrial struggles and to the notorious brutality of its police force. To the second Congress of the International, held in Pittsburgh during 1883, Chicago sent more delegates than any other city, and after the discussions at Pittsburgh the movement in Chicago took an immediate upsurge, both in members and in activity. The actual number of anarchists in Chicago groups was probably about 3,000, out of the International's total American membership of 6,000. Most of them were Germans and Czechs, but there was also a vigorous American group of a hundred members, led by the flamboyant orator Albert Parsons. But the membership of the groups does not in itself give a full idea of the following the anarchists could command in Chicago between 1883 and 1886; this is perhaps better suggested by the fact that the International published five papers in the city—a German daily and two German weeklies, a Bohemian weekly, and an English fortnightly, *Alarm*. The aggregate circulation of these five journals was over 30,000. A Central Labour Union was founded in 1883 under the influence of the International, and by the beginning of 1886 it had already won the support of most of the organized labour in the city.

When the Eight-Hour movement started in the spring, the International was virtually in the lead, and 65,000 men went on strike or were locked out by their employers. Meanwhile, both sides had been assiduously whipping up feelings of violence. The police continued to deal brutally with strikers and demonstrators. The International called loudly for counter-violence. In October 1885 the Central Labour Union passed a resolution proposed by the anarchist August Spies:

> We urgently call upon the wage-class to arm itself in order to be able
> to put forth against their exploiters such an argument which alone
> can be effective—*Violence!*

And on 18 March 1886 *Die Arbeiter Zeitung*, the International's German daily, declared:

> If we do not soon bestir ourselves for a bloody revolution, we cannot leave anything to our children but poverty and slavery. Therefore, prepare yourselves! In all quietness, prepare yourselves for the Revolution!

As May Day drew near, the centre of strife became the McCormick Harvester Works, which had locked out its men and hired blacklegs, with 300 Pinkerton gunmen to protect them. Meetings were held regularly outside the works, and as regularly the police broke them up. On 3 May the police opened fire on the crowd and killed several men. The next day a protest meeting was called in Haymarket Square. The rain began to fall and the crowd was breaking up peaceably when 200 police marched into the square. They had just begun to break up the meeting when a bomb was thrown from a side-alley. The police started to shoot into the crowd, some of the workers shot back, the police shot at each other in the confusion, and when it was all ended some seven policemen were mortally wounded, mostly by the explosion, and probably three times as many demonstrators were killed, though the exact number has never been published.

A great round-up of anarchists followed immediately, and eight of the local leaders, including Parsons, editor of *Alarm*, and Spies, editor of *Die Arbeiter Zeitung*, were tried for murder. There was no attempt to prove that any of the men had thrown the bomb. The prosecution concentrated on exposing their revolutionary beliefs and their violent statements of which there was no lack, and on the strength of its case seven were condemned to death. Four were actually hanged. The survivors were released a few years later when Governor Altgeld ordered an inquiry into the case and found no evidence that showed any of the accused men to have been involved in the bombing. A judicial murder of the four hanged men had in fact taken place.

But the recognition of the injustice the Chicago anarchists suffered, which made them into classic martyrs of the labour movement, has tended to obscure one point. No one, as I have said, has ever known who threw the Haymarket bomb. It may have been an *agent provocateur*. It may just as easily have been some unknown anarchist, as Frank Harris suggested in *The Bomb*, the novel he wrote about the incident. But it would never have been thrown, and Parsons and Spies and their comrades would not have been hanged, if it had not been for the crescendo of exhortations to violence that had poured from the Chicago anarchist papers and from Most's *Die Freiheit* during the critical years between 1883 and 1886.

The Chicago incident was the beginning of the popular American prejudice against anarchism of any type. In later years anarchists in the United States indulged in very little violence, but unfortunately two of the few incidents in which they were involved became so notorious that they vastly increased the general and sweeping unpopularity of anarchism. In 1892 the Russian Alexander Berkman attempted unsuccessfully to shoot the financier Henry Clay Frick in revenge for the killing of strikers by Pinkerton men during the Homestead steel strike. And in 1901 a Polish youth, Leon Czolgosz, shot and killed President McKinley. Czolgosz still remains, after sixty years, a rather enigmatic figure. He claimed at his trial to be an anarchist, and bore himself with the same stoicism as Ravachol and Henry. But he belonged to no anarchist group and had only recently been denounced as a spy by a libertarian paper, *Free Society*, in Chicago. He was most probably a neurotic who had brooded solitarily over the world's injustice and had decided independently to perform a symbolic act by killing the relatively inoffensive McKinley, who seemed to him a personification of the system he hated. It is certain that the rather frantic police efforts to implicate anarchist groups and individual anarchist celebrities like Emma Goldman were completely unsuccessful.

However, in the eyes of Theodore Roosevelt, who followed McKinley in the presidency, Czolgosz became the typical anarchist, and the incident led to the abandonment in 1903 of the good American tradition of asylum for political refugees, no matter what their opinions; in that year the law was passed which banned the entry of alien anarchists into the United States.

The anarchist movement within the country was inevitably affected by this series of sensational and tragic events. The Haymarket affair ended the brief period in which anarchism could command even a limited mass following. The Black International disintegrated, and most of its journals disappeared. The native American workers held more aloof than ever before, and from 1887 anarchism became principally a movement of immigrants and the children of immigrants. Even the Germans fell away, and it was only with great difficulty that Most kept alive *Die Freiheit*, which vanished after his death in 1906. It was mainly among the Russian refugees from Tsarist persecution that anarchism survived. Except for the Union of Russian Workers, with its 10,000 members, and a large federation of Jewish groups, it became a movement of small and relatively isolated circles. A few dynamic personalities, like the Russians Emma Goldman and

Alexander Berkman, both of whom reached America just after the Chicago tragedy, and the Italian Carlo Tresca, kept anarchist doctrines in the public eye, and it was mostly these outstanding individuals who produced its best periodicals—such as Emma Goldman's *Mother Earth*, which ran from 1906 to 1917, and Berkman's *Blast*, which had a brief but lively existence from 1916 to 1917. Berkman contributed a minor classic to libertarian literature, *The ABC of Anarchism*. Emma Goldman, with her emotional oratory, her enormous courage, and her generous advocacy of unpopular causes, really belongs in a frame larger than the anarchist movement alone can give her, for, Russian though she was by birth, she represented in a very broad sense the best traditions of American radicalism. She faced many a hostile crowd for the sake of free speech, she went to prison for her advocacy of birth control, and she helped to introduce Ibsen and his contemporaries to the American public.

During this period many individual anarchists were active in organizing Jews and Italian immigrant workers into unions and in leading strikes, but no true anarcho-syndicalist movement appeared, though in 1912 the future communist leader, William Z. Foster, founded the abortive Syndicalist League of North America under the influence of the French CGT. After 1905 the anarchists who were interested in labour organization tended to join the Industrial Workers of the World, which was to some extent influenced by French syndicalism. However, they formed only one of a number of groups in that chaotic organization, and they never controlled it. In fact the IWW, which drew so much of its vigour and its methods from the hard traditions of the American frontier, was at most a parallel movement to anarchism. It contained too many Marxist elements ever to be truly libertarian, and its central idea of the One Big Union was fundamentally opposed to the anarchists' passionately held ideals of localism and decentralization.

The First World War, the Russian Revolution, and the anti-radical repression which reached its high point in the Palmer raids of 1919, all took their toll of what remained of anarchism in America. The No Conscription League which Emma Goldman and Berkman started during the war years was suppressed in 1917 and many of its members were imprisoned. The February Revolution of the same year was the signal for thousands of anarchists to return to Russia, and in 1919 there began a series of deportations in which hundreds of active anarchists, particularly from East Europe and Italy, were sent back to their own countries; they included Emma Goldman and Alexander Berkman. Finally there was the advent of communism, which in the United States as in other countries attracted many of the younger anarchists and syndicalists into its ranks.

What remained of American anarchism during the decades between the wars entered into the condition common to sects that pass their age of militancy, lose the missionary urge, and settle down into self-contained inactivity. There were thousands of anarchists left in the country, as there still are, and anarchist papers like the Jewish *Freie Arbeter Shtimme* and the Italian *L'Adunata die refratteri* continued to appear. But it was the communists who in the Depression years took the kind of initiative that in the past the anarchists and the IWW would have taken with a rather different intent. The anarchist groups became largely social and educational circles for the ageing faithful, and no new and vibrant personalities arose to take the place of Goldman and Berkman, deported out of harm's way, or Benjamin Tucker, self-exiled in Europe's last absolute principality.

Yet even in its period of decline between the wars American anarchism produced a tragedy that stirred the world to anger and admiration; I refer, of course, to the case of Sacco and Vanzetti. The condemnation to death of these amiable idealists on scantily supported charges of banditry, and the seven years of agony that followed before they were finally electrocuted, in defiance of worldwide protests, by the State of Massachusetts in 1927, have become part of American and even international history, described so often that there is no need to retell them here. So has the dignity with which Sacco and Vanzetti endured the long cruelty of legal process, and so also has Vanzetti's statement on hearing the sentence of death, that statement which echoed in the hearts and consciences of an American generation and which seems even now to distil in essence the faith that for so many men has made anarchism more than a political doctrine.

> If it had not been for this, I might have lived out my life, talking at street corners to scorning men. I might have died, unmarked, unknown, a failure. Now we are not a failure. This is our career and our triumph. Never in our full life can we do such a work for tolerance, for justice, for man's understanding of man, as we now do by an accident. Our words—our lives—our pains—nothing! The taking of our lives—lives of a good shoemaker and a poor fish-peddler—all! The last moment belongs to us—that agony is our triumph!

As in Britain, anarchism in the United States began to revive during the 1940s, largely as a result of resistance to the war. While the veteran Jewish and Italian groups continued, publishing their journals in their own languages, the new recruits consisted largely of younger intellectuals, including writers and artists; many of them were led to anarchism by the fact that they were already resisting the state as conscientious objectors to military service.

New York and its vicinity and the Pacific Coast were the principal areas of this renaissance. In New York itself David Wieck and a group of his associates, including Paul Goodman, brought out *Why*, which later became *Resistance*, while in upstate New York Holley Cantine and Dachine Rainer published an anarchist review entitled *Retort*, which attempted with some success to unite the two worlds of anarchist theory and literary creation. The *Catholic Worker* group, led by Dorothy Day, veered at the same time towards a Christian anarchism, most notably represented by Ammon Hennacy, who proclaimed himself the 'one-man revolution', and by his highly publicized resistance to the tax authorities gave a new turn to Gandhi's belief that a single person acting resolutely can awaken thousands. One notable new adherent was Dwight Macdonald, the former editor of *Partisan Review*, who in 1944 founded *Politics* as a journal of philosophic anarchism and pacifism and attracted some remarkable contributors, including George Orwell, Ignazio Silone, and Simone Weil. Macdonald borrowed a title from Kropotkin when he published his radical essays in 1957 as *Memoirs of a Revolutionist.*

In California the main centre of activity was San Francisco, though a secondary focus was the camp for conscientious objectors at Waldport in Oregon, where a number of young poets brought together by circumstances—the most notable among them was William Everson—published at least two magazines with libertarian inclinations and established contact with like-minded literati in San Francisco. San Francisco provided a fruitful soil for such activities, since there was a tradition of working-class radicalism deriving from the IWW; many Italian anarchists had found their way there to cultivate vineyards and orchards, and a strong literary movement had arisen under the leadership of the poet Kenneth Rexroth, himself a longtime anarchist. The San Francisco Anarchist Circle, which Rexroth founded in the early 1940s, was a heterogeneous group in which veteran Italian and Jewish anarchists would mingle and sometimes clash with young intellectuals. Among the poets linked with the Circle and its magazine, *The Ark*, were Kenneth Patchen, Robert Duncan, and Philip Lamantia, and it was certainly one of the main sources of the so-called beat movement, whose writers were among the more vocal spokesmen for the counter-culture of the 1960s.

During the 1960s anarchism was among a number of influences on the student radicalism of the 1960s, and Paul Goodman, hitherto a comparatively unknown writer, gained a certain national celebrity as one of its spokesmen. I shall discuss Paul Goodman's ideas and the way they helped to change the course of anarchist thought in the Epilogue to this volume. But before I leave the matter of literary influences a word must be said of another writer then resident in California.

Undoubtedly one of the factors that made anarchism popular among the young—and not merely among students—was its opposition to the increasingly technological cultures of Western Europe, North America, Japan, and Russia. In this case one is inclined to forget—because the orthodox anarchists never accepted him—that the principal mediating figure was Aldous Huxley, whose experimentation with psychedelic drugs, whose pacifism and early recognition of the perils of population explosion, of ecological destruction, and psychological manipulation, all combined in a vision that anticipated many elements of the counter-culture of the 1960s and the early 1970s. In *Brave New World* during the 1930s Huxley had already presented the first warning vision of the kind of mindless materialistic existence a society dominated by technological centralization might produce. In his Foreword to the 1946 edition of that novel, Huxley concluded that only by radical decentralization and simplification in economic terms, and by a politics that was 'Kropotkinesque and cooperative', could the peril implicit in modern social trends be avoided. In later writings like *Ends and Means, Brave New World Revisited,* and his novel *After Many a Summer,* Huxley explicitly accepted the validity of the anarchist critique of existing society, and his last novel, *Island,* was the nearest any writer approached to an anarchist Utopia since William Morris wrote *News from Nowhere.*

In the great kaleidoscope of New Radical trends and organizations that emerged in the United States during the counter-cultural 1960s, there is no doubt that anarchism played an important role, though it is not always easy to establish its presence, since explicit statements of anarchistic loyalties were rare and the groups of avowed anarchists remained few and scattered. Yet the influence was strongly there. In an article—'Anarchism Revisited'—which I contributed to *Commentary* in 1968, I remarked:

In practice many observers regard anarchism as an important and central element in the pluralistic spectrum of New Radical thought. Perhaps the best study of the movement from the inside is Jack Newfield's *A Prophetic Minority* (1966), and Newfield has no hesitation at all in placing anarchism, with pacifism and socialism, as one of the three basic influences on the New Left. Sometimes the influence becomes a long but concentrated beam stretching across centuries; that of seventeenth-century Winstanley, for example, on the modern Diggers. In general, however, it is hard to find North American New Radicals who have read an anarchist classic as recent as Kropotkin's *Mutual Aid* or *Memoirs of a Revolutionist*, though many have read that surviving but untypical Old Anarchist, Paul Goodman. In general, the basic ideas of anarchism, like those of traditional socialism and pacifism, have come down to the New Radicals (that generation of voluntary semi-literates) not through direct reading, but in a kind of mental nutrient broth of remnants of the old ideologies which pervade the air of certain settings in New York, the Bay Area, Los Angeles, Vancouver, and Montreal. But the key tenets that have been on anarchist lips for generations are there: the rejection of the state, and abandonment of the comfortable in favour of the good life, direct action, decentralization, the primacy of the functional group, participation.

Also present, though I underestimated them at the time, were vestiges of Bakuninist insurrectionism, which towards the end of the decade, at the very time when the counter-culture was beginning to disintegrate, came to the fore as the Yippies under Abbie Hoffman and Jerry Rubin resorted to street violence and the Weathermen to bombings and burnings. However, in this direction the signals of the New Radical movement in the 1960s were perhaps most confusing, since those who resorted to Bakuninist tactics were often attracted at the same time to Leninist notions of disciplined conspiracy, with their authoritarian implications, as happened also in the case of the left-wing terrorist groups in Italy and Germany.

In the 1980s anarchism in the United States is in a phase of temporary retreat so far as activity is concerned, though the continued flow of books about anarchist personalities and events of the past shows that a considerable public interest in the doctrine and the people who propagated it remains. Despite the conservatism that seems to be temporarily enthroned in Washington and to have the support of a vast fundamentalist following, the basic ideas of anarchism—linked as they are with current trends in the directions of environmental responsibility, of civil liberties, and of the rights of minorities—are considered more seriously and less fearfully than at any time since the 1880s. It is an example of the contradictions of American society that anarchists from abroad are still excluded from the United States under the immigration laws, while their writings and ideas circulate freely under the protection of the First Amendment.

15. Epilogue

THE narrative I have just completed leaves two questions in one's mind. Why did classic anarchism, the historical movement created by Bakunin and his associates a century and a quarter ago, fail in the early twentieth century? And why and how did the anarchist idea, which is a much wider thing, survive it and re-emerge in new forms in the later twentieth century?

To answer the first question, I suggest, we must begin with a contradiction between self-image and reality. The anarchists have always regarded themselves as revolutionaries, and so they are in theory. In practice, however, organized anarchism in the nineteenth and twentieth centuries was really a movement of rebellion rather than a movement or revolution. It was a protest, a dedicated resistance to the worldwide trend since the middle of the eighteenth century towards economic and political centralization, with all it implies in terms of the replacement of personal values by collective values, of the subordination of the individual to the state. The real social revolution of the modern age has in fact been this process of centralization, towards which every development of scientific and technological progress has contributed, which has welded nations out of regions and which today is creating a single world where the fundamental differences between regions and peoples and classes are being levelled into a characterless homogeneity.

The anarchists protested against this negative revolution in the name of human dignity and individuality, and their protest was necessary; it was perhaps their greatest achievement. But it placed them in a line of opposition to the dominant trend in modern history. They stood outside to criticize, and their criticism was given power and edge by their disappointed idealism. They defied the materialism of modern society, its regimentation, its drive towards conformity, and, while they looked towards an idyllic future, they also stood for the better aspects of a dying past. This residual conservatism is a feature of all forms of anarchism, both old and new.

Their ruthless criticism of the present was always the great strength of the classic anarchists. It was their urges towards the past and the future that weakened them as a movement. For they drew their support mainly from those social classes that were out of tune with the dominant historical trend and were also steadily declining in influence and in numbers. We have seen already how many of their leaders were conscience-stricken gentlemen and clergymen revolting against their churches in the name of a literal Christianity. We have seen how much of the rank-and-file of the movement was made up of artisans, of poor and primitive peasants, of those shiftless, rebellious sections of the lower classes whom Shaw hailed as 'the undeserving poor' and whom Marx dismissed as the *Lumpenproletariat*. In one of its aspects, anarchism became the great uprising of the dispossessed, of all those who were thrust aside by the Juggernaut of nineteenth-century material progress. Each of these classes stood, in its own way, for independence and individuality, but even in the 1860s, when they first began to rally to the black banners of anarchism, they were already being superseded as a result of profound changes in the structure of society, in the distribution of wealth, and in the methods of production.

In the same way, the countries and regions where anarchism was strongest were those in which industry was least developed and in which the poor were poorest. As progress engulfed the original fatherlands of anarchism, as the factory workers replaced the handicraftsmen, as the aristocrats became detached from the land and absorbed into the new plutocracy, anarchism began to lose the original sources of its support.

Meanwhile, it failed to win over the classes which were most closely involved in the trend towards centralization and uniformity. In the classic era, down to 1939, bureaucrats and businessmen, professionals and shopkeepers and clerks provided few recruits to the anarchist cause, in spite of Marx's dismissal of it as a *petit-bourgeois* phenomenon. Even among the industrial workers, the anarchists won only temporary and limited victories. It is true that the factory workers of Barcelona remained under anarchist leadership until the end of the Spanish Civil War, but they were largely, by origin, Andalusian peasants driven from the land by their extreme poverty. It is true also that anarcho-syndicalism for a long period dominated the French trade unions and played an important role in the Dutch and Italian labour movements. But these were equivocal triumphs, since syndicalism in fact represented a compromise with the trend towards centralization. It sought, as Malatesta suggested, to imitate too closely the political and industrial forms of the time, to oppose the massive organizations of the state and industry by massive organizations of the workers, which eventually moved away from anarchism to become part of the centralist order they had originally opposed. The French CGT passed from anarchist control into the hands of reformists like Jouhaux and at last into those of the communists. Even the CNT, always tempted by reformism, eventually sent its leaders into the Spanish coalition government during the Civil War, and there seems little doubt that if the Republic had survived it would have moved in the same direction as the French CGT; its alliance with the socialist UGT in 1938 was a sign of the direction in which it was moving. Thus, in the long run, the anarchist movement suffered an almost complete defeat in its attempts to win over the industrial workers. In general, its mass followings, when they appeared, consisted of people in desperate circumstances and they tended to dissolve quickly when those circumstances changed and the lives of those to whom such an extreme doctrine appealed showed some improvement; the failure of the CNT, once an organization running to well over a million members, to re-emerge as a mass movement in Spain during the 1970s is a good example of what happens to anarchist movements of the old kind when standards of living change.

The classic anarchist movement also suffered from the weakness of its own revolutionary tactics. Anarchist action, which had the virtue of spontaneity, also had the weakness of an almost complete lack of coordination. In the minds of the more conspiratorial anarchists there doubtless existed programmes for the great strategy that would finally encompass the millennial social revolution. But the history of anarchist rebellion shows only a bewildering confusion of small insurrections, individual acts of violence, and strikes which sometimes served to keep society in a state of tension, but which had no lasting results. The typical anarchist rebellions were local risings like those of Benevento, Saragossa, and Lyons, easily defeated because of their isolation and leading by their failure to the discrediting of the anarchist cause in the eyes of the populace in general. The propaganda of the deed turned out all too often to be negative propaganda.

It is true that in Spain something like a revolutionary situation did exist after the anarchists and their allies of the CNT had defeated the uprising of the generals in Catalonia and Levante at the beginning of the Spanish Civil War. But the event was thrust upon the anarchists, not created by them, and their lack of organizational coherence prevented them from retaining the advantages they had gained; within a few months the revolution had slipped from their hands. Everywhere, in fact, the anarchists during the classic period showed themselves to be highly individualistic amateur rebels, and in this role they were sometimes successful, but on no occasion did they demonstrate any capacity for the sustained effort that wins and consolidates a revolution.

Linked to the failure of the anarchists as revolutionary actionists was the weakness of their practical proposals for the society that would follow their hypothetical revolution. There was much honesty in their refusal to make elaborate blueprints of the new world they hoped to create, but their disinclination to attempt specific proposals led to their producing a vague and vapid vision of an idyllic society where the instinct of mutual aid would enable men to create a variety of cooperative relationships unimaginable in the enslaved present. Primitive and evangelically-minded people like the Andalusian peasants could accept this vision and give it life by their own millenarian longings for the earthly Kingdom of God where all men would live in simple brotherhood. Intellectuals and artists could also accept it as a kind of working myth around which their own fantasies and speculations might crystallize. But ordinary working- and middle-class people, influenced by nineteenth-century factualism, rejected the anarchist vision because, unlike the prophetic imaginings of H.G. Wells, it lacked the reassuring concreteness and precision they desired.

Another disturbing feature of the anarchist future was that its achievement was indefinitely postponed until the millennial day of reckoning; it was a kind of revolutionary pie-in-the-sky, and one was expected to fast until mealtime. For the anarchists who followed Bakunin and Kropotkin were political and social absolutists, and they displayed an infinite and consistent contempt for piecemeal reform or for the kind of improvements in working conditions which trade unions sought and benevolent or sensible employers offered. They believed that all such gains must be temporary and illusory, and that only in the anarchist millennium would the poor really better themselves. Many of the poor thought otherwise and followed the reformists. How right they were—and how wrong the anarchists—in purely material terms has been shown by the radical change in the character of modern capitalism, which has led to a remarkable broadening in the standard of living and the scope of leisure in the Western world, and also to the appearance of the welfare state, with its insidious dulling of the edge of resentment and its weakening of the forces of natural social cooperation.

Thus the historic anarchist movement failed to produce an alternative to the nation-state or to the capitalist economy that lastingly convinced any large section of the world's population. It also failed in the long run to compete effectively with the other radical movements that were its historical contemporaries: the varieties of Marxism on the Left and the varieties of Fascism on the Right.

Initially, during the 1870s and the early 1880s, the anarchists won considerable gains over the Marxists in the Latin countries, but after that time, except in Spain, they were in steady retreat before the stronger political parties and unions created first by the social democrats and then by the communists. The organization of the Marxists was more unified, efficient, and reliable, their promises were more concrete and immediate; they were willing to fight for reformist goals, and they offered in their dogma of the dictatorship of the proletariat that illusion of wielding power without accepting responsibility which had earlier seduced the workers into seeking in universal suffrage a universal panacea. To all these Marxist advantages was finally added the success of the Bolshevik revolution, which put the anarchists, who had succeeded in no revolution, at an ultimate disadvantage; the glamour of Russia lasted long enough to draw away from anarchism those very radical elements among the youth of countries like France and Italy from which its most devoted militants had once been drawn.

As for fascism and Nazism, those crude and primitive manifestations of the centralist urge that marks our age, the anarchist movement showed itself powerless to combat them effectively in the countries that they dominated and invaded, though individual anarchists often asserted themselves with self-sacrificing heroism. Only in Spain, against Franco's hybrid of militarism and fascism, did organized anarchism put up a determined resistance, and even there, despite its enormous following, it collapsed with dramatic suddenness on the day General Yagüe and his column marched into Barcelona without a single factory going on strike or a single barricade going up in the streets. This was the last, greatest defeat of the historic anarchist movement, the movement founded by Bakunin within the ranks of the International three-quarters of a century before. On that day it ceased to exist as a living cause. There remained only anarchists, scattered individually and in small groups over the world, and the anarchist idea.

Lost causes may be the best causes—they usually are—but once lost they are never won again, and it was only as a kind of fossil faith, kept by Italian grocers and vine-growers in the United States and ageing Spanish refugees in Languedoc and Mexico, that the ghost of the historic anarchist movement lingered on for a couple of decades after 1939. And that is probably all to the good. For movements are like men, and they should be allowed to die peacefully so that room can be made for the new movements that will take their place and perhaps learn from both their virtues and their errors.

For now we must ask whether the record was so entirely negative as I may seem to have suggested? Were there not positive aspects of historic anarchism from which we can still learn useful lessons? In fact, the anarchist movement did achieve limited and local successes when it was content to leave the future to itself and to attempt the application of libertarian ideas to immediate and concrete tasks. The taking over and the running of factories and public services in Barcelona, the effective creation of well-working peasant collectives in Spain and the Makhnoist Ukraine, the movements for adult and juvenile education in Spain before the Civil War and anarchist involvement in free school experiments in Britain, France, and other countries, the mutual aid institutions created by Jewish anarchists in Britain and the United States; these may have been modest achievements in comparison with the great revolutionary aims of the anarchist movement in its more optimistic periods, and they certainly did not prove that a complete anarchist society such as Kropotkin, for example, envisaged could come into existence or would work if it did. But they did show that in certain circumstances voluntary methods of organizing economic and industrial relations may be more practical than authoritarian methods, and that anarchism had a concrete aspect which could offer an immediate alternative to the totalitarian way.

But there is another positive factor to be found in any anarchist movement whether of the past or of the present, and that is its role as a touchstone, posing in its logical extremity and purity an attitude that is necessary for the survival of a free and humanist society. To acknowledge the existence and the overbearing force of the movement towards universal centralization that still grips the world is not to accept it. If human values are to survive, a counter-ideal must be posed to the totalitarian ideal of a homogeneous world, and that counter-ideal exists precisely in the vision of pure liberty that has inspired the anarchist and near-anarchist writers at least from Winstanley in the seventeenth century down to the present. Obviously it is not immediately realizable, and, since it is an ideal, it may never be realized. But the very presence of such a concept of pure liberty can help us to judge our condition and see our aims; it can help us to safeguard what liberties we still retain against the further encroachments of the centralizing state; it can help us to conserve and even enlarge those areas in which personal values still operate; it can help in the urgent task of mere survival, of living out the critical decades ahead until the world trend towards centralization loses its impetus like all historical movements (including Bakunin's anarchism), and the moral forces that depend on individual choice and judgement can reassert themselves in the midst of its corruption.

Implicit in what I have said is a considerable modification of the revolutionary purist attitude of many classic anarchists. For when we turn to history we realize that the essential features of the anarchist idea are not merely older than the historical movement. They have also spread far beyond its boundaries, in the sense of both giving and receiving. Godwin, Tolstoy, Stirner, Thoreau: none of them accepted the label of anarchist. Their contributions came from outside the historic movement, and in some respects, notably violence in the case of Godwin and Tolstoy, they were even opposed to the arguments of activists like Bakunin and Malatesta. On the other hand, the influence of the basic libertarian and decentralist features of anarchist doctrine have been found not only in the organized anarchist groups, but also in movements like Russian and American populism, Spanish federalism, and Mexican radical agrarianism. It provided Gandhi and his associates in the Indian National Congress with the techniques of non-cooperative resistance that won the great conflict against the British overlords, and with the liberation of India started the collapse of empires all over the world. And it helped to inspire some movements of our own period that have presented encouraging alternatives to the general centralist trend, such as the Israeli kibbutzim, the village community movement in India, and even the Credit Unions of North America which are the remote descendants of Proudhon's People's Bank.

I have drawn out these often neglected features of historic anarchism—its recognition of the strong mutualist elements that survive in human societies despite governments, its occasional brilliant improvisation of piecemeal solutions to immediate problems, its often reluctant openness to ideas and impulses that come from outside, and its tendency often unknowingly to contribute vital ideas to movements beyond its own arbitrarily conceived bounds—since I believe they represent a current of pragmatic activism that has continued without much regard for the purity of dogma that has continued among real if not named anarchists from Winstanley in the seventeenth-century English Commonwealth down to the young rebels who, from the 1960s onward, began to act like anarchists—even if they did not assume the label—because they were extracting from experience the same truths as earlier anarchists had derived from reflecting on their own lives and worlds.

What we have seen in the last quarter of a century on an almost worldwide scale has not been the revival of the historic anarchist movement, with its martyrology and its passwords all complete. The significant contemporary phenomenon has been something quite different, an autonomous revival of the anarchist idea, whose extraordinary power of spontaneous renewal, as I remark in the Prologue to this book, is due to its inability to establish lasting dogmas, to its variability, and hence to its adaptability.

Because anarchism is in its essence an anti-dogmatic and unstructured cluster of related attitudes which does not depend for its existence on any enduring organization, it can flourish when circumstances are favourable and then, like a desert plant, lie dormant for seasons and even for years, waiting for the rains that will make it burgeon. Unlike an ordinary political faith, in which the party becomes the vehicle of the dogma, it does not need a movement to carry it forward; many of its important teachers have been solitary men, dedicated individuals like Godwin and Stirner, and even Proudhon, who refused to countenance the suggestion that he had invented a 'system' or that a party might be built up around his teachings. What happened during the recent revival of anarchism was an explosion of ideas which carried the essential libertarian doctrines, and the methods associated with them, far beyond the remnants of the old anarchist organizations, creating new types of movements, new modes of radical action, but reproducing with a surprising degree of faith—even among young people who hardly know what the word 'anarchism' means—the essential ideas on the desirable reshaping of society that have been taught by the seminal thinkers of the libertarian tradition.

The upsurge of the anarchist idea in fact took place mainly outside the groups that after 1939 had tenuously carried on the tradition stemming from Bakunin and Malatesta. The crucial decade was the 1960s. The 1950s, the decade of cautious careerist youth, had been—as we have seen—a period of hibernation for anarchist ideas. Anarchism perhaps contributed a little to the literary and artistic life of the times; its influence was certainly evident among the New Apocalyptics and New Romantics in Britain and the 'beat' poets and novelists of the United States, while surrealism revived on the European continent with clearly anarchistic orientations. But not until the end of the 1950s did a renewed interest in the doctrine as a whole begin to emerge. The idea then seemed suddenly to be in the air again. It developed in two ways.

First, there was a scholarly interest. Classic anarchism had by the beginning of the 1960s receded far enough into the past to make it material for historians, and from early in the 1950s, in France, in Britain, in the United States, biographies of the leading anarchist thinkers—Kropotkin and Godwin, Proudhon and Bakunin—had begun to appear, not merely recounting their often exemplary lives, but re-establishing anarchism as a tradition of political thought to be studied and discussed on the same level as Marxism and other socialist teachings. Next were published the first objective histories of the tradition, seeking neither to adulate nor to condemn. The first appeared in France: the uncompleted *Histoire de l'anarchie* by Alain Sergent and Claude Harmel in 1949 and Jean Maitron's definitive

Histoire du mouvement anarchiste en France in 1955, followed by Daniel Guérin's partisan and restrictive but lively account, *L'Anarchisme*, in 1965. Of works in English, the present book (*Anarchism*) first appeared in the United States in 1962 (a year before the British edition) and James Joll's *The Anarchists* appeared in 1964. A number of anthologies during the 1960s and the 1970s also brought back to a modern public not only the more celebrated anarchist texts, but also many that were forgotten, because they had long been out of print, and so an introductory selection of anarchist ideas became available even before the classic works were reprinted, as inevitably happened, so that new and scholarly edited versions of Godwin and Kropotkin, Proudhon and Bakunin began to come off the press; of Godwin's *Political Justice*, unreprinted for almost a century, three new editions came out in rapid succession. The best of the anthologies were *The Anarchists*, edited by Irving Horowitz (1964), *Patterns of Anarchy*, edited by Leonard Krimerman and Lewis Perry (1966), *The Essential Works of Anarchism*, edited by Marshall Shatz (1971), and *The Anarchist Reader*, edited by George Woodcock (1977).

Since that time, scholarly endeavour has rummaged far in the past of anarchism. Lesser but interesting figures like Gustav Landauer and Élisée Reclus, Paul Brousse and Voltairine de Cleyre have been brought into the light, and so many books have been written on Emma Goldman and Alexander Berkman since Richard Drinnon's *Rebel in Paradise* appeared in 1961 that one can begin to talk of a romantic cult. Histories of national movements have also appeared, like Paul Avrich's *The Anarchists in the Russian Revolution* (1973) and John Quail's *The Slow-Burning Fuse: The Lost History of the British Anarchists* (1975), and dramatic incidents in anarchist history, like the Haymarket Tragedy and the anarchist collectives in Spain, have become the subjects of detailed study. Anarchism has become, as is evident, a favoured hunting-ground of academic and popular historians alike, but it has by no means become merely their preserve, for their endeavours have not only given it respectability as a philosophy and an influential movement during an important period of European and North American history. They have also—as I record with pleasure when I remember how little had been written in a serious vein on anarchism even by the 1940s and how few texts were then in print—made available a vast amount of knowledge and original material for those who are nowadays inclined to study or perhaps to embrace anarchist beliefs.

As the revised and updated historical chapters of this book will have shown, anarchism itself re-emerged parallel to this activity among scholars as a rapidly spreading faith among young people, and especially among intellectuals and students, in many European and American countries. Since I have already outlined what happened in these areas in specific terms, it seems appropriate at this time to move on to more general questions relating to the anarchist renaissance of the 1960s and onward. Who were the young people who made up the revived movement? Where did they come from? What was it in anarchism that appealed especially to them?

To begin, the social background of the new anarchists is markedly different from that of the old anarchists in their heyday. They are no longer recruited from the poorest classes, the illiterate peasants of Andalusia and the Ukraine, the hard-run French and Lombard factory workers of the turn of the century, the marble-cutters of Carrara, the dock-workers of Ancona and Genoa, the makers of watchcases in the Jura. Nor are they led by a mixed élite of renegade aristocrats, unfrocked clergymen and working-class autodidactic intellectuals, with impressionist painters and symbolist poets skirmishing on their flanks. Now the conscience-stricken noblemen and the desperate peasants have been replaced by the conscience-stricken middle class, whose desperation, real as it may be, is usually not material, and these, with a vastly increased bohemian contingent, have almost completely displaced the old anarchist constituency of the peasants and the poor.

During the 1960s the British anarchist magazine *Freedom* conducted an enlightening survey of its readers. Out of 457 who replied to the questionnaire, forty were engaged in industry, but six of these were managers. Twenty-three worked on the land, but of these eight ran their own farms and one was an estate manager. Nineteen worked in communications and transport. And that—15 per cent when one had counted out the managers and owners—was about the total of those who belonged to the traditional groupings of workers and peasants. On the other hand, there were fifty-two teachers, thirty students, twenty architects, sixteen journalists and writers, twenty-three involved in the arts and entertainments, twelve in the book trade, twenty-five in scientific research and twenty-five in health and welfare; forty, finally, in various administrative and clerical jobs. The preponderance of white-collar or at least non-manual workers was striking. So was the predominance of youth. Anarchists in the 1940s had included a high proportion of the elderly, nostalgic moss-backed veterans, but of this batch in the 1960s, 65 per cent were under forty, and I suspect that if such a count were taken of anarchists in the 1980s it would show no less a proportion and probably a higher one. Even more significant was the stronger class shift among the young. Forty-five per cent of those over sixty were working-class, as against 23 per cent of those in their thirties and 10 per cent of those in their twenties. The new anarchists in Britain—and this applied as much to the Kabouters in Holland and the New Radicals in the United States and the students who revolted in Paris in 1968—were creating a movement of dissident middle-class youth.

The new anarchists not only tended to come from different classes; they also came from different places. The historic anarchist movement was strongest in countries which, apart from France, were technologically and socially backward and where authority took on a reactionary and half-feudal form, like Spain and Italy and the Ukraine. The new anarchism, on the other hand, has made the greatest advances in technologically advanced countries where the state has assumed a bland welfare face and where its corrupting influence on daily life as it operates in association with multinational corporate capitalism is what offends the young, rather than its occasional overt expressions of brutality. My own country of Canada, benevolently over-governed and economically dominated by multinational corporations (largely American) is a fair example. When I first returned to the country in 1949 there was not a single anarchist group in operation, not a single anarchist sheet being published, and until the 1960s I did not discover more than a dozen unorganized individuals who even called themselves anarchists. Now, to judge from the circled As one sees on walls, there are fairly active sympathizers in all Canadian towns of any size. I am in touch with four groups who publish intermittent propaganda sheets, two in Toronto and two in Vancouver, while a theoretical quarterly that emerged out of the student revolt of the 1960s, *Our Generation*, continues as an anarchist journal in Montreal. In Montreal there is also a flourishing libertarian publishing house, Black Rose Books, while the strong academic presence in the Canadian anarchist movement is shown by the existence in that city of an Anarchos Institute with broad international connections. But scholarly interest is not the only aspect of anarchism in Canada. Five Vancouver militants, members of a group who called themselves Direct Action, are now serving prison sentences for varied acts of sabotage, including an explosion at a plant in Toronto that was making components for the Cruise missiles. This group was characteristically linked not only with the anti-war movement, but also with the environmentalists (it blew up a controversial power sub-station on Vancouver Island) and radical feminism (it fire-bombed video stores selling tapes showing violence towards women).

In considering why anarchism should have appealed to such different classes and in such different areas, and especially to the young, one cannot dismiss the possibility that even the failures of anarchism, splendid and comic as they have variously been, may have spoken in its favour. Anarchism can claim, almost alone among modern ideologies, the equivocal merit of never having been really tried out. Not having come to power, it was never discredited in power, and in this sense it presents an untarnished and pristine image, the image of an idea which, in practical terms, has had nothing but a future. Success has not sullied it, and with the young—especially in their mood of the 1960s—this was a unique and powerful advantage. 'Flowers for the rebels who failed,' the old anarchists used to sing. Their successors appropriated the flowers and pushed them into the barrels of guns.

Though its ideas were originally framed in situations totally different from those in which the youth of the later twentieth century have found themselves, anarchism—with its cult of the spontaneous—has always shown a strikingly protean fluidity in adapting its approach and methods to special historical circumstances. Winstanley in civil-war England concentrates on direct action to cultivate the wastelands; Godwin at the height of the Enlightenment interests himself in the spread of discussion groups; Proudhon works through the pioneer credit unions (his People's Banks); Bakunin's romantic insurrectionism is balanced by Kropotkin's scientific-sociological approach, from which arose some seminal insights on the relations between town and country, industry and agriculture; the tragically flamboyant gestures of the terrorists in the 1890s gave way to the syndicalists' myth of the regenerative general strike; the Andalusian peasants in the early months of the Spanish Civil War set up communes of idyllic and altruistic simplicity. The means were always fluid, adapting to changing social norms, but always keeping close to the ground, to the ideal of a deep-rooted society, and always keeping away from ordinary politics, away from power.

None of these specific phases of the anarchist past seems to matter greatly to the new anarchists. They have relatively little historical inclination, and what mainly concerns them about ideas is applicability to their own situation. Here anarchism certainly seems to have a great deal to give them.

Consider that situation. Since the 1960s, in varying numbers at difference times, they have been in revolt against a society dominated by material goals, by established power. They are facing—perhaps more realistically than most of their elders—the great revolution which automation has wreaked on our concepts of the dignity and necessity of toil; they see that the world which provides material security and increased leisure for many millions, leaves—even in North America and Europe—other millions in poverty and alienation, with unemployment as a permanent condition until we entirely change our concepts of arranging work. If they were Americans in the 1960s they saw the most condemned war in their country's history, that in Vietnam, being fought in their name and—for many—with their blood and suffering. Afterwards they lived protesting under the growing shadow of a nuclear war to end war and everything else. They have seen the traditional political parties concerned everywhere with despicable goals of power and material reward, yet they have also revolted, in Poland and Czechoslovakia and Hungary as much as in the West, against the hierarchic institutionalization of revolutionism by the Old Left. They have seen labour unions concerned almost entirely with money, and uninspired by the radical visions of a transformed society that once led the syndicalists and the Wobblies to their desperate struggles.

What the anarchist tradition had to give the radical young was perhaps, first of all, the vision of a society in which every relation would have moral rather than political characteristics. The anarchist believes in a moral urge in man powerful enough to survive the destruction of authority and still hold society together in the free and natural bonds of fraternity. Many events in the latter half of the present century—the civil-rights campaigns, the revolts in the black ghettos of the United States, the defiant behaviour of have-not countries towards their prosperous benefactors, the Solidarity movement in Poland, the great protests that continue against the folly of nuclear armaments—have shown that, even in a materialist society, non-materialist values will make an irrational but convincing clamour. The relations among men are moral in nature, and neither politics nor economics (*pace* Marx) can ever entirely embrace them. This, the anarchists have always insisted.

Within such a non-materialist purview they have always posed, in contradiction to social-democratic and orthodox unionist drives to bring the workers into line materially with the rich, the ideal of a dignified poverty. Paul Goodman wrote a great deal on this, but we should not forget those magnificently poetic passages of *La Guerre et la paix* in which Proudhon draws the distinction between pauperism and poverty. Pauperism, he contends, is destitution; poverty is the state in which a man gains from his work just enough for his needs, and this condition Proudhon praises in lyrical terms as the ideal human state, in which we are most free, in which—masters of our senses and our appetites—we are best able to spiritualize our needs. In material terms anarchists have never asked for more than the sufficiency that will allow men to be free; the collectives of the Spanish Civil War showed men willing to live in the most austere of conditions so that they might gain their freedom and the dignity of managing their affairs according to their own judgements.

The great anarchist thinkers laid a constant stress on the natural, the spontaneous, the unsystematic. For them individual judgement held primacy; dogmas impeded men's understanding of the quality of life. That life, they believed, should be as simple and as near to nature as possible. This urge towards the simple, natural way of life made men like Kropotkin urgently concerned over the alienation of men in modern cities and the destruction of the countryside, themes that were dear to the young radicals of the 1960s and their successors. The anarchists were also ever conscious of the danger of rule by experts. Bakunin was frankly hostile to scientists. Kropotkin, scientist by training, stressed the great role of the amateur in scientific development, and when it came to the organization of a trade or a village or a city quarter to fulfil its material needs, he believed that responsibility should lie with those nearest to the problem. People must learn to make their own decisions. This strong sense of the appropriateness of those directly concerned deciding on all matters affecting them alone became the basis of Proudhon's federalism. He saw society organized in functional groups, industrial and social in character, in which people would decide what should be done at their place of work or their place of living; above these primary levels, and dependent always upon them, would be constructed—in the most loosely federal manner possible—the few national and international institutions that might be necessary. At every level the people would participate as widely as possible, but at the lowest level, in workshops and living areas, participation would be complete.

It is easy to see how such views would appeal to the new radicals from the 1960s onward, with their concern for participatory democracy, communal and community organization at the grassroots level, and spontaneous movements of protest, and indeed to see how far these basic concepts of the counter-culture derived half-consciously from those of the anarchist past. But perhaps they way in which the anarchists have most interestingly anticipated the preoccupations of the aware young, and indeed of all concerned people today, is in their emphasis on what they firmly believed would be the death of the relation between man and his work as we have known it. As long ago as 1793, writing *Political Justice*, Godwin foresaw with great accuracy the age of automation and forced leisure which today seems upon us.

When we look at the complicated machines of human contrivance, various sorts of mills, of weaving engines, of steam engines, are we not astonished at the compendium of labour they produce? Who shall say where this species of improvement must stop? ...

With a daring that seemed more astonishing 190 years ago than it does today, Godwin ventured the prophecy that one day man might have to work no more than an average of half an hour a day. The rest he could devote to the cultivation of his nature. Kropotkin, writing almost a century later in *The Conquest of Bread*, was more cautious than his predecessor, merely making a suggestion whose fulfilment is now almost upon us in the Western world: the physical comfort of society might be assured, he ventured, if all men worked 'five hours a day from the age of twenty or twenty-five to forty-five or fifty'. But Kropotkin also realized what is becoming steadily more clear to us today, that the small amount of work necessary in the near future will be of far less concern than the long hours away from the factory and the office. We are faced with the problem of what happens—to borrow phraseology from that other old libertarian, William Morris—when Useless Toil is eliminated and we have to find Useful Work. Kropotkin believed optimistically that when the problems of excessive toil had been solved, men would adjust themselves, creatively.

Man is not a being whose exclusive purpose in life is eating, drinking, and providing a shelter for himself. As soon as his material needs are satisfied, other needs, which generally speaking may be described as of an artistic nature, will thrust themselves forward. These needs are of the greatest variety; they vary in each and every individual, and the more society is civilized, the more will individuality be developed, and the more desires be varied.

So Kropotkin wrote in 1892. I think the new anarchists today would see the problem in exactly the same terms, though I doubt if many would be as optimistic about an easy solution.

I still share many of the libertarian attitudes I have been describing as constant to the tradition, though my propagandist days have long been ended. But, as a historian, I am extremely interested in the phenomenon of a group of ideas, which only a decade ago seemed tied to the dying animal of a nineteenth-century working-class movement, but which today has taken on new company among the young and the middle class, and which seems to be giving both groups some at least of the answers they need to contemporary questions.

I am also interested in the absence of some of the elements that were part of classic anarchism. Despite the brief period of Yippie and Weatherman violence, it is long since we have heard much talk of barricades and revolutionary heroism, and while 'direct action' is a phrase continually on the lips of modern anarchists and other libertarians, it usually means something very near to Gandhian civil disobedience. Terroristic tactics have been left strictly in recent decades to extreme nationalist or Islamic groups or to the authoritarians of the Left. Anarchists have long recognized, I think, that to kill is the worst form of tyranny. In fact, the anarchists of the past were too much inclined, despite their fervent anti-Marxism, to accept the stereotypes of nineteenth-century left-wing thinking; the idea of the class struggle as a dominant and constructive force in society, the romantic cult of insurrectionism and terror, and even—though this they rarely admitted—a vision of proletarian dictatorship that lingered particularly among the anarcho-syndicalists who envisaged a society run by monolithic workers' unions. Those who openly or unwittingly advocate anarchistic ideas today have mostly shed these outdated and irrelevant concepts, together with much else of the ideological baggage of the Old Left.

As to the kind of society their efforts might lead to, the anarchists were never great Utopians; they liked to keep the future flexible and felt that elaborate plans laid burdens on generations that had not devised them. But there was nevertheless, as I have already noted, an unbending rigidity about one aspect of the old anarchist view of the future. It was a hard, no-compromise view; either the completely non-governmental society or nothing at all. Anything less was labelled reformist and duly condemned. The old anarchists never came within light years of attaining such a goal; hence the glorious record of unsuccess which is now so much to anarchism's advantage.

Today I doubt if anyone in the West seriously believes in the possibility of creating a uniform society of any kind, and I suspect the Russians too are fast abandoning such a hope, as the Chinese communists have already done. We no longer think terminally, thanks paradoxically to the threat of nuclear destruction. The future is open-ended, open-sided, and as far as we can see ahead we are likely to be involved in pluralistic social permutations that will embrace many philosophies, many institutional patterns, many nuances of approach.

The anarchists, in other words, will never create their own world; the free society of which they have dreamed is as pleasant and as remote a myth as the idyllic and aesthetic libertarian society that William Morris portrayed in *News from Nowhere*. The material and social complexity of the modern world obviously precludes such simplistic solutions. But this does not mean that the ideas which have emerged within the libertarian tradition are—outside the context of an anarchist Utopia—irrelevant in the real world. Taken individually they often have, in fact, a striking relevance to current problems. At the same time, they can only be put to use if those who respect the positive and constructive aspects of anarchist thought are willing to make a number of radical admissions.

Classic anarchists, for instance, believed that the destruction of an authoritarian society must precede the creation of its libertarian successor. But history in the past seventy years—ever since the Russian Revolution—had tended to show that the revolutionary destruction of an authoritarian society was likely to end in the creation of a more efficiently coercive society in its place. The liberation of a society is, in fact, an evolutionary and not an apocalyptic process, and can only be attained by resolutely seizing the opportunities for piecemeal changes. Such changes are to be attained not by rejecting all laws, since some restraints are manifestly necessary in any foreseeable future society, but by searching out those areas in which authoritarian and bureaucratic measures have manifestly failed or over-extended themselves, and by endeavouring to give practical expression and application to libertarian concepts of decentralization, voluntarism, and direct participation in decision-making. Such an admission implies that it is time for those who still find some virtue in basic libertarian teachings to recognize that anarchism has never been genuinely non-political, as its apologists used to argue; it has always represented politics carried out by other means. A recognition of this kind sets those who hold libertarian convictions free to seed the social changes they think necessary within an existing political framework, which, needless to say, is also changeable. And in fact, during the 1960s and the early 1970s, many essentially libertarian changes were effected. On a broad scale they extended sexual and artistic freedoms and improved the status of women and of many minorities. On a more local and regional scale, municipal, educational, and environmental advances were made through the initiative and participatory action of ordinary citizens. Even in the more reactionary atmosphere of the 1980s many of the gains of that radical period have not been lost; it is impossible, for example, to think of a retrogression that would put the status of women or gays or blacks back to what it was in the 1950s, or to think of *Lady Chatterley's Lover* again coming before the courts.

One has finally, I suggest, to accept a more existential view of human nature than the historic anarchists upheld. Their assumption that all men, if not naturally good, were naturally social, presupposed ideal circumstances. Given freedom and sufficiency and time to heal their psychic wounds, men would perhaps begin behaving with perfect sociability. But this, again, is a Utopian vision, unlikely to be realized in foreseeable circumstances. We live in a present where most men are probably better fitted for responsibility than the pessimists assume, and where a few are more chronically anti-social than the optimists wish to admit; this, impossible to define as it may be, is the only human nature we know from experience, which suggests that human beings are improvable but not—as Godwin seems once to have thought—literally perfectible. We must accept the probability of imperfection and limit anti-sociality where it impinges on the lives of others. Our aim should be to offer as much freedom as possible to men as they are, rather than dream of a hypothetical total freedom for men as they at present are not.

Classic anarchists, I am sure, would complain that what I have left is no longer anarchism. But it is an attempt to bring the constructive insights of anarchist thinkers, too often neglected in the past because of the tactics they were wedded to, into a context where they may at last wield some positive and beneficial influence on the shaping of our society. And it does come close to the arguments of the most originative of recent anarchist writers, such as Colin Ward, Paul Goodman, and Murray Bookchin.

In *Anarchy in Action* Colin Ward, who so brilliantly edited *Anarchy*, develops an effective criticism of pie-in-the-sky anarchism, of the argument that we have to wait for fundamental social changes before we can begin the liberation of society. Ward argues that this arises from an erroneous posing of an opposition between existing society and a libertarian future. In fact, as he shows by applying Kropotkin's arguments on mutual aid and Proudhon's on federalism to society as it exists, most of our institutions originated in voluntary cooperation and still operate most effectively when that principle is maintained. The factor of free cooperation in fact permeates every sphere of life, even though it is hidden under authoritarian structures which impoverish society by discouraging and destroying popular initiatives, by doing things for people instead of letting them do for themselves. 'Do-it-yourself' is in fact the essence of anarchist action, and the more people apply it on every level, in education, in the workplace, in the family, the more ineffective restrictive structures will become and the more dependence will be replaced by individual and collective self-reliance. Ward quotes what he calls 'a profound and simple' statement of Gustav Landauer, the German anarchist and friend of Martin Buber. 'The state is not something that can be destroyed by a revolution, but is a condition, a certain relationship between human beings, a mode of human behaviour; we destroy it by contracting other relationships, by behaving differently.' The more we build and strengthen an alternative society, the more the state is weakened. An example of what can be done, without elaborate organization, is the barter economy that has developed during recent years in communist as well as capitalist countries, depriving the state of taxes and other emoluments; put to more constructive uses, the same kind of popular initiative could radically extend the area of social action taken out of the hands of governments and put into the hands of the people acting cooperatively.

A similar attitude inspired the numerous books of Paul Goodman, including *Compulsory Miseducation* and *People or Personnel: Decentralizing and the Mixed System.* Goodman stressed the conservative element in true anarchism. Anarchism, he argued, was not essentially a destructive tradition. In fact it sought to conserve and extend those positive social factors which the state set out to destroy. Goodman adopted a pragmatic, piecemeal approach similar to that which Gandhi advocated when he adopted as his motto John Henry Newman's phrase, 'One step enough for me!' Goodman argued that it is in the nature of anarchism to resist change that reduces the naturalness of a society (which is a conservative act) and to promote change that makes society more free (which is a radical act). He recognized that people live largely by anarchist principles even in the most authoritarian society, and that small steps in the direction of simplification often immensely enlarge the scope of freedom. The process of anarchism, he said,

> is always a continual coping with the next situation, and vigilance to make sure that past freedoms are not lost and do not turn into the opposite, as free enterprise turned into wage-slavery and monopoly capitalism, or the independent judiciary turned into a monopoly of courts, cops and lawyers, or free education into School Systems.

Goodman's realistic assessment was that the best we can expect in any foreseeable future is a vigorously pluralist society.

Goodman tended to concentrate largely on education. Murray Bookchin, in *Post-Scarcity Anarchism* and *Towards an Ecological Society*, links the aims of anarchism to those of the environmentalists and the advocates of an alternative technology. Essentially, just as Colin Ward developed in a modern context Kropotkin's insights in *Mutual Aid*, so Bookchin, with scanty acknowledgement, develops those of *Fields, Factories and Workshops*, in which Kropotkin talks of industrial decentralization, the harmonization of urban and rural life and the integration of work and education. Bookchin's books are especially useful because in them he demonstrates how far technological advance since Kropotkin's day has made possible a society that is no longer dependent on centralized industry and can therefore begin on an economic level the transformations that will lead to a freer society.

Such books as these show that anarchists are now thinking in political and social matters alike more openly and more pluralistically than in the past. And this makes it possible for the ideas that emerged within the libertarian tradition to play a vital part in shaping not an anarchist Utopia, but a society that takes full advantage of the liberative possibilities of technological change. But this can only happen if, as Paul Goodman does so admirably, libertarians are willing to make their social criticisms and their proposals for reform relevant to our concrete and rapidly changing present and not to some idealized future. In this way anarchism can retain its force as an inspiring power, an activating vision, whose true importance was stated by Herbert Read, the anarchist poet, when he surveyed his life and its relevance—and the relevance of anarchism as well—in the book he completed shortly before his death in 1968, *The Cult of Sincerity:*

> My understanding of the history of culture has convinced me that the ideal society is a point on a receding horizon. We move steadily towards it but can never reach it. Nevertheless we must engage with passion in the immediate strife.

Index